SHIFTING GROUNDS

The Ground between Form and Practice in Beirut

Carla Aramouny
Sandra Frem

table of contents

prolog

ard

hashim sarkis

In Arabic, the word *ard* أرض is used interchangeably to mean 'ground' and 'floor' and is also used to mean foundation or property, as well as the planet Earth. Its meaning is therefore shifting all the time, making this book a great lexicon at two levels: spatial and semantic. The book demonstrates how these multiple grounds and their multiple meanings intersect daily to produce unique spatial practices that are ingrained in the way the streets and public spaces of Beirut are designed, built, experienced, and used.

One example: The fact that the interior floor and exterior ground share the same name makes the interiors and exterior grounds of the city, its paved and asphalted surfaces, difficult to distinguish. They are all the same ground, even if covered differently or trodden by different heels. The raised floor is also the same as the ground floor. When you are on level one or two, the floor you are walking on is also *ard*. This continuity is vital to understanding the spatial practices illustrated in many of this book's case studies. This is explored at length in the essay "Sampling the Ground" through the reinterpreted Nolli[1] map of the ground, as well as in "Anatomy of Ground Sections" through the sectional explorations of the studied urban fragments.

This is not to say that there are no boundaries between the two. As this book shows, the potential of continuity is latent in the lexicon of spatial practices, coming to life during events like a parade, a demonstration, or a riot. Where it exists, the space between the two grounds—the sidewalk—is the space of ebb and flow, of animated erasure and redrawing of boundaries.

Another example: The property one owns, even if sequestered by fences, deeds, vigilances, and all its surrounding properties, are part of the same earth. Simultaneously, they each constitute an earth on its own. Despite their apparent contradiction, these two possibilities work together, as illustrated in the essay "Architecture as Ground Shaper" with its exploration of Beirut's privatized production of space. They are bound to each other, as if through the labor theory of John Locke.[2] If you till the land with your sweat, you walk on it, you build on it, then you own it, but by doing so, you reunify it with all the other lands you are separating it from. Here again, and in its exploration of geographic and natural conditions that inform the spatial practices of making the city, this book, especially in the essay "Ecology of the Ground," articulates the spatial practices that reconnect the city to the earth. The ground you are standing on is, in fact, the whole earth. In every step you take, you are aware that this is a continuous surface and not just delimited by the journey you are making on that stretch of street or sidewalk. There are very few clues on this earth that make you aware that it is connected and continuous. The horizon is one, and Beirut's is very present and unifying once you are on the corniche by the sea. In the inner city, the ground instead takes on the role of the horizon.

1 In reference to the 18th c. figure-ground map of Rome by Giambattista Nolli.
2 "The Project Gutenberg eBook of Second Treatise of Government, by John Locke." Archived from the original on 30 May 2024. Retrieved 3 June 2024.

At the 17th Architecture Venice Biennale, the Beirut Shifting Grounds installation was installed on the ground. Visitors had to look down on the display, a series of projections on a surface that was slightly lifted from the Arsenale floor and that interrupted both the continuity of the floor and the vertical logic of the display. This shift also highlighted the significance of nuanced measurements when dealing with the ground. A ten-centimeter difference in level is probably more difficult to navigate than a 15-centimeter difference, being less than a step but more than a bump in the ground. This subtle variation, as the installation demonstrated, creates an awareness of the ground's articulation, making it differentiated if not divided.

The public takeover of Martyrs' Square during the revolution of 2019, was perhaps the event that demonstrated the significance of these nuances the most, as studied in the essay "From Streets to Strategies" and explored further in the expanded timeframes of evolution in "Metamorphosis and Manifestations of the Ground." When the ground of the different properties of the destroyed city center was turned into stocks in a real estate holding company by decree, the ground —whether public or private— was liquified into assets with the idea that it would be redrawn, re-parcelled, and redeveloped as a contemporary city with wider boulevards, bigger blocks, and taller buildings. What has been achieved in this plan's public spaces resembles more of a drawing on the ground and a hopscotch game but with the thicknesses of sidewalk edges and changes in paving. The way these subtle but significant surface differentiations were trespassed by the demonstrators —and sometimes magnified to completely reimagine the public space— reveals how much urban information there is in those few centimeters that define the section of the ground.

Drawing on events that have marked the city in the past decade, and on neighborhoods that reveal the intersections of the multiple meanings of 'ground', this book reveals how the constant negotiations of the ground are what makes a city —in times of normalcy but more often of exception. This book also demonstrates how social practices, whether triggered by events, habits or both, become urban practices and how urban practices come back to reshape the habits of citizens. It also explains how these urban practices replicate themselves through code, zoning, and the building economy to shape the city's fabric and pulse. It is this nuanced ground that makes Beirut Beirut.

Figure 1 - Beirut's Ground. Axonometric depicting built densities and the collective realm in Beirut

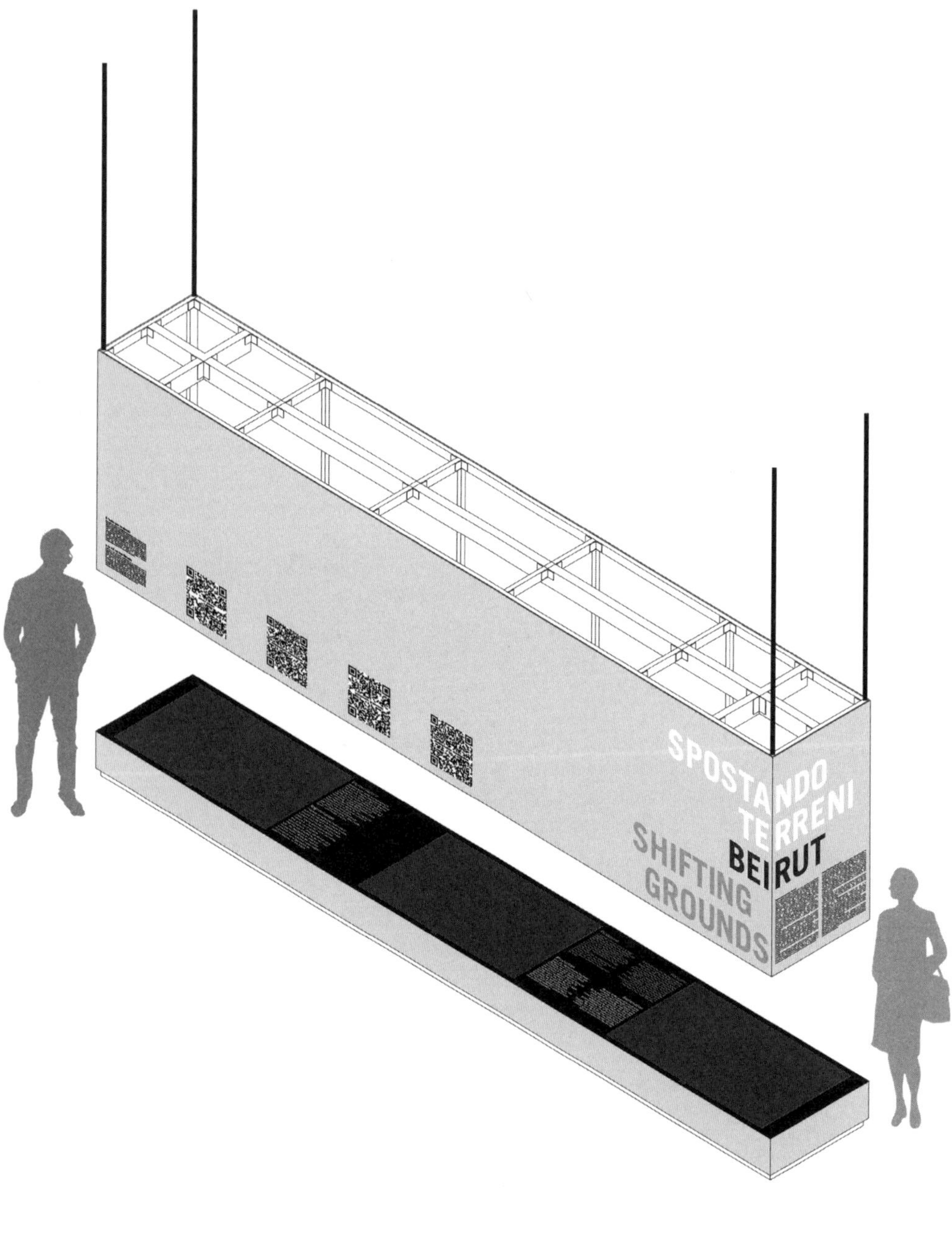
SPOSTANDO
TERRENI
BEIRUT
SHIFTING
GROUNDS

preface

The research presented in this work initially started as —Beirut Shifting Grounds—[1] a biennial participation in 2019-2021 that developed in parallel to the shifting conditions of that period. It was commissioned shortly after October 2019 for the Co-Habitats exhibition at the 17th Venice Architecture Biennale "How Will We Live Together?" which hosted multiple academic institutions, each looking at a different city through the cohabitation lens. The research was initiated as Beirut's streets were flooded with public dissent and was presented a year and 6 months later, in May 2021, in Venice, after what seemed to be an eternity to the city and the world. The research was conducted with *platau* | platform for architecture and urbanism and faculty from the Department of Architecture and Design at the American University of Beirut. The research itself was symptomatic of the period and the city in constant flux; its narrative continuously changed and was repositioned to reflect on the fast-paced transformations that Beirut was going through.

The research premise investigated the city through its ground level to reveal how spatial and social practices created co-habitats that characterized its ground experience and filled the gaps between top-down planning and the unmet needs of people at multiple scales. The argument was that, despite all its shortcomings, Beirut's value resided in its adaptable ground that allowed improvisation and appropriation by the people—the last being the collective occupation of public space during the October 2019 revolution and the mass mobilization that followed the Port blast. Such practices changed the ground from built matter and residual space to a cultural habitat that allowed cohabitation and collective assembly, much-needed attributes in times of uncertainty. The research was organized through four lenses—urban, architecture, human, and temporal, and attempted to convey the shifting dynamics of the ground as a layer that permeates all the studied scales and time-frames.

Presented mainly through video narratives, composite visuals, timelines, and axonometric drawings, the four lenses each revealed a different reading of the ground of Beirut, structuring its evolution and revealing the guiding mechanisms, whether social, political or economic, that enforced and enabled various social practices to emerge and adapt to its surfaces. The work was presented in two formats, physically through an installation at the Biennale and digitally through an online platform launched with the Biennale's opening, providing access to a larger global audience.[2]

1 The Beirut Shifting Grounds project was presented in 2021 in the Co-Habitats section of the 17th Venice Architecture, co-curated by Sandra Frem, Boulos Douaihy, Carla Aramouny, Rana Haddad, Nicolas Fayad, and Joanne Hayek.
2 www.beirutshiftinggrounds.com

introduction

shifting grounds: transformative periods and emergent spatial practices

carla aramouny / sandra frem

"There are decades where nothing happens; and there are weeks where decades happen" vladimir lenin

October 2019 marked the end of abundant living in Beirut. In the decades that followed the end of the civil war in 1990, life in Lebanon was enabled by spending in a socioeconomic bubble supported by sectarian clientelism, public debt accumulation, lira-dollar peg, and Ponzi schemes. The political economy and governance system of the country, and Beirut in particular, was undermined by incestuous relationships between political, economic, and private development interests. This bubble burst in 2019 with the financial meltdown and bank crisis. People lost access to their savings. Real estate markets crashed. The myths of the "Lebanese Miracle," Beirut's "Creative Chaos," and other anecdotes that accompanied decades of post-war development ended in mere days.

In the following three years and ever since, Beirut was caught in a spiraling downfall: the financial meltdown was quickly followed by the Covid-19 lock-down, and the Beirut Port Blast in August 2020, all against the backdrop of an ongoing currency devaluation that radically changed the life and ethos of the city. More than 70% of the population fell into poverty, and decreasing access to essential commodities including food, energy, services, and money disrupted lifestyles and cultural values.

Never had a city faced such compounded extremes in a non-war context as Beirut did between 2019 and 2022. It was during this period that the seeds of this book were initiated. Looking at the ground during this volatile period was highly disconcerting. Transition occurred at a rapid and almost elusive pace. Ground uses constantly changed due to the economic crash from shop closures, people's daily rituals, and the movement of matter and resources in neighborhoods. Routines were suspended by financial and quarantine limitations, and the destruction/ reconstruction that followed the Port blast upended urban settings and the socioeconomic dynamics associated with them. The economic crash placed additional strains on an already flimsy infrastructure, as power outages rendered the city and its streets dark and unsettling.

Yet observing the city's ground level between its urban form and practice during this period helped reveal the inherent properties of Beirut's urban life, its culture, and its ability to deal with both normality and exception.

A brief history of the ground

Spatial practices of the urban ground in Beirut were affected by various social, political, and economic upheaval through time (Fig. 1, 2, 3). The first appropriation practices of the ground date to the early 19th century, when Beirut was still a small city bounded by medieval walls, with various quarters characterized by religious landmarks, occupational affiliations, and mercantile exchange. Unplanned and organic, appropriative practices emerged through incidental public spaces extending from religious and public buildings or at specific *souk* intersections. The city operated around these spatial 'loci' of communication and social relations.[1] "Public" was the natural continuity of private.[2]

The late Ottoman period was significant in propelling Beirut from a mercantile city to the capital of the Wilayet, a first-level province of the Ottoman Empire. During this period, the city expanded beyond its walls, and major rail networks connected it to the rest of the Empire. The Tanzimat reforms[3] were instrumental to the organization of the city's 'commons' or *'Mashaa'*, communal land outside the city walls that was distributed equally among farmers with the premise of cultivating the land together. This concept of collective management through common use disappeared during the process of the city's modernization in subsequent decades. This period witnessed the urbanization of Beirut's hills—particularly on the Eastern side—by the first extra-muros neighborhoods, where the relation between architecture and ground shifted from scattered villas among orchards to the structuring of urban streets. Simultaneously, this urban growth instigated sectional morphologies adapting to the city's topography and the emergence of urban stairs as connectors and public spaces.

After the end of the Ottoman period, several events prompted rapid transformations in Beirut's ground, starting with the influx of Armenian refugees, the creation of settlement zones, and their bottom-up adaptation from Armenian planning principles. Such experiences resulted in fine grain quarters that adapted to flat land east of the Beirut River (Bourj Hammoud) and Beirut's eastern hill (Karm El Zeitoun). Expansive planning continued further in the following two decades during the French Mandate, juxtaposing Haussmannian logic over the city's ground, cutting wide avenues, and bisecting arteries into the urban fabric. Guided by the building code that was introduced in 1919 and updated in 1940, the character of the city's first urban quarters was molded to adapt to the ground's topographical features, using architectural archetypes to create porous transitions between public and private.

1 May Davie, "The History and Evolution of Public Spaces in Beirut Central District," Solidere publication (1997).

2 Marlène Ghorayeb, *Beyrouth sous Mandat Français*, (New York, Khartala, 2014), 53.

3 Ottoman development laws that comprised expropriation and the first version of a building code

4 Oussama Kabbani, "Public Space as Infrastructure," in *Projecting Beirut*, in Sarkis, H. et al., (Prestel, 1998).

5 The postwar boom in real estate led to massive destruction of the urban fabric in return for higher exploitation factors, resulting in gated high-rises in the different neighborhoods. See: Marieke Krijnen. Creative economy, Social justice and Urban strategies (Beirut: Issam Fares Institute for Public Policy and International Affairs, American University of Beirut, 2016), 15.

6 Samir Khalaf, "Post-War Barbarism in Lebanon," *Annahar*, February 22, 2019, https://en.annahar.com/article/940004-postwar-barbarism-in-lebanon.

After Lebanon's independence in 1943, the port boom following the 1948 Nakba and the influx of Palestinian capital into Beirut caused the city to expand rapidly to an extent that planning processes were unable to keep pace with its growth. Since this period, Beirut has grown perpetually, with the private sector preceding formal planning in shaping its development and ground experience.

Between 1954 and 1975—a period known as the "golden age—Beirut's ground underwent divergent transformations as the city's planning and ground practices grew further apart. On one hand, the state focused on honing the public sphere through the modernization of infrastructure, public transport, and public institutions while sponsoring public architecture competitions. Major competitions were held in key sites in the city, with briefs favoring approaches of porosity, modern identity, and the openness of the ground to its context. Simultaneously, neighborhoods witnessed their second wave of densification under the impact of the city's first master plan and its inflated zoning coefficients. On the other hand, the city's construction boom triggered massive migration to its peripheral areas and contributed to the emergence of informal areas, populated by rural migrants in search of livelihoods and immigrants escaping regional instability. Due to the lack of affordable housing policies, municipal regulatory powers, and a private sector that privileged the middle and upper class, these areas expanded on agrarian land south and east of the city without formal planning. This created inadequate subdivisions within large agricultural lots, resulting in high urban density and poor living conditions. The socio-political climate at the time, combined with the vulnerability of these low-income groups and lack of official authorities, made those areas the first battlegrounds of the civil war.

With the onset of the civil war in 1975, Beirut's ground was transformed into a divisive battleground as streets were seized, public spaces turned into sniper strongholds, and ground floors barricaded. The city's urban space turned into barricaded enclaves entrenching social division and political dissent. Haphazard buildings not adhering to the building code became common practice. Private development repeatedly and casually encroached upon the public domain and resources through political backing.

After the war and the ensuing reconstruction process, the rift between formal planning and informal practices shaped the urban ground. As major reconstruction projects completely reshaped the destroyed city center, the segregation of the city into socio-political enclaves was further normalized through the implementation and upgrading of existing and new road infrastructures (such as the Fouad Chehab highway/Ring, Salim Salam highway, to name but a few). This resulted in the subdivision of the ground and local neighborhoods into a patchwork of fragmented entities, which, paired with the forces of land speculation, slowly eroded the social structure of these localities. The rebuilt center, in contrast, became a neutral ground,[4] a high-end real estate endeavor targeting the elite and international investors, a tabula rasa with a ground plane disconnected from its adjoining quarters.

Militarization and privatization became key forces that reshaped the ground during the following decades, whether through reinforcing political and socioeconomic divides or channeling global capital into the city's built environment. Consequently, capital reshaped the interface between private and public, gentrifying the city over successive episodes[5] and converting the urban experience of the ground through new financialized ownership, alienating its original inhabitants in favor of a new elite. Urban life thus became increasingly delegated to the private realm, gated from the chaos of street life through a myriad of "sanitized" air-conditioned typologies. As a result, private development erased the geographical features of the ground, reducing the city's open spaces to a mere 600000 sqm —less than 5% of the overall city area.[6] As it downsized to a simple grid of streets, Beirut's public ground became faster, tending to vehicular transit rather than people and pedestrians. In many parts of the city, the ground was transformed into a complicit control agent, encompassing aspects of security and exclusivity.[7,8]

All such trends were temporarily halted with the financial meltdown that hit the country in October 2019. This can be seen as an opportunity to reflect on the duplicity of the ground between the destructive development paths and the bottom-up spatial practices that can hold positive lessons for inclusive planning and co-production of space.

The book

This book builds on this framing of the ground and furthers the former research developed during the 17th Venice Architecture Biennale, towards more substantive findings. First, it expands on the evolution of the city's ground level, tracing through original drawings, archival materials, and essays, its transformation through the twentieth and twenty-first centuries. Through these mappings and drawings, it emphasizes the incremental aspect of evolutionary processes in the production of urban spaces and the shaping of the ground. Second, it synthesizes the earlier research through reflective essays that relate urban form to different spatial and social practices, revealing relations between the entrenched appropriative culture of people in Beirut and their role in molding their ground space. Third, the book considers how planning in Beirut can devise new approaches to co-produce the city, taking cues from spatial practices and bottom-up methods documented through this work.

The ground is a well-documented topic across multiple disciplines dealing with the city. Several urbanists and philosophers have taken on the topic of the ground as a conveyor of urban life, and the social appropriation and reproduction of built form in different lenses: Walter Benjamin's accounts of 1920s Naples, Siegfried Kracauer's writings on 1930s Marseilles, Jane Jacobs' writings on Greenwich Village and New York in the 1950s, Henri Lefebvre's production of space, Richard Sennett's numerous books, and Jan Gehl's life between buildings, to name but a few. Social and urban science has perfected methods of studying the ground through the lens of transportation, urban form, spatial syntax, ecology, ethnography, socio-economic studies, planning, etc. Mapping and analytical methods have ranged from empirical developing metrics for evaluation to qualitative mental mapping, urban transects, and analogous representation, with examples as early as the 1750 Nolli map of Rome. Other studies have focused on social and common practices in the city, examining how they play a niche role in the city's urban development. As

7 Mona Fawaz, Mona Harb, and Ahmad Gharbieh, "Living Beirut's Security Zones: An Investigation of the Modalities and Practice of Urban Security," *City & Society*, 24 (2012): 173-195.

8 Valet parking companies usually monopolize on-street public parking in Beirut's hotspots, making it compulsory to give them one's car.

a term, the ground has been designated in multiple ways: the urban level, the city at eye level, the plinth of the city, the third space, and so forth.

This book contributes to this discussion by exploring the ambivalent relationship between the architecture of the ground and its appropriation in Beirut through four key practices. Each is explored with a set of methods zoomed to its appropriate scale(s) of investigation. The four practices and corresponding sections in this book include Appropriation, Commoning, Production, and Activism.

The first section investigates appropriation as a cultural and spatial practice that has given Beirut its distinct character and vitality. Stemming from a strong culture of improvisation that emerged as a response to weak governance, appropriation became a tool to reclaim the everyday ground as a supportive realm for its inhabitants.

This section examines the taxonomies of appropriation found in Beirut. Some materialize from the necessities of the lived space and the logic of daily urban rituals that reshuffle urban space with improvised add-ons. Others emerge from people's conceived space, projecting their identities onto the ground through cultural or religious markers that mirror their diverse communities. Fewer result in environments amenable to non-human interactions, such as appropriated urban nature or homegrown farming that, in turn, supports urban biodiversity.

In "Sampling the Ground," a comparative urban sampling investigates the diverse appropriations that emerge from the multiplicity of urban patterns and social strata found in Beirut, probing the different correlations between form and use to produce interpretive cartographies of the ground. In "Ecology of the Ground," a particular emphasis is given to the role of landscape in Beirut in generating localized atmospheres. The chapter examines the relationship between urban landscapes and their appropriation through four analytical layers: the spatial, the ecological, the agricultural, and the human, which impact inhabitation very differently across the studied grounds. In "Appropriation as the New Aesthetic," a visual essay explores appropriation as the new identity of the ground, enacted by individuals and communities to differentiate themselves from their surroundings and project their ideologies and beliefs onto the urban space.

The Commoning section reviews commoning practices and common spaces of the urban ground in Beirut as spaces for collective practices, shared uses, and cultural production. It delves into spaces of tension and transformation that possess symbolic significance for people and shape their understanding of the city. Through a time-based overview, commoning is considered a bottom-up dynamic, evolving from people's free and shared use of city space and influenced further by key events and spatial transformations, whether constructive or disruptive, that validate its relevance in time. Under this premise, the first part of this section explores commoning as a time-based narrative, zooming in on a particular area of ground, Martyrs' Square, as a central public space that has retained its symbolic importance and use as common ground despite its severe transfiguration.

The chapter "Metamorphosis and Manifestations of the Ground as Commons in Martyrs' Square" delves into the square's morphological transformation and elaborates on its evolution and commoning practices that have persisted until today.

Furthermore, in "Cultural Commons and Retaining Collective Memory," the conversation engages with local scholars and activists and discusses the notion of cultural commons and their various manifestations in the city. It explores various significant city spaces and considers their correlation to collective memory. It further highlights the role repositories can play in reinforcing collective commons, whether physical or digital.

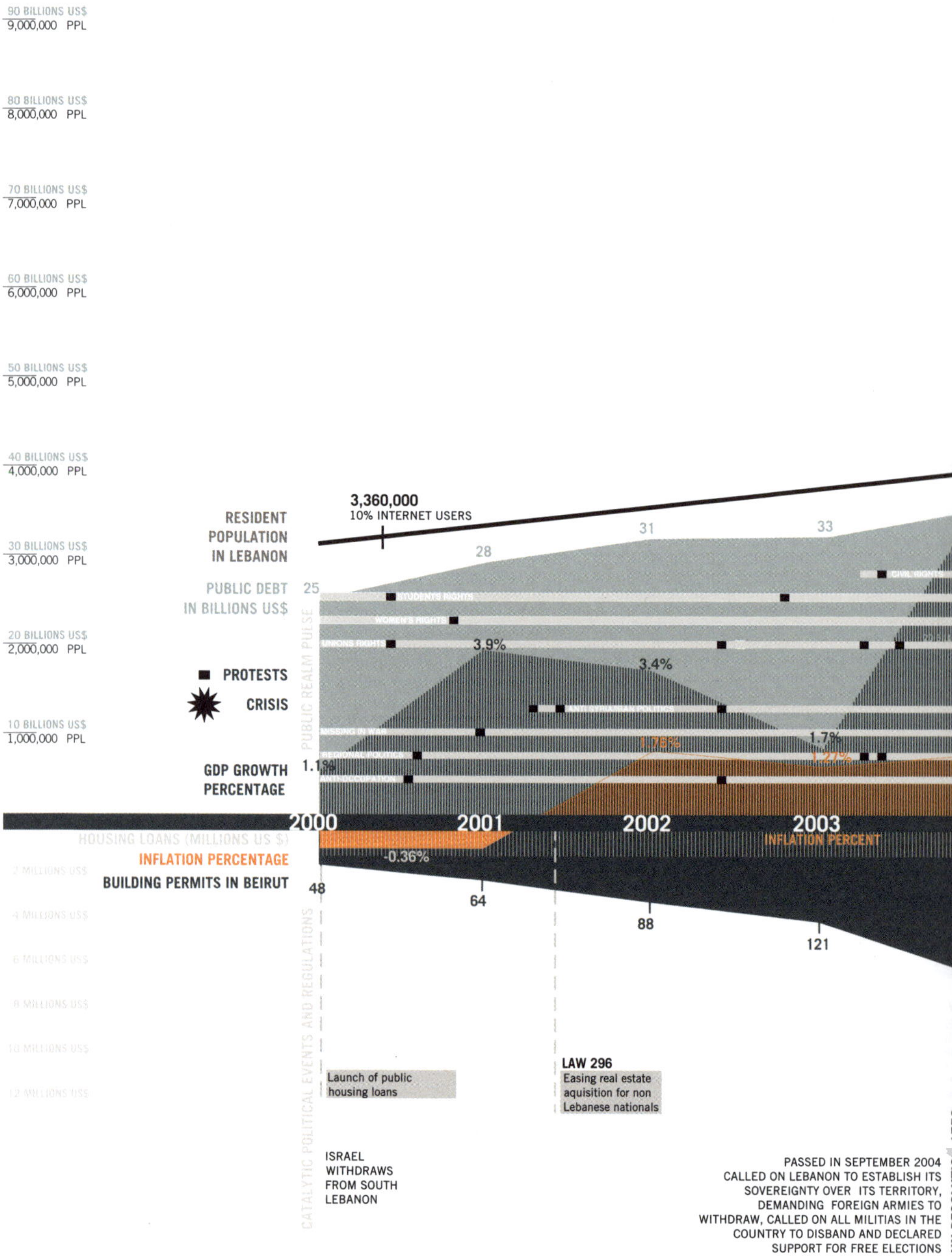

90 BILLIONS US$
9,000,000 PPL
80 BILLIONS US$
8,000,000 PPL
70 BILLIONS US$
7,000,000 PPL
60 BILLIONS US$
6,000,000 PPL
50 BILLIONS US$
5,000,000 PPL
40 BILLIONS US$
4,000,000 PPL
30 BILLIONS US$
3,000,000 PPL
20 BILLIONS US$
2,000,000 PPL
10 BILLIONS US$
1,000,000 PPL
RESIDENT POPULATION IN LEBANON
3,360,000
10% INTERNET USERS
PUBLIC DEBT IN BILLIONS US$
25
28
31
33
PUBLIC REALM PULSE
STUDENTS RIGHTS
WOMEN'S RIGHTS
UNIONS RIGHTS
CIVIL RIGHTS
MISSING IN WAR
REGIONAL POLITICS
ANTI-OCCUPATION
PROTESTS
CRISIS
GDP GROWTH PERCENTAGE
1.1%
3.9%
3.4%
1.7%
1.75%
1.27%
2000
2001
2002
2003
INFLATION PERCENT
HOUSING LOANS (MILLIONS US $)
INFLATION PERCENTAGE
BUILDING PERMITS IN BEIRUT
-0.36%
48
64
88
121
2 MILLIONS US$
4 MILLIONS US$
6 MILLIONS US$
8 MILLIONS US$
10 MILLIONS US$
12 MILLIONS US$
CATALYTIC POLITICAL EVENTS AND REGULATIONS
Launch of public housing loans
LAW 296
Easing real estate aquisition for non Lebanese nationals
ISRAEL WITHDRAWS FROM SOUTH LEBANON
PASSED IN SEPTEMBER 2004 CALLED ON LEBANON TO ESTABLISH ITS SOVEREIGNTY OVER ITS TERRITORY, DEMANDING FOREIGN ARMIES TO WITHDRAW, CALLED ON ALL MILITIAS IN THE COUNTRY TO DISBAND AND DECLARED SUPPORT FOR FREE ELECTIONS

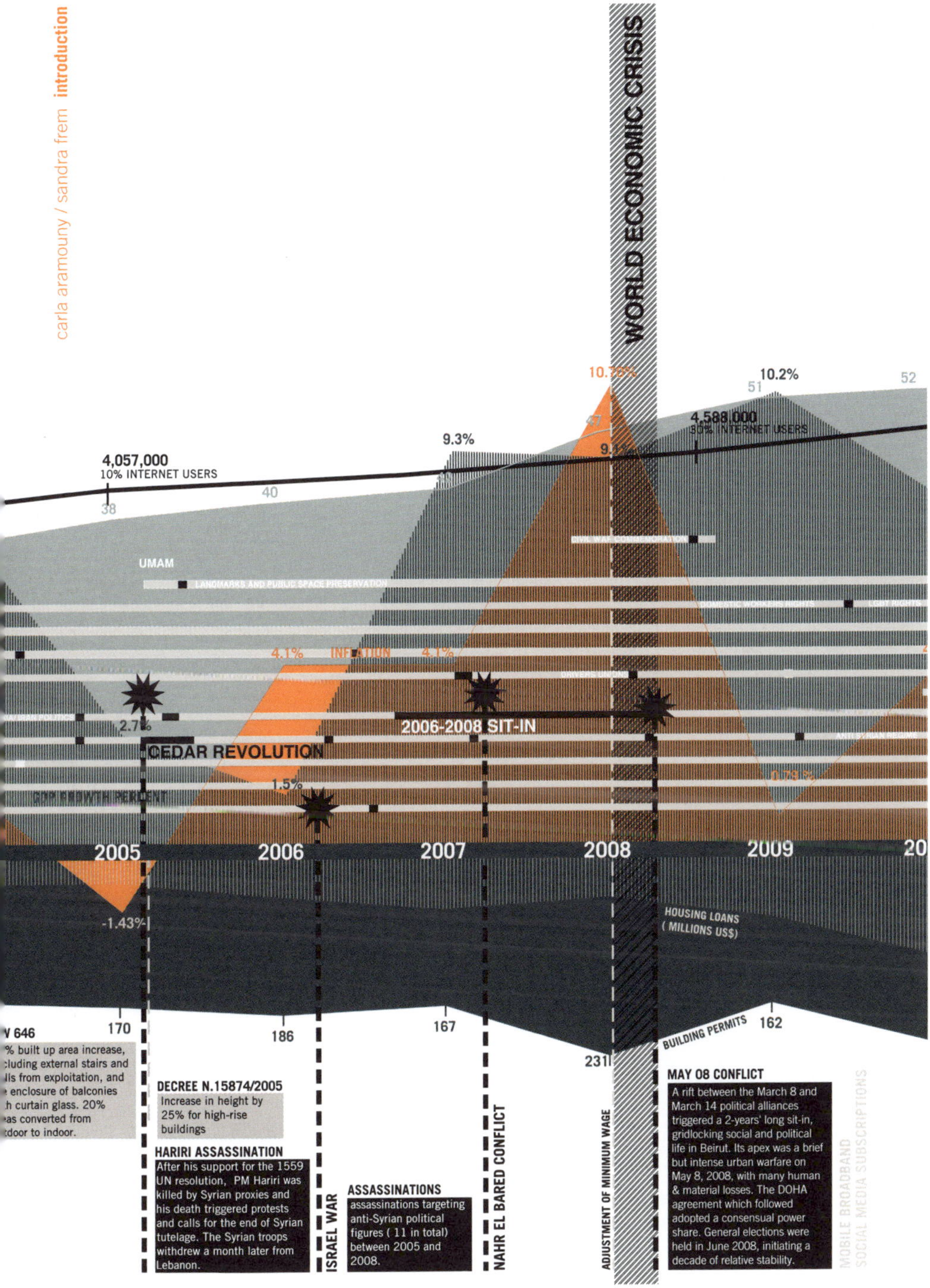

Figures 1, 2, 3 - Timeline of urban transformations in Beirut (2000-2021)

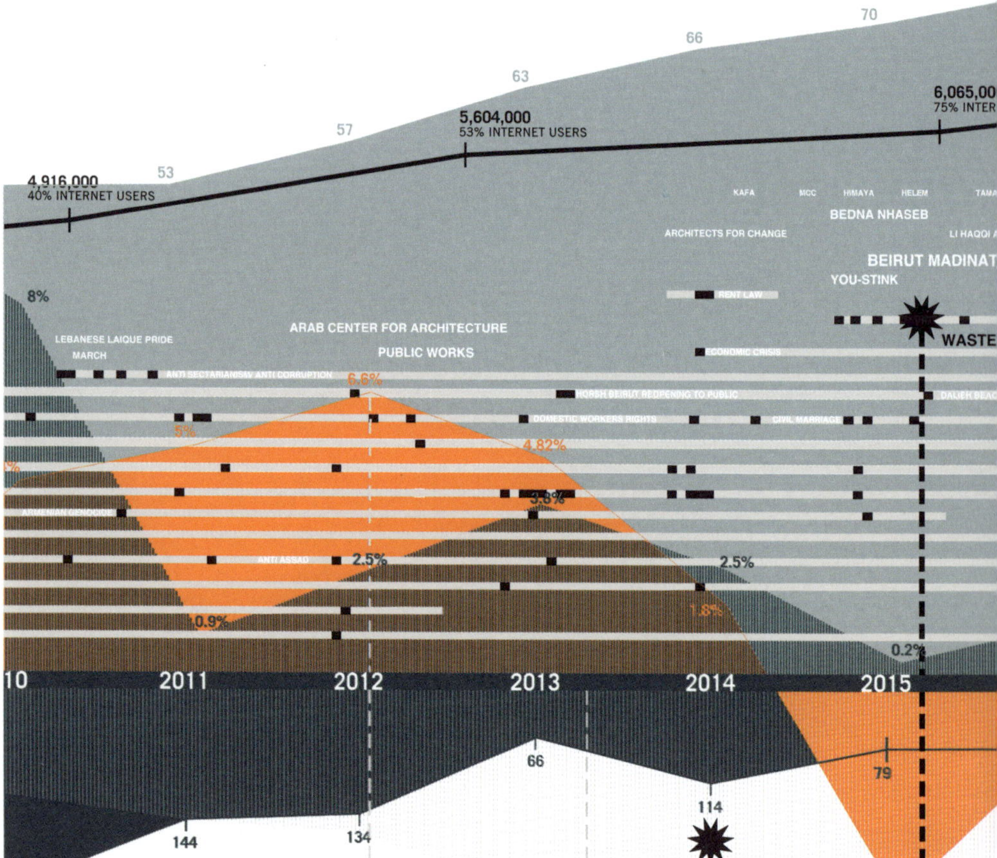

THE WAVE OF UPRISINGS IN THE ARAB WORLD WAS ACCOMPANIED LOCALLY BY UNPRECEDENTED DEMONSTRATIONS BY APOLITICAL GROUPS, ORGANIZED SOLELY THROUGH FACEBOOK- CALLING FOR A SECULAR POLITICAL SYSTEM AND THE FALL OF SECTARIANISM.

IN SYRIA, THE ARAB SPRING PROTESTS AGAINST THE REGIME QUICKLY EVOLVED INTO A CIVIL WAR WITH INTERNATIONAL PLAYERS, DISPLACING MORE THAN ONE MILLION CIVILIANS TO LEBANON. THIS BROUGHT NEW DYNAMICS TO BEIRUT, WITH PALPABLE IN THE DEMOGRAPHIC PRESSURE ON PUBLIC INFRASTRUCTURES AND ECONOMY.

ARAB SPRING
SYRIAN CIVIL WAR

ADJUSTMENT OF MINIMUM WAGE

LAW 230
Tax exemptions for housing loans recipients

Crisis between public housing corporation and commercial banks

WASTE CRISIS
The closure of the Naameh landfill triggered a nation wide waste crisis, and mass protests chanting "You stink!" at the government. It became a glaring symbol of the failures of a sectarian power system unable to meet basic needs like electricity and water and waste, and for the first time, the rise of numerous civic and movements that ran for municipal elections.

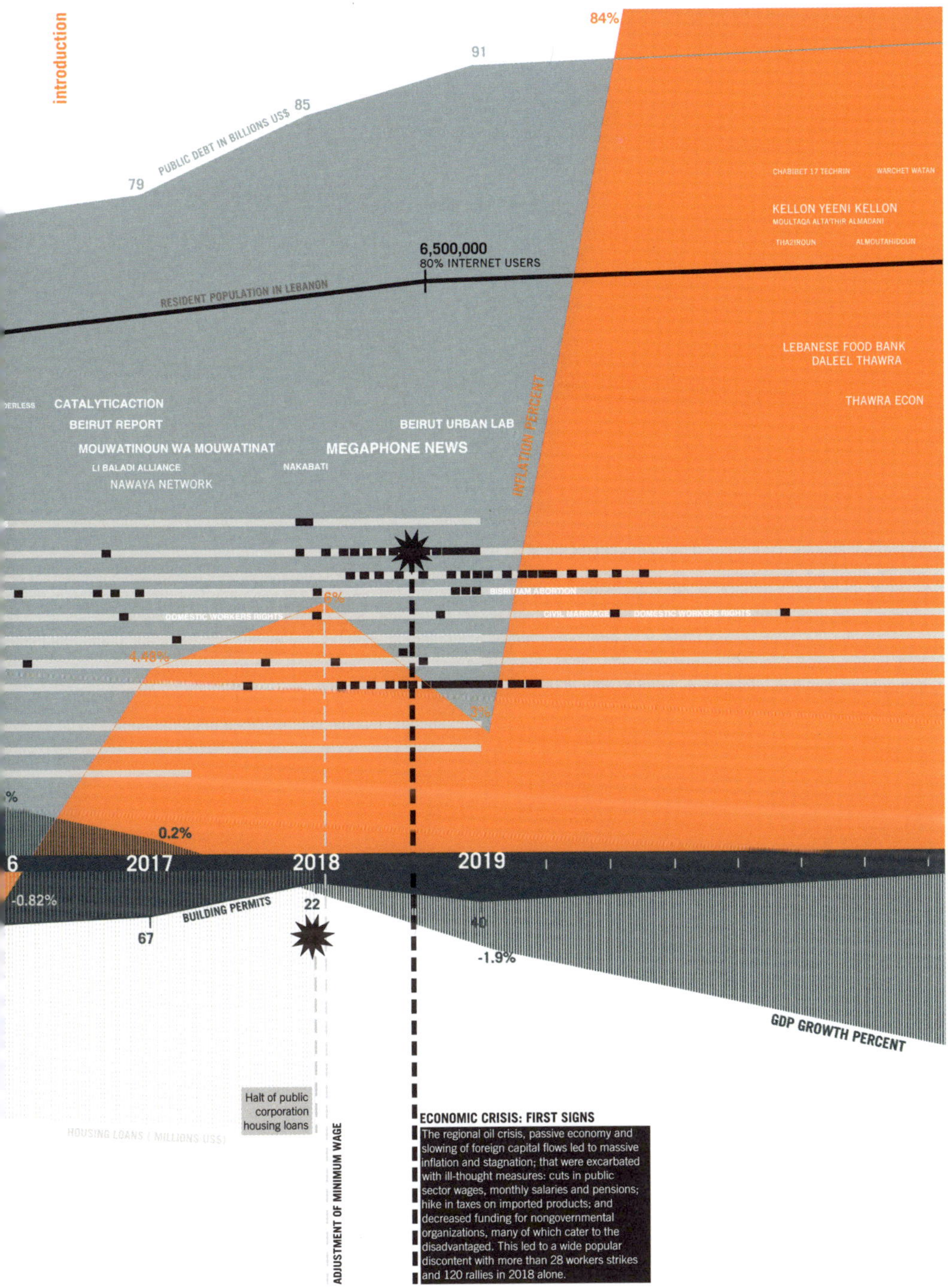
84%
91
85
PUBLIC DEBT IN BILLIONS US$
79
CHABIBET 17 TECHRIN
WARCHET WATAN
KELLON YEENI KELLON
MOULTAQA ALTA'THIR ALMADANI
THA2IROUN
ALMOUTAHIDOUN
6,500,000
80% INTERNET USERS
RESIDENT POPULATION IN LEBANON
LEBANESE FOOD BANK
DALEEL THAWRA
THAWRA ECON
INFLATION PERCENT
CATALYTICACTION
BEIRUT REPORT
MOUWATINOUN WA MOUWATINAT
LI BALADI ALLIANCE
NAWAYA NETWORK
NAKABATI
BEIRUT URBAN LAB
MEGAPHONE NEWS
6%
4.48%
DOMESTIC WORKERS RIGHTS
CIVIL MARRIAGE
DOMESTIC WORKERS RIGHTS
0.2%
2017
2018
2019
-0.82%
BUILDING PERMITS
67
22
40
-1.9%
GDP GROWTH PERCENT
Halt of public corporation housing loans
HOUSING LOANS (MILLIONS US$)
ADJUSTMENT OF MINIMUM WAGE
ECONOMIC CRISIS: FIRST SIGNS
The regional oil crisis, passive economy and slowing of foreign capital flows led to massive inflation and stagnation; that were excarbated with ill-thought measures: cuts in public sector wages, monthly salaries and pensions; hike in taxes on imported products; and decreased funding for nongovernmental organizations, many of which cater to the disadvantaged. This led to a wide popular discontent with more than 28 workers strikes and 120 rallies in 2018 alone.

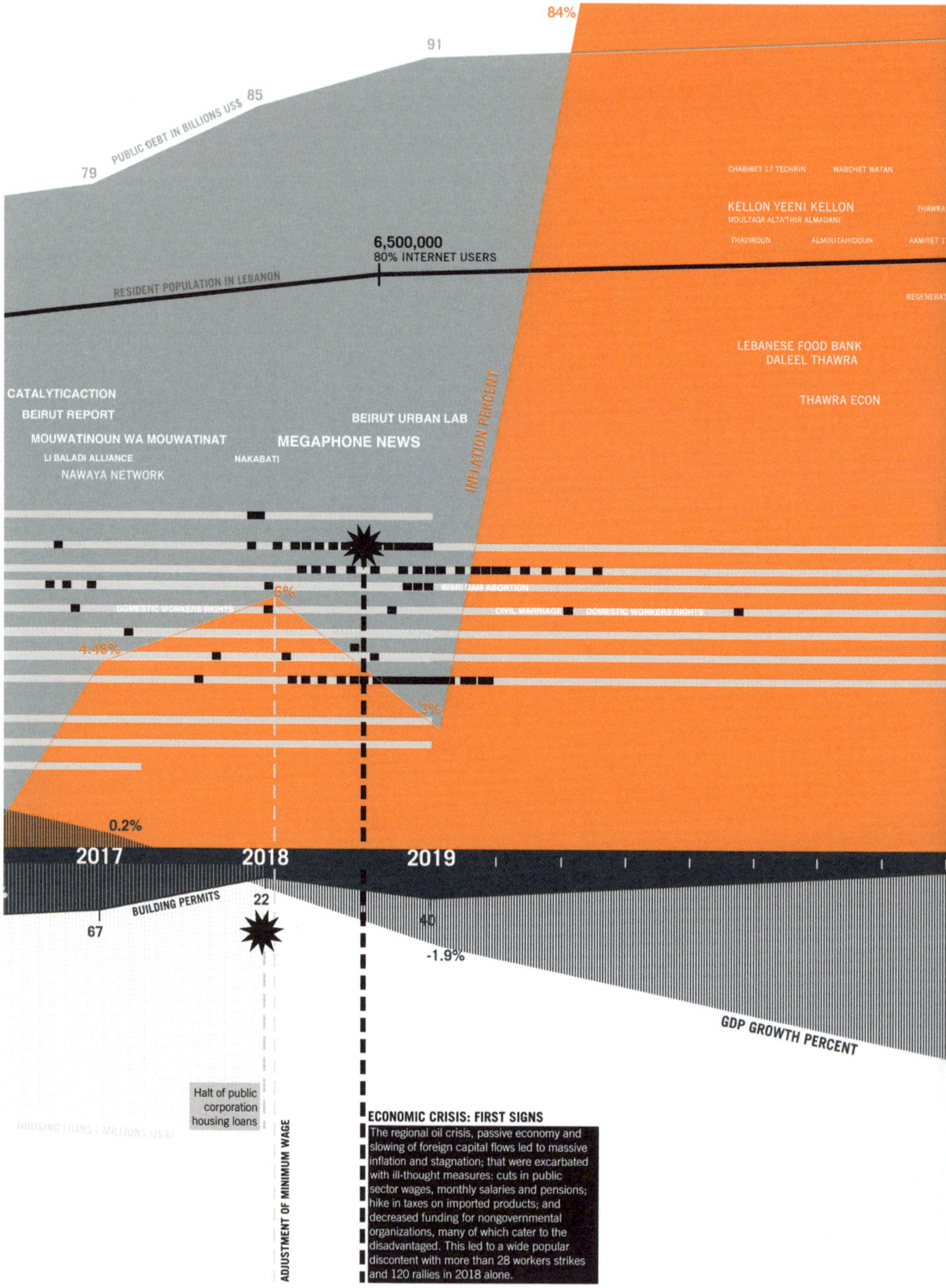
84%
91
85
PUBLIC DEBT IN BILLIONS US$
79
CHABIBET 17 TECHRIN
WARCHET WATAN
KELLON YEENI KELLON
MOULTAQA ALTA'THIR ALMADANI
THA2IROUN
ALMOUTAHIDOUN
6,500,000
80% INTERNET USERS
RESIDENT POPULATION IN LEBANON
LEBANESE FOOD BANK
DALEEL THAWRA
THAWRA ECON
CATALYTICACTION
BEIRUT REPORT
MOUWATINOUN WA MOUWATINAT
LI BALADI ALLIANCE
NAWAYA NETWORK
NAKABATI
BEIRUT URBAN LAB
MEGAPHONE NEWS
INFLATION PERCENT
6%
DOMESTIC WORKERS RIGHTS
CIVIL MARRIAGE
DOMESTIC WORKERS RIGHTS
4.48%
3%
0.2%
2017
2018
2019
BUILDING PERMITS
22
67
40
-1.9%
GDP GROWTH PERCENT
Halt of public corporation housing loans
HOUSING LOANS (MILLIONS US$)
ADJUSTMENT OF MINIMUM WAGE
ECONOMIC CRISIS: FIRST SIGNS
The regional oil crisis, passive economy and slowing of foreign capital flows led to massive inflation and stagnation; that were excarbated with ill-thought measures: cuts in public sector wages, monthly salaries and pensions; hike in taxes on imported products; and decreased funding for nongovernmental organizations, many of which cater to the disadvantaged. This led to a wide popular discontent with more than 28 workers strikes and 120 rallies in 2018 alone.

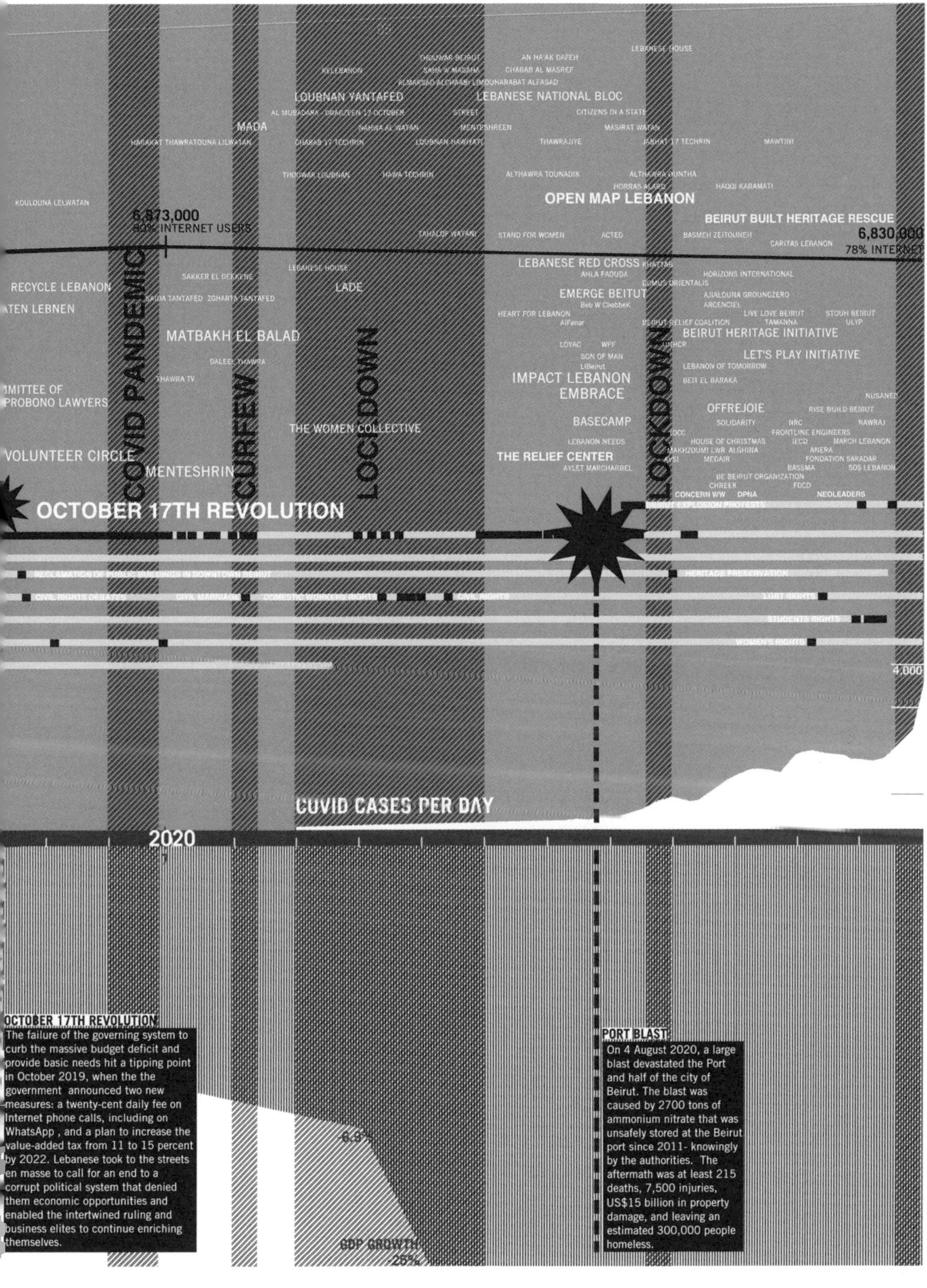

OCTOBER 17TH REVOLUTION

The failure of the governing system to curb the massive budget deficit and provide basic needs hit a tipping point in October 2019, when the the government announced two new measures: a twenty-cent daily fee on Internet phone calls, including on WhatsApp , and a plan to increase the value-added tax from 11 to 15 percent by 2022. Lebanese took to the streets en masse to call for an end to a corrupt political system that denied them economic opportunities and enabled the intertwined ruling and business elites to continue enriching themselves.

PORT BLAST

On 4 August 2020, a large blast devastated the Port and half of the city of Beirut. The blast was caused by 2700 tons of ammonium nitrate that was unsafely stored at the Beirut port since 2011- knowingly by the authorities. The aftermath was at least 215 deaths, 7,500 injuries, US$15 billion in property damage, and leaving an estimated 300,000 people homeless.

Finally, commoning is further extended towards the issue of collective memory and remembrance through a visual essay, "Port Silos as Common Ground," narrating the Port Silos as a recently emerged commons of shared trauma. The essay reflects on the exposed disconnection between the city, the port, and the sea and highlights the importance of the silos as a necessary space for acknowledgment and reconciliation.

The Production section looks at the ground's production through the lens of architecture. In the absence of planning in Beirut, private development and architecture became the ground's form givers, guided by an opportunistic building code and regulatory tools that generated discordant relationships to increase built-up areas. This section expands on the role of architectural production, from a didactic process (building code and general practice), an intuitive process (isolated urban fragments), to a process of co-production (an unfinished form that encourages multiple alliances in co-producing urban space).

In "Architecture as Form Giver," the chapter examines the evolution of architecture under the impact of development forces and how they shaped the ground level. It links historical typologies, development dynamics, and building code criteria from the early 1930s until 2020 through a typological repertoire that examines buildings and their ground. It charts the evolution of architecture from a discipline that engages with the public realm through spatial conditions of the ground to a gentrifying tool of development that resulted in mundane and privatized environments in recent decades.

Amid this general trajectory, the second chapter, "Anatomies of Ground Sections," focuses on specific typologies that foster meaningful connections with the ground by examining sectional relationships of selected architectural fragments in Beirut. The fragments come from a mix of commercial, residential, and public projects that, through their form and use, became analogous assemblies with transient and often intangible urban spaces, offering new possibilities for the urban ground.

In the third chapter, "The Collective Ground," such possibilities are explored in a design experiment, speculating how an assemblage of collective infrastructural networks, open systems, flexible/multi-use forms, and co-design processes can create amenable social and spatial environments that can form a new collective ground in Beirut.

The final section and practice revolve around Activism, particularly collective activism, that is actively enabled and supported by the urban ground. Activism is explored as a practice that manifests on the streets, whether in the form of mobilization and organization or as a political act of place-making and spatial appropriation. This section also considers activism through design, where design interventions become the mode for critiquing or reflecting on the city's conditions and livability.

The first chapter, "Pulsing Grounds," examines the 2019 revolution's activism and the 2020 post-blast relief efforts in Beirut as ground-level manifestations that rose from assemblies in urban spaces and were further strengthened by active appropriations of open grounds as nodes and grass-root society bases. The chapter incorporates mappings and critical visual analysis that narrate the unfolding of the revolution and its protocols of collective as well as the ground-level mobilization and coordination of grassroots in the aftermath of the Beirut port blast. Through these two episodes, the chapter highlights how ground-level activism became the mechanism for urban regeneration and citizen engagement and how it can inform top-down planning.

The second chapter in this section further sheds light on the role of design and art practice in public engagement and urban activism. The chapter "Public Art as Activism" reflects on how public art can engage citizens as active participants in socio-political debates and how it can enable the ground to serve alternative uses beyond conventional practice. In conversation with Rana Haddad, the chapter delves into her installation art practice and its relationship to Beirut's ground. It reflects on the political role that art installations can play in shaping the city's public sphere and revealing urban disruptions and disconnections.

By breaking the complexity of Beirut's grounds into a set of spatial practices that are dismantled and synthesized, the material in this book offers a form of—almost analogous—knowledge that can serve as a reference for any serious discussion on the future of Beirut, from large scale planning to micro-interventions that take into account the dynamics of life at the ground level. It aims to bring together various readings of the ground in Beirut during a tumultuous, transformative period, offering insight into how culture, social practices, politics, and urban life can help transform the city through its ground.

Addendum: This book—as the title suggests—was conceived during a period of significant change for Beirut and, unfortunately, is being completed during another momentous shift: In September 2024, Israeli air strikes destroyed large parts of Beirut, escalating a conflict in Lebanon that began in October 2023 and spread from its South to encompass the entire country. This tragic event, marking yet another profound transformation, underscores the vulnerability of urban life in Beirut. However, it also lays witness to the practices that people never cease to resort to in times of normalcy but, most crucially, in times of crisis —to reclaim and re-appropriate their ground as a support infrastructure.

section 1

appropriation

Appropriation is a complex term with two conflicting connotations. The first refers to exclusive possession or use, often criticized as confiscation. The second refers to adapting existing spaces to one's needs, generally seen as empowerment. In Beirut, appropriation as a spatial practice is pervasive and closely linked to daily urban rituals. Encouraged by a culture of informality and spontaneity, appropriation in Beirut has taken many forms. Generally, it refers to the informal —often unauthorized—use of urban space, which can be permanent or temporary. It also refers to practices that engage with or nurture the natural and urban ecosystems. Additionally, it registers in Beirut's complex socio-political context through symbolic spatial markers that demarcate communal or political territories, transforming the ground into a coded environment.

In design and social sciences, appropriation is interpreted through its dual meanings, but often within a Marxist framework, which considers that appropriation is opposed to alienation in re-appropriating the human essence through praxis and work. Scholars such as Sennett[1] and Lefebvre[2] argue that appropriating the built environment is a fundamental socio-spatial demand, enabling citizens to participate actively in urban production beyond the private sphere. A more nuanced framing in the recent work of Lara Hernandez, Melis, and Lehman[3] has linked appropriation to the assemblage theory of Deleuze and Guattari[4] and further developed by DeLanda,[5] which considers appropriation as a product of synergies between various components. In geography, Ripoll and Veschambre[6] have developed a typological understanding of appropriation between i) material forms (enclosing or transforming space), ii) ideal and subjective forms, and iii) institutionalized forms, which refer to the legal attribution of space with symbolic and material markings (signage, objects, bodies, architecture, etc.).

Based on these cumulative readings, we identify appropriation practices in Beirut as an assemblage that emerges from multiple urban relations: the built environment, the cultural context, and the legal regulations that allow it to occupy many spaces within Beirut's ground. Under such a theoretical framework and within this book section, we explore Beirut's ground as an emergence of appropriations, breaking down the spatial complexity embedded in its form and use and searching for connections between this spatial practice and long-term social and environmental sustainability for the city.

1 Richard Sennett, *The Uses of Disorder: Personal Identity and City Life* (Yale University Press, 2008).
2 Henri Lefebvre, *The Production of Space* (Blackwell, 1991), and *Le droit à la ville* (Anthropos, 1968).
3 J. A. Lara-Hernandez et al., "Temporary Appropriation of Public Space as an Emergence Assemblage for the Future Urban Landscape: The Case of Mexico City," *Future Cities and Environment 5*, no. 1 (2019): 10-12.
4 Gilles Deleuze and Félix Guattari, "A Thousand Plateaus: Capitalism and Schizophrenia," trans. Brian Massumi (University of Minnesota Press, 1989), 55.
5 Manuel DeLanda, *Assemblage Theory* (Edinburgh University Press, 2016), 93.
6 Fabrice Ripoll and Vincent Veschambre, "L'appropriation de l'espace comme problématique," *Norois*, no. 195 (2005): 25-30.

Figure 1 - Informal appropriations are an intrinsic layer of Beirut's ground

sampling the ground

sandra frem

"The value of cities is determined according to the number of places where improvisation is permitted." [1]

The ground in Beirut is a complex urban mosaic resulting from successive phases of unplanned development that allowed diverse urban textures to emerge (Fig. 2, 3). Added to this initial stratum, informality and appropriation are living layers that give Beirut its distinct character, repurposing its urban fabric into "co-habitats": lived spaces amenable to host spontaneous activities and living needs of different users, that manifest in various forms of appropriations at ground level and in mixed pulses and intensities (Fig. 1, 4).

This chapter aims to dismantle the complexity of the appropriated ground in Beirut between its physical form and urban life, through a comparative urban sampling. It zooms at the micro-scale to observe seven ground samples with different characteristics, mapping their appropriation patterns as highly contextual, intrinsically social, and reflective of the ground's "pulse" as it is lived. To understand how and why appropriation unfolds differently in each locality, the chapter adopts unified urban metrics and methods to observe the seven grounds. The sampling methodology combines field surveying, morphological analysis, social-economic profiling, typological taxonomy, and data collection, recording the dynamics of each ground sample.

The goals for this mapping are two-fold:
First, compare how the studied metrics lead to different ground appropriations, putting them in relation to one another to broaden the understanding of urban life from a surveyed perspective, and generate a new reading of the city through its ground.
Second, interpret how the different metrics influence each ground's inclusivity by showing what types of ground spaces are inherently connected to the city through their engagements, and what appropriation typologies can unlock the ground as a collective space.

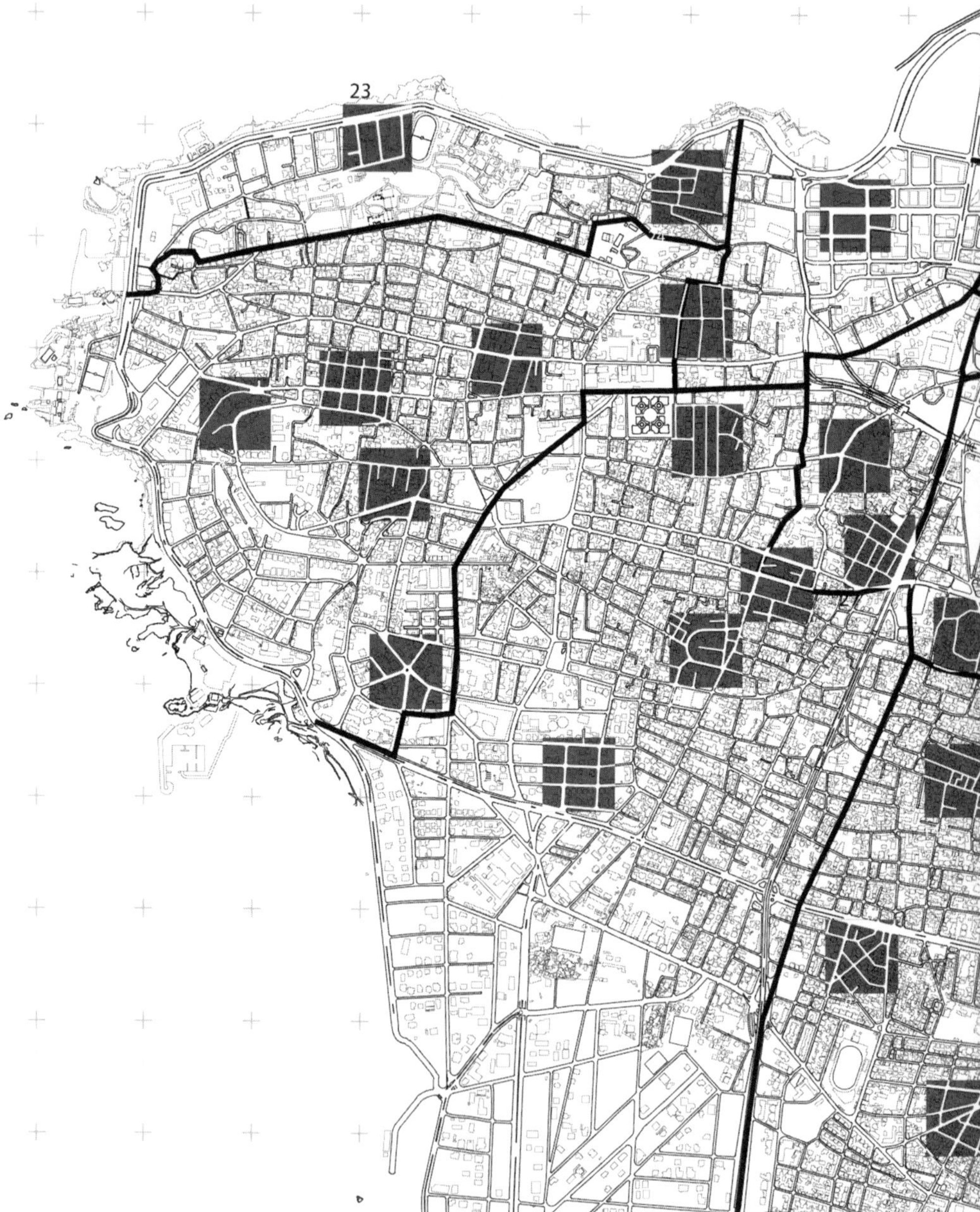
23

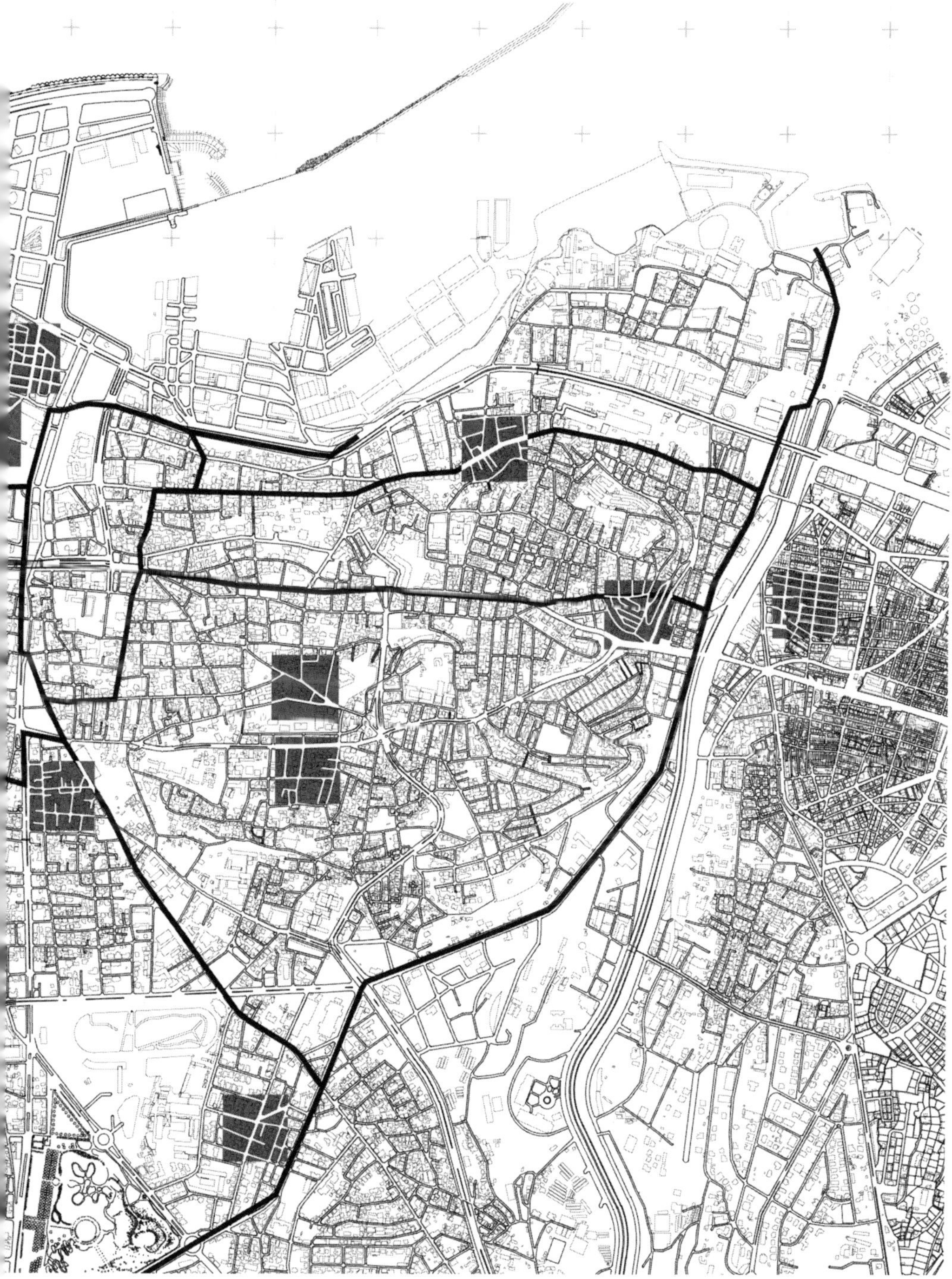

Figure 2 - The multiplicity of urban fabrics found in Beirut

The ground in a city of fragments

A contemporary reading of Beirut's plan reveals a city of urban fragments that originate from localized instances of development, operating primarily at the local scale (Fig. 4). This present-day phenomenon derives from a history of growth with no regulating master plan: Most of the city's past plans were partially implemented, prioritizing at ground level the creation of mobility corridors that produced divisive road infrastructures and anchored the fragmentation of the urban grid, with little to no overlap between the different urban parts.[2]

A closer look at Beirut's urban grid shows a lack of directionality in many districts. Today, only a tiny percentage of its grid comes from the geometric logic of a planned fragment—such as Hamra, Karm El Zeitoun, Beirut Central District, or Badaro. The remaining streets' patterns are irregular, emerging from the adaptation of agricultural lots and topography shifts into buildable land. These disparities add to the self-containment of each district, making it challenging to establish connectivity with other parts. Adding to this physical fragmentation is a division of governance, which is oddly divided between two separate executive and administrative authorities with little coordination between them.[3] However, the lived city does not necessarily circumscribe to the fragmentations of its built form or its governance. Borrowing from Lefebvre's notions of the perceived, conceived, and lived space,[4] the lived in Beirut always preceded the planned in informing ground realities, creating a gap between planned visions, which take years to materialize, and everyday experiences, which are faster to appear, largely informal, and always in flux. Equally, the lived has always succeeded over the conceived, adding a layer of usage to urban or architectural forms catering to their users' needs.

Informality as second nature

As a city with weak regulatory frameworks, Beirut thrives on urban informality as a cultural practice of space. In fact, what users experience first-hand—and often value—in Beirut is the vibrancy of its street life that emerges from spontaneous encounters. Its ground is not designed but largely improvised by its inhabitants.

The term "informal" has been used in planning disciplines to distinguish between regulated and unregulated sectors, often describing activities walking the line between legal and illegal. However, this connotation usually downplays the formal attributes of informal manifestations and the socio-economic and environmental values they bring to the ground. It can be argued that informal practices emerging from people's rituals often give legibility to the ground and clues to how the city could function holistically.[5] Today, informality largely contributes to how Beirut works on levels of mobility, services, and labor. It exists as a second nature in its urban space and is not only confined to its informal settlements. It manifests as an assemblage of unwarranted additions to its buildings and ground. It shows up as millions of cables that clutter the skyline, as a daily reminder of the alternative economy of water and power networks that became formalized through decades of state neglect. It overrides formal definitions of space (Fig. 5). Emerging as a cultural assemblage, the informal manifests at ground level with a taxonomy of appropriations that blur the boundaries between public and private spaces along main streets and inner city fabrics in answer to different needs and daily rituals.

1 Siegfried Kracauer, *Streets in Berlin and Elsewhere* (Polity Press, 2007).
2 See: Hashim Sarkis and Colin Rowe, *Projecting Beirut* (Prestel, 1997).
3 Beirut is the only city in the world which is governed by separate executive (*Mohafez*) and administrative (municipal council) authorities.
4 Henri Lefebvre, *The Production of Space* (Blackwell, 1991).
5 The same is true for numerous predominantly informal cities from the Global South, such as Sao Paolo, Mumbai, Cairo, and many others.

Figure 3 - Informal appropriations in different areas of Beirut

	01	02	03	04	05	06	07

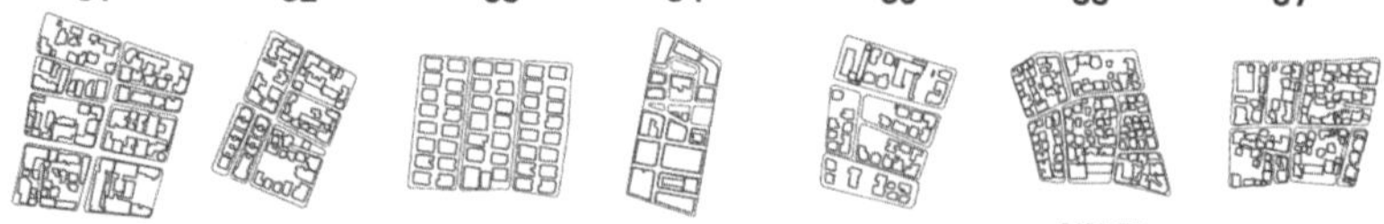

NEIGHBORHOOD	**HAMRA**	**MAZRAA**	**JNAH**	**BCD**	**BADARO**	**AIN EL REMMANEH**	**SASSINE**
ZONE	3	4	50 / 2.5	1	5	50 / 2	3
TOTAL EXPLOITATION RATIO	4	3.5	2.5	6	2.5	2	4
GROUND EXPLOITATION RATIO	60%	50%	50%	100%	40%	50%	60%
THIRD SPACE RATIO	17%	14%	6%	35%	15%	6%	13.7%
PEOPLE DENSITY /KM2 (ESTIMATION)	40,000 P/KM2	30,000 P/KM2	25,000 P/KM2	10,000 P/KM2	20,000 P / KM2	45,000 P/KM2	20,000 P/KM2

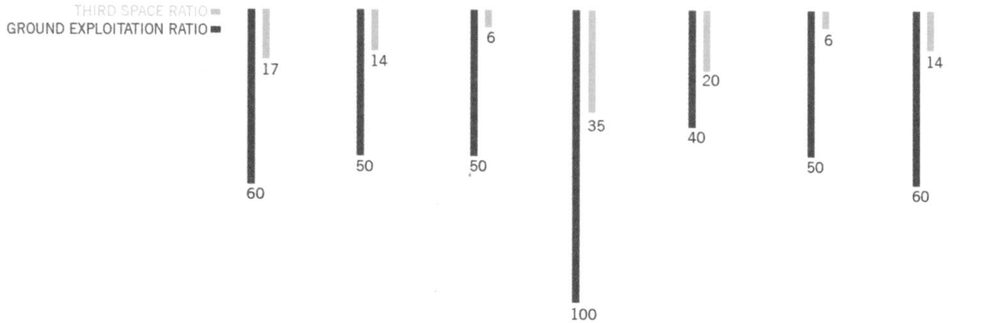

08	09	10	11	12	13	14	15	16
MAR MIKHAEL	KARM EL ZEITOUN	BOURJ HAMMOUD	SAIFI	ZOKAK EL BLAT	MINAT EL HOSN	BASHOURA	MOUSSAITBEH	AIN EL MRAYSEH
3	6	50 / 2	2	3	1	2	5	3
4	3 (AS BUILT)	6-7 (AS BUILT)	2	2.5	3	2.5	1	2.5
60%	90% (AS BUILT)	90% (AS BUILT)	40%	40%	29%	52%	18%	40%
15%	40%	20%	6%	12%	17%	6%	13%	12%
30,000 P/KM2	43,500 P/KM2	63,000 P/KM2	4,500 P/KM2	19,500 P/KM2	2,500 P/KM2	20,300 P/KM2	65,000 P/KM2	9,000 P/KM2

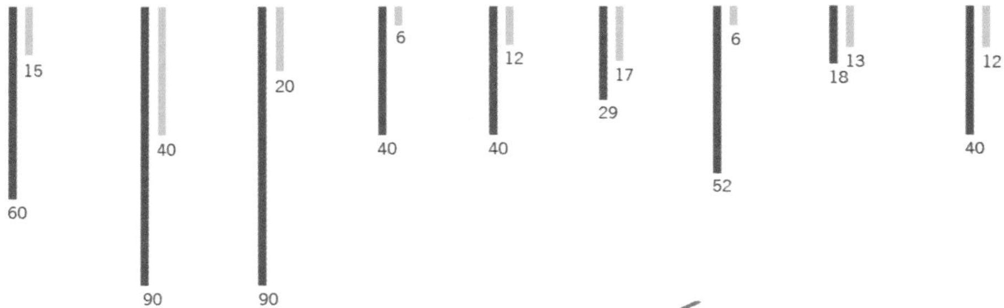

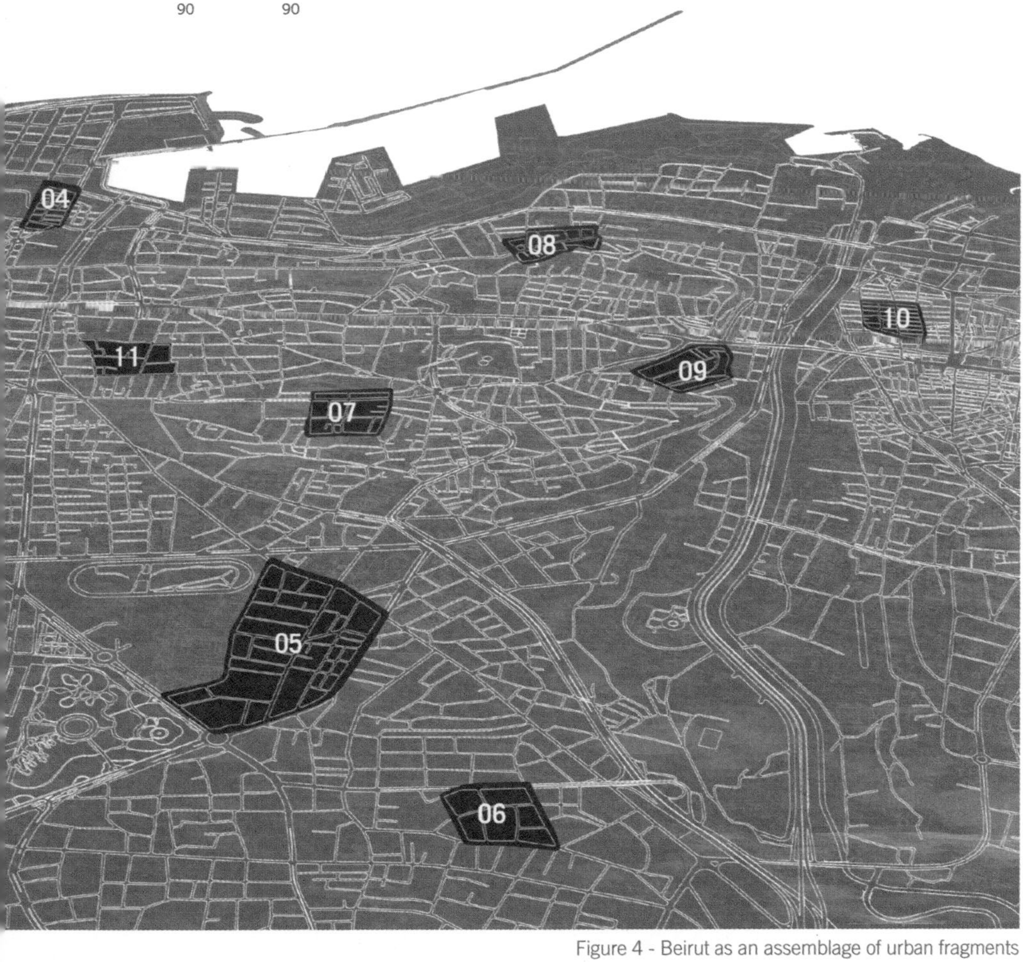

Figure 4 - Beirut as an assemblage of urban fragments

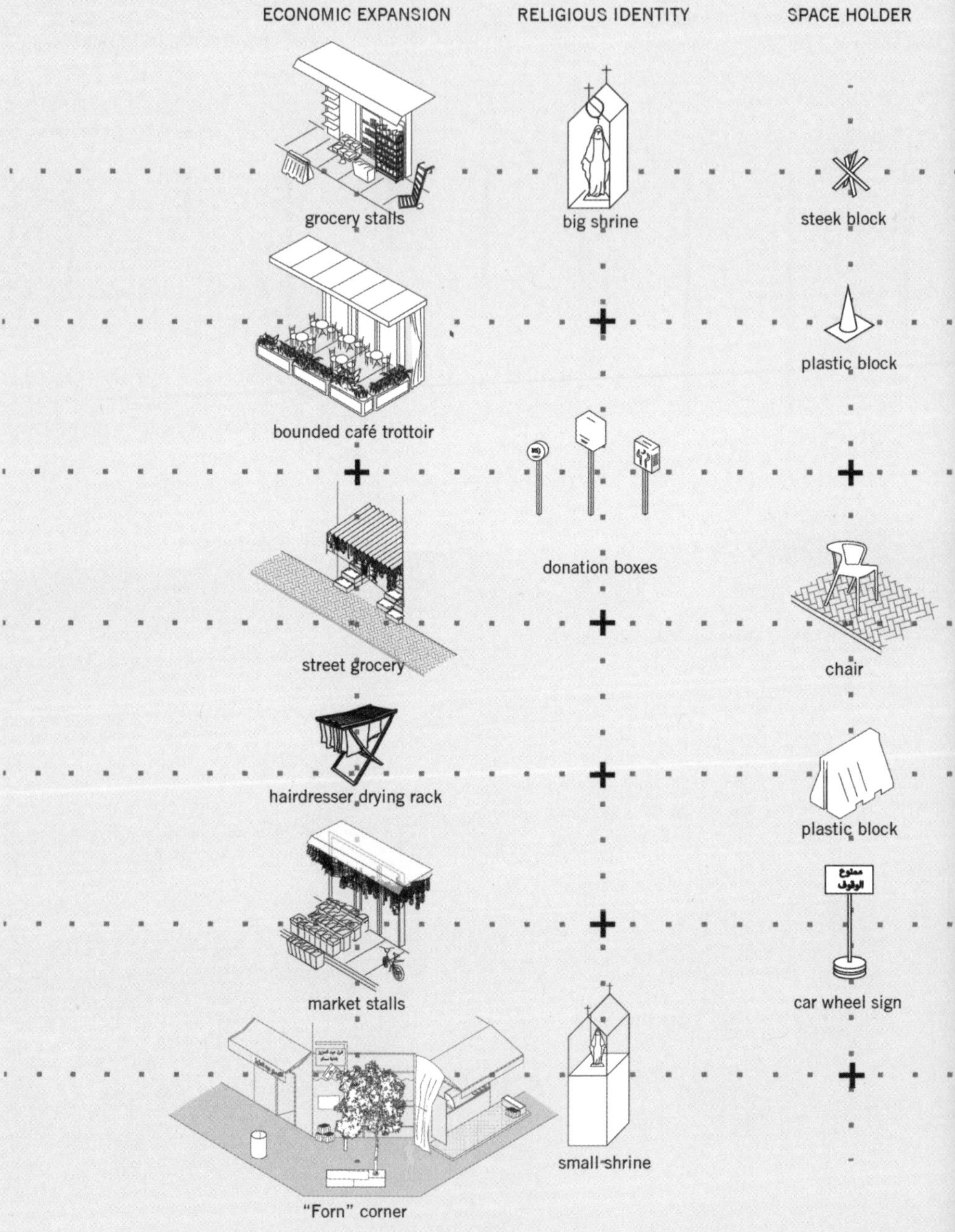
ECONOMIC EXPANSION
RELIGIOUS IDENTITY
SPACE HOLDER
grocery stalls
big shrine
steek block
bounded café trottoir
plastic block
donation boxes
street grocery
chair
hairdresser drying rack
plastic block
ممنوع
الوقوف
market stalls
car wheel sign
"Forn" corner
small shrine

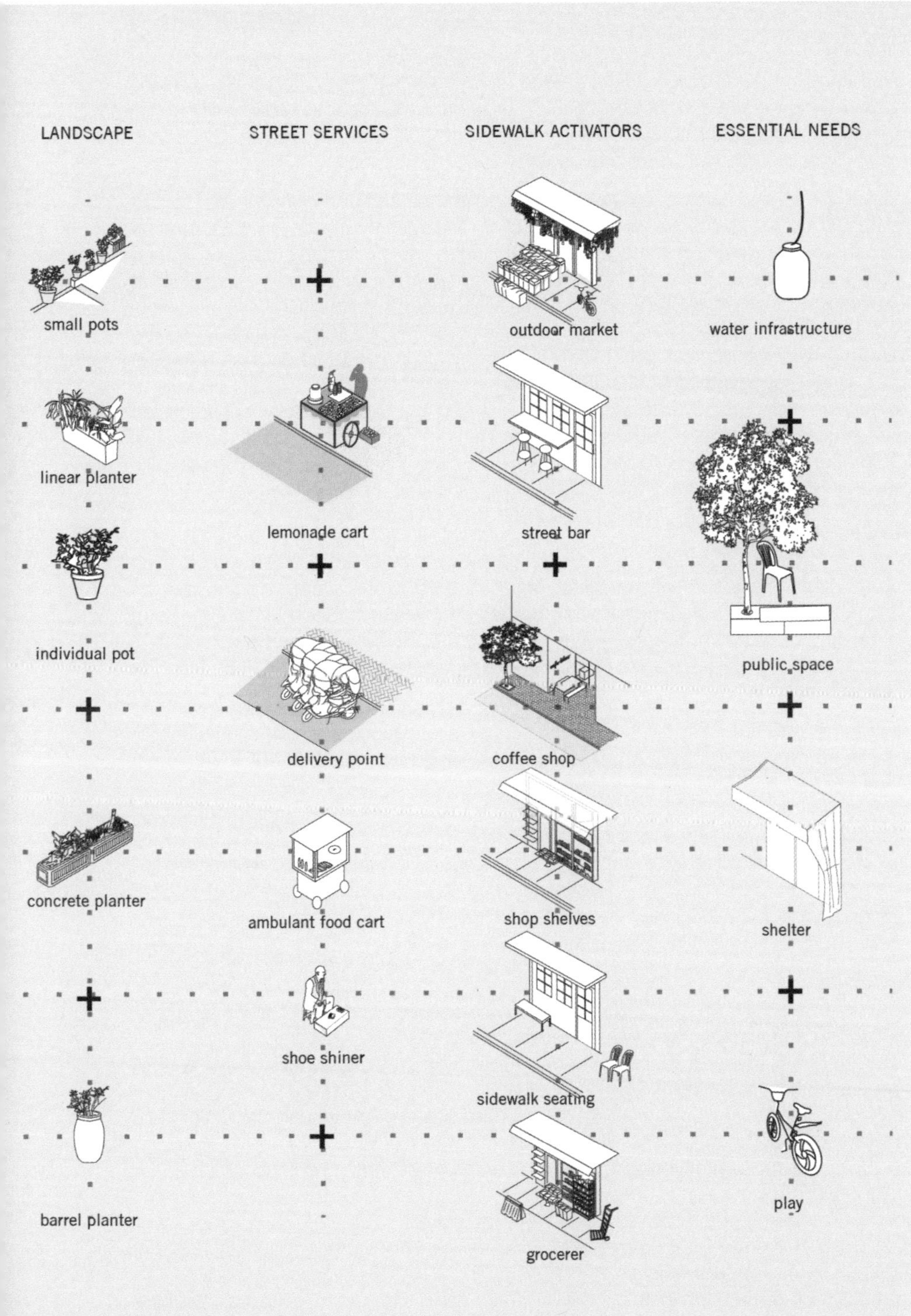

Figure 5 - Taxonomy of urban appropriations found in Beirut

Methodology

To measure appropriation as an informal phenomenon, urban mapping methods have shifted in recent decades to evidence-based techniques that generate real-time sensing of urban performance and growth, people's usage of urban space (accessibility, social hotspots, mobility patterns, etc.), using a myriad of tools (remote sensing, GIS, social media, AI, etc.) and methodical approaches.[6]

However, for the comparative study of ground form and urban pulse in a data-poor context like Beirut, the chapter proposes urban sampling[7] as a general framework that relies on observational methods.[8] Sampling in this study involves using a limited number of "ground samples" to investigate, compare, and synthesize instead of trying to acquire information on all variable conditions found in Beirut. This framework absorbs, on one hand, the multiplicity of urban fabrics and their socioeconomic nuances and, on the other hand, the lack of equally available data for the different areas of the city. With such constraints, observational methods come out as easy to implement, and their surveyed data encompass a wide spectrum of information—including physical, social, typological, and intangible qualities of appropriated urban space. Within this framework, the mapping joins methods of urban morphology to study the form of the ground, social sciences to study its economic and demographic composition, and observational methods of field surveying to measure its usage.

Samples selection

Ground samples are all selected to the same measurements of 250 x 250 meters, picked from residential neighborhoods of Beirut, each comprising one active commercial main street. They include Achrafieh (Sassine), Badaro, Mar Mikhael, Karm El Zeitoun, Bourj Hammoud (Nor Marash), Mazraa, Hamra, Jnah, Ain El Remmane, and Downtown.
The selected ground samples are representative of diverse criteria that can be found in other parts of the city:

urban forms resulting from planned fragments (grids of Badaro, Jnah, Bourj Hammoud, and Hamra) and unplanned growth (additive/ infilled patterns of Ain El Remmaneh, Achrafieh, and Mar Mikhael);
urban grains ranging from the small (Bourj Hammoud) to the large (Jnah), resulting in different building/ housing unit/ open space ratios;
diversity between historic urban fabrics (Mar Mikhael, Bourj Hammoud, Hamra), versus more recent urban fabrics (Ain El Remmane, Jnah);
diversity of socio-economic patterns, ranging from low-income areas (Bourj Hammoud, Ain El Remmane) to more affluent ones (Jnah, Badaro) (Fig. 6).

Hypothesis

Many initial questions were departure points for the selection of metrics according to their influence on appropriation forms and pulses. For example:
Are urban pulses primarily generated from the built form or spatial practices? i.e., do they come first from an advantageous/compact urban form that favors daily interactions or from the dynamics of social groups that take their cultural rituals to the ground and adapt them to their needs?
How does social class influence the intensity and type of interactions occurring in the public realm?
How do climate and urban nature influence ground usage?
What types of architectural spaces and economic activities produce higher levels of interactions and appropriations?
Does a vibrant pulse (high interaction levels, high pedestrian fluxes) reflect accessibility and inclusivity?

The mapping compares information that addresses these questions and provides metrics for comparison and interpretation.

Metrics

On the temporal level, the mapping looks at historic versus daily rhythms:

History of the ground's emergence reviews social groups who succeeded in it, investment sources that contributed to its economy, political events that affected it, and built typologies that contributed to its making.

Daily rhythm simulates recorded rhythms of users over 24 hours, noting overlaps or segregation between them (Fig. 26).

On the usage level, short-term metrics show transient patterns of usage/urban life, visualizing surveyed data from the seven ground samples. Surveying took place systematically at the same time in all seven samples, a mid-weekday between 2-5 pm, during the transitional period of December 2019 and March 2020.[9] The selected timing coincided with different users and patterns: high-intensity moments like lunch breaks, school exits, and commuter induced traffic, as well as low-intensity periods in between.

Speeds and Flows were recorded through car and pedestrian counts. Their numbers were quantified and translated in a pro-rata ratio into lines of different colors based on their speed (Fig. 7).

Activities and Interactions were recorded by category, density of occurrence, and location on the ground (Fig. 8).

Noise and Sounds were recorded every 50 meters using a decibel counter. Noise sources were mapped and noted (Fig. 9).

Taxonomy of Gound Appropriations was recorded in relation to its use and causality (replacing missing infrastructure, make-shifting public space, space-holding, etc.).

Long-term metrics show slower phenomena like landscape patterns, exposure to climatic elements, and economic mixity—latent but highly influential on ground occupation patterns and atmospheres beneficial to appropriation.
Landscape mapped existing urban patches found in each ground, explored in the following chapter.

Economic Mixity mapped economic activities at ground level, ranked by the level of accessibility from the least accessible (banks and jewelery shops) to the most accessible (essential services, food/health outlets, and social infrastructure) (Fig. 10).

Exposure mapped the ground's vulnerability to climatic elements through human thermal comfort. A detailed 3d model of each ground is used to perform geospatial analysis, simulating climatic factors like solar insolation, radiative temperature, dry bulb temperature recorded humidity, and relative wind, synthesizing outdoor urban comfort in winter and summer and the resilience of each ground to the elements due to its urban form (see Fig. 12, 14, 16, 18, 20, 22, 24).

6 A comprehensive panorama of these methods and approaches is covered in the following paper: Marc Fleischmann, Olivera Romice, and Salvatore Porta, "Measuring urban Form: Overcoming Terminological Inconsistencies for a Quantitative And Comprehensive Morphologic Analysis of Cities," *Environment and Planning B: Urban Analytics and City Science* 48, no. 8 (2021): 2133-50.

7 Sampling is usually a measuring method adopted in a context where every instance is closer to being an exception rather than a rule.

8 Observational tools have been employed by numerous urbanists like Jan Gehl to study urban life. See Gehl Institute, "How to Use the Public Life Tools," accessed July 1, 2024, https://gehlpeople.com/tools/ and Jan Gehl and Birgitte Svarre, *How to Study Public Life* (Island Press, 2013), 45.

9 This was a shifting period in Beirut after the October 2019 revolution/ financial crash and just before the beginning of the pandemic's extended lockdown.

On the formal level, the urban morphology mapping includes:

*A variation of the Nolli plan,*maps the built ground's porosity, highlighting an elastic public realm to include spaces that are "working" with the ground— physically/ visually and programmatically accessible. The plan shows these spaces in the same color as the public realm and the types of appropriations found in them (see Fig. 11, 13, 15, 17, 19, 21, 23).

Urban block massing, shows the scale and spatial porosity of a block from the studied ground sample. This criterion shows built density, the scale of buildings, the ratio of open-close and built-unbuilt at ground level, and the type of facades and interfaces between inner and outer blocks (see Fig. 11, 13, 15, 17, 19, 21, 23).

Sample grounds

Mar Mikhael's ground offers the earliest 20th-century typologies of ground commercial space in residential buildings, with an urban grid that meets the hill through staircases and cascading residential quarters. As the neighborhood reemerged as a creative district and culinary destination in the last decade, it underwent a gentrification process that reflected in its ground floor form and life. Its current ground registers discordances between the porosities of the historic architecture versus its new gated developments, the segregated daily cycles of old residents versus new users, and the intense development of its main spine (Armenia Street) versus its neglected residential edges. This temporal and spatial segregation is also evident in the appropriations through which new users monopolize the ground level for their usage (Fig. 11, 12).

Badaro is a residential neighborhood with a regular urban grid that was planned in the 1940s. Dotted with distinctive modernist architecture, it has also reinvented itself as a hip café and bar scene, in addition to its banking and institutional character. Home to a more established social class, gentrification is less evident than in other neighborhoods like Mar Mikhael. Badaro's newest uses appropriate sidewalks for café extensions, protruding in some cases to widen their indoor areas and reshaping the ground on the main spine to one that is less porous and more frequented, in contrast with the intersecting residential streets that retained their original character and pace (Fig. 13, 14).

Bourj Hammoud is a neighborhood that was established in the early 1920s as a settlement for Armenian refugees on the eastern bank of the Beirut River. Characterized by long linear blocks, it went on to become the Armenian enclave of Beirut with a vibrant street life and pedestrian scale, with a ground porosity between public and private uses that recalls Walter Benjamin's writings on Naples: "Just as the living room reappears on the street, with chairs, hearth, and altar, the street migrates into the living room." On an average day, people/ residents are on the street, living, working, and interacting (Fig. 15, 16).

Hamra is the case of a highly mixed-use ground that draws its raison d'être from its proximity to academic, commercial, and official institutions. With a regular urban grid populated by diverse uses such as commerce, banking, food, and shops, it is a daily destination for Beiruties from all classes, students, professionals, and a cosmopolitan crowd. On any given day, its ground is an intense place for social and economic interactions with considerable pedestrian and vehicular traffic. The use of the ground reflects perimeter blocks' activity patterns, with the edges used as commercial frontages and the centers used as service spaces (Fig. 17, 18).

Achrafieh-Sassine reflects the neighborhood's history as an enclave that emerged in Eastern Beirut during wartime and has undergone gentrification since 2004 with the development of large institutional projects at the neighborhood edges (LAU- Rizk Medical Center, AUST, etc.). Achrafieh provides a mix of fabrics between its 1980s residential buildings on Independence Street and an infill fabric of old and newer residential buildings that vary in access and interaction at the ground level. Its large lots became urbanized through the cul-de-sac typology, resulting in residential uses (pilotis, ground floor units, residents' parking) at the lots centers and essential services (groceries, pharmacies) at the lots' edges (Fig. 19, 20).

Jnah is an upper-class enclave that emerged at the end of the 1990s. Its ground shows a segregation between its lower and its upper floors. The ground is characterized by large-scale commerce, punctuated by vehicular ramps leading to undergrounds used for warehousing, fulfilment, and storage services. This differs significantly from the upper levels' luxury residential identity. As a result, the ground pulse is drastically different on weekdays during business hours than during afternoons and weekends when ground occupations cease, and it becomes an upper-residential ground with reduced pedestrian activities (Fig. 21, 22).

Ain El Remmaneh presents the case of a ground that densified haphazardly from agricultural land to a low-income residential neighborhood. Its first users were rural migrants coming to Beirut in the 1950s during the first construction boom. Undergoing several waves of densification, its urban fabric is characterized by large lots with underserviced inner parts, in an ad-hoc network of access roads and building entrances. In any given lot, the ground at the edges is a mix of shops that draw dense pedestrian activitiy contrasting with the strictly residential center (Fig. 23, 24).

Figure 6 - Selected ground samples to study of appropriation in Beirut: 1. Mar Mikhael, 2. Badaro, 3. Bourj Hammoud, 4. Hamra, 5. Achrafieh (Sassine), 6. Jnah, 7. Ain El Remmaneh.

SPEED AND FLOWS

0 KM/ HOUR 1 PERSON/DOT
05 KM/ HOUR 20 PEOPLE/HOUR
07 KM/ HOUR 20 PEOPLE/HOUR
30 KM/ HOUR 20 CARS/ HOUR
50 KM/ HOUR 20 CARS/ HOUR

Figure 7 - Speed and flows

INTERACTIONS

	WALKING		CHILDREN PLAYING
	STOPPING LOOKING		DOG WALKING
	ENTERING LEAVING		EATING
	GATHERING		GREETING
	STANDING IN DOORWAY		TALKING
	SITTING		PEOPLE WATCHING

Figure 8 - Activities and interactions

ECONOMIC MIXITY

USES WITH LOW ECONOMIC ACCESSIBILITY
- BANKING
- JEWELLERY
- CLOSED SHOPS

USES WITH DECLINING ECONOMIC ACCESSIBILITY
- PERSONAL ARTICLES
- RETAIL
- SERVICES
- HOME APPLIANCES
- OFFICES
- CRAFTS
- LIGHT INDUSTRY
- CREATIVE INDUSTRY

GROUND "ANCHOR" USES WITH HIGH GROUND ENGAGEMENT
- SOCIAL INFRASTRUCTURE
- CLUBS AND LEISURE
- COFFEE SHOPS/ BARS
- RESTAURANTS
- FOOD SHOP/STREET FOOD
- GROCERY STORE
- SPICES SHOPS

Figure 9 - Economic mixicity

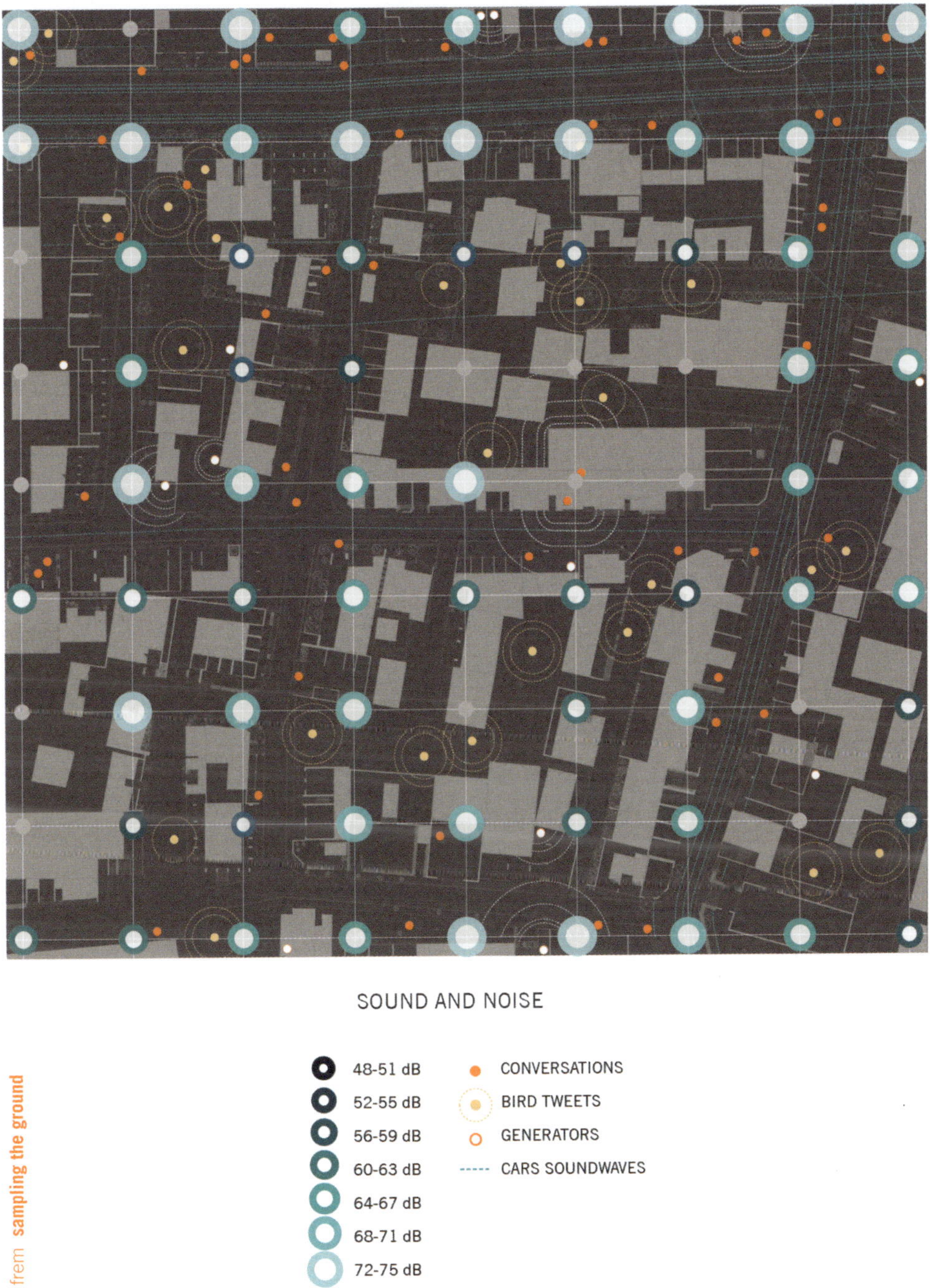

Figure 10 - Noise and sounds

MAR MICHAEL

GROUND PLAN

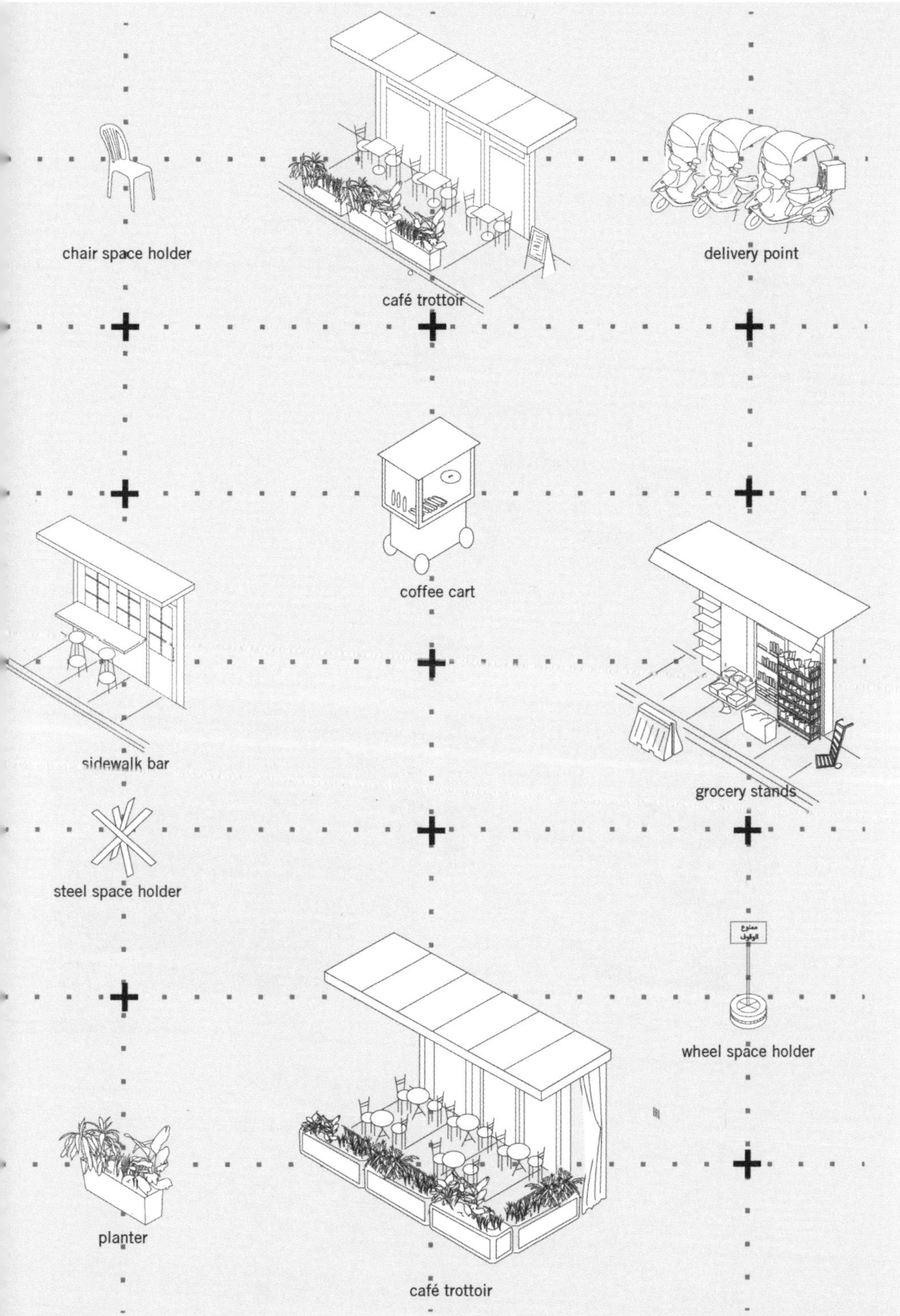

Figure 11 - Mar Mikhael plan and appropriations

USERS

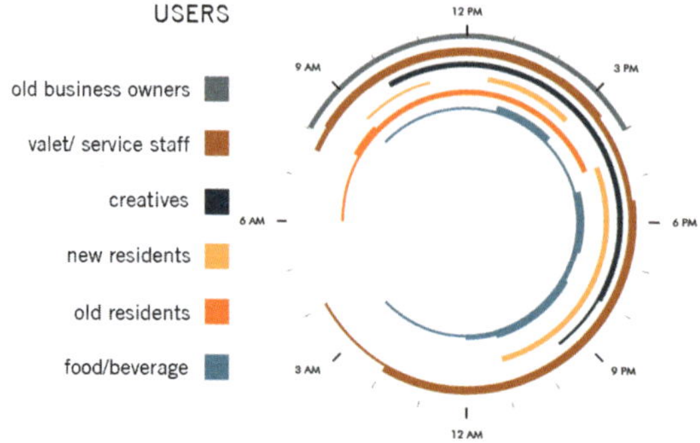

FLOOR RATIO

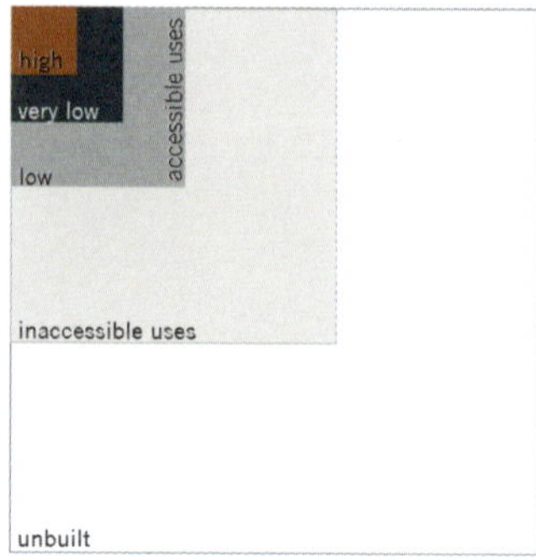

SPEED/FLOWS

INTERACTIONS

MIXITY

NOISE

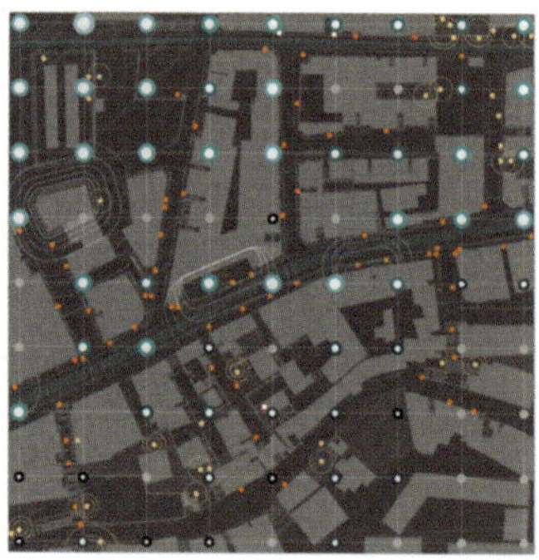

EXPOSURE

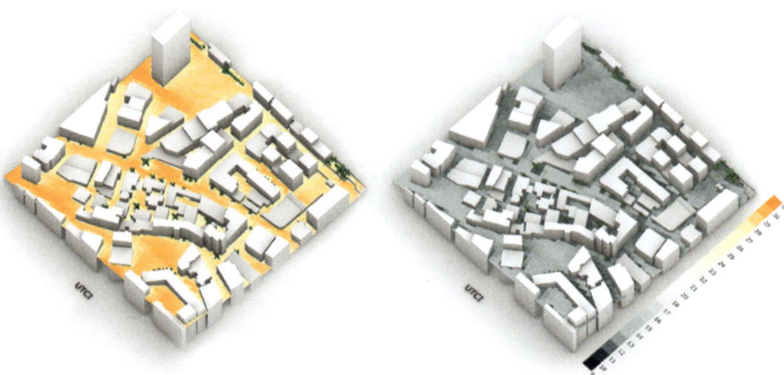

URBAN BLOCK

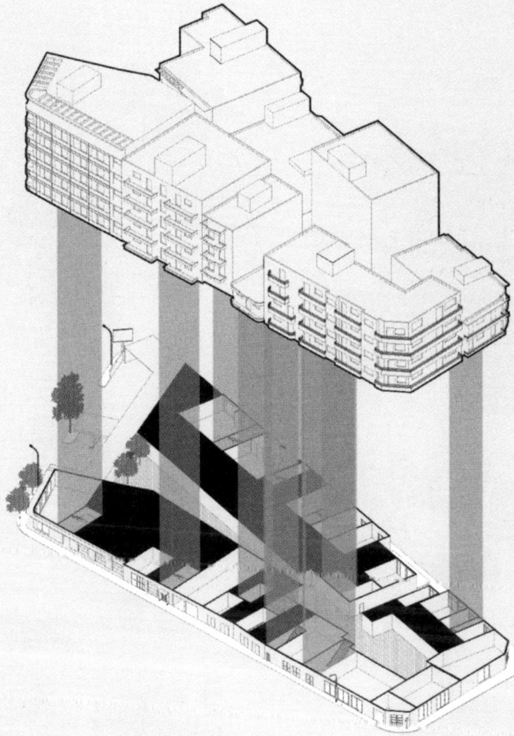

ZONE	3	GROUND ACTIVITY RATIO	
EXPLOITATION RATIO	4	Eat + Drink	23.8 %
GROUND EXPLOITATION	60%	Services	12.3 %
		Creatives	7.8 %
BUILT/NON BUILT	73/29	Grocery	1 %
Built (m2)	3699	Light Industry	7.8 %
Non Built (m2)	1396	Restaurants:	1 %
Total Block Area (m2)	5095	Housing/Circulation	46.3 %
PEOPLE AND URBAN DENSITY		HOUSING	
People density /km2	30000	Av. Unit area	120 m2
Nb of buildings	9	Av. Unit Price / m2	4000 $/ m2
Nb of housing units	60	Av. Persons per unit	3
Av. Person on Ground	180	** sources available in credits*	

Figure 12 - Mar Mikhael metrics

BADARO

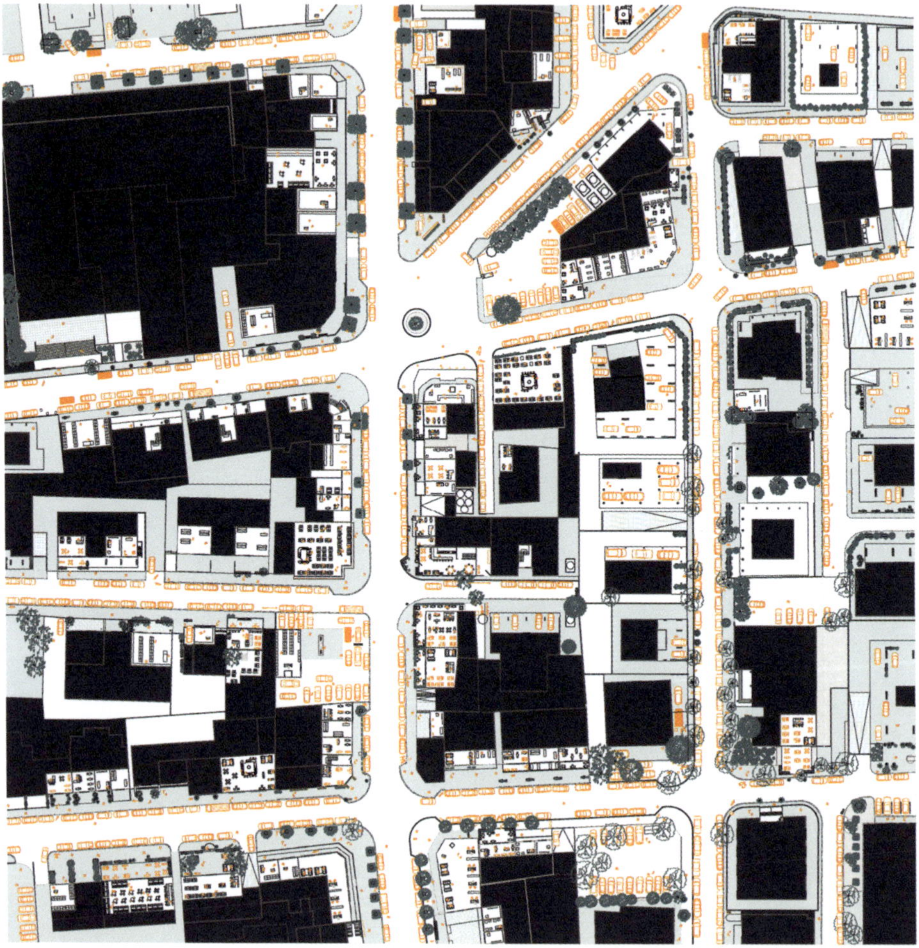

GROUND PLAN

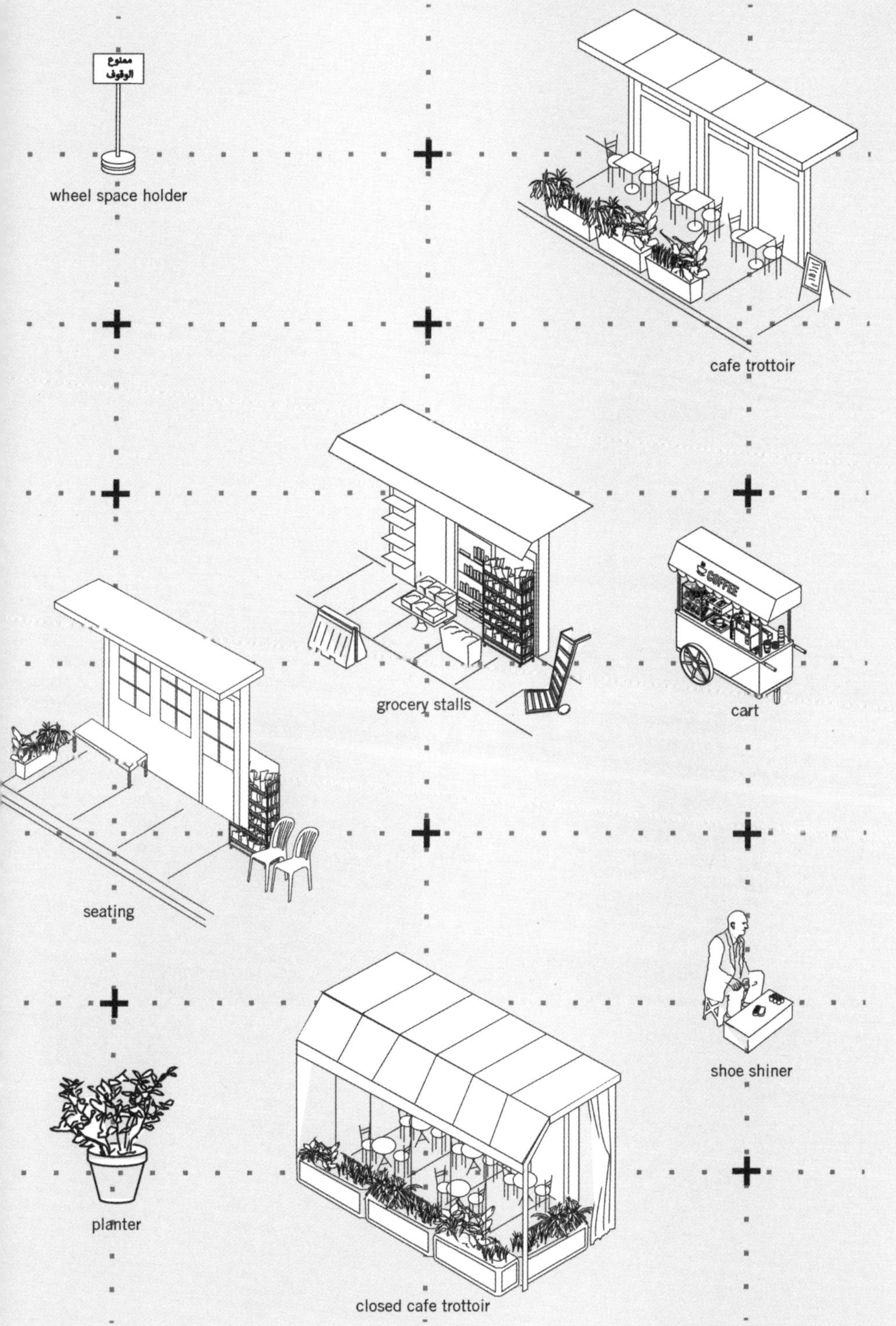

Figure 13 - Badaro plan and appropriations

USERS

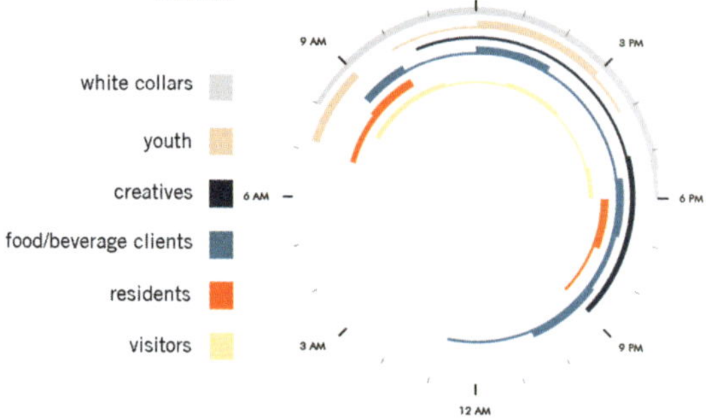

FLOOR RATIO

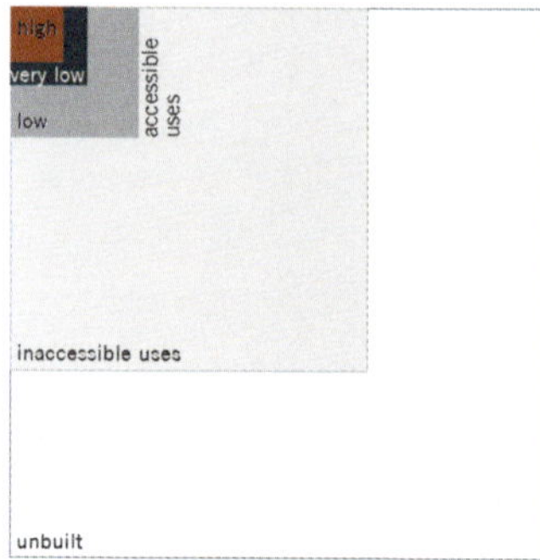

SPEED/FLOWS

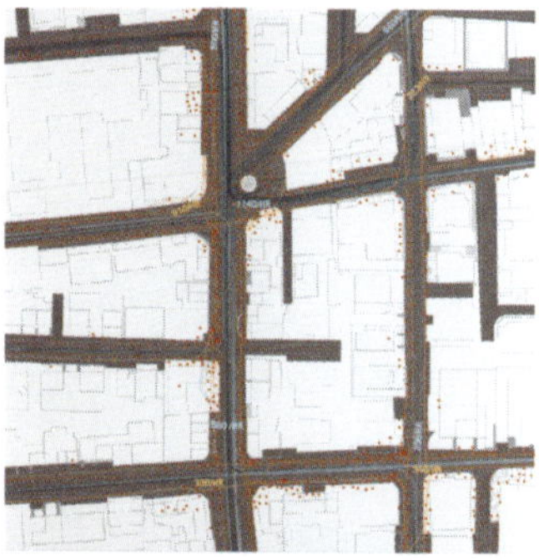

INTERACTIONS

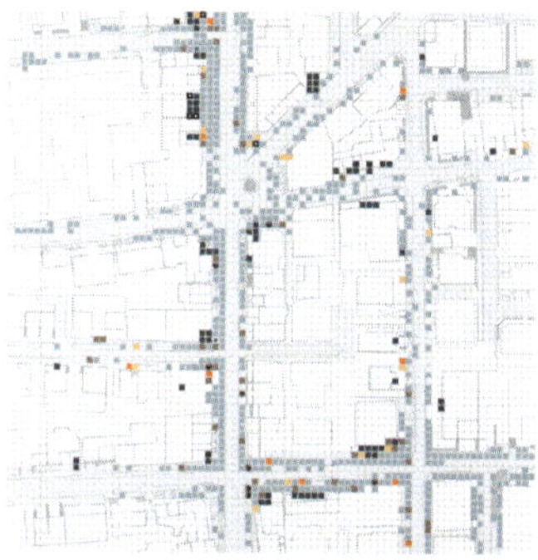

MIXITY

NOISE

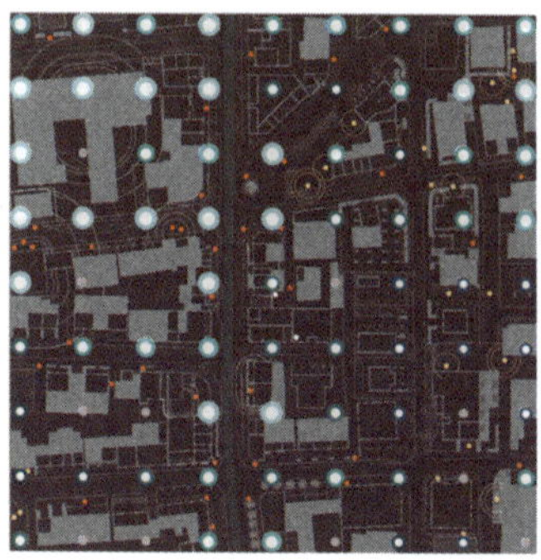

EXPOSURE

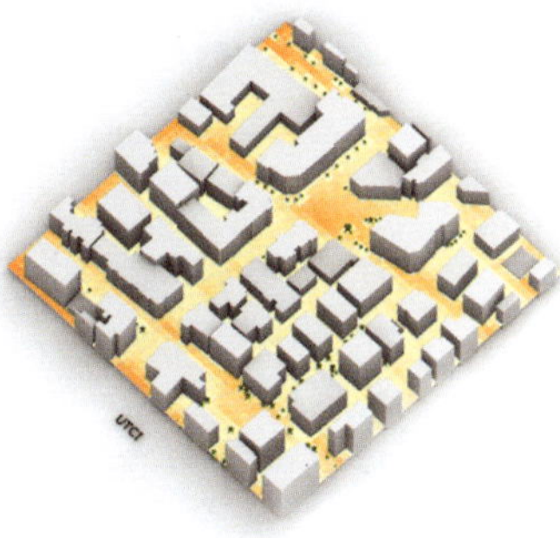

URBAN BLOCK

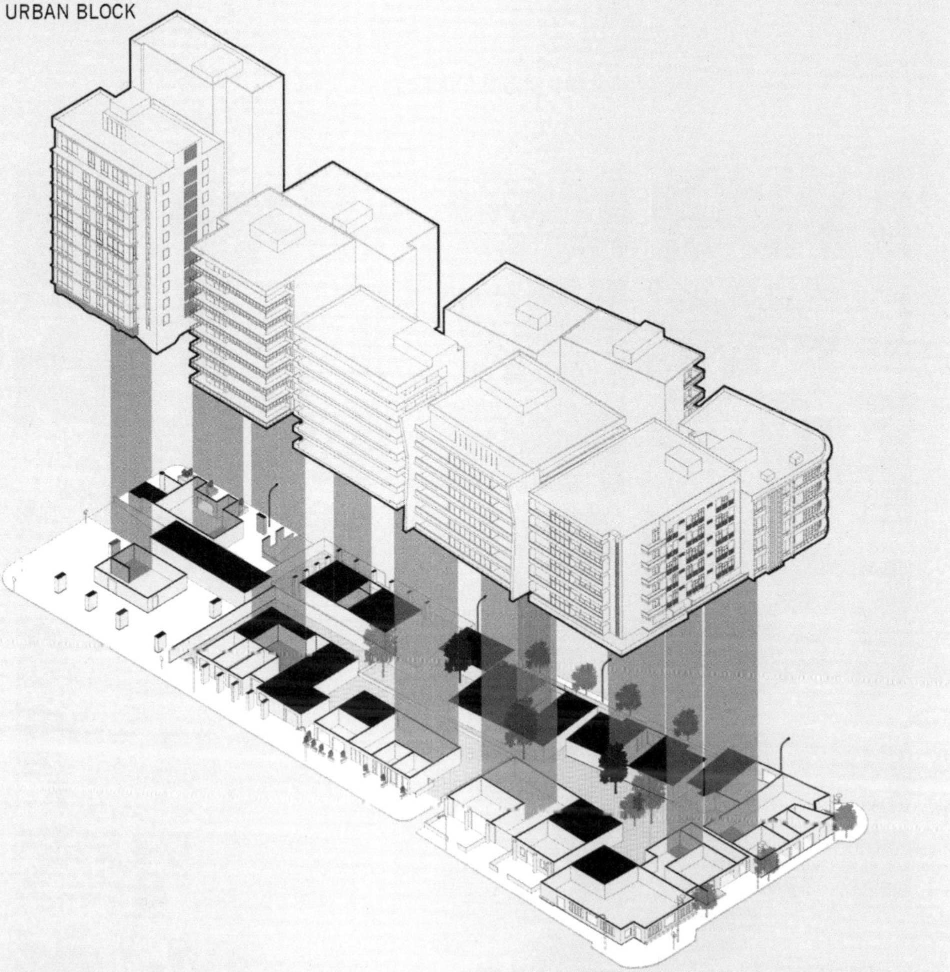

ZONE	5	GROUND ACTIVITY RATIO	
EXPLOITATION RATIO	2.5	Eat + Drink	0.8 %
GROUND EXPLOITATION	40%	Services	3.5 %
		Grocery	3 %
BUILT/NON BUILT %	49/51	Restaurant	8.1 %
Built (m2)	3688	Closed Shops	4.3 %
Non Built (m2)	3492	Homes Furnishes	2.4 %
Total Block Area (m2)	7180	Housing/Circ	76.09%
PEOPLE AND URBAN DENSITY		HOUSING	
People density /km2	35000	Av. Unit area	180 m2
Nb of buildings	10	Av. Unit Price / m2	3300 $/ m2
Nb of housing units	112	Av. Persons per unit	5
Av. Person on Ground	290	** sources available in credits*	

Figure 14 - Badaro metrics

BOURJ HAMMOUD

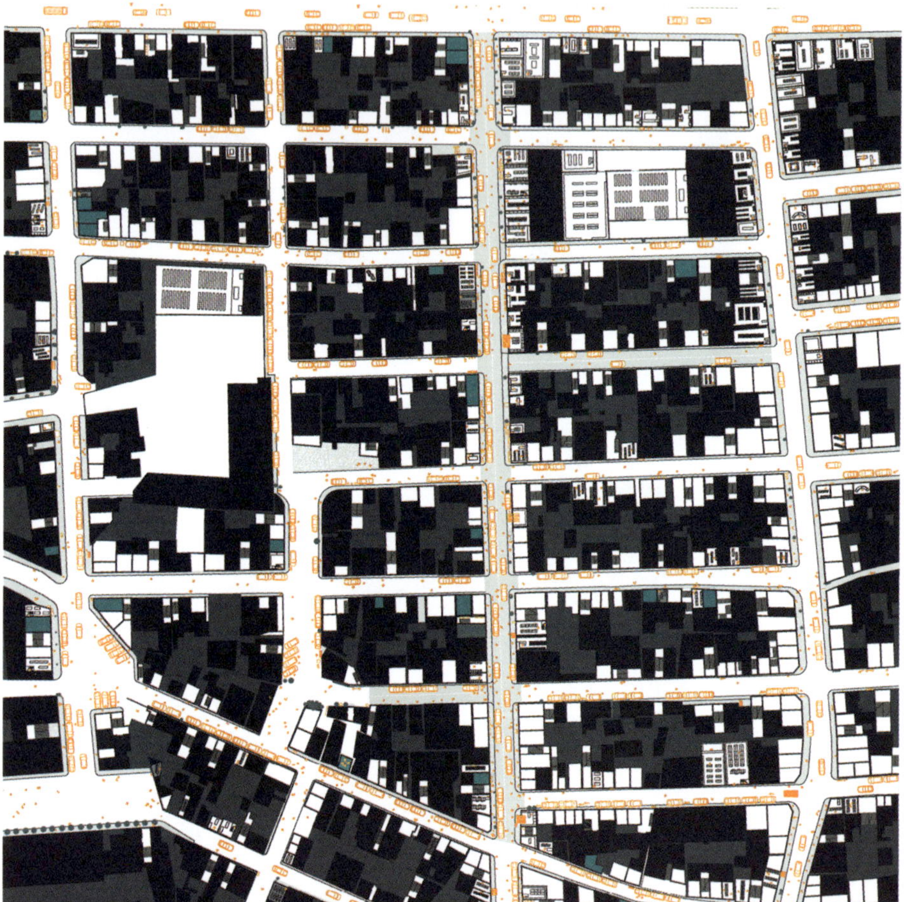

GROUND PLAN

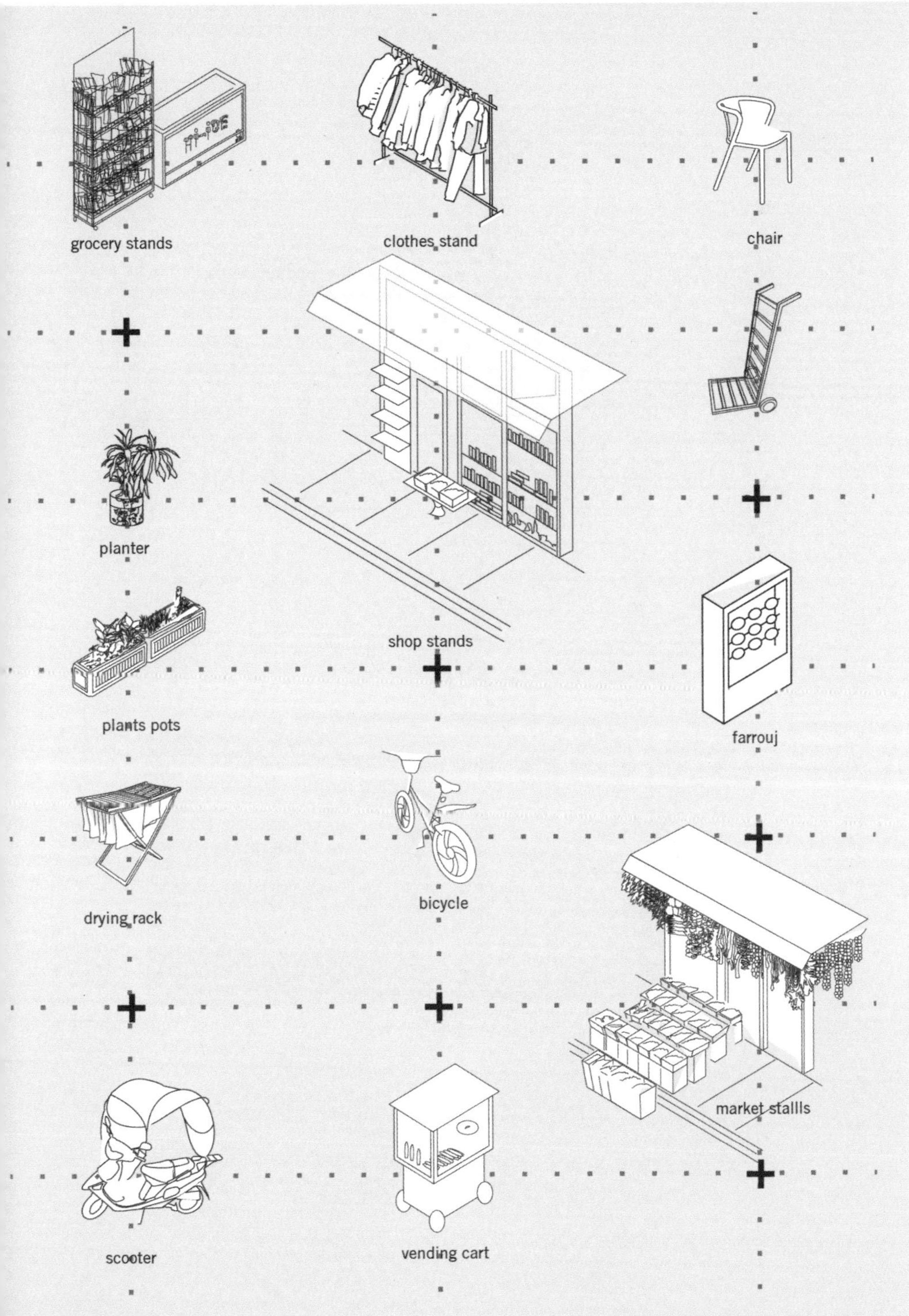

Figure 15 - Bourj Hammoud plan and appropriations

USERS

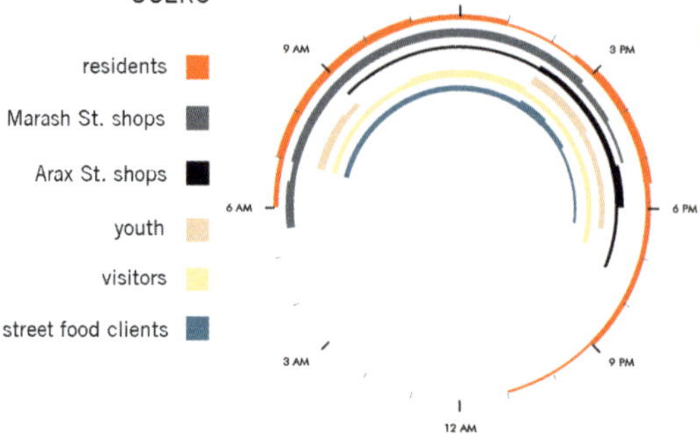

FLOOR RATIO

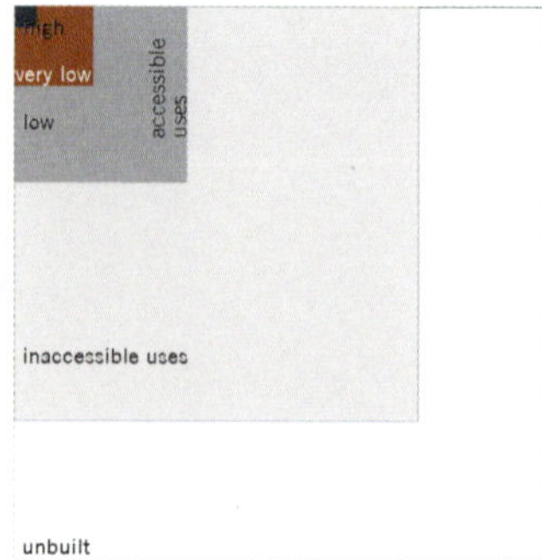

SPEED/FLOWS

INTERACTIONS

MIXITY

NOISE

EXPOSURE

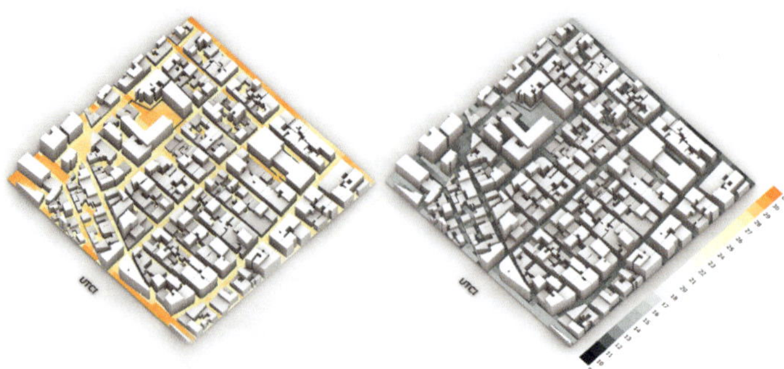

URBAN BLOCK

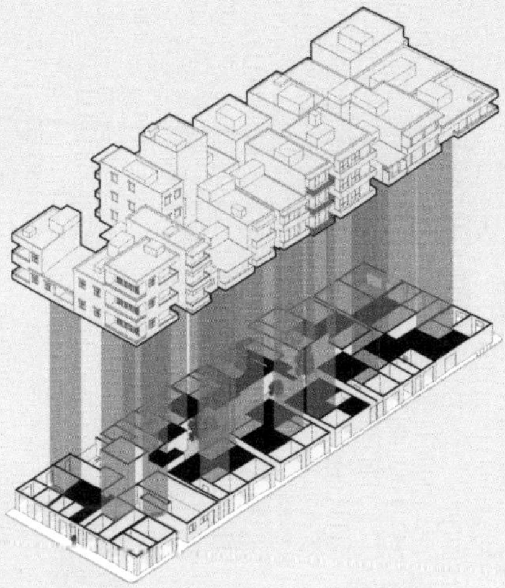

ZONE	50/2	GROUND ACTIVITY RATIO	
EXPLOITATION RATIO	2	Spices:	1.4 %
GROUND EXPLOITATION	90%	Grocery :	3.8 %
		Clothes & Shoes :	23.5 %
BUILT/NON BUILT	78/22	Services :	1.4 %
Built (m2)	1507	Housing/Circ :	69.9 %
Non Built (m2)	419		
Total Block Area (m2)	1926		
PEOPLE AND URBAN DENSITY		HOUSING	
People density /km2	63000	Av. Unit area	90 m2
Nb of buildings	19	Av. Unit Price / m2	500 $/ m2
Nb of housing units	46	Av. Persons per unit	4
Av. Person on Ground	184	** sources available in credits*	

Figure 16 - Bourj Hammoud metrics

HAMRA

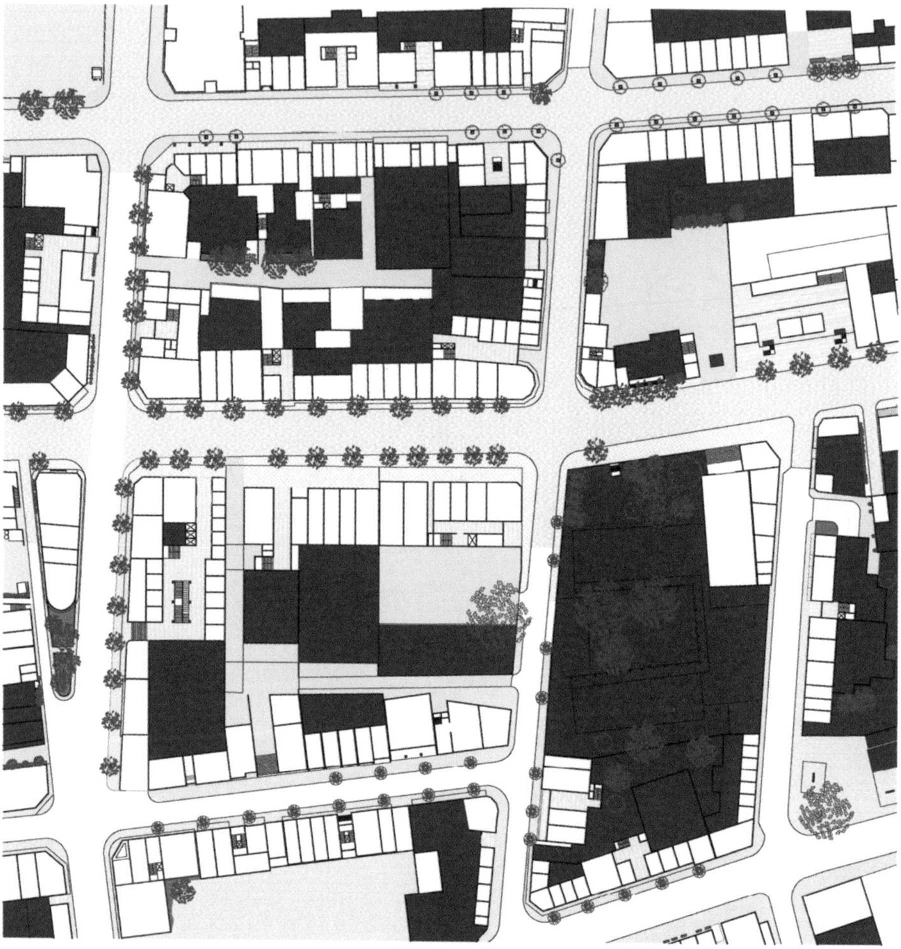

GROUND PLAN

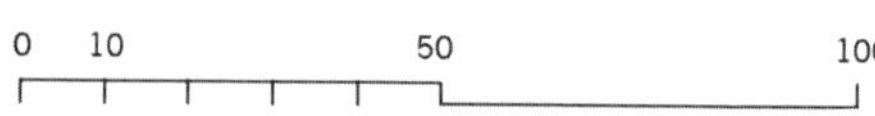

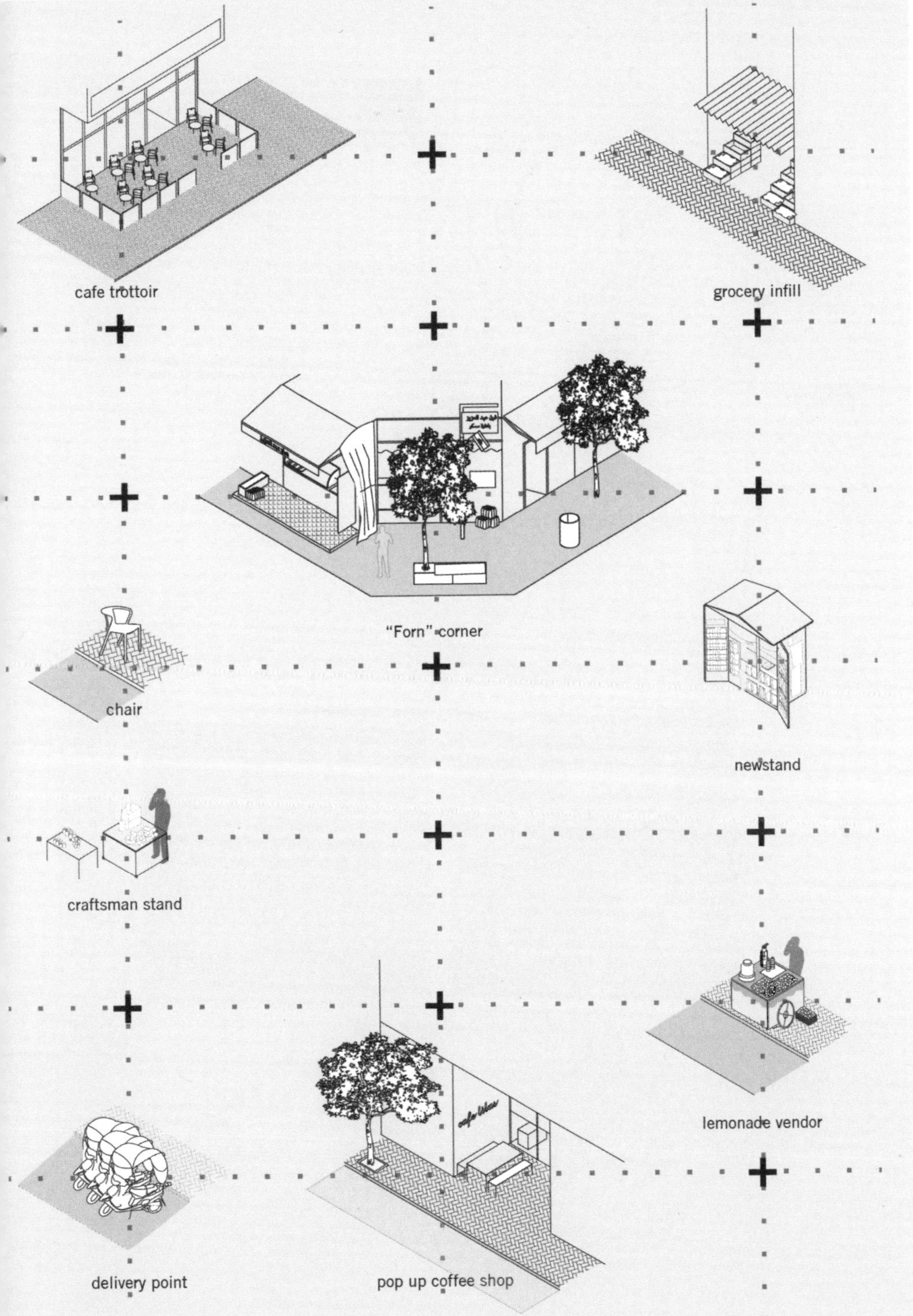

Figure 17. Hamra plan and appropriations

USERS

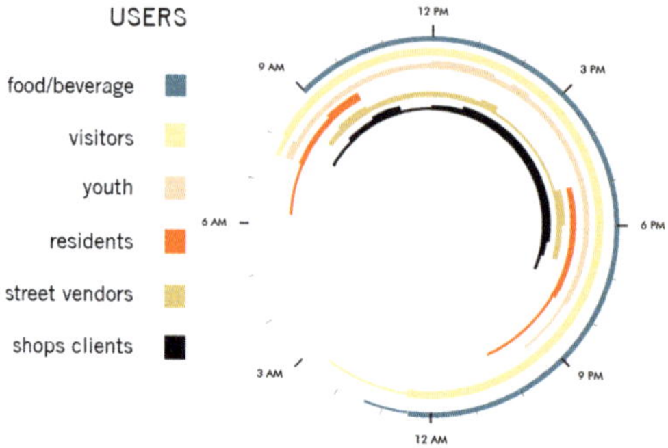

FLOOR RATIO

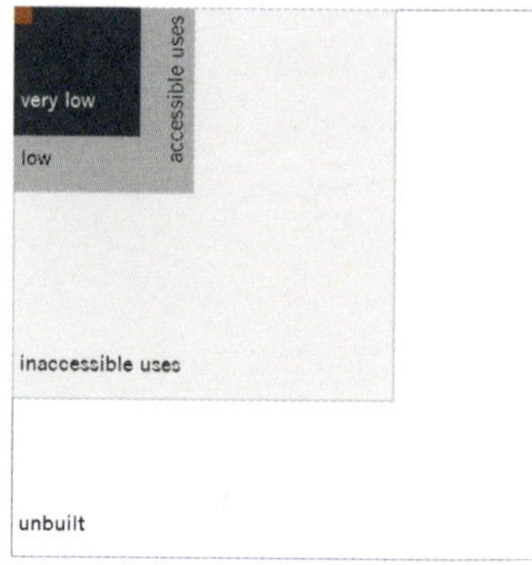

SPEED/FLOWS

INTERACTIONS

MIXITY

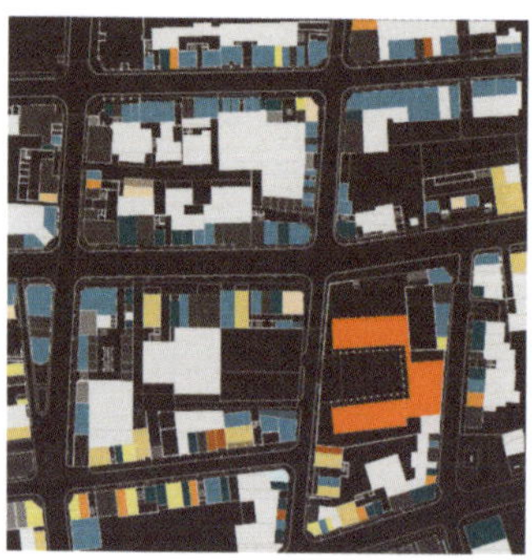

NOISE

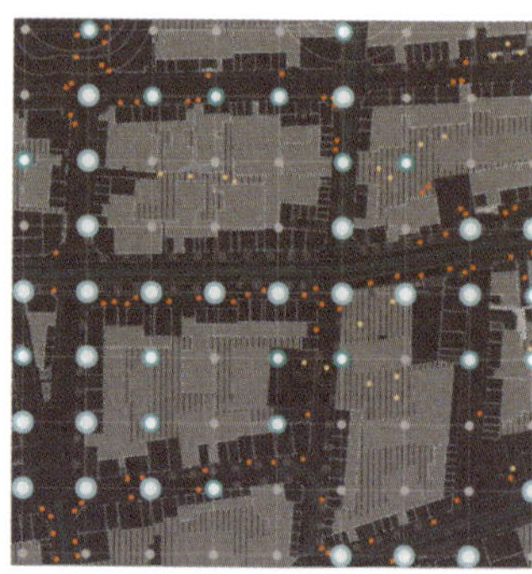

EXPOSURE

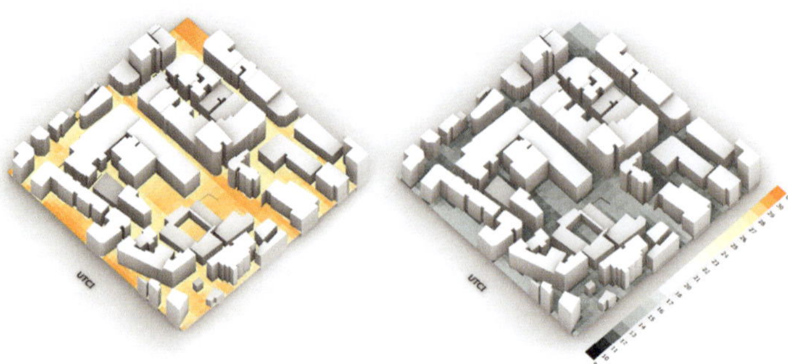

URBAN BLOCK

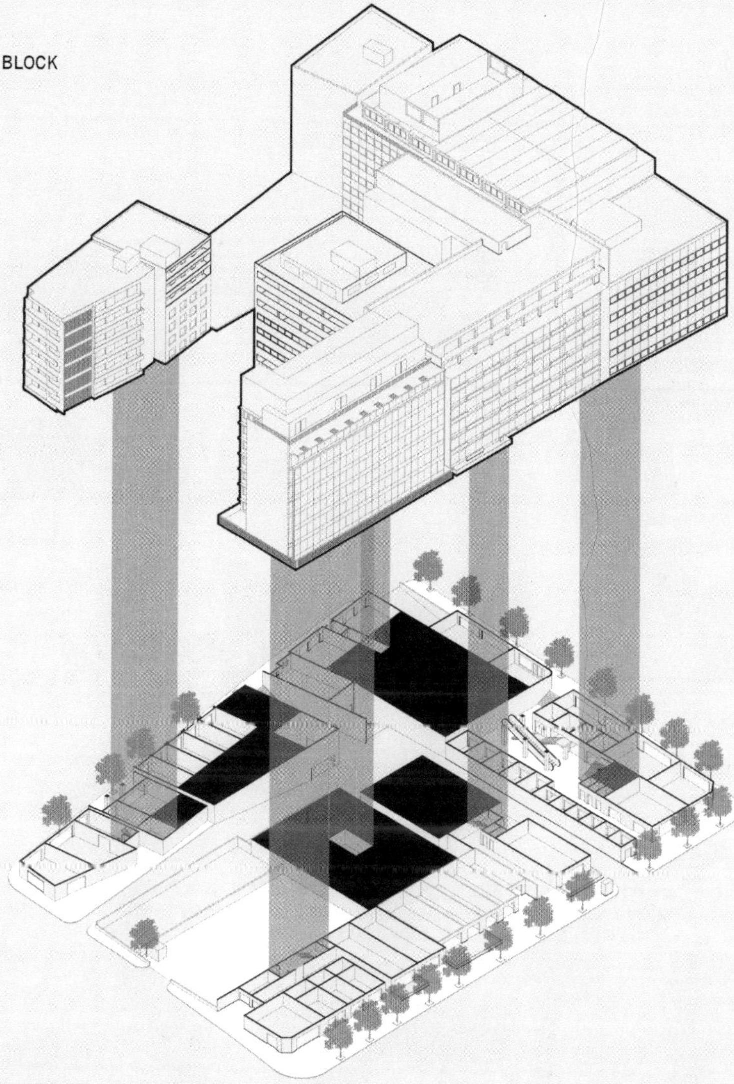

ZONE	3	GROUND ACTIVITY RATIO	
EXPLOITATION RATIO	4	Closed Shops	8.1 %
GROUND EXPLOITATION	60%	Services	2.4 %
		Grocery	1.4 %
BUILT/NON BUILT	66/ 34	Eat+Drink	9.6 %
Built (m2)	6220	Jewellery	1.1 %
Non Built (m2)	3196	Food Shops	0.7 %
Total Block Area (m2)	9416	Clothes & Shoes	14 %
		Housing/Circulation	62.51%
PEOPLE AND URBAN DENSITY			
People density /km2	40000	HOUSING	
Nb of buildings	9	Av. Unit area	120 m2
Nb of housing units	54	Av. Unit Price / m2	4300 $/ m2
Av. Person on Ground	180	Av. Persons per unit	4

** sources available in credits*

Figure 18 - Hamra metrics

ACHRAFIEH (SASSINE)

GROUND PLAN

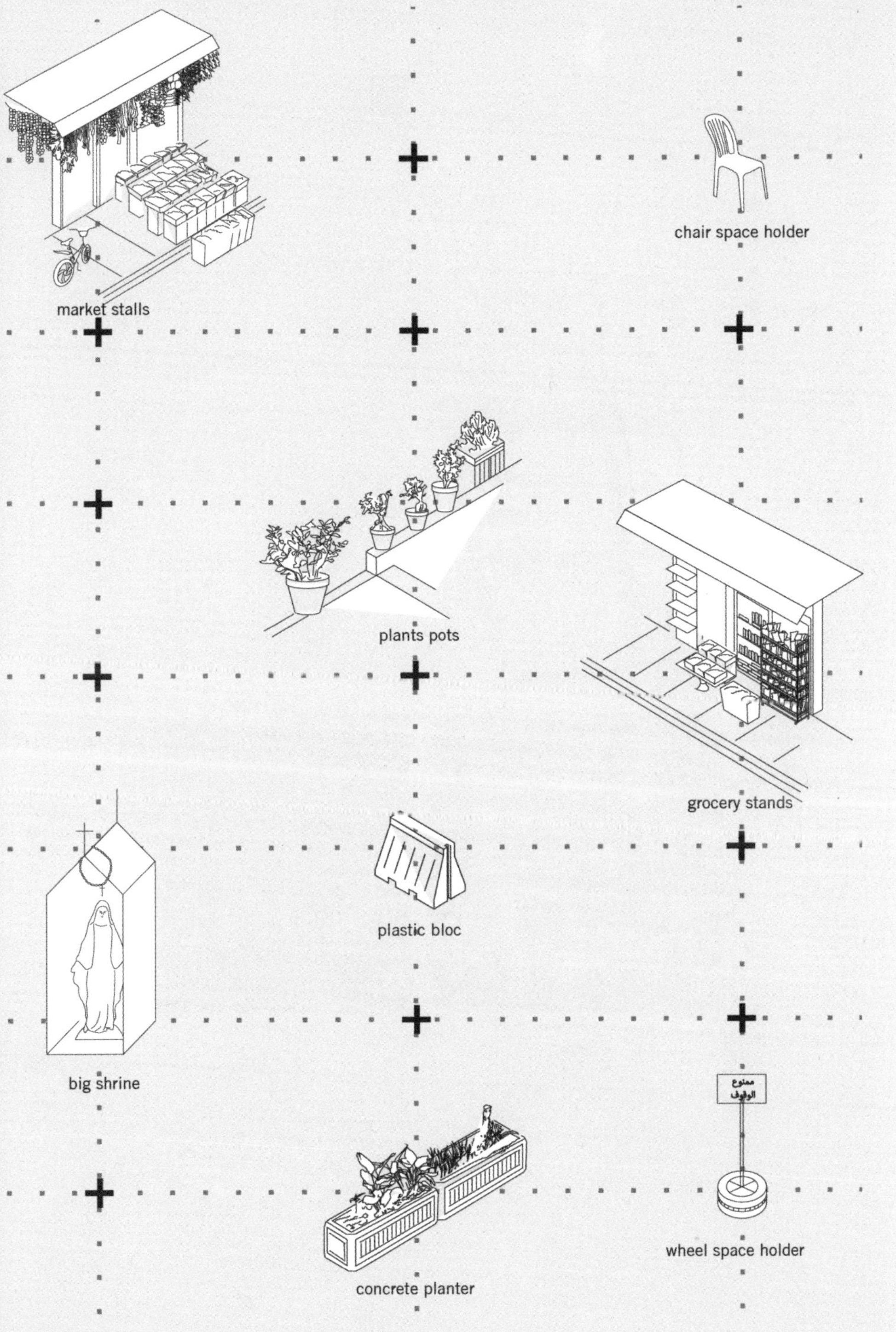

Figure 19 - Achrafieh plan and appropriations

USERS

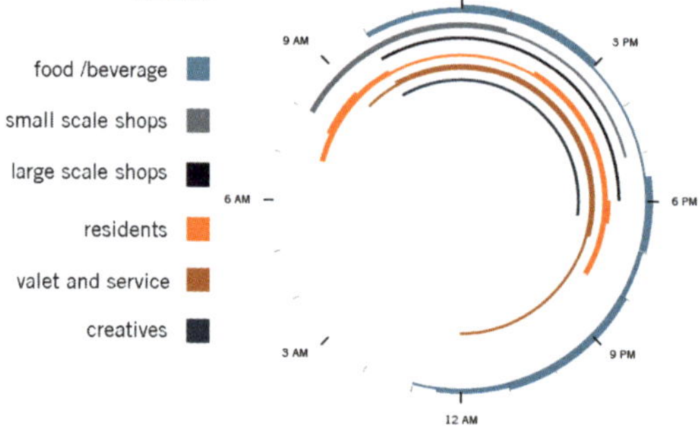

FLOOR RATIO

SPEED/FLOWS

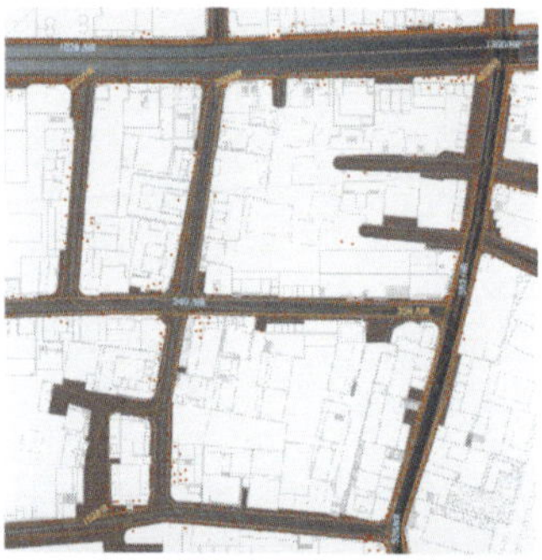

INTERACTIONS

MIXITY

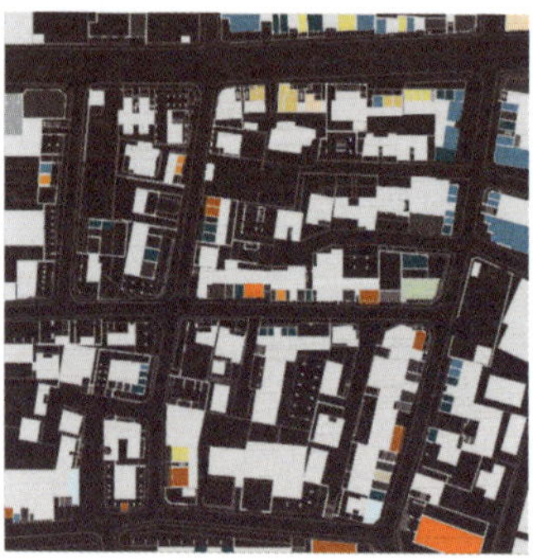

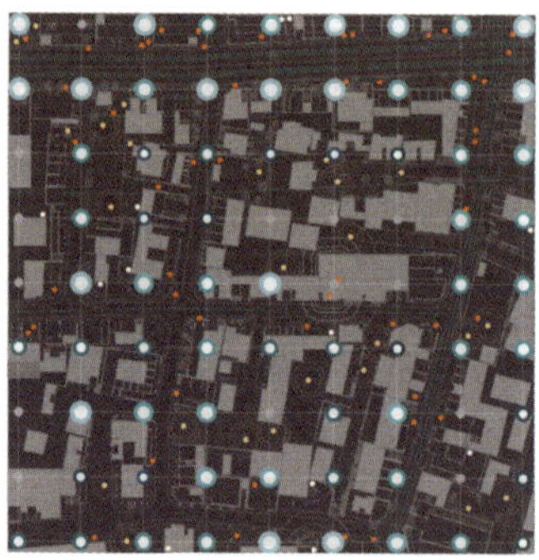

NOISE

EXPOSURE

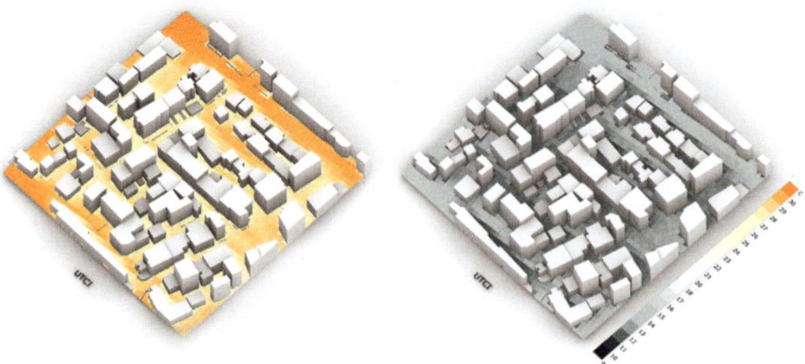

URBAN BLOCK

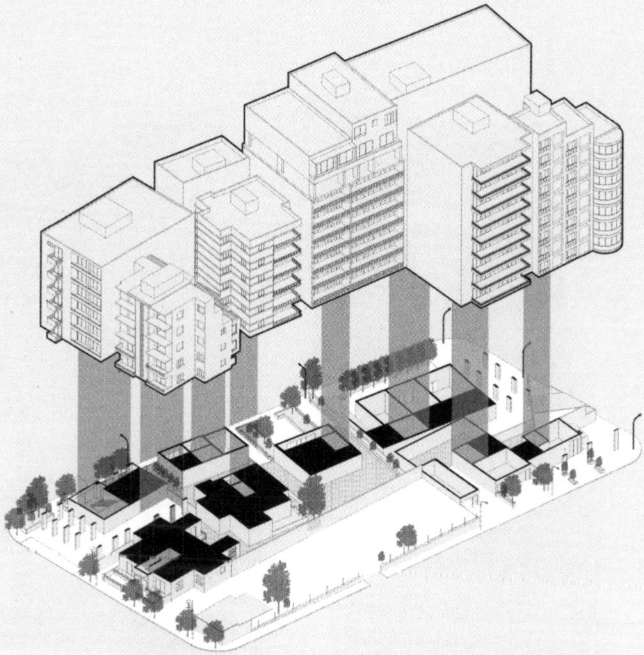

ZONE	3	GROUND ACTIVITY RATIO	
EXPLOITATION RATIO 4		Services	4.7 %
GROUND EXPLOITATION	60%	Closed Shop	5.5 %
		Creatives	1.6 %
BUILT/NON BUILT	36/64	Housing/Circulation	88.2 %
Built (m2)	1888		
Non Built (m2)	3333		
Total Block Area (m2)	5221		
PEOPLE AND URBAN DENSITY		HOUSING	
People density /km2	20000	Av. Unit area	150 m2
Nb of buildings	8	Av. Unit Price / m2	3382 $/ m2
Nb of housing units	77	Av. Persons per unit	5
Av. Person on Ground	151	** sources available in credits*	

Figure 20 - Achrafieh metrics

JNAH

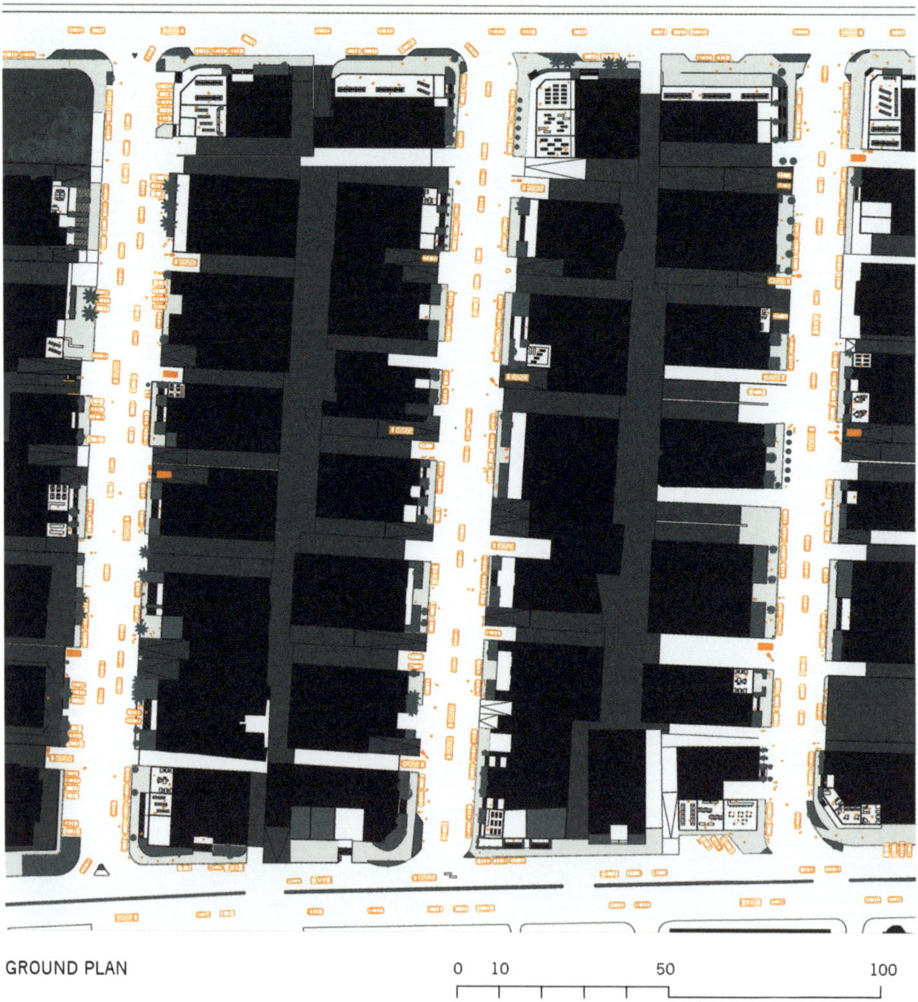

GROUND PLAN

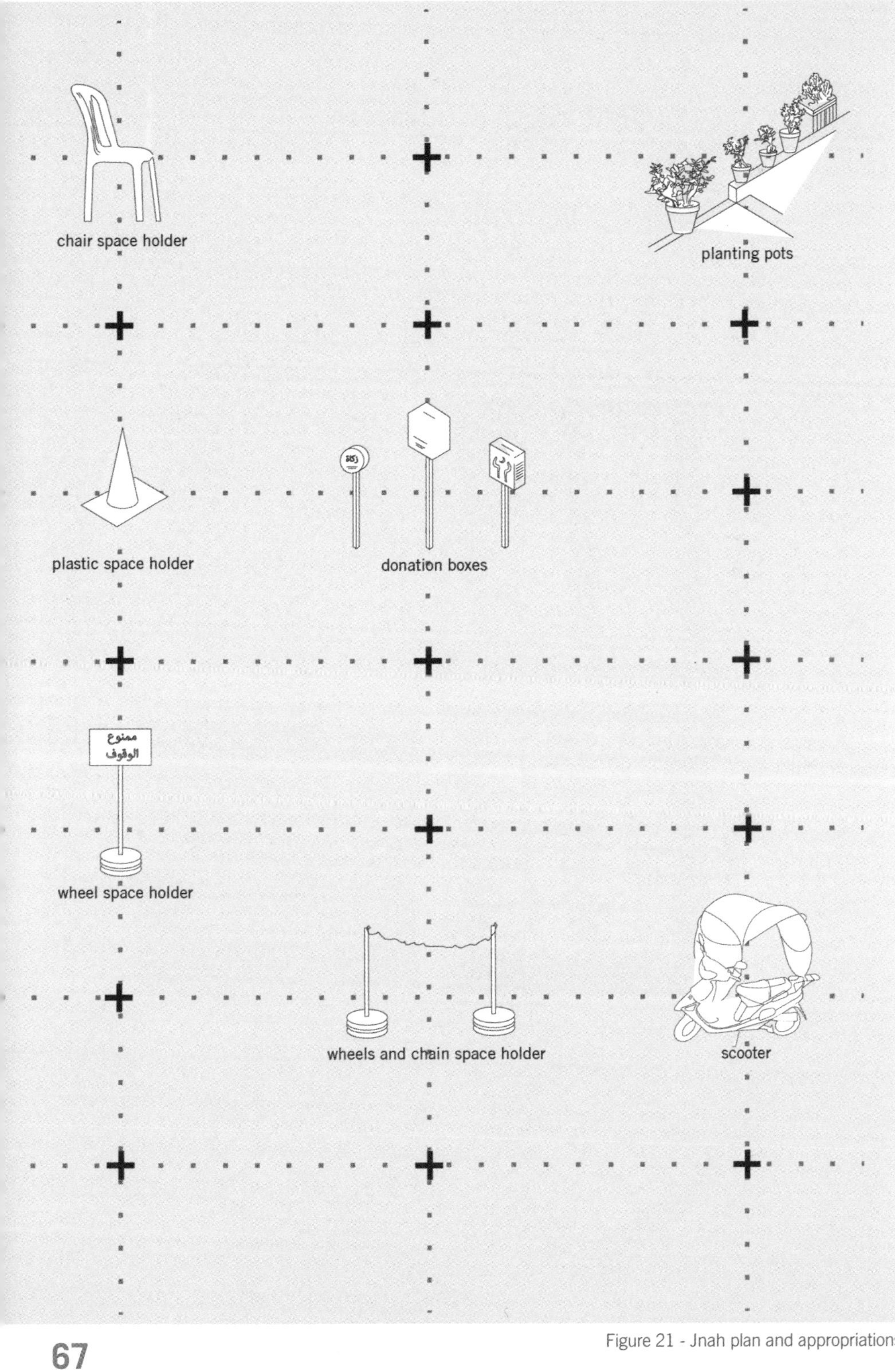

Figure 21 - Jnah plan and appropriations

USERS

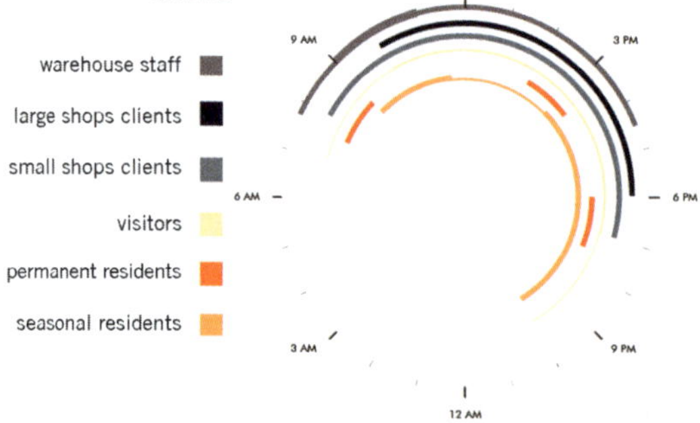

FLOOR RATIO

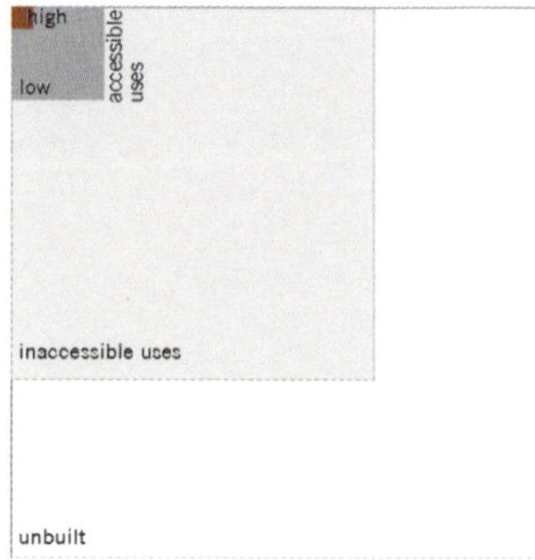

SPEED/FLOWS

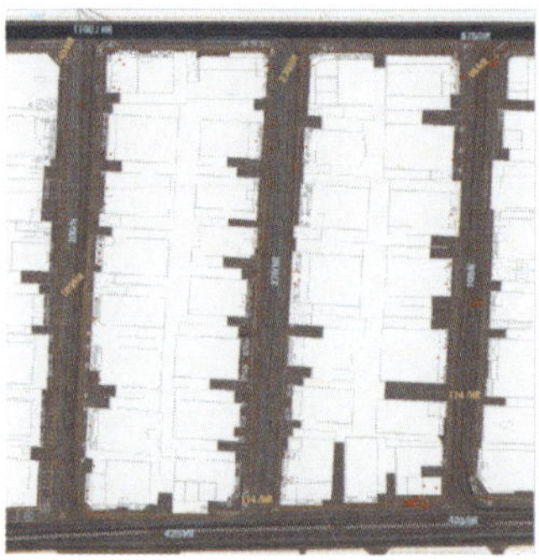

INTERACTIONS

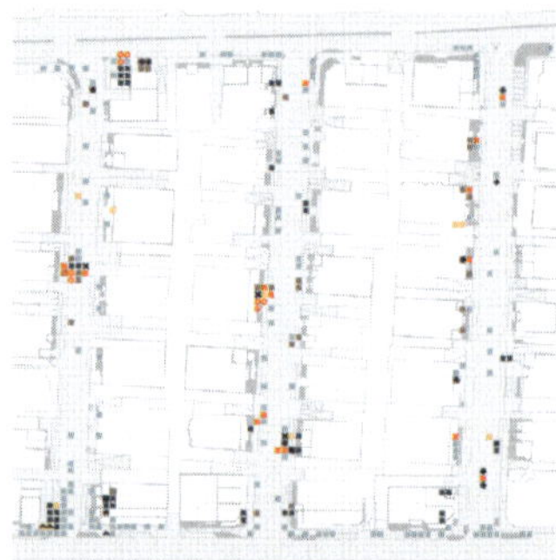

MIXITY

NOISE

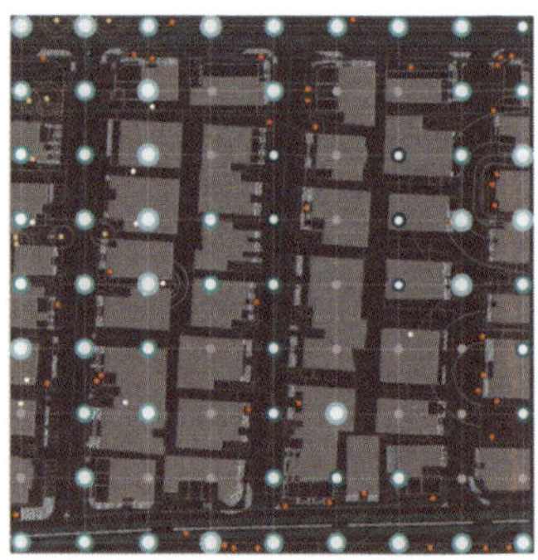

EXPOSURE

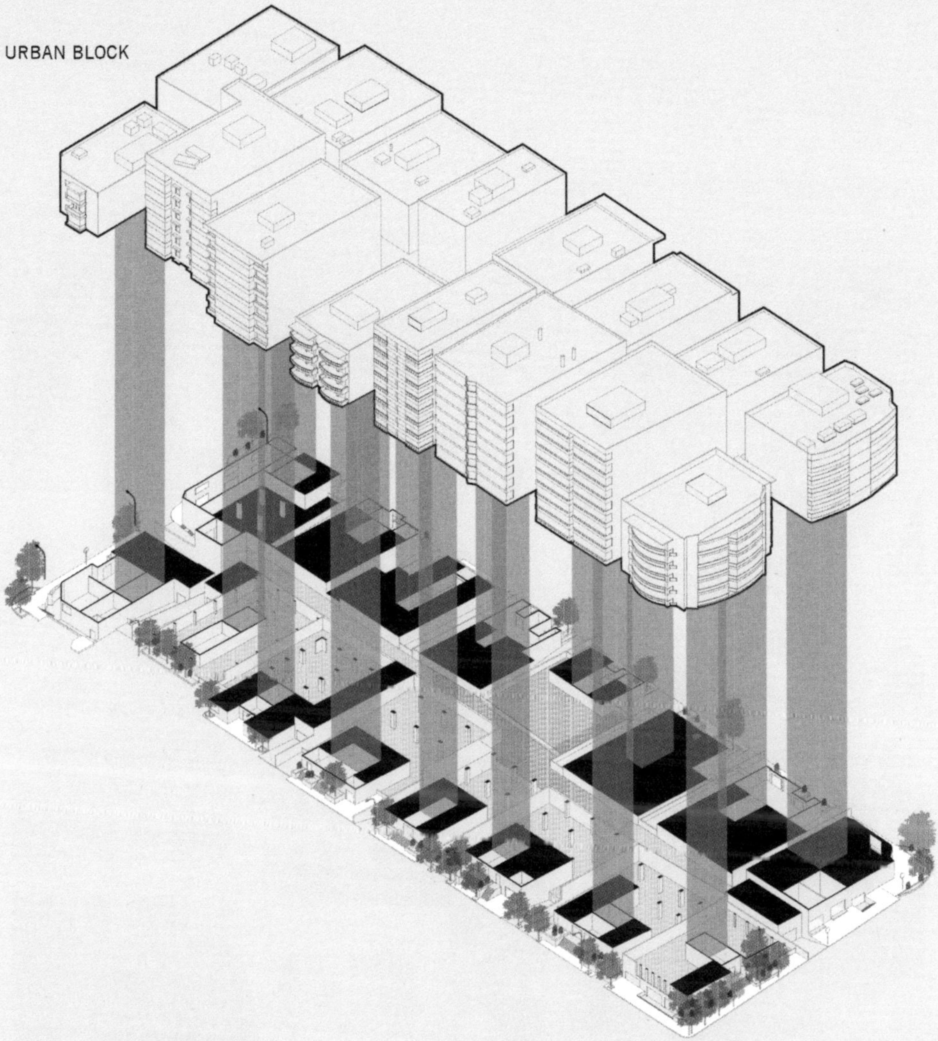

ZONE	50/2.5	GROUND ACTIVITY RATIO	
EXPLOITATION RATIO	2.5	Services	1.8 %
GROUND EXPLOITATION	60%	Closed Shops	1.6 %
		Clothes & Shoes	0.19 %
BUILT/NON BUILT	56/44	Homes Appliances	3.5 %
Built (m2)	9591	Housing/Circ	91.66 %
Non Built (m2)	5400		
Total Block Area (m2)	16891		
PEOPLE AND URBAN DENSITY		HOUSING	
People density /km2	25000	Av. Unit area	250 m2
Nb of buildings	16	Av. Unit Price / m2	4775 $/ m2
Nb of housing units	160	Av. Persons per unit	6
Av. Person on Ground	160	** sources available in credits*	

Figure 22 - Jnah metrics

AIN EL REMMANEH

GROUND PLAN

0 10 50 100

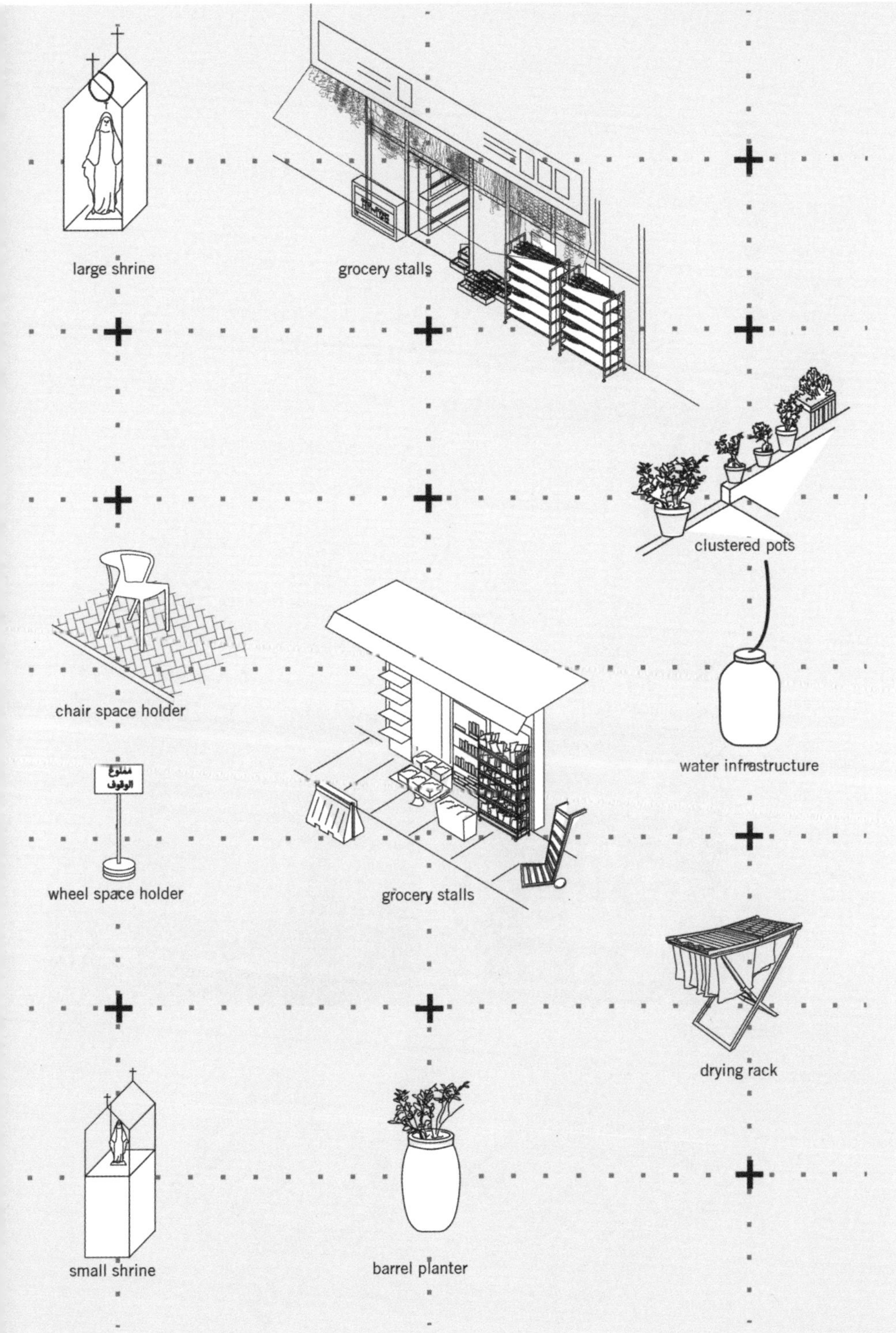

Figure 23 - Ain El Remmaneh plan and appropriations

USERS

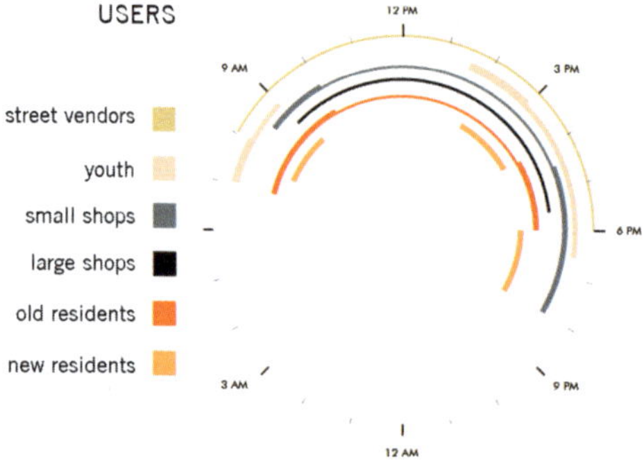

FLOOR RATIO

SPEED/FLOWS

INTERACTIONS

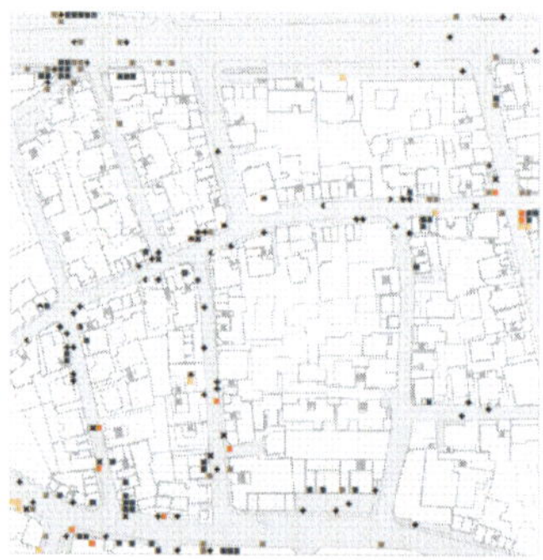

MIXITY

NOISE

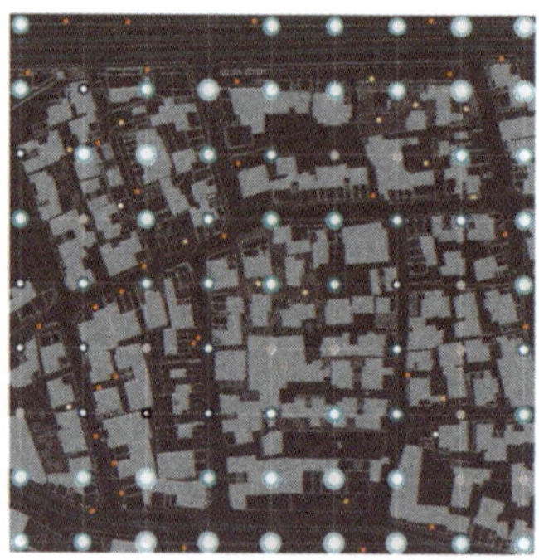

EXPOSURE

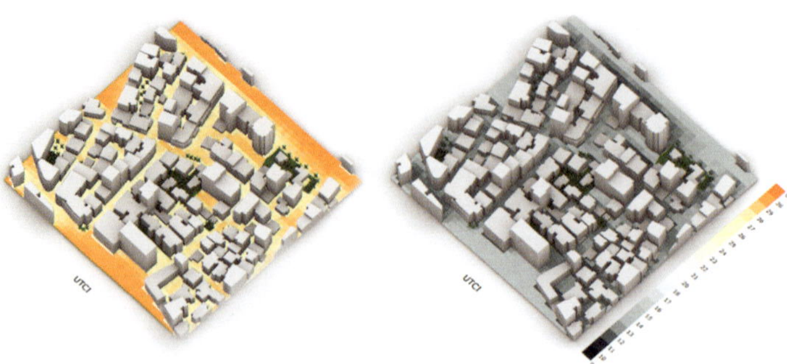

URBAN BLOCK

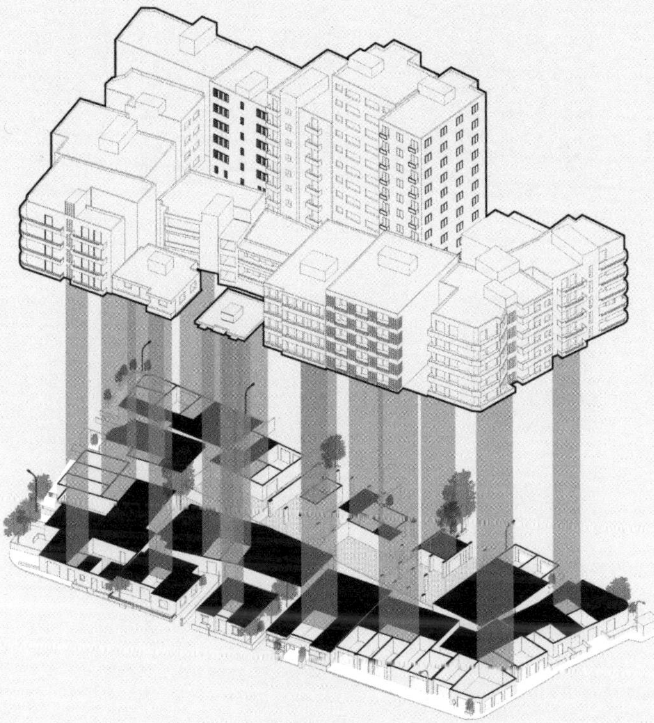

ZONE	50/2	GROUND ACTIVITY RATIO	
EXPLOITATION RATIO	2	Grocery	3.5 %
GROUND EXPLOITATION	50%	Creatives	3.1 %
		Services	4 %
BUILT/NON BUILT	64/36	Closed Shops	4.3 %
Built (m2)	3570	Food Shops	1.65 %
Non Built (m2)	1986	Housing/Circ	83.45 %
Total Block Area (m2)	5556		
PEOPLE AND URBAN DENSITY		HOUSING	
People density /km2	40000	Av. Unit area	120 m2
Nb of buildings	16	Av. Unit Price / m2	2000 $/ m2
Nb of housing units	102	Av. Persons per unit	4
Av. Person on Ground	180	** sources available in credits*	

Figure 24 - Ain El Remmaneh metrics

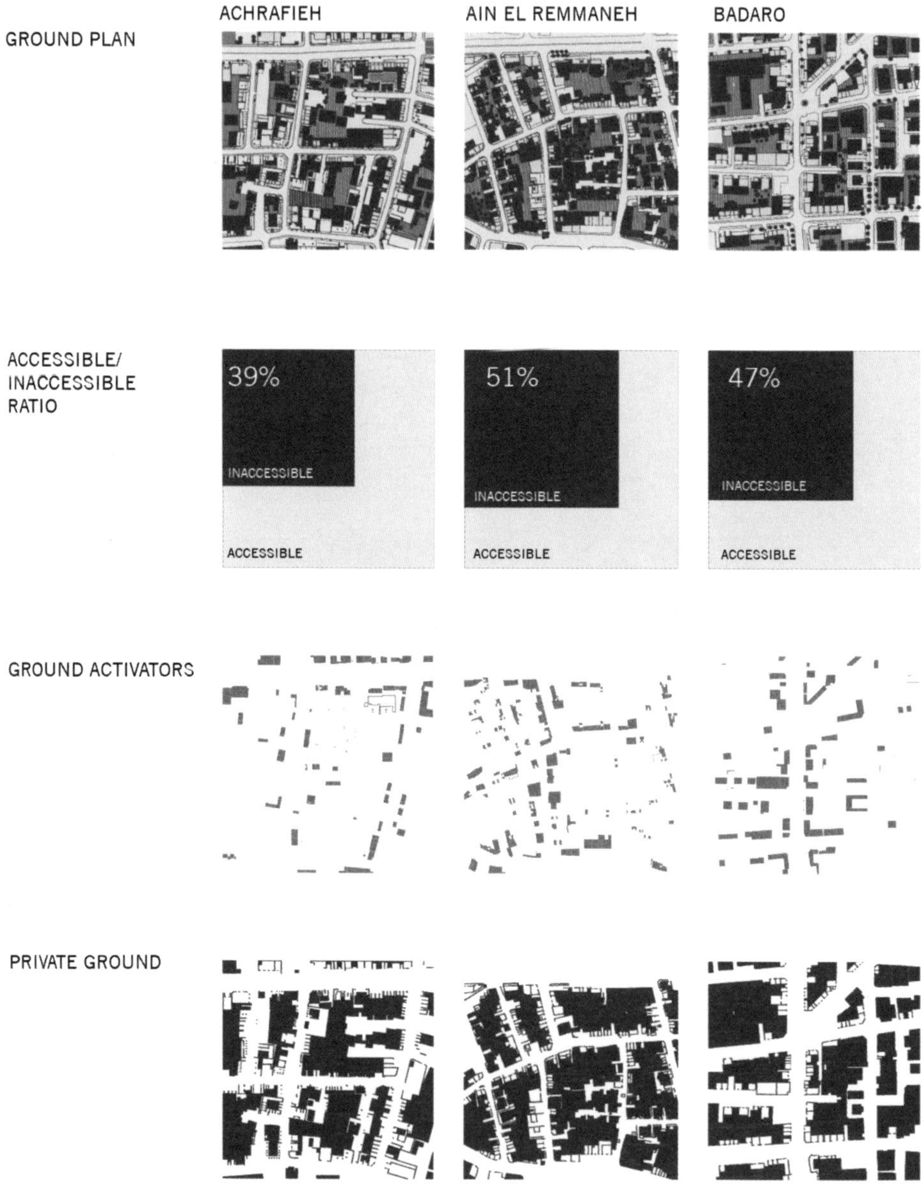
ACHRAFIEH
AIN EL REMMANEH
BADARO
GROUND PLAN
ACCESSIBLE/
INACCESSIBLE
RATIO
39%
INACCESSIBLE
ACCESSIBLE
51%
INACCESSIBLE
ACCESSIBLE
47%
INACCESSIBLE
ACCESSIBLE
GROUND ACTIVATORS
PRIVATE GROUND

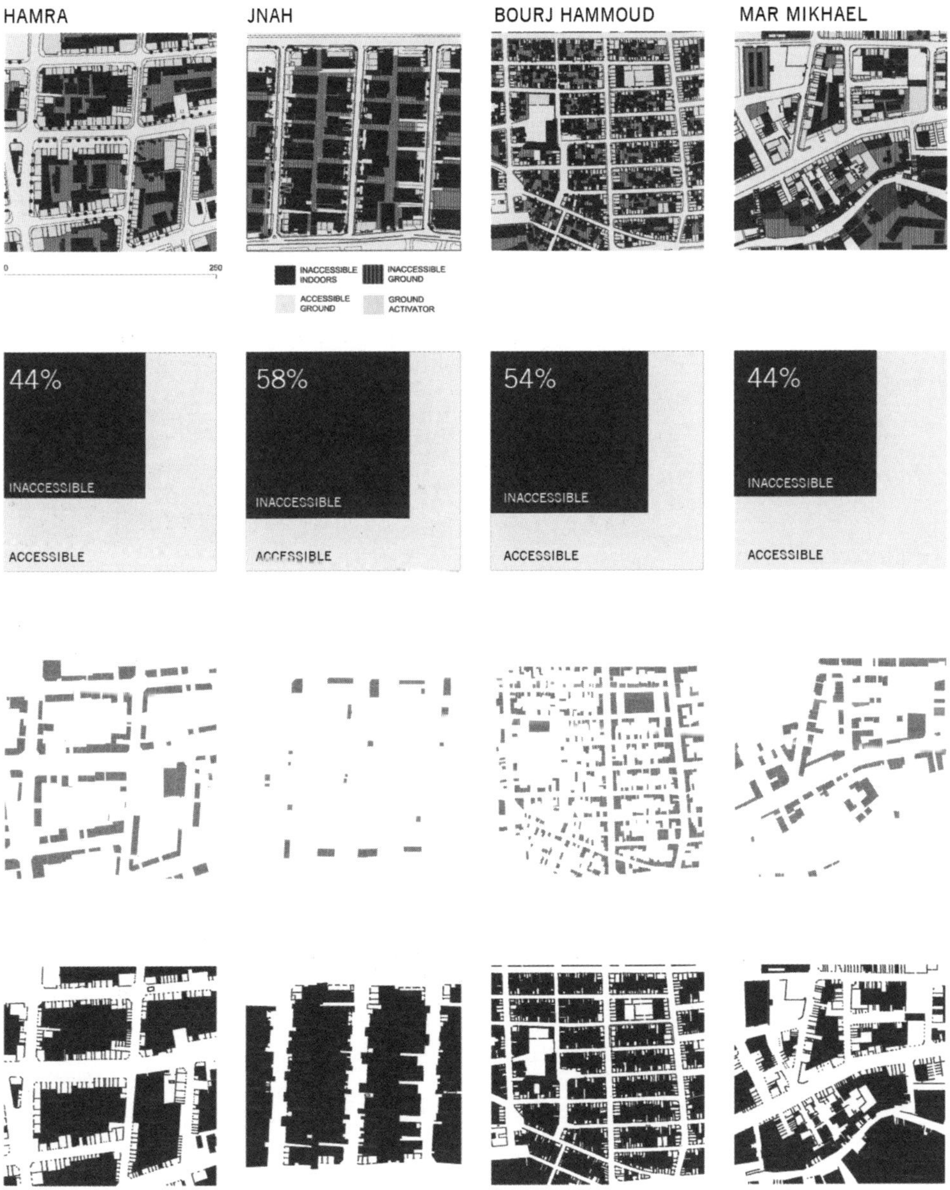

Figure 25 - Comparative metrics 01- Form

ACHRAFIEH | AIN EL REMMANEH | BADARO

ECONOMIC ENGAGEMENT RATIO

- HIGH ENGAGEMENT
- VERY LOW ENGAGEMENT
- LOW ENGAGEMENT
- NO ENGAGEMENT/ PRIVATE

GROUND USES

LOW ACCESS
- BANKING
- JEWELLERY
- CLOSED SHOPS
- PERSONAL ARTICLES
- RETAIL
- SERVICES

DECLINING ACCESS
- HOME APPLIANCES
- OFFICES
- CRAFTS
- LIGHT INDUSTRY
- CREATIVE INDUSTRY
- SOCIAL INFRASTRUCTURE
- CLUBS AND LEISURE

HIGH ACCESS
- COFFEE SHOPS/ BARS
- RESTAURANTS
- FOOD SHOP/STREET FOOD
- GROCERY STORE
- SPICES SHOPS

INTERACTIONS

- WALKING
- STOPPING LOOKING
- ENTERING LEAVING
- GATHERING
- STANDING IN DOORWAY
- SITTING
- CHILDREN PLAYING
- DOG WALKING
- EATING
- GREETING
- TALKING
- PEOPLE WATCHING

NOISE PATTERNS

- 48-51 dB
- 60-63 dB
- 72-75 dB
- CONVERSATIONS
- BIRDS TWEETS
- GENERATORS
- CARS SOUNDWAVES

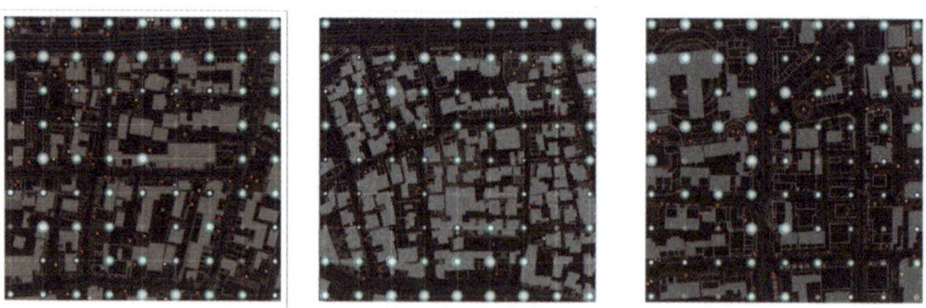

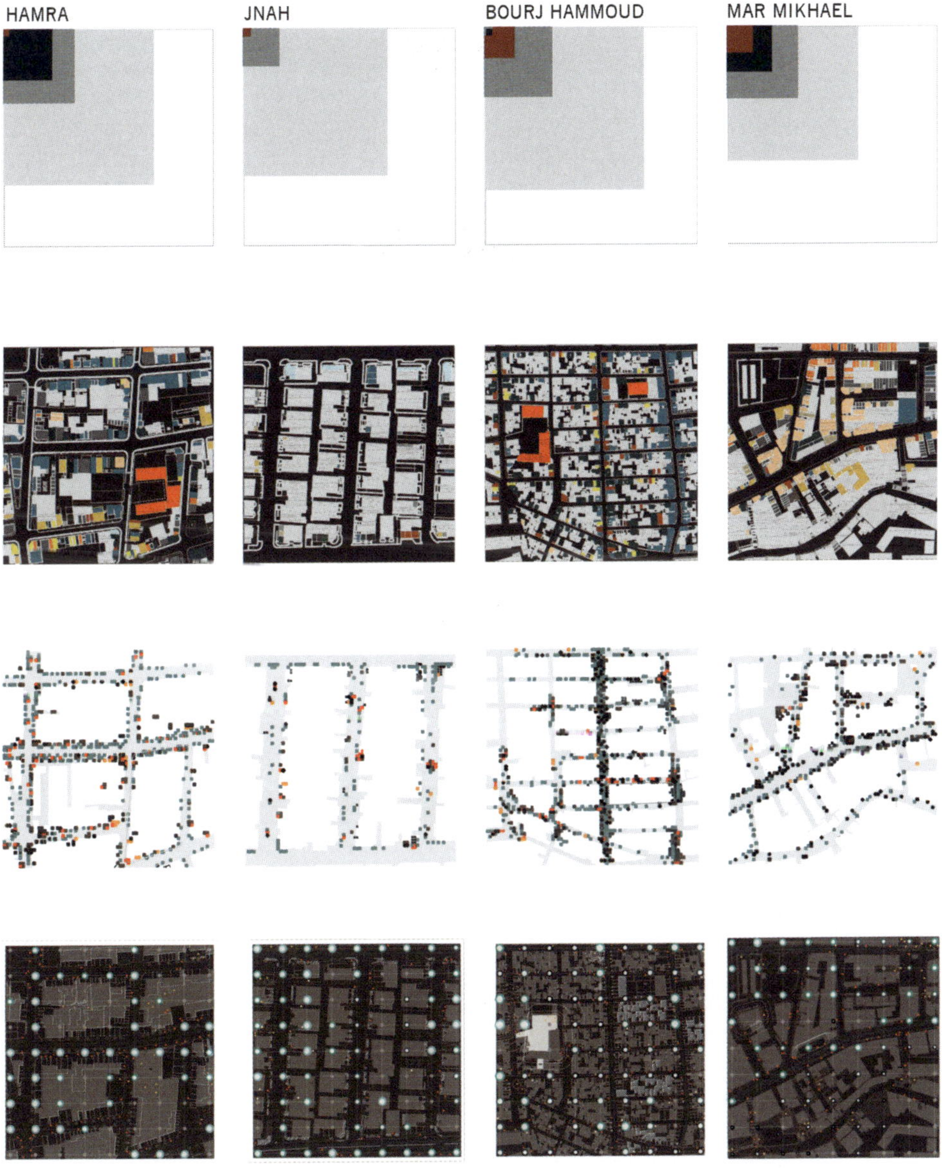

Figure 26 - Comparative metrics 02- Usage

MAR MIKHAEL

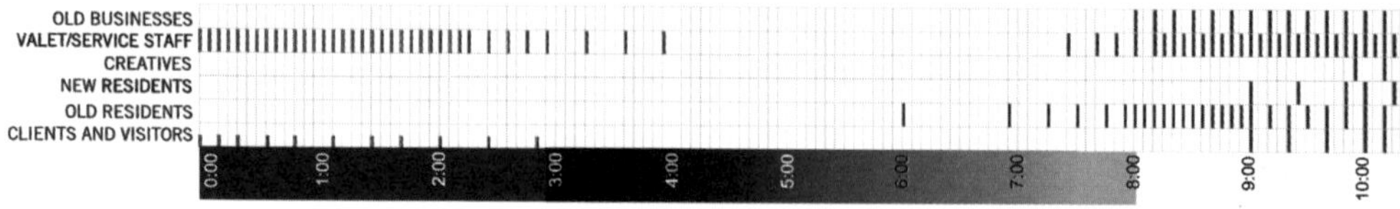

HAMRA

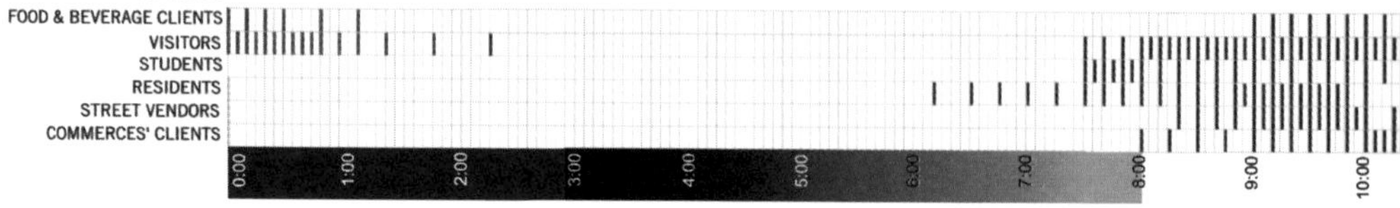

BADARO

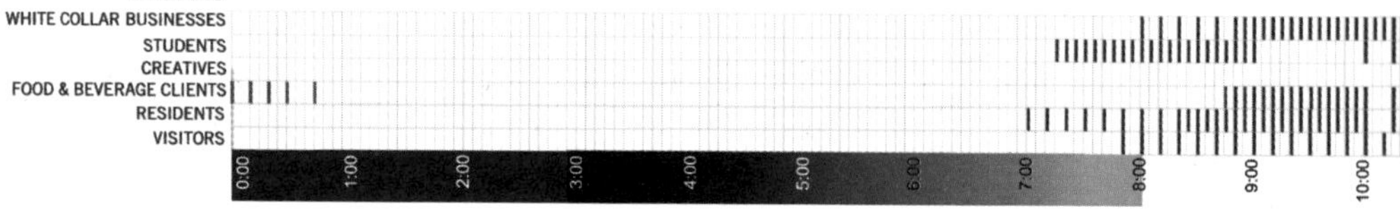

JNAH

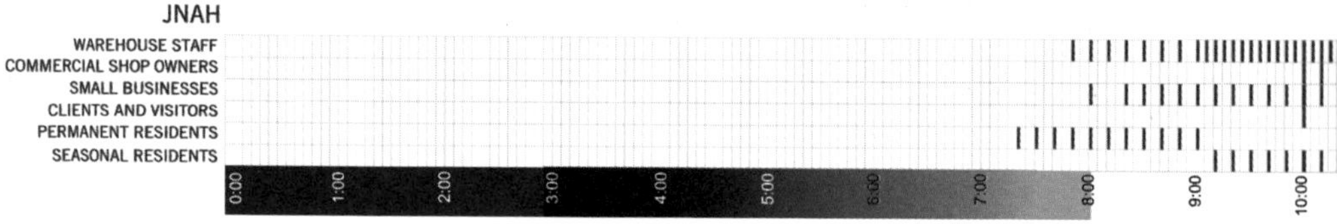

AIN EL REMMANEH

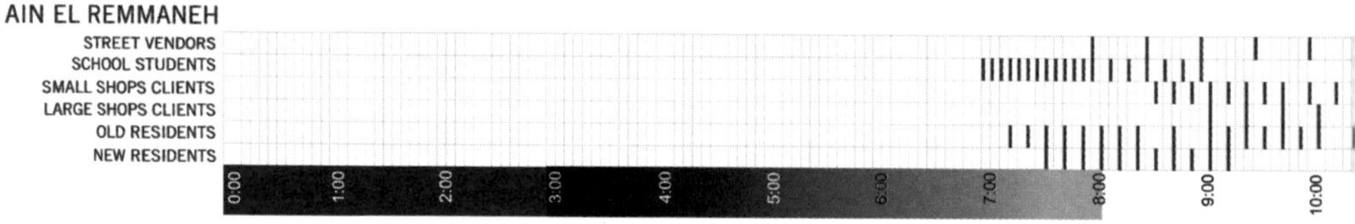

ACHRAFIEH

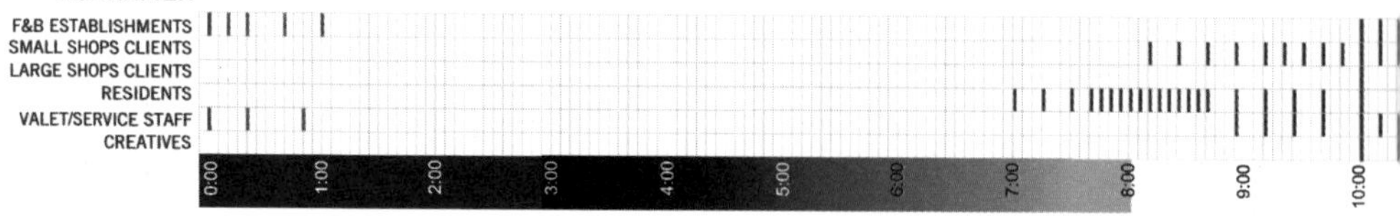

BOURJ HAMMOUD

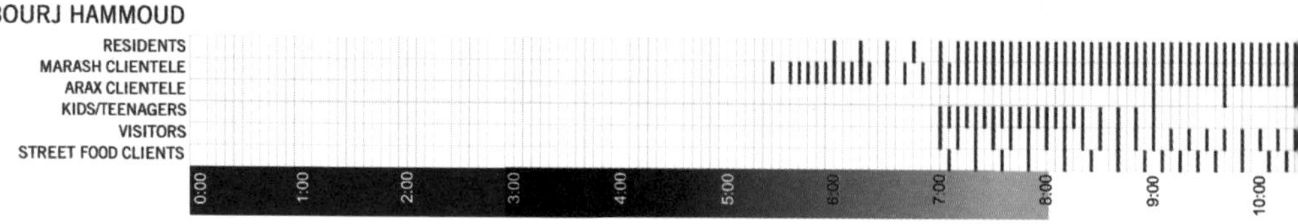

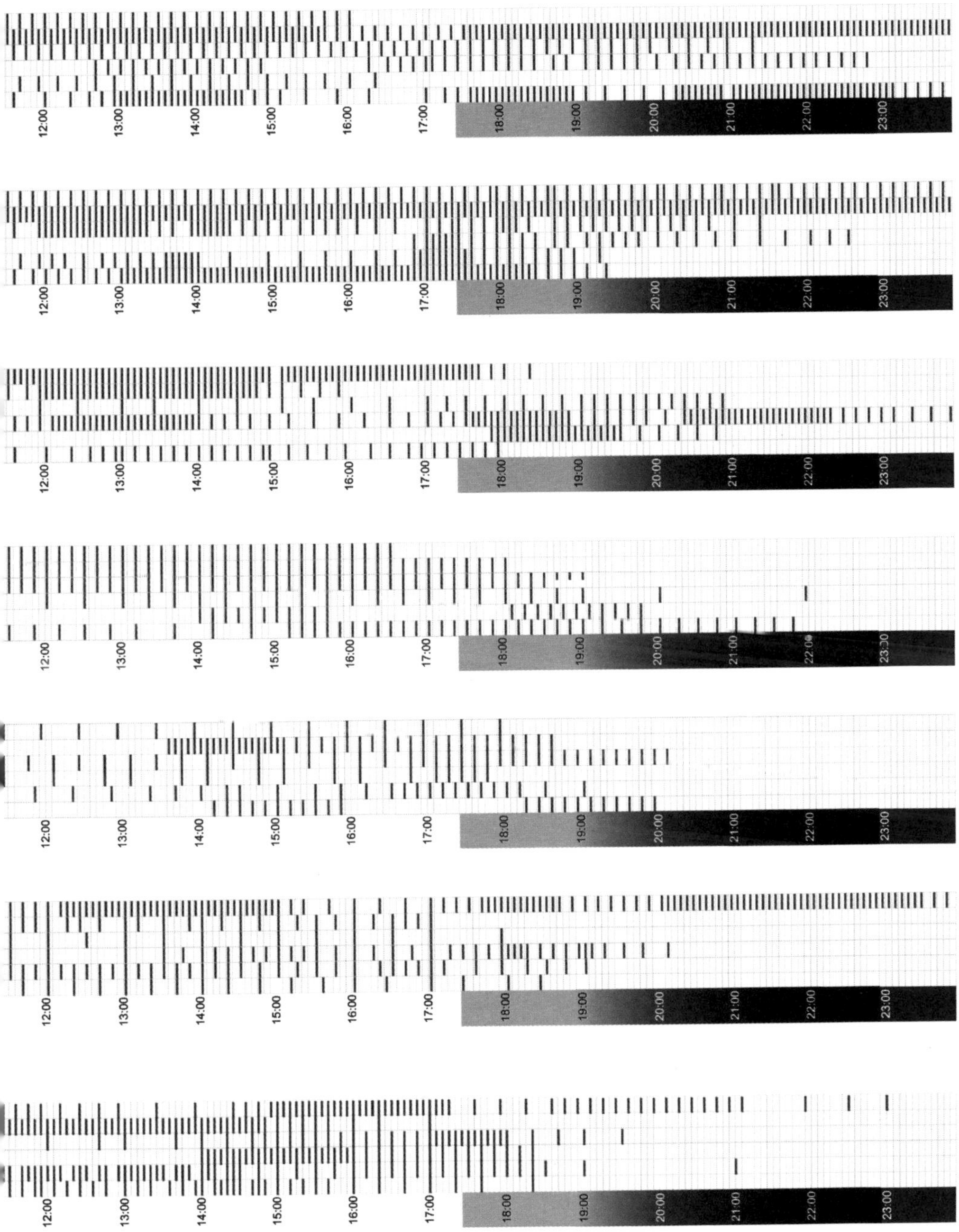

Figure 27 - Comparative metrics 03-Time

Comparison

Several observations emerge upon comparison of the different grounds (Fig. 25, 26, 27).

Spatial organization is essential to a vibrant urban pulse (Fig. 25)

Urban Structure: Due to their current spatial structure, areas like Achrafieh, Badaro, Hamra, and Mar Mikhael have the highest ground accessibility and porosity. The flexible thresholds between their streets, ground interiors, and inner lots are hybrid datums that allow for most of their appropriations but, most importantly, hold potential for adaptation to future scenarios and uses.

Rhythm and grain: The urban grain is crucial in shaping the ground's rhythm and façade diversity, which, when paired with appropriate uses, results in higher interactions and appropriations at ground level. Areas like Badaro and Hamra have a better rhythm and diversity than Achrafieh, Ain El Remmaneh, or Jnah, as evidenced by their ground plan and appropriations. Despite a low ratio of accessible ground, Bourj Hammoud scores the highest in appropriations due to its fine grain and façade engagement.

Streets: Streets have a direct impact on a vibrant ground. Their character, proportions, and intersection intensity affect walkability, depending on factors such as sidewalk width, scale, rhythm, and vehicular pace. They also affect thermal comfort levels as a result of their urban form's climate mitigation. When considered together, these aspects affect the frequency of pedestrian flows of each ground and their related interactions, which peak in grounds like Bourj Hammoud, followed by Hamra, Badaro, and Ain El Remmane.

Ground Activators: Ground activators act as catalysts that directly reflect the intensity of appropriations and interactions in each ground. They are measured as a spatial metric (frequency of occurrence) and an economic metric (level of economic engagement). A comparison shows different ratios of activators in a 250 x 250 m area, with Bourj Hammoud and Jnah showing stark exceptions.

Economic inclusivity and pedestrian accessibility at ground-level can enable broader access to the city

As observed in the different ground samples, a mix of economic activities centered on essential services and social infrastructure leads to increased ground usage. Likewise, providing pedestrian access to a wide range of ground-level amenities has been shown to promote more inclusive access to the city. For example, in Bourj Hammoud, ground activators extend from essential services (food and spice market) to include social infrastructure (school, church, youth club, and parish hall). This contributes to a wider range of mapped appropriations and interactions like meetings, conversations, and leisurely activities. During the observed period, a diverse range of age groups and genders were using the entire streetscape rather than just sidewalks, encouraged by the minimal car traffic on this ground.

On the other hand, in areas like Mar Mikhael, Hamra, and Badaro that are pedestrian-friendly but experiencing gentrification, activities are primarily related to paid economic activities, such as upscale cafes and commerce. While these uses generate vibrant ground atmospheres, interactions/appropriations are more limited in scope due to the upscalet nature of their uses, where more affluent groups tend to monopolize ground appropriations (parking space holders, greenery-enclosed cafes) and interactions. In Jnah, the economic mixity and pedestrian continuity observed in other areas were largely absent, resulting in fewer appropriations/interactions.

Affordable housing and ground vibrancy go hand in hand

The relationship between housing and ground usage is most noticeable in extreme conditions such as Bourj Hammoud and Jnah. However, this connection is not as apparent in other areas despite being validated across different contexts.[10] In Bourj Hammoud, it is evident that affordable housing[11] is linked to lower-income demographics and high-density occupancy. It corresponds to small housing units and limited private space, paired with increased ground use and interactions, where resilience and creativity make the most of the limited accessible space at ground level. On the other hand, affluent neighborhoods like Jnah are characterized by large housing units, medium-density occupancy, and minimal ground use. Ground space is mainly utilized for beautifying building entrances, and it lacks the intimacy of human scale and the necessity of uses that are intrinsic to appropriation patterns in working-class grounds.

Conclusion

The mapping of ground appropriations in Beirut has revealed their inherent potential to support socio-economic capital, endowing areas with a vibrant urban environment full of value and potential. However, in many of the studied grounds, appropriation is used as a tool for separating and monopolizing by more affluent groups. This mapping approach and its findings can serve as a starting point for making more inclusive decisions that bridge between formal and grassroots initiatives to result in appropriation practices that bring social, spatial, and economic value to Beirut's ground. Some examples are:

Preserving the hybrid space between private and public by encouraging open uses and creative programming through neighborhood alliances;

Promoting a variety of urban elements (such as play areas, seating, and shelters) that are open for free appropriation and in support of marginalized social groups and their right to the ground;

Reducing the impact of cars and prioritizing pedestrian-friendly environments in collaboration with municipal and planning agencies;

Enhancing the ground's climate mitigation and outdoor activities through greening and urban shading campaigns, Lastly, increasing social infrastructures as ground anchors for an inclusive ground in Beirut across social spectrum.

10 Ivan Nasution, "Urban Appropriation: Creativity in Marginalization," *Procedia - Social and Behavioral Sciences* 184 (May 2015): 4-12, https://doi.org/10.1016/j.sbspro.2015.05.04

11 Housing access is based on a 2015 map of average asking prices of apartments from 71 neighborhoods in Beirut, developed by real estate advisory firm RAMCO. Ain El Remmane and Bourj Hammoud – as low-income areas which are not mentioned on the map - are below the average of mentioned prices. See: "Apartment Prices in Beirut I Beirut RE," Beirutre.com, accessed May 20, 2024, https://www.beirutre.com/real-estate-group-reveals-average-apartment-prices-in-beirut/.

Figure 1 - Peripheral landscapes in Achrafieh

ecology of the ground

microscale urban landscapes of beirut neighborhoods

nayla al-akl

Introduction

The importance of landscape and ecosystem services in promoting the sustainability and well-being of cities, urban regions, and their inhabitants cannot be overstated. Urban landscapes play a critical role in providing a wide range of ecosystem services, including provisionary services such as direct products or resources to humans, regulating services that ensure the continuity of healthy environmental processes, cultural services that provide non-material human benefits, and supporting services that lay the foundation for a functioning ecosystem.[1,2]

This chapter investigates the ground in Beirut as an urban ecosystem fragmented by waves of unplanned urbanization and reduced to the scale of microscale urban landscapes. The chapter probes how the remaining urban landscapes can generate value in their built environment and influence how the ground level is inhabited and experienced. The chapter examines such landscapes at the micro-scale, looking at ground samples selected from the following neighborhoods: Achrafieh, Ain El Remmaneh, Badaro, Bourj Hammoud, Jnah, Hamra, and Mar Mikhael. This examination is conducted through a mapping that abstracts and reinterprets the existing landscapes under four analytical layers to reveal their multifunctionality and correlation with the ecosystem services mentioned above.

Landscapes of Beirut neighborhoods

The different neighborhoods in Beirut have unique urbanization and development patterns that significantly impact the city's current landscape morphology. A study of the urban landscape in Beirut reveals heterogeneous and fine-grained landscape patterns across the city, with often more complex structures in the older parts of the city. In such areas, the remains of historical and cultural landscapes have been preserved, either intentionally as heritage landscapes or unintentionally within private and semi-private holdings, as well as within peripheral land and infrastructural areas awaiting future development due to city growth (Fig. 1).

Neighborhoods such as Badaro, Mar Michael, and Achrafieh are part of the earlier wave of 20th-century urban growth in Beirut, showcasing remnants of older and larger ecosystems. For instance, in Badaro, remains of the city's historic pine forest are scattered across its neighborhood along main streets and within its semi-private yards (Fig. 2). Similarly, the green hills and natural topography of Achrafieh, which once accommodated urban orchards, gardens, and viewsheds, continue to exist on the peripheries of the neighborhood, shaped by new forms of temporary use, sports and recreation (Fig. 1). And finally, urban agriculture, which was once found abundantly along the city's waterways and within residential neighborhoods, mainly was reduced to small-scale infills and impact, within peripheral lots and conserved private landscapes resulting from individual rather than communal practices with few remnants of earlier agricultural practices (Fig. 3).

When looking at newer landscapes in areas that have shifted to more intensive construction practices,[3] reliance on a beautification approach is evident, using an often-limited vegetation palette focused on streetscaping. For example, in the Jnah neighborhood, tropical trees and low-maintenance shrubs are utilized to provide the neighborhood with its 'preferred' greenery (Fig. 4). This trend is also seen in commercial districts and newly developed parts of older neighborhoods, making landscape identities more complex and diverse within these mixed areas (Fig. 5).

These diverse landscape patterns are influenced by top-down land use and planning policies as well as urban growth patterns. They are also the results of ad-hoc incidents of organic applications, socioeconomic contexts, and aesthetic expectations, which strongly impact the landscape function and its values. A nuanced multidimensional analysis is needed to understand the impacts of these micro-scale patterns on ecosystem services through four key layers: spatial composition, ecological, agricultural, and human values. This mapping approach requires a level of generalization and simplification of ecological landscape concepts to provide a conceptual framework for understanding the remaining urban landscapes in the city.

Spatial composition of urban landscapes

The spatial composition layer in the studied neighborhoods is based on the "pixelation" of the urban ground pattern and is divided into built, open, and vegetated areas (Fig. 6). It highlights green patches, corridors, and landscape matrices, a prominent categorization method in landscape planning.[4] The availability and proportion of green spaces within a neighborhood are crucial indicators of ecological value and urban health. Large and multi-scalar landscapes remain key assets in urban landscapes.[5] Nevertheless, in Beirut, where vegetated spaces are extremely limited and found at the micro-scales of the neighborhoods,

from top to bottom
Figure 2 - Remnant heritage pine ecosystem in Badaro
Figure 3 - Urban agriculture in Sin El Fil
Figure 4 - Jnah's street vegetation
Fiigure 5 - Mixed landscapes at the peripheries of Achrafieh

1 Brendan Fisher and R. Kerry Turner, "Ecosystem Services: Classification For Valuation," *Biological conservation* 141, no. 5 (2008): 1167-1169.
2 Marion Potchin and Roy Haines-Young, "Defining and Measuring Ecosystem Services," In *Routledge Handbook of Ecosystem Services* (Routledge, 2016), 25-44.
3 Marieke Krijnen and Mona Fawaz, "Exception as the rule: High-end developments in neoliberal Beirut," *Built environment* 36, no. 2 (2010): 245-259.
4 Richard TT. Forman, *Land Mosaics: The Ecology of Landscapes and Regions* (Cambridge University Press, 1995).
5 Briony A. Norton, Karl L. Evans, and Philip H. Warren, "Urban Biodiversity and Landscape Ecology: Patterns, Processes and Planning," *Current Landscape Ecology Reports* 1 (2016): 178-192.

Vegetation
Open
Built

Figure 6 - Landscape patches in Ain El Remmaneh, Badaro, Mar Mikhael and Achrafieh

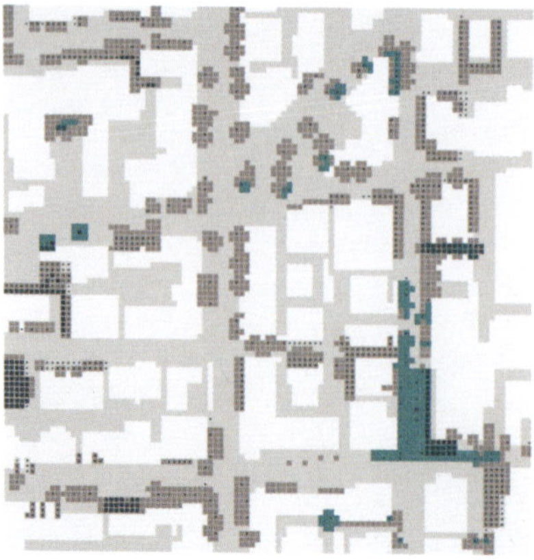

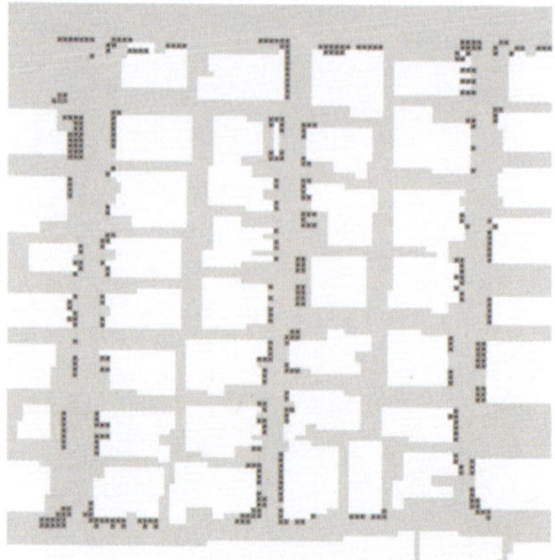

- Native species
- Diverse groundcovers (3+ species)
- Soil

- Native species
- Diverse groundcovers (3+ species)
- Soil
- Hard soil with full sun exposure
- Low maintenance fruit tree

from top to bottom
Figure 7 - Patch heterogeneity comparison: Badaro (left) and Jnah (right)
Figure 8 - Unmaintained urban soil (left) vs protected urban soil in an urban cemetery in Achrafieh (right)
Figure 9 - Urban Agriculture as mapped in Mar Mikhael, Ain El Remmaneh, Hamra, Bourj Hammoud, and Achrafieh

the matrix and connectivity of green patches become the main promoters of localized ecosystem services (Fig. 7).

Neighborhoods like Badaro, Mar Mikhael, Ain El Remmaneh, and Achrafieh rely on this matrix to create microclimates, reduce the heat island effect, and promote water (and potentially carbon) storage. Depending on their size, organic morphology, edge location, and multilayered landscape values, landscape patches within these neighborhoods help blur the boundaries of the public and private urban realms and impact the neighborhood community. These patches also enhance the visual and sensory experience for the resident and passerby, contributing to overall well-being and ensuring habitat opportunities.

Ecological value and patch heterogeneity

The perceived ecological value is heavily linked to the heterogeneity of landscape patches, which sheds light on ecosystem services and, more specifically, on the level of biodiversity present at the micro-scale, particularly in fragmented patches[6] across the city (Fig. 8). There is a positive correlation between the level of environmental heterogeneity, especially one related to the diversity of land cover and vegetation, and the positive impact on landscape ecology and biodiversity.[7,8] This is particularly visible in neighborhoods such as Badaro, where larger landscape patches contain high diversity and richness in plant species across scales and within patches. These diverse and complex setups allow for a combination of manicured landscapes and aesthetically guided interventions, as well as a spectrum of managed/unmanaged vegetation, leading to a wide range of aesthetic and ecological benefits as well as spatial qualities and natural resources that promote human, ecological, and environmental values within the same space.

The more homogenous the patch, the fewer ecosystem services it provides, and this is particularly visible when comparing Badaro to Jnah's smaller and more standardized front yards of exotic species. These species primarily serve aesthetic purposes while providing limited environmental benefits. This also applies to Bourj Hammoud's street planters, which provide a level of social benefit and affirm ownership and community appropriation.

Under this layer, soil mainly contributes to urban ecology and health. Today, the availability of protected soil within dense urban fabrics requires particular interest, especially as populations increase and cities densify, losing the availability of this critical resource within the urban realm. Urban soil is core for human and ecological health and provides human and water-related services as well as opportunities for climate regulation, recreational benefits, and food production.[9,10,11]

Extensive human activities, including construction, transportation, and other daily polluting activities, modify soil composition in cities and lead to contaminated soils.[12] In the studied sidewalks, and building fronts, rendering their risk for over-exploitation, over-saturation, and contamination relatively high. Nevertheless, within older neighborhoods with large institutional plots such as schools or cemeteries, as well as in newly planned residential and mixed-use areas of medium to large scales, there is a growing potential for soil protection, especially in residential backyards and semi-public spaces that would provide health and recreational activities as well as agricultural benefits (Fig. 9). These landscapes will be key to clean and protect from soil and environmental pollutants. They currently have medium to low maintenance and management levels, rendering them ideal for ecological services. Once protected, landscapes within the urban environments become key features for the city of Beirut and may represent a landscape of high interest that highlights a complex mosaic of environmental, agricultural, and cultural values.

Agricultural value and urban productive landscapes

Throughout different neighborhoods, a variety of agricultural interventions have been observed, ranging from small-scale edible plantings to medium-scale food production initiatives (Fig. 9). No longer at the fringe of the city, productive landscapes are identified within a variety of patches and typologies across neighborhoods with various socioeconomic demographics. They take the form of planted fruit-producing street trees, edible gardens, and productive agricultural lands (Fig. 10). In all three cases, there is a strong emphasis on cultural practices and heritage landscapes as integral parts of this particular urban landscape. While productive trees, such as loquat, citrus, and olive, are prominent as street vegetation and garden plants, they are used mainly for aesthetic and cultural reasons. This emphasizes a deep awareness and interest in preserving the heritage and practice of productive landscapes. It also indicates a potential willingness to reintegrate productive landscapes in more formal ways and establish them as a comprehensive infrastructure, a practice reminiscent of the historic city. These currently scattered interventions have the potential to be part of a larger, more strategic, and multilayered 'continuous productive urban landscape' (CPUL) and edible city framework,[13] where food and the city become more strongly intertwined, and where public spaces are re-envisioned into new economic, community-based and health-related urban landscape systems.

The human value of mixed urban landscapes

Research indicates that urban green spaces have significant value for human social and ecological health and overall well-being.[14] In cities like Beirut, where formal green spaces are scarce, both formal and informal urban landscapes, whether private or public, offer greater value to residents when visible and accessible. Many neighborhoods in Beirut rely on private and semi-private green spaces and street vegetation (Fig. 11) to create a cooler environment, more pleasant views, increased interactions with urban fauna and flora, and a stronger connection between community and nature (Fig. 12). The higher the number of green spaces and vegetation, the stronger the impact on human wellbeing.[15] The higher the proximity and quality of green spaces, the higher the value.[16] In Beirut, older neighborhoods like Badaro meet these criteria more closely due to the diversity, density, and proximity of their green patches and the intentional preservation of historical and cultural landscapes.

6 Yongzhi Yan, Scott Jarvie, Qing Zhang, Shuangshuang Zhang, Peng Han, Qingfu Liu, and Pengtao Liu, "Small patches are hotspots for biodiversity conservation in fragmented landscapes," *Ecological indicators* 130 (2021): 108086.
7 R. A. Francis, Millington, J. D., Perry, G. L., & Minor, E. S. (Eds.), *The Routledge handbook of landscape ecology* (Routledge, 2022).
8 Anke Stein, Katharina Gerstner, and Holger Kreft, "Environmental Heterogeneity as a Universal Driver of Species Richness Across Taxa, Biomes and Spatial Scales," *Ecology letters* 17, no. 7 (2014): 866-80.
9 Gang Li, G- X. Sun, Yin Ren, X- S. Luo, and Y- G. Zhu, "Urban soil and human health: a review," *European Journal of Soil Science* 69, no. 1 (2018): 196-215.
10 Richard TT. Forman, *Urban Ecology: Science of Cities* (Cambridge University Press, 2014).
11 Roisin O'Riordan, Jess Davies, Carly Stevens, John N. Quinton, and Christopher Boyko "The Ecosystem Services of Urban Soils: A Review," *Geoderma* 395 (2021): 115076.
12 Helmut Meuser, *Contaminated Urban Soils*, Vol. 18 (Springer Science & Business Media, 2010).
13 Katrin Bohn and André Viljoen, "The Edible City: Envisioning The Continuous Productive Urban Landscape (CPUL)," *Field* 4, no. 1 (2011).
14 Rodney H. Matsuoka and Rachel Kaplan, "People Needs In The Urban Landscape: Analysis Of Landscape And Urban Planning Contributions," *Landscape And Urban Planning* 84, no. 1 (2008): 7-19.
15 Rosa Reyes-Riveros, Adison Altamirano, Francisco De La Barrera, Daniel Rozas-Vásquez, Lorena Vieli, and Paula Meli, "Linking Public Urban Green Spaces and Human Well-Being: A Systematic Review," *Urban forestry & urban greening* 61 (2021): 127105.
16 E. Dinand Ekkel and Sjerp de Vries, "Nearby Green Space and Human Health: Evaluating Accessibility Metrics," *Landscape and Urban Planning* 157 (2017): 214-20.

Conclusion

While there is a growing awareness of the importance of creating publicly accessible urban green spaces at the ground level of the city, for both human and ecological health, the Beirut neighborhoods that have been the most successful in this approach were those developed in the earlier 20th-century development waves. These grew through a more organic and contextually responsive development pattern that allowed high diversity and extensive microscale landscape interventions with a stronger complexity and diversity of green cover and landscape typologies, lower maintenance requirements, and a conservation approach to historic and cultural ecosystems. Such features are key for advancing the impact and relevance of urban landscapes of the future where cities will be exposed to denser urban patterns and smaller spaces.

For Beirut, contrary to popular belief, it is not the socioeconomic status of the neighborhood that primarily dictates the extent and ecological value of its urban green spaces; rather, it is the ability of neighborhood development to protect existing landscapes and adopt a microscale landscape strategy within a comprehensive, value-driven system focused on ecological and human objectives.

As the concerns over food security in Lebanon grow and as discussions on the need for urban food production advance, it becomes critical to evaluate the requirement to design and implement a comprehensive, effective, and sustainable urban landscape infrastructure that advances biodiversity and human health, reduces waste and energy consumption, while remaining economically viable.

Figure 10 - Agricultural production in an urban lot in Achrafieh *(top)*

Figure 11 - Semi-private green spaces (left) and street vegetation (right) reflecting localized landscape values and preferences *(bottom)*

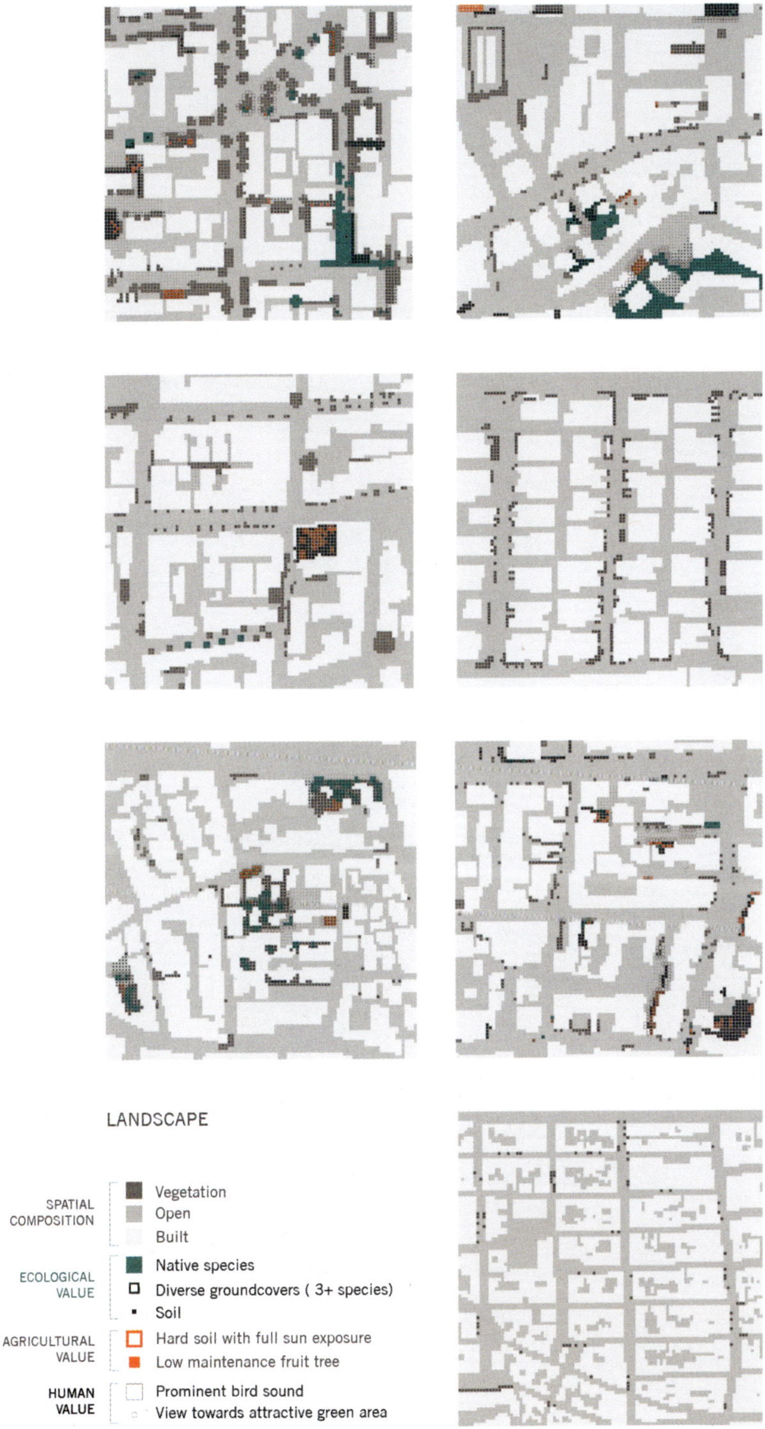

Figure 12 - Human value mapping of the seven urban landscapes

Figure 1 - In Nabaa, a historically Christian low-income neighborhood, a portrait of "Bashir," a Christian warlord and leader of a right-wing political party, hangs on display. The poster serves as a reminder of his short-lived presidency in 1982, as he was assassinated shortly after taking office as president of the Lebanese Republic. However, as the neighborhood's demographics shifted and incoming Shia Muslims replaced its Christian majority with differing political and religious beliefs, the poster took on a new significance.

APPROPRIATION AS AESTHETIC

wissam chaaya

I used to start my day with a peaceful moment on my balcony. Unfortunately, a foul odor of trash from across the street often disrupted my daily routine. This area had been an informal dumping ground for years despite residents' numerous complaints and local authorities' efforts to address the issue. Now, this spot is immaculate and well-organized, complete with a statue of a saint at its center.

This is a traditional tactic commonly used in public areas in Beirut to alter people's perception of a particular place. In this specific case, the appropriation of the space through a religious figure created a sense of ownership within its community by incorporating its symbols and aesthetics while simultaneously improving the cleanliness of the urban space. As proved in this example, informal appropriation plays a key role in the social construction of this public space, translating the community's identity and its interactions with the urban environment and creating a bond between people and place.

Home to different communities and in a context of weak regulation enforcement, informal appropriation of the ground by individuals and communities in Beirut is a common practice, taking various forms that vary from the more mundane to the most ideological.

Mundane activities encompass gardening or beautifying areas adjacent to privately owned establishments or homes as dominant forms of individual appropriation. Indeed, many residents take pride in cultivating small gardens or green spaces near their commercial establishments or ground floor apartments to enhance their appeal and set them apart, resulting in privately managed public spaces. Landscaping and fencing privately owned ground floors next to public spaces are also routine practices used to create a buffer from the gaze and noise of the street.

St. Francis
School

MANGO
Master

Figure 2 - A literary kiosk alongside a graffiti-clad school fence in the vibrant district of Hamra serves as a testament to the diverse array of individuals frequenting the area. The street is renowned for its reputation as a hub for intellectualism.
Figure 3 - Flashy colors and crates spill over on the sidewalk in front of a grocery store in Hamra.
Figure 4 - Vibrant commercial posters and lively decorations adorn the storefronts on this busy street in Nabaa.

In contrast, commercial appropriation of the ground usually takes more temporary dimensions, such as ambulant vending or daily extensions to the sidewalk space in the form of shading, kiosks, temporary seating, and potted plants, with eye-catching features to entice potential customers.

Ranging between the mundane and the ideological, graffiti and murals are popular mediums of appropriating public space to express artistic creativity or quirky political statements; they tend to reveal popular representations played out routinely on urban surfaces such as walls, bridges, and other structures throughout the city.

However, as a city with a strong cultural and religious background comprising 17 different sects whose history often intertwines with political and sectarian identity, Beirut's urban ground is more particularly appropriated as an ideological platform to broadcast convictions or mark territories of different groups in the urban space.

Flags, banners, and photographs are more routinely used as temporary and cost-effective means to leave a strong imprint on the city, especially in areas where more permanent forms of space-marking are prohibited. As a result, Beirut's urban landscape is pervasive, with visual markers like political parties' logos, slogans, and portraits of sectarian leaders deployed by various political parties and factions to mark their territory and promote their messages. However, in areas with more unified religious or political affiliations, such expressions take on more permanent manifestations, such as monuments, shrines, statues of saints, memorials of martyrs, or even symbolic war artillery representing the community's past legacy or preparedness for resistance.

Between the mundane and the ideological, appropriation in Beirut gives the ground its ultimate aesthetic. This visual layer reflects the city's multiple cultural identities and the wide range of perspectives that find their accommodation in urban space. Through their informal expressions, appropriations imbue the ground with a cultural grounding that reflects the strong links and rituals between Beirutis and how they associate with and shape their urban environment.

Figure 5 - Passersby cannot miss the sight of the cross that hangs above this street in Bourj Hammoud, an Armenian neighborhood in the eastern suburb of Beirut. The disproportionate scale of the size of the cross and the narrow streets contrasts with the community's deep-rooted religious and cultural heritage.

Figure 6 - The presence of political figures of the Amal party on the corner wall in Nabaa expresses the recent demographic shift of this neighborhood into a Shia Muslim quarter.

Figure 7 - A Christian figurine shrine is juxtaposed with a poster bearing an inscription that reads, "Do not throw garbage in this area." The joining of religious appropriation with civic responsibility in proximate placement is one of the recurrent appropriative practices of urban space in Beirut.

Figure 8 - Military symbols are frequently used in Beirut's urban space as memorials to Civil war martyrs, such as this artillery cannon, here exhibited in the "Mkalles" roundabout to commemorate fallen soldiers of the Lebanese Army.

Figure 9 - A figurine of Saint Charbel is placed to upgrade an area near residential buildings, formerly used as a trash disposal site.

section 2

commoning

Commoning is generally understood as the practice of producing 'commons', those shared and often necessary communal resources. The 'commons' as a spatial practice has been widely debated in architecture and urban discourse and typically refers to the work of Garrett Hardin[1] and Elinor Ostrom,[2] which focus more on the organization and management of commons, mostly natural resources, whether through top-down private mechanisms or bottom-up collective practices. Through a critical reading of the commons, David Harvey in "The Future of the Commons"[3] depicts an interesting shift from both previous works in expanding the concept of commons, moving beyond natural or even physical resources to larger constructs of culture, society, and urban space. He further advocates for the collective agency in reclaiming and creating new commons, challenging privatization approaches and restrictions on commoning practices.

The more recent work of Stavros Stavrides[4] argues that commoning practices involve the creation of new relations between people and enable creative encounters and a shared organization of urban life. In addition, he distinguishes common spaces from public or private spaces, as those sites whose ways of use are not typically dictated by the governing authority. These particular approaches frame our understanding of commons and commoning in this section. Thus, Commoning is explored as a people-centered practice and a means to reclaim urban space through collective coming together and shared practices. This is evident in the historical transformation of Martyr's Square, where informal practices, cultural production, and spatial reorganization have enabled it to remain a core collective space that is constantly and creatively reclaimed as 'commons'. We further extend the meaning of commons to encompass larger cultural and social connotations, looking at creative cultural production, collective repositories, and symbolic sites as places of common value. Recently emerged spaces, particularly Beirut's Port Silos as a contested space of shared trauma, further contribute to the framing of commons and practices of commoning, situating urban scars and collective resistance as core attributes.

1 Garrett Hardin, "The Tragedy of the Commons," in *Science 162*, no. 3859 (1968): 1243-48.
2 Elinor Ostrom, *Governing the Commons: The Evolution of Institutions for Collective Action* (Cambridge University Press, 1990).
3 David Harvey, "The Future of the Commons," *Radical History Review*, no. 109 (2011): 101-7.
4 Stavros Stavrides, *Common Space: The City as Commons* (Zed Books, 2016).

Figure 1a - Place Des Canons showing the Petit Serial, 1930, courtesy of the Arab Image Foundation.
Figure 1b - Celebration of the Independence Day at the "Place des Canons," 1944, courtesy of the Arab Image Foundation.

metamorphosis and manifestations of the ground as commons in martyrs' square

carla aramouny

Martyrs' Square, a symbolic space in the heart of Beirut, has always retained a unique capacity to serve as a collective space. A central connective node at the intersection of key city arteries, its identity as commons has historically sustained, despite various episodes of transformation, destruction, and reconstruction. Though currently a road junction at the intersection of Weygand, Bechara El Khoury, and Damascus Streets, the square as a public node materialized around 180 years ago during the late Ottoman period. Its evolution reflects Beirut's urban development; its history is rife with urban transformation, reflected in its name, morphology, and usage, which were outcomes of strategic shifts affecting the city and the region. Acts of commoning continuously manifested through various collective initiatives, whether political, social, or cultural (Fig. 1a & 1b).

This essay narrates the square's transformation through three key sections of strategic regional developments and their impact on the square, its spatial metamorphosis, and commoning acts that allowed it to remain a collective public symbol. The research is supported by visualization and drawings, narrating the different episodes of transformation through various modes from archival photographs and maps, 3d simulations, and drawing overlays, to time-based mappings. The verification of the research and visual narration relied on scholarly references, in addition to an extensive collection of archival photos and postcards sourced from online sources, local special archives, and private collectors. The aim is to produce an evolutionary visual archive of the square, unpacking its various socio-spatial manifestations and symbolic representations in time.

Strategic developments

Several strategic shifts were fundamental in spurring the transformation in the field known as 'maidan' into Martyrs' square mirroring Beirut's growth and development (Fig. 2).

Originally a small intramural city of 6000 people, Beirut's growth was first catalyzed during Egyptian rule (1832-1841) with its designation as the capital of Wilayet Sidon. Port modernization, the silk trade, and the opening of the Suez Canal in 1869 spurred its economic and urban growth.

The city grew outside its walls and over adjacent hills as a local merchant culture flourished. This growth further accelerated after the influx of refugees fleeing the 1860 Mount Lebanon massacres.[1] Within this context,[2] the maidan formed a connective space at the city's eastern plateau that served as a traveler's stop, a busy marketplace,[3] a field for walks, and a military training ground, flanked by the Bourj El Kashef watchtower on its southern edge and the Mohammadin cemetery on its northern edge.

The Tanzimat reforms (1839-1876) of the Ottoman Empire modernized Beirut, including street widening, installation of gas lighting, parcelization, and planning regulations to guide urban growth.[4] Establishing the Beirut-Damascus road in 1863 further solidified the maidan's role as a pivotal node in regional trade.[5]

However, the most substantial transformation of the city came during Sultan Abdul Hamid's rule. The city was developed to reflect the imperial government's ambition for a modern public image, with ambitious public edifices, exemplified by the inaugural formation of the square.[6]

The establishment of Wilayet Beirut in 1888 gave the city further regional importance, supported by municipal establishment, a new building code, and the inauguration of the tramway system in 1909.

With the fall of the Ottoman Empire at the end of World War I, the French took over the mandate of the Levant[7] and proclaimed the State of Greater Lebanon in 1920, with Beirut as its capital. They initiated their mandate with ambitious urban renewal projects to westernize the city, reshaping its historic quarters, including the square. Their main urban projects included widening Maarad Street,[8] applying a Haussmannian star-shaped grid over the old city, and implementing the Place de l'Etoile at its center.[9]

The mandate also included cadastral reforms, extensive city land surveys, and the production of a new building code in 1940, which organized building regulations, including building heights and plot setbacks.[10] It also brought about

1 Robert Saliba, *Beirut 1920-1940: Domestic Architecture Between Tradition and Modernity*, (Order of Engineers and Architects, 1998).

2 This period of rapid development also witnessed the establishment of schools by French and American missionaries in the city and the development of a city quarantine area .

3 Baptisin Poujoulat, "La Place du Canon en 1861," in *El Bourj Place de la liberté et porte du Levant*, ed. Ghassan Tueni and Fares Sassine, (Beirut: Dar Annahar, 2000), 10-11.

4 Toufoul Abou Hodeib, "Home is Where the Investment is," in *A Taste for Home: The Modern Middle Class in Ottoman Beirut.* (Stanford University Press, 2017), 49-82.

5 Nadine Hindi, "Urban forms at the intersection of Imperialism and Colonialism: A Perspective on Beirut," *The 18th International Planning History Society Conference*, (Yokohama: July 2018).

6 Jan Hanssen, "Your Beirut is on my Desk: Ottomanizing Beirut under Sultan Abdülhamid II (1876-1909)," in *Projecting Beirut. Episodes in the Construction and Reconstruction of a Modern City*, ed. Peter Rowe and Hashim Sarkis, (Prestel, 1998), 41-67.

7 Following the Sykes Picot agreement in 1916, which divided the region into French and British control.

8 The Maarad street's widening was initially begun by the Ottomans to implement hygiene measures in the intramural city.

9 The star-shaped grid was however executed as a truncated star in order to avoid the religious awqaf - Khalaf.

10 Saliba, *Beirut 1920-1940*, 2-4.

11Assem Salam, "The Role of Government in Shaping the Built Environment," in *Projecting Beirut. Episodes in the Construction and Reconstruction of a Modern City*, ed. Peter Rowe and Hashim Sarkis, (Prestel, 1998), 122-133.

12 Hashim Sarkis, "A Vital Void," in *Two Squares*, ed. Hashim Sarkis, ed. (Harvard University Press, 2006), 19.

13 Sarkis, "A Vital Void," 20.

several urban planning studies that implicated future visions of the city and its square, initially with Plan Danger, which represented the first attempt at a comprehensive study of the city and its outskirts, highlighting the need for decongesting the center.[11] One key vision by Delahalle incorporated re-imagining the square as a gateway to the city with a cascading piazza open to the sea.[12] Furthermore, in 1943, a master plan proposal by French urbanist Michel Ecochard reinforced a shift from the city to its outskirts and incorporated main transportation arteries connecting the square to the sea while strengthening its east/west connection.[13]

Following independence from the French in 1943, the early years of the Lebanese Republic ushered in a period of unregulated, exuberant urban growth.[14] A significant plan, approved in 1954, focused primarily on road networks and densification but completely neglected the city's future growth or its natural and cultural heritage. This resulted in severe long-standing repercussions on city density, exacerbating congestion. New buildings with increased height and widening of the Damascus and Bechara el Khoury roads further characterized the square as a congested transport hub.

The Fouad Chehab period that followed (1958-1964) was important for its infrastructural modernization and establishment of public institutions. It included the approval of a new master plan by Ecochard in 1963, focusing more on the city's outskirts and main extending arteries.[15] Attempting to revive the congested city center, the Chehab administration launched an architecture competition for the square's redesign.[16]

A key development during this era was the establishment of the Directorate of Town Planning with new urban planning regulations, enforcing processes of review and approvals on large-scale projects in the city. One aspect of these regulations enabled the setup of public-private real-estate companies for land expropriation and public projects while turning landowners into shareholders. This particular legislation was a key predecessor to the city's future development after its devastation by the 1975 civil war.[17]

The war inflicted city-wide divisions and vast destruction, particularly in Beirut's center and square, turning it into a conflict zone and demarcation line between East and West Beirut. During 15 years of strife, two periods of calm allowed reconstruction planning to commence, mainly in 1977 and 1983.[18] The 1977 efforts included the development of the first Beirut Central District (BCD) master plan and the establishment of the Council for Development and Reconstruction (CDR), controlling processes for future project planning and reconstruction. In the brief period of the ceasefire in 1983, initial rebuilding efforts executed the first demolitions of heavily destroyed buildings, particularly around the square, but were halted as fighting resumed.

At the war's end in 1990, a private company, Solidere,[19] was consigned with Beirut's reconstruction through a long-term lease of BCD and its future maintenance. Benefiting from previous expropiation laws, the company was established as a public-private initiative, converting former landowners into shareholders.[20] The resulting master plan instituted the westernization of the city with the intentional demolition of the vast majority of its remaining Ottoman and Arab fabric. Instead, it proposed high-end development targeting foreign capital and tourism.

14 Salam, "The Role of Government in Shaping the Built Environment," 126.
15 Salam, "The Role of Government in Shaping the Built Environment," 127-128.
16 Competition in *El Bourj Place de la liberté et porte du Levant*, ed. Ghassan Tueni and Fares Sassine, (Dar Annahar, 2000), 206-207.
17 Salam, "The Role of Government in Shaping the Built Environment," 129.
18 Deen Sharp, "Lebanon and the fog of reconstruction," *The Politics of Post-conflict Reconstruction* (September, 2018), 44-50.
19 Owned by Rafik Hariri, Lebanese-Saudi businessman later prime minister, and considered as mastermind behind BCD's development.
20 Sharp, "Lebanon and the fog of reconstruction," 48.

WW1 WW2

OTTOMAN RULE	FRENCH MANDATE	LEBANESE REPUBLIC
1832-1841 Egyptian rule and modernization of Beirut as port city with Ibrahim Pasha 1839-1876 Tanzimat reforms to modernize the Ottoman empire ending with constitution in 1876 1860 Mutasarrifyate Mount Lebanon after massacres and influx of refugees to Beirut 1876 - 1909 Despotic rule of Abdul Hamid II until Young Turks revolution 1888 Beirut as capital of Wilayat Beirut stretching along the Mediterranean coast 1915-18 Great Famine of Mount Lebanon under Jamal 'Saffah' Pasha	1920 State of Greater Lebanon declaration by the French mandate 1926 Republic of Lebanon under French mandate and first constitution draft 1930-40 Urban developments of the old city by the French and the creation of Place de L'Etoile	1943 End of French mandate and Lebanon's independence 1946 Withdrawal of last French troops 1958 Short civil war amid regional clashes 1960s Beirut's golden age and establishment of modern institutions under the presidency of Fouad Chehab

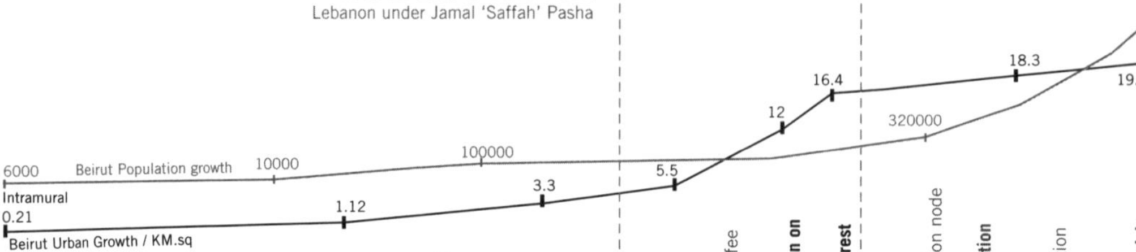

- 1770 — **Russian Fleet canons occupy the square**
- 1780 — open 'sahl' plain outside city walls and Fakhreddine's place with Bourj Al Kashef on its corner
- 1810 — the maidan as merchants and travelers stop
- 1840 — growth of city beyond city walls
- 1850 — cafes, locandas, transit stop, houses and villas outside city walls
- 1860 — **French canons and camps in square**
- 1880 — mulberry plantations within the square
- 1890 — Fakhry Bey transforms square into a muntazah garden as a place for leisure and strolling
- 1910 — shoe shiners and merchant shacks around garden
- 1916 — **Martyrs hanged by Jamal 'Saffah' Pasha in square**
- 1921 — Beirut International fair hosted by the French
- 1925 — **January demonstrations demanding national governer**
- 1930 — hotels,restaurants, theaters, and coffee shops as public sphere
- 1935 — **clashes with police against ban on leagues and associations**
- 1943 — **demonstrations denouncing leaders arrest**
- 1943 — independence celebrations
- 1950 — commercial hub, cinemas, theaters, prostitution, and central transportation node
- 1958 — **revolt against the Chamoun administration**
- 1963 — square as public sphere for demonstrations and political opposition
- 1973 — **student demonstrations on economic crisis**

1770 1780 1790 1800 1810 1820 1830 1840 1850 1860 1870 1880 1890 1900 1910 1912 1915 1916 1918 1920 1921 1925 1928 1930 1933 1935 1938 1940 1943 1945 1948 1950 1953 1955 1958 1960 1963 1965 1968 1970 1973

maidan — sahlat (sahat) al bourj — place du canon — muntazah / al hamidiyah — union square — place des canons — place des martyrs / bourj square

1772
Russian canons placed in Sahat al Bourj

1874
demolition Bourj el Kashef (al hashash)

1883/4
Menchiyyeh garden and Petit Serial

1921
transformation of garden to host Beirut International fair

1925
removal of garden kiosks and redesign of square

1930
first martyrs monument (two weeping women)

1950
destruction of Petit Serail / Rivoli construction

1960
square redesign & second martyrs monument

1975
heavy w toll on square buildin

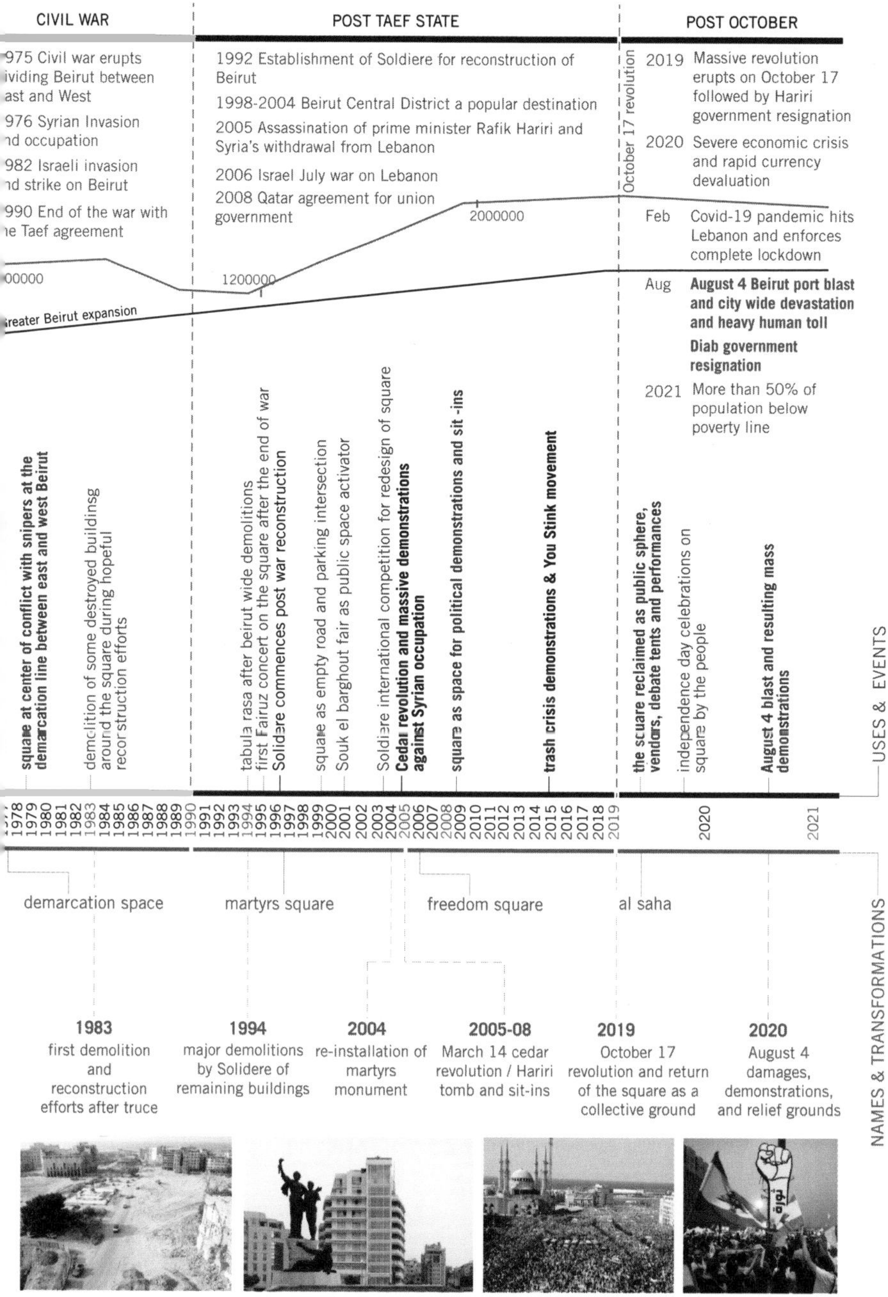

Figure 2 - Timeline diagram of the square and city's evolution

This was particularly enforced on the old souks and the square, where most of the latter's buildings were demolished.

The reconstruction period continued for over two decades, during which the square mainly remained an open space flanked by roads and parking lots. A competition was launched in 2004 for the square's design but was halted after the assassination of Rafik Hariri a year later. The assassination marked a major transformation point for downtown Beirut, as development stopped for many years, with the square remaining in limbo as a vehicular junction. Eventually, new constructions resumed, particularly high-end residential blocks designed by international architects, following Solidere's aim for an international image for the city.

That period, however, was marked less by the impact of planning and more by the square's transformation into a ground for bottom-up activism. Its open character and symbolic history enabled it to serve as a central manifestation hub for several resistance movements culminating in the 2019 'Thawra' Uprising.[21] In recent years, Lebanon and Beirut witnessed multiple compounding crises impacting development and public spaces. The severe economic crash in 2019, the restriction of power in the hands of a corrupt government, the COVID pandemic lock-down, and the port blast in 2020 all detrimentally halted all forms of development or planning (Fig. 3).

Spatial metamorphosis: The square's morphology & uses in time

These transformative developments metamorphosed the square in time and heavily impacted its spatial morphologies and urban activities (Fig. 4). Its ground shifted from an open field to a structured and connective urban node. At the same time, later violent episodes of war and reconstruction returned it to a residual space. The changing nature of the square's morphology was equally reflected in typological shifts of its buildings, as variations of style, height, and articulation reflected modernization objectives and regulations. As the square transformed in shape and structure, various key programs and activities, from commerce and leisure to trade and political administration, further reinforced its role and significance.

The city's development in the mid-1800s maintained the maidan's open characteristic as a public free space. The abundance of *azdarahit* trees,[22] it's informal functioning as a travelers' rest point, as an area for city dwellers to take a stroll, its use as a training ground for Ottoman cavalry, and its subjugation to foreign military landings might have all attributed to its remaining an open space while the city expanded. Furthermore, its relationship to markers such as Bourj El Kashef, the Damascus-Beirut artery, and the Mohammadin cemetery allowed it to function as an enclosed node (Fig. 5).

As it was to the city, the reign of Sultan Abdul Hamid was equally significant to the maidan's development, enabling its first transformation into an urban square. The new square incorporated the building of strategic edifices of administrative and cultural significance, following new urban planning regulations, building codes, and façade guidelines, notably the Petit Serail, an administrative facility initially serving as the seat of the Wali.[23] The change of building heights around the square transformed its morphology, as red tiled roofs and embellishments inspired by the West adorned the different facades[24] (Fig. 6).

21 The 2019 revolution 'Thawra' ignited in October in protest to the dire economic situation and political stagnation the country was living.
22 Chinaberry or zinzalakhit trees as identified by Jens Hanssen - referred to as Mulberry plantations by in J. Loytved's map of 1876.
23 The building later served as the municipality headquarters.
24 Saliba, *Beirut 1920-1940*, 10.
25 Arabic word meaning strolling area or leisurely park .
26 Designed by sculptor Yousef El Houwayek. The public criticized the monument for its representation, and it was vandalized later, before its vandalism in 1950 and its later removal.
27 May Davie, The History and Evolution of Public Spaces in Beirut Central District. (Solidere Report, 1997).

Other key buildings included new hybrid structures built over existing edifices, such as the Khan Tayan showing traces of its predecessor, the demolished Bourj El Kashef, or the Kawkab Al Sharq Hotel built over earlier informal marketplaces (Fig. 8).

The transformation also included incorporating a delineated public park in its center, the *muntazah*,[25] as a lush garden with the original *azdaharit* trees. The ground in this period served as a public sphere, extending from the leisurely park to the commercial ground of adjacent buildings and a political ground represented by the local government's seat.

The French mandate period had a lesser impact on the square's built fabric. However, it did heavily alter the park's nature and the relationship of its ground to the surroundings (Fig. 7). In their inaugural year, the French launched the Beirut International Fair, disfiguring the square and cutting down its trees to house the different pavilions, while inserting a circus area over the northern cemetery grounds. In 1926, the park was reshaped into a disconnected landscaped area with a central fountain and an alignment of palm trees, intended as a beautification project rather than an outlet for inhabitants. Later, in 1934, a Martyrs' monument, the Weeping Women,[26] was installed on the square as a memorial for the 1916 martyrs, giving the square its infamous name, Martyrs' Square. The French mandate, however, did set the ground for future visions of the square, many of which were translated during the early republic. Its focus on the Place de L'Étoile played a major role in diverting the political character and centrality of the square, which accordingly converted towards a cultural and transportation role[27] (Fig. 9).

This role continued well into the period of independence and the early republic. Changes in building code and zoning regulations brought new construction and more modern typologies that gained further height over the square. Continuation of activities like the infamous brothel area, police station, restaurants and cafés, including the notorious Kahwet Al Kazaz on its southwest corner, travel agents, low-budget hotels, souks, and theatres, all made the square a dense bustling commercial hub (Fig. 10 a&b). Its ground operated mainly as a transportation network busy with pedestrian and private and public vehicular traffic. A key event during this period included the demolition of the Petit Serail to increase the square's surface area and connect it visually with the sea. Following the competition launched during the Chehab era, the center of the square was transformed once again, this time into an elevated detached piazza and a new iconic Martyrs' monument in its center (Fig. 11). The eventual building of the new Rivoli Cinema at the northern edge re-framed the square as an enclosed space.

Vast urban destruction ensued during the following 15 years of civil war, causing a complete deformation of the square. From a connective ground to a battlefield, the square turned into an amorphous space with sniper posts, as buildings stood in ruin and wild greenery took over. A no man's land with a scarred Martyrs' monument, its previous bustle was completely eradicated (Fig. 12).

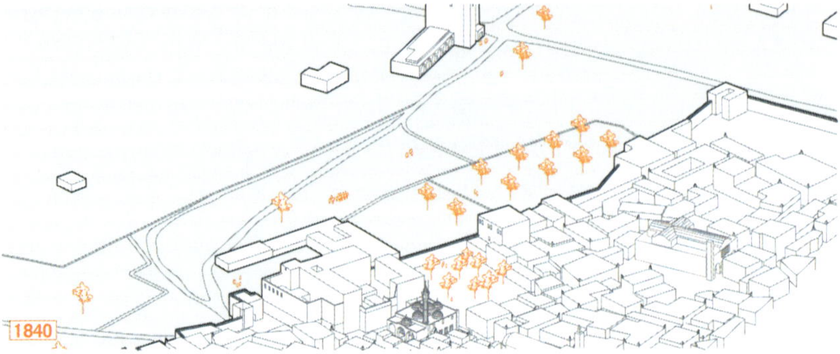
1840

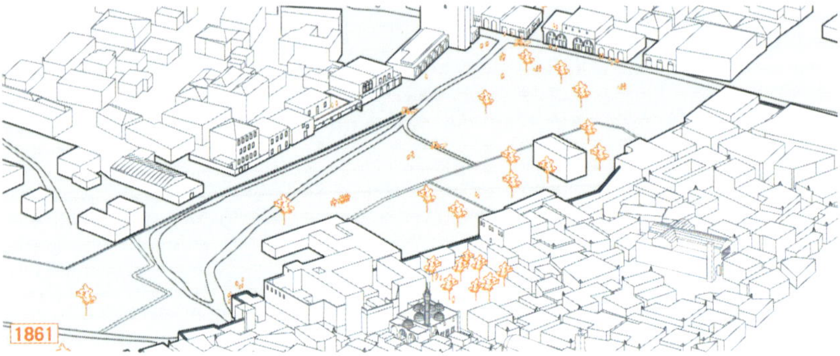
1861

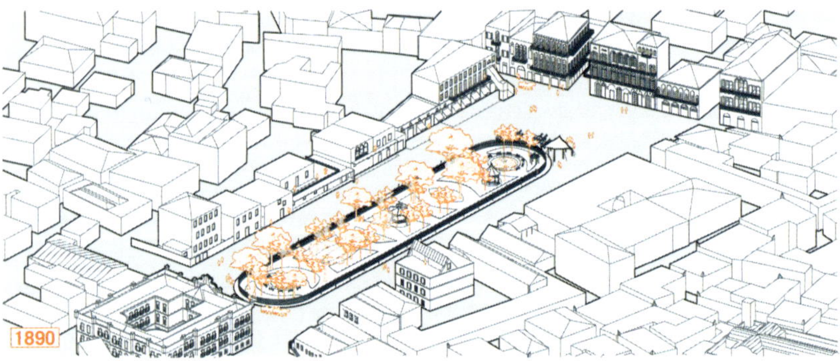
1890

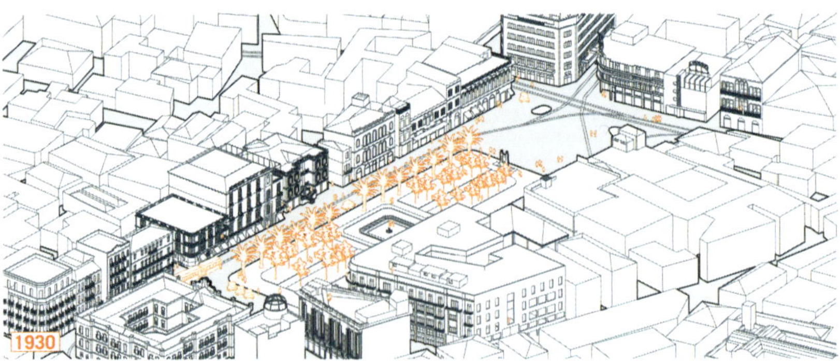
1930

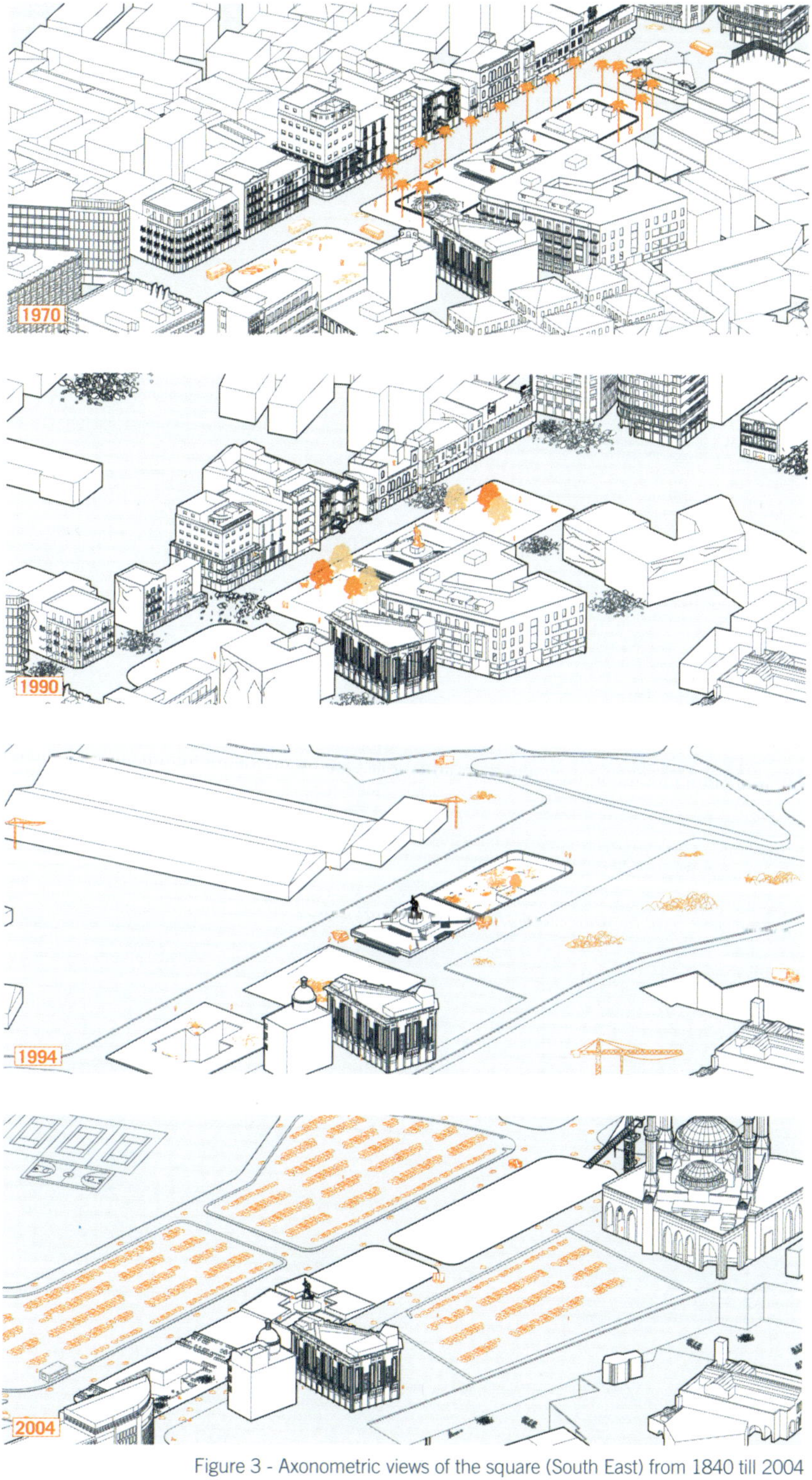

Figure 3 - Axonometric views of the square (South East) from 1840 till 2004

1841
Maidan / Sahat Al Bourj

The 'maidan' outside the old city walls, with Bourj El Kashef on its south east edge, a meeting place for travelers and merchants

*based on map by M. Davie

1876
Sahat Al Bourj / Place des Canons

City growth beyond walls and the square as a contained urban space with mulberry trees and cemetery on north edge

*based on map by J. Loyvted

1920
Muntazah / Al Hamidiyah Square

Square redesign, initiation of tramway lines, and development of central garden 'muntazah' - named Al Hamidiyah and briefly Union square

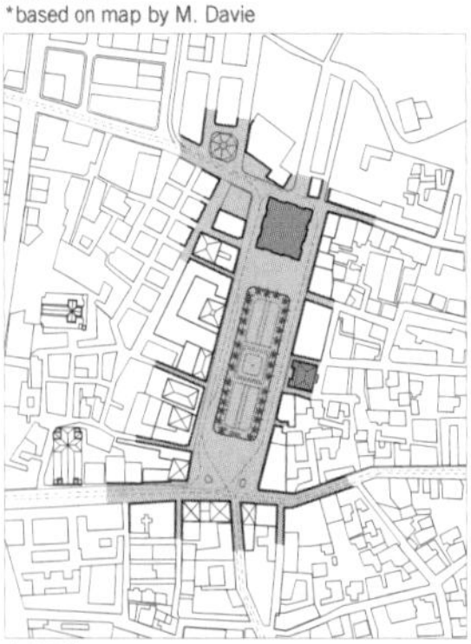

1930
Place Des Canons / Martyrs Square

Square redesign under mandate as enclosed pond and green scape with memorial for martyrs on its southern edge

*based on map by C. Durrafourd

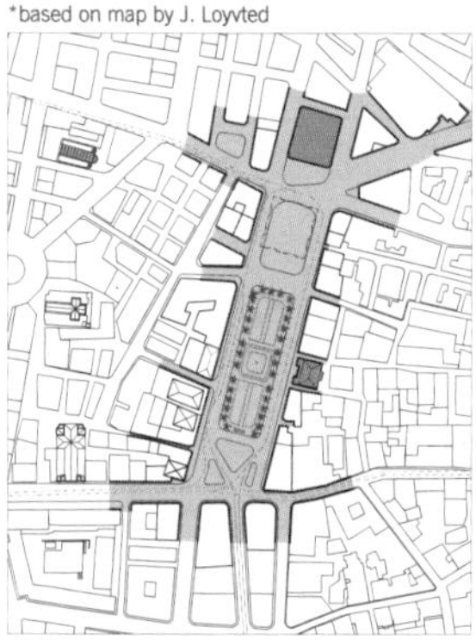

1950
Place Des Martyrs

Square enlarged with the demolition of Petit Serail, building the new Rivoli Cinema on north, and development of wider street networks

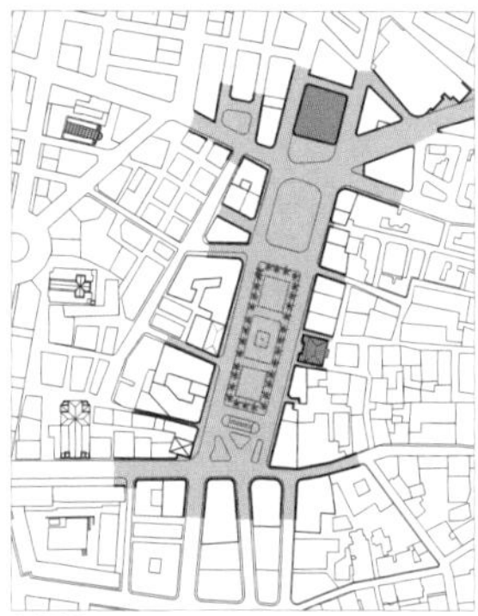

1970
Place Des Martyrs / Bourj Square

Redesign of the square as a leveled platform and the installation of a new memorial for martyrs in its center, bus lines replace the tramway network

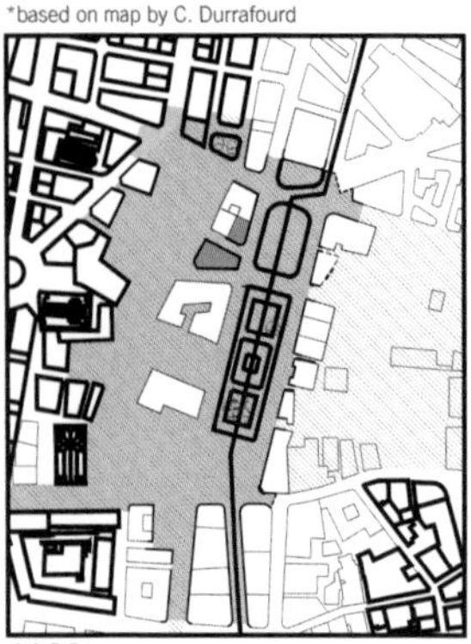

1990
Demarcation space

Demarcation line cutting through the square with snipers taking over buildings / massive war toll on the urban fabric

*based on aerials from the period

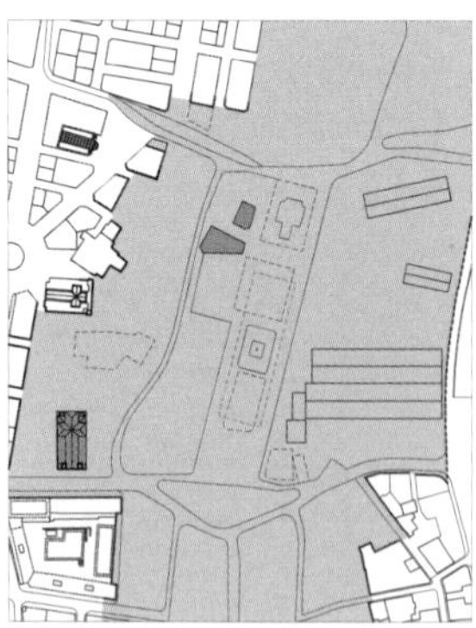

1994
Reconstruction field

Square as a 'tabula rasa' space after major demolitions by Solidere of the surviving fabric in preparation for reconstruction

*based on aerials from the period

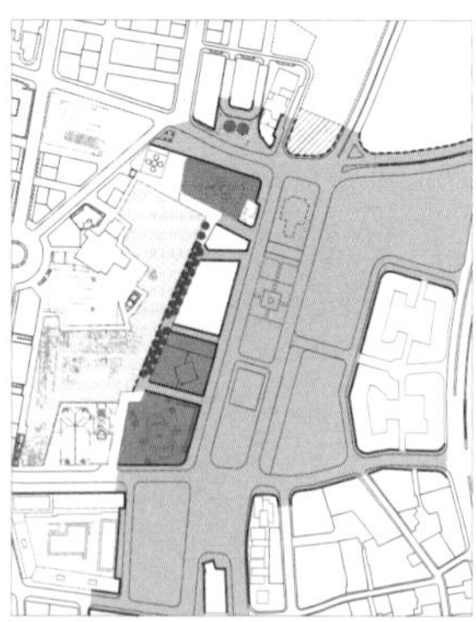

2019
Freedom Square / Martyrs Square / Al Saha

Square as an isolated road junction / The tomb and memorial of Hariri and high-end residential surround the empty square / Square regained post Oct. 17 as a Saha

Figure 4 - Metamorphosis of Martyrs Square's urban ground in time

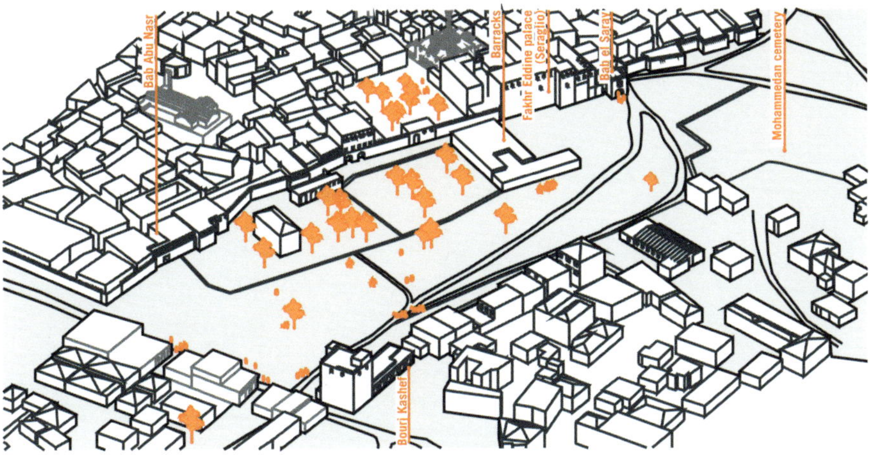

Figure 5 - Axonometric drawing of 1861 showing the Maidan outside the intramural city and key landmarks

Figure 6 - View of the square's southern blocks in 1920

Figure 7 - Ceremony during the French Mandate in Place des Canons with Kahwet Al Kazaz in the background, 1921, courtesy of the Arab Image Foundation

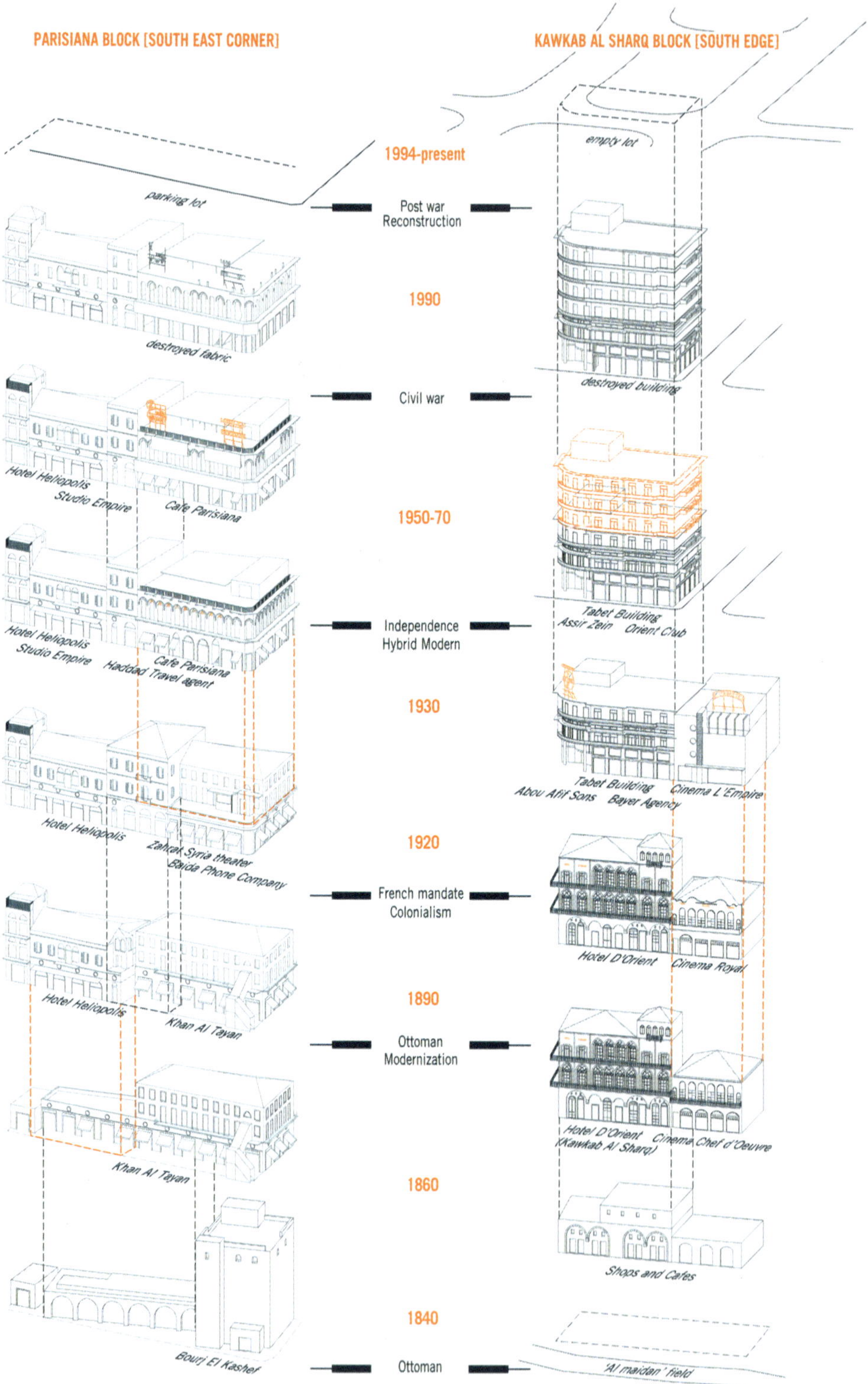

Figure 8 - Shifting Block typology of Khayan Tayan into Parisiana restaurant and Kawkab El Shark Hotel into Tabet office building

1890 Muntazah / Al Hamidiyah / Union Square

1930 Place des Canons / Place des Martyrs

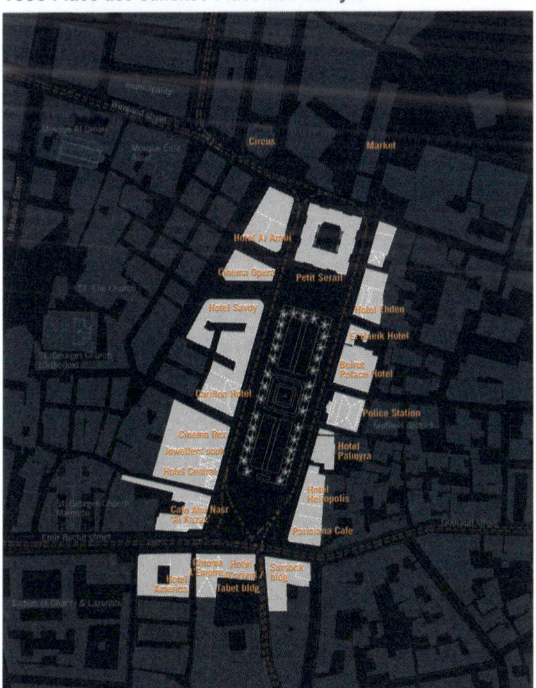

URBAN CHANGES		PUBLIC EVENTS
Urban Alignment of plots around square	1890	Community-funded 'Muntazah' as central garden accessible with fee
	1895	
	1900	
Paving the square		Horse carriage stops serving the city and beyond
	1905	
Inauguration of Beirut Tramway with lines intersecting on square	1910	
Demolition of wood shacks around the square	1914	
	1916	Martyrs hanged by Jamal 'Saffah' Pasha in square
		Period of the Great Famine of Mount Lebanon
	1918	
Welcoming General Gouraud on square	1920	French mandate & Great Lebanon Declaration
Zahrat Syria Theater / Khan Tayan burns down	1921	Beirut International fair hosted by the French with city and square transformation
Removal of pavilions and French redesign of square	1925	January demonstrations demanding national governer
Serail as new seat of Lebanese government		
	1927	
Martyrs' Square naming and inauguration of first monument	1930	
		Hotels,restaurants, theaters, and coffee shops as public sphere
	1933	
Collapse of Kawkab Al Sharq/Hotel d'Orient building		
	1935	Clashes with police against ban on leagues and associations
Fire destroys Cinema Royale		Square's centrality shifts to new Place de L'Etoile
	1938	
	1940	
Plan "Danger" to decongest square		
	1943	Demonstrations denouncing leaders' arrest - followed by Independence celebrations
	1945	
Widening of Bechara El Khoury street	1946	Withdrawal of last French troops

Figure 9 - Plans and timeline of public events and urban transformations, 1890-1930

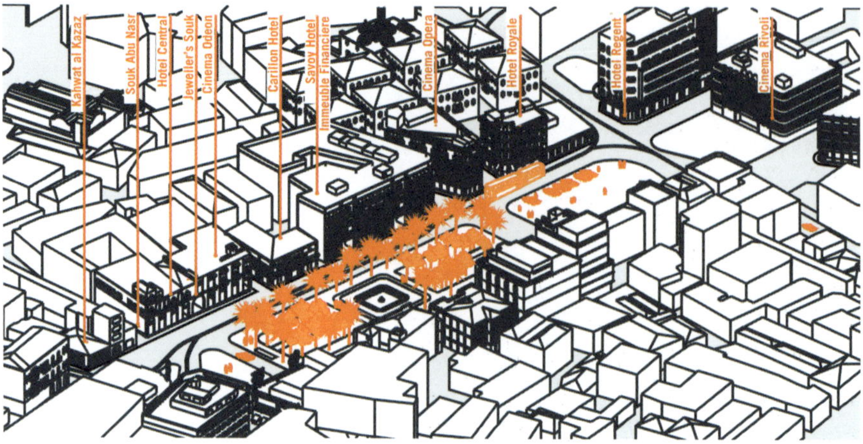

Figure 10a - Axonometric view in 1950 showing the city bustle around the square

Figure 10b - View of the square in 1950 after the removal of the Weeping Women monument

Figure 11 - Axonometric view in 1970 with the new square platform and monument

Figure 12 - The square as a space of conflict and division in 1990

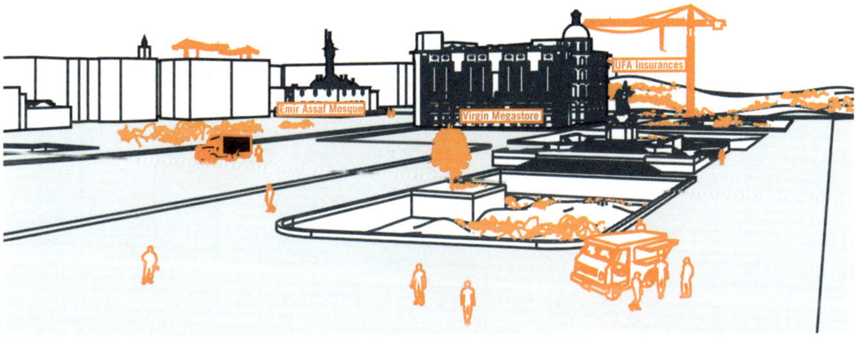

Figure 13 - View of the square as a reconstruction field in 1994

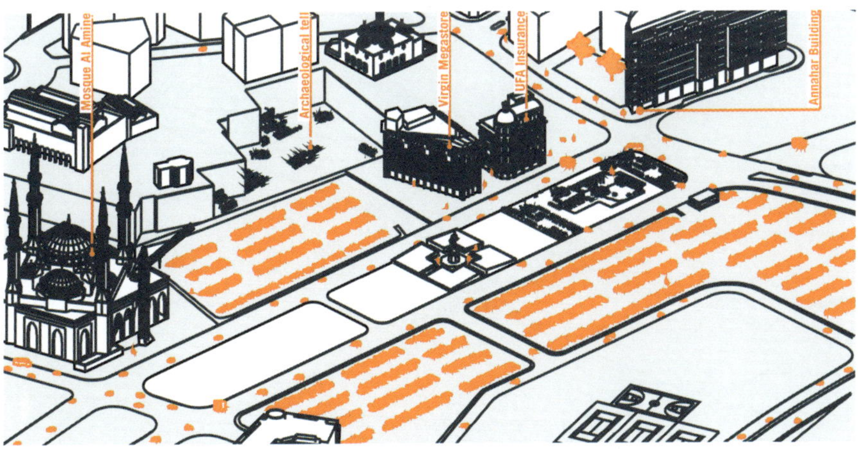

Figure 14 - The reconstructed city in 2004 in an axonometric view showing landmarks and parking lots

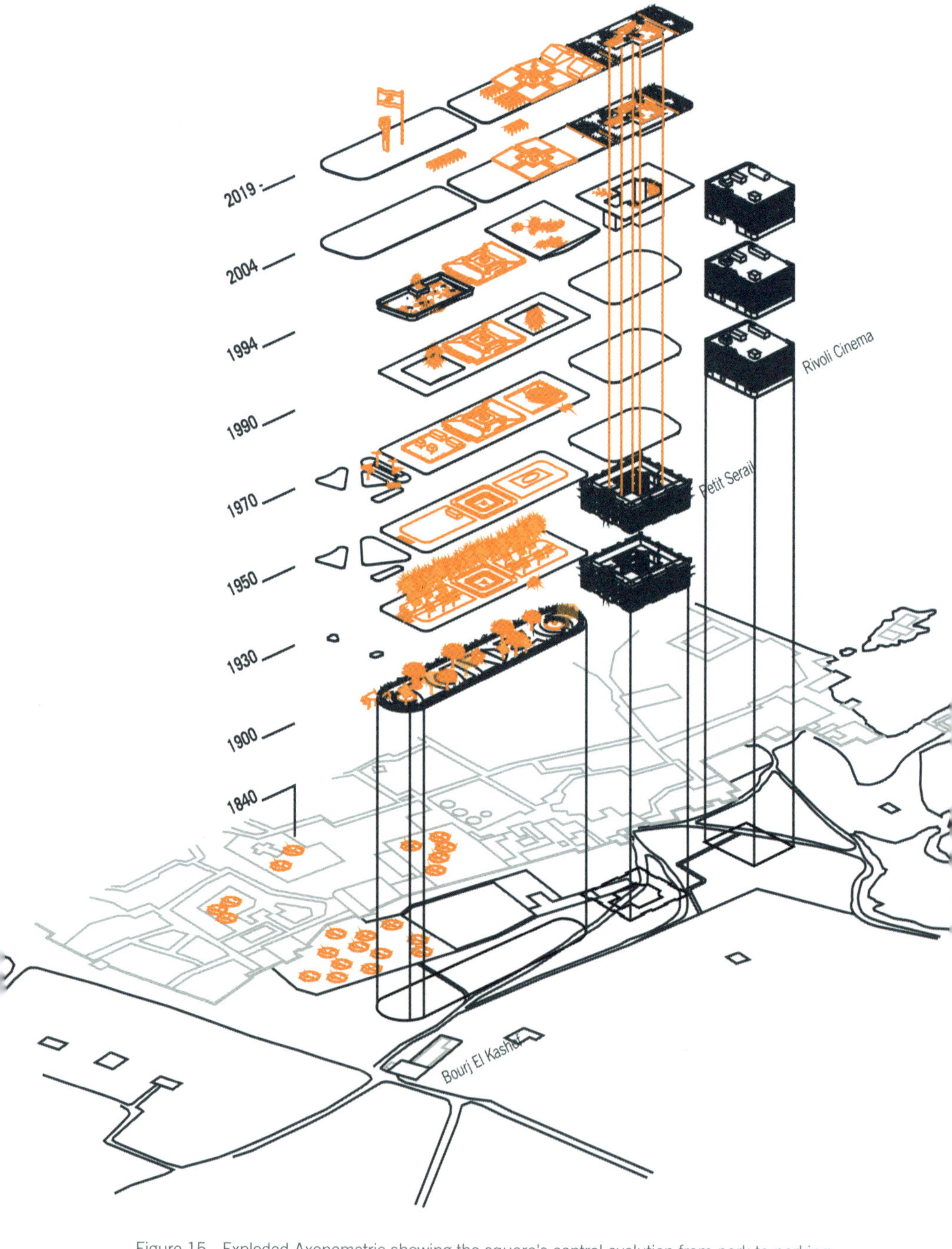

Figure 15 - Exploded Axonometric showing the square's central evolution from park to parking

1990 Demarcation line / Greenline

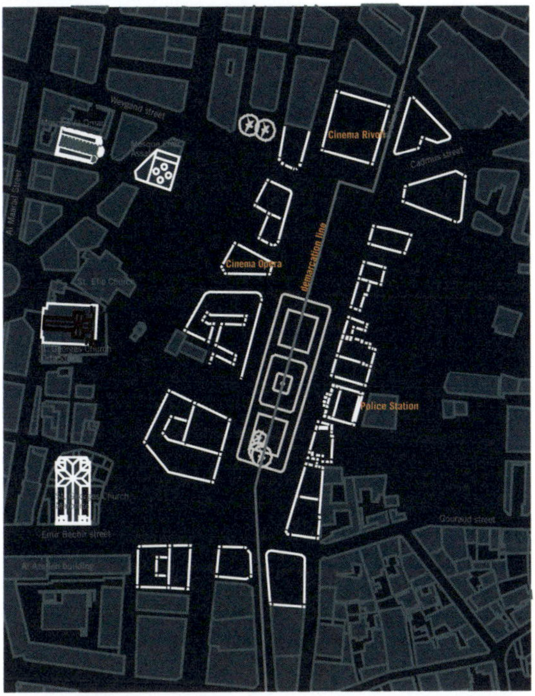

1994 Martyrs Square / BCD

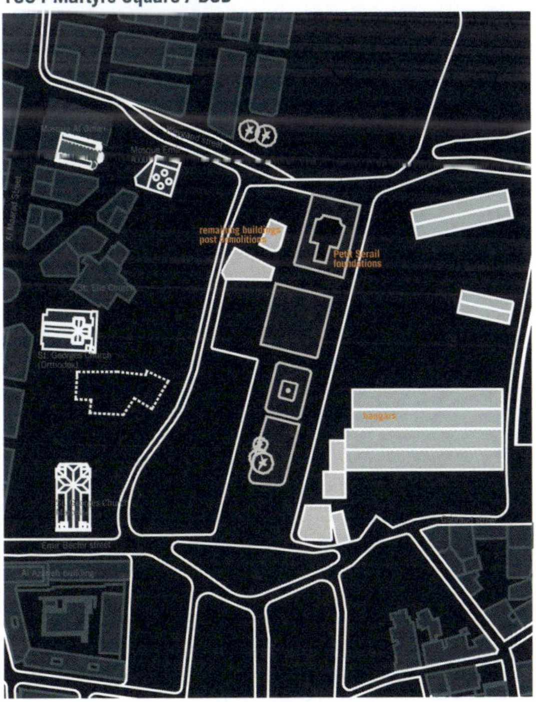

URBAN CHANGES		PUBLIC EVENTS
	1976	Syrian invasion and occupation
	1979	Square at center of conflict with snipers at the demarcation line between east and west Beirut
	1980	
	1982	Israeli invasion and strike on Beirut
First demolition and reconstruction efforts after truce	1983	
	1986	
	1988	
	1990	End of the war with the Taef agreement
	1992	Establishment of a private real-estate company 'Solidere' for reconstruction of Beirut
	1993	
Major demolitions by Solidere of remaining buildings	**1994**	Square asTabula rasa after city-wide demolitions
	1995	First Fairuz concert on the square after the end of the war
Removal of Martyrs' monument from square	1996	Solidere commences post war reconstruction
Temporary sculptural artwork installed on square	1997	
	1998	
Square as empty road and parking intersection	1999	
Annahar newspaper building completion	2000	
Virgin Megastore opens in old Cinema Opera	2001	Souk el Barghout flee market as public space activator
	2002	
	2003	

Figure 16 - Plans and timeline of public events and urban transformations 1975-2004

Figure 17 - Al Hamidiyah square in 1890 in axonometric view, with the Petit Serail at the back

Figure 18 - The modernized square with the first martyrs' monument in 1930

Figure 19 - View in 2019 showing Thawra ground reclamation and activists' practices

With the reconstruction process, a new vision for the square was put in place; its entire ground was cleared to make way for new high-end construction, creating a disruptive break from its urban and social fabric (Fig. 13). The master plan revived the vision of the square as an open city piazza connecting to the sea and maintaining only two surviving buildings with new high-end residential constructions, a large mosque over the Kahwat Al Kazaz site, and some surrounding commercial functions.

The central area of the square became a void, a clearing between new wide roads that operated as a parking area, except for the lone Martyrs' monument. The early construction period included executing several buildings around the square, such as the monumental Mohammad Al Amin Mosque, Le Grey Hotel, and the Annahar newspaper building, as well as the renovation of the two remaining buildings (Fig. 14). Later, high-end residential buildings were built adopting a distinctly contemporary aesthetic. Except for the mosque and the Hariri memorial piazza, none of the buildings connected to the square's ground nor provided an extension for public engagement. Instead, they operated as enclaves, reinforcing the square's detached character with no role except to serve vehicular needs.

As such, the square's morphological transformation turned in full circle, from an open free space in the 1800s into today's open vehicular field (Fig. 15). This field-like characteristic is enabled not only by its openness but also by the disconnection between its ground and the adjacent buildings. It thus operates as a free plane, irrelevant to its surroundings, except for a few markers that occasionally serve as communal meeting points during main political or social events, such as the Martyrs' monument, the mosque, and the Hariri memorial.

Collective commons and shifting identity

Throughout time, the square remained a collective ground. Its earlier form as a maidan allowed it to be a free negotiable ground, a collective space at the intersection of vital city arteries with a long-standing predisposition for re-appropriation, adaptability, and commonality.[28] Its continual interpretation as 'commons' can thus be observed as an outcome of its open spatial characteristic, centrality, and historical significance.

While pre-war development constituted a linear history of the square and its functions, the war and reconstruction periods were two episodes of evident disruption in its transformation, severely altering its operation as commons (Fig. 16). More recent changes imposed by the heavy demolition and Solidere's master plan instated a radical break from the city and the square's visual urban history. This included the shift of programming of its ground into solely vehicular, incorporating mainly residential building blocks, disregarding easy pedestrian traversability, and imposing regulations impeding informal street-level practices such as street vendors or gatherings.

Despite these episodes of erasure, the square's significance and symbolism solidified and remained in people's memory. The history of the square lays witness to various acts of commoning, whether through formal top-down planning or informal, bottom-up practices of reclamation and

28 referencing M. Mathur, in Samir Khalaf, "The Bourj as a Cosmopolitan Public Sphere," in *Heart of Beirut: Reclaiming the Bourj*, Samir Khalaf (Saqi Books, 2006), 180.

organization. Its identity was never static but continuously evolved into various meanings and representations, whether political, cultural, or social. This shifting identity was reflected in its changing name, always redefining its status and designation.

The publicness of the maidan field first manifested through informal acts of strolling and resting outside the city walls. Poujoulat, in 1861, described its popularity later as a busy marketplace and center of trade and transport, depicting its multi-confessional character, French-operated facilities, and its name: Place du Canon.[29]

The late Ottoman planning period initiated a more formal publicness, enforcing public use as a citizen's right.[30] The structured square was conceived as a common ground necessary for "public" good and popularly designated Sahat Al Bourj.[31] This commons aspect was furthered through a bottom-up public effort by the citizens of Beirut to turn the center of the sahat into the muntazah, labeled Menchiyeh.[32] The Ottomans further reinforced its public and political symbolism by building the Petit Serail as the city's seat of power on the square while renaming it Al Hamidiyah Square in honor of Sultan Abdul Hamid (Fig. 17). However, this also allowed it to become a center for political protests and organization. The hanging of revolutionary liberals in the square in 1916 tarnished its centrality yet gave the square a new symbolic meaning for martyrdom and resistance.[33]

This symbolic aspect of martyrdom was formally instated on the square during the French period, when the first memorial for martyrs was installed in 1934, changing thereafter the square's identity from a public ground to a symbolic commons (Fig. 18). The French attempted through this act to enforce a national narrative unifying various confessions and distancing them from Ottoman identity.[34] This constructed symbolism allowed the square to remain significant to people through time despite the erasure of its built fabric. Its marking as Martyrs' Square continued well through the early Republic period, with a renewed Martyrs' monument and the more recent installation of the Hariri memorial in 2005.

The political symbolism also became the drive behind the continuous re-appropriation of the square as a center for protest at various political events. From the manifestation against French rule in 1943, the 1958 civil clashes, to the 1970s massive student protests,[35] political assembly was strong in and around the square, whether through its open center or its cafés, locales, and surrounding hotels.[36] The war, however, forced the conversion of this political symbolism into that of conflict and division. The commons aspect of its ground became obsolete as it became the space for violent demarcation. In recent years, however, major protests such as the 2005 Cedars revolution, the 2015 "You Stink" movement, and the 2019 Thawra regained the square as a collective common despite losing its centrality within the urban fabric. The Thawra reclaimed the square as a sahat for the people, moving beyond its symbolic value to a common ground manifested in various activities and appropriations (Fig. 19 a&b). The square functioned once more as a uniting ground, as protesters transformed it organically into a vital center for activism reconnected to its surroundings.

Beyond its political symbolism, the square's history incorporated various cultural and leisure spaces that enabled its operation as a cultural commons, from cinemas, theaters, and hotels for local and international travelers to marketplaces and souks. Bringing back the bustle of its pre-war history, the Thawra re-envisioned the square as a cultural hub, temporarily installing markets, food stalls, and debate tents and transforming existing structures into spaces of exhibitions, events, and performances. The Thawra thus expanded the meaning of the square as commons beyond its mono-symbolism for martyrs, renaming it Al Sahat as a shared space for coming together and mobilizing in the city.

Conclusion

The evolution of Martyrs' Square, from its origins as an open field to its current state as a vehicular junction, reflects its enduring historical significance as a collective space. Its temporal metamorphosis reveals the relationship and impact of historical shifts, politics, and social dynamics. These various episodes of transformation, from the late Ottoman period to the French mandate, from independence to civil war and post-war reconstruction, caused profound changes that impacted the square's form, building typologies, and operation. Despite these various phases of transformation, destruction, and reconstruction, the square has retained its significance as a commons at cultural, political, and social levels. Its continuous reclamation by the people has enabled it to emerge as a site of collective action and protest during pivotal moments in history.

Today, while it stands empty, serving solely vehicular traffic, the square presents a unique opportunity as a collectively formed common ground that can be redefined and reclaimed. Despite losing its centrality, it continues to act as an amorphous field, able to connect, divide, or re-adapt to various public imaginaries. It is important to recognize that its free and adaptable characteristic can serve as a valuable reference for the city's future planning and development; this field-like quality should be retained instead of imposing top-down planning visions, and the informalities it enables should be valued as reflections of public life. While the square has lost its historical continuity and urban fabric, it has enabled a new condition to form, an adaptable ground that continues to shape and be shaped by the local collective.

29 A designation referencing the French canons that took post on the Maidan in 1860, and previously the landing of Russian canons in 1772.

30 Or mnafa3a 3amma (public benefit) as described in Toufoul Abou Hodeib, "Home is Where the Investment is," 51-52.

31 'Sahat' Arabic word for open square, and 'Al Bourj' designating the Bourj El Kashef tower.

32 Tueni and Sassine, *El Bourj*, 222-223.

33 Executed by Jamal 'Saffah' Pasha (1913-1919) in the square during a period of great famine and local discontent.

34 According to Lucia Volk, in Lucia Volk, *Memorials and Martyrs in Modern Lebanon*, (Indiana University Press, 2010), 39-77.

35 Tueni and Sassine, *El Bourj*, 164-165.

36 Such as Pharmacy Gemmayel run by Pierre Gemmayel, head of the Phalangist political party, In Tueni and Sassine, *El Bourj*, 176-177.

Figure 1 - Panoramic view of Martyrs Square and downtown Beirut during Thawra in October 2019

cultural commons and retaining collective memory

editors in conversation with
farès el-dahdah*
& abdul-halim jabr**

This conversation discusses cultural commons in Beirut and their significance for inhabitants and collective memory. The talk explores various manifestations of cultural commons, from those that are "lived" to those that are constructed from archives, virtual repositories, and local collectives. It distinguishes cultural commons between places holding significant social memory and the instruments employed for retaining it. Through highlighting two significant spaces of cultural and socio-political relevance, Martyrs Square and the Port Silos, the discussion revolves around the ephemerality of these spaces as part of the collective imagination. The conversation further delves into the role of archives and digital repositories in retaining collective memory and how local collectives help substantiate cultural commons from a bottom-up approach.

* levantCarta Initiative / Rice University.
** Beirut Heritage Initiative / ALBA.

Carla Aramouny: We'll begin with the notion of 'Commons', generally defined as a necessary resource that is shared by a community. That resource could be an actual physical element, like land or water, or understood more broadly through expanded cultural and social connotations. We can think of spaces or instruments that retain collective memory as part of this larger understanding of commons. Repositories of collective memory can be defined as two types: Places of shared memory (such as city landmarks) and instruments of shared memory (such as narratives, archives, virtual repositories, and collectives). Whether places or instruments, both can be permanent or ephemeral, experienced or imagined, physical or virtual.

In Beirut, how can we define current modes of cultural commons? What constitutes, in that sense, 'commons', and how can they play a part in retaining collective memory?

Abdul-Halim Jabr: I will focus on places rather than instruments, pointing to examples of cultural commons in Beirut that have gained significance in recent years due to collective events, whether spontaneous or planned. The center of Beirut, including Martyrs Square, devastated during the civil war,[1] holds, for example, immense importance. It witnessed Fairuz's first concert post-war in 1994, its reconstruction becoming a subject of national debate, and it was the center for most protest movements. In recent protests, and particularly the "Thawra"[2] in 2019 (Fig. 1), several landmark 'commons' carried significance, like the "Azariyye"[3] building, for instance, that had its own nuance as a place of debate. Similarly, the City Center dome (the Egg)[4] had more elitist connotations as a cultural hub, while the Grand Theatre[5] presented an alternative underground function. These are essential spaces of social and cultural meaning that should not be overlooked.

There are also transient cultural commons, like "matbakh el balad,"[6] which involved countless meetings, whether online or in apartments, emphasizing the centrality of the protest. Another is Antoine Atallah's potent visual brilliantly capturing the first few days and events of the Thawra, showcasing the diverse subcultures inhabiting the city center (Fig. 2). It was intended to be the starting point of a contemporary archive. I suggest we expand our collective definition to those places of significance representing milestones in our social debate.

Farès el-Dahdah: Wherever these culturally significant places may exist, in Beirut or elsewhere, their essence cannot be fully grasped without acknowledging the ephemera they produce. This ephemeral aspect can extend beyond the online realm to include public displays such as billboards, movie posters from the 70s, or the iconic Rivoli cinema in Martyrs Square during the 60s. These transient elements serve as meaning markers that it would be wonderful to recapture. Reflecting on the recent protests in Martyrs Square, I am reminded of the artwork, jokes, and graffiti that emerged around these spaces, adding layers of significance that qualified their meaning as commons (Fig. 3).

If there is an effort to capture the memory of these places, I would focus less on the space and more on the ephemera that the circumstances produced. I see these ephemera as central to the qualification of a place as culturally meaningful more so than the actual form; the experiences they generate trigger our emotions and become deeply ingrained in our imaginary.

CA: I would like to continue the discussion on ephemera by looking at the distinction between commons in the cloud (virtual) and commons on the ground (physical). Ephemera encompasses not only actual artifacts but also intangible virtual productions that emerge from events and contribute to their cultural significance. Fares, could you elaborate on this?

FD: I want to re-emphasize that ephemera can take various forms, whether newspaper headlines, WhatsApp conversations, etc. WhatsApp groups, for example, have played a crucial role in mobilizing people quickly and facilitating synchronized reactions. While I cannot confirm this in Beirut's protests, in Brazil's back in 2013, protesters created "spontaneous" slogans shared via WhatsApp for collective chanting. This idea of a collective is further enhanced by the ability to have these social media networks that are live, fueled by tools like WhatsApp, Facebook, or others, and that give the impression of general mobilization, which is, in effect, ephemeral in nature.

Massive mobilization does fade over time, though, as seen in many of these movements. They emerge, gain momentum, and eventually lose steam, and this could be linked to these tools that create an illusion of vaster impact.

CA: Can we see both Fares's ephemera and Abdul-Halim's expanded meanings of commons broadening what constitutes collective memory? Should we prioritize the city's collective memory through preservation or accept a *tabula rasa* approach of erasure (as witnessed in several previous reconstruction episodes of Beirut) as an opportunity to reclaim new meanings in the city?

AHJ: Should we prioritize collective memory? I believe we should, though the question is how to approach it. This requires innovative, inclusive, and interdisciplinary thinking that transcends traditional boundaries. How can we counter the concept of *tabula rasa*? While it becomes a call to resistance, it is important to recognize that it often results in defeat. Real-estate dominance and centralized decision-making often outweigh sporadic decentralized movements.

Referring to Fares's term ephemera, I would like to highlight two ephemeral experiments that are relevant for archiving and preserving collective memory, though they differ in intention and success.

The first example, the 'Allo Beirut' exhibition,[7] showcased an extensive collection of authentic memorabilia from Beirut's material history, serving as a place of consumption, with different generations perceiving it in distinct ways. The second example is the exhibition 'Memory of a Paper City' by Alfred Tarazi.[8] It is a remarkable personal archive featuring paper publications spanning from the 1930s to the 1980s, exploring the exploitation of women and their portrayal in media and focusing on three recurring themes during those five decades: sex, violence, and rock and roll.

Overall, these examples represent attempts to document and anchor shared and evolving narratives.

1 The Lebanese Civil War was a sectarian war that lasted 15 years from 1975 to 1990 and resulted in vast destruction and the division of Beirut between dominantly Christian East and Muslim West parts.

2 The 2019 revolution, or Thawra in Arabic, was the mass uprising that ignited in October of that year in Beirut, spreading to other cities around Lebanon. The revolution was against the dire economic situation and government measures that increased taxes without reforms.

3 Azarieh building, an office building in downtown Beirut built in 1954 by architect André Leconte.

4 The Dome, a remaining ruin from the City Center complex that was destroyed by the Civil War and demolished during the reconstruction phase, is a symbolic building remnant of old Beirut and its history of conflict.

5 The Grand Theater in Beirut remains currently abandoned; built in late 1920s, architect Yousef Aftimos.

6 Arabic for Town's Kitchen, a make-shift pro-bono kitchen distributing food in the city for people in need.

7 Held at Beit Beirut Sodeco in 2022, (https://allobeirutexhibition.com/).

8 Exhibition by Alfred Tarazi housed at the Umam Documentation Center in Haret Hreik, in 2023, (https://www.umam-dr.org/event_detail/114/114/).

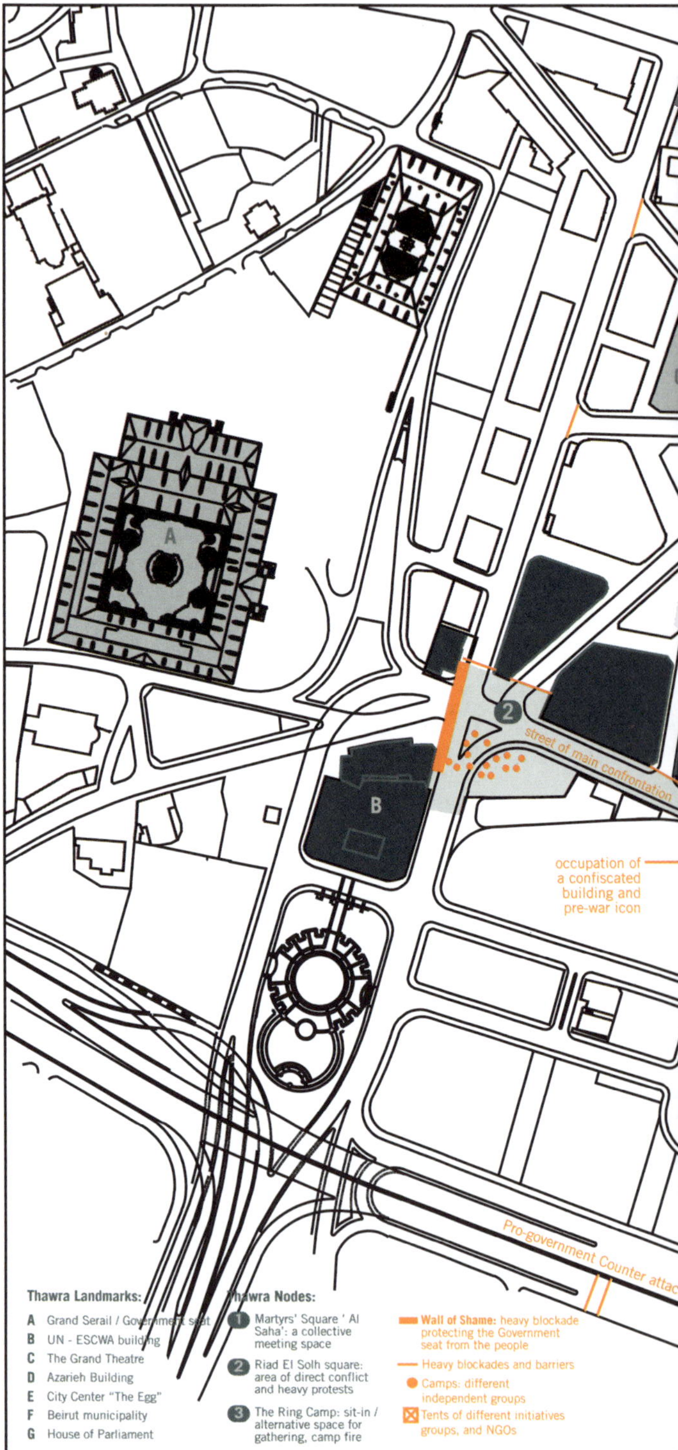

Figure 2 - Drawing based on Antoine Atallah's 2019 drawing of the Thawra's informal practices in Martyrs' Square and the surrounding areas

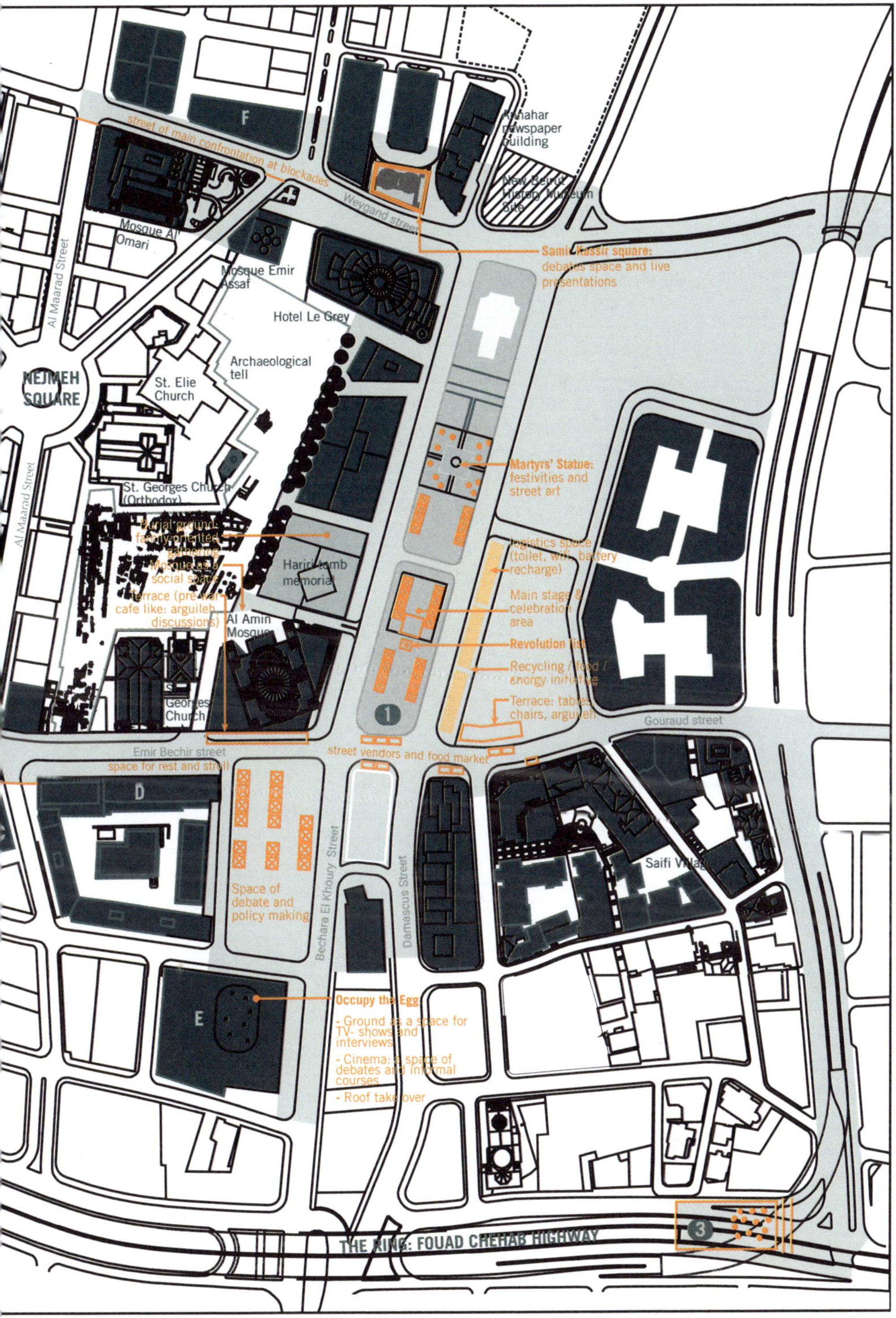
F
An-nahar newspaper building
street of main confrontation at blockades
New Beirut History Museum Site
Weygand street
Mosque Al Omari
Al Maarad Street
Samir Kassir square: debates space and live presentations
Mosque Emir Assaf
Hotel Le Grey
Archaeological tell
NEJMEH SQUARE
St. Elie Church
Martyrs' Statue: festivities and street art
St. Georges Church (Orthodox)
Al Maarad Street
Burial ground: family-oriented gathering
Mosque as a social space
Terrace (pre-war cafe like: arguileh discussions)
Hariri tomb memorial
Logistics space (toilet, wifi, battery recharge)
Main stage & celebration area
Al Amin Mosque
Revolution fist
Recycling / food / energy initiative
St. Georges Church
Terrace: tables, chairs, arguileh
1
Gouraud street
Emir Bechir street
space for rest and stroll
street vendors and food market
D
Bechara El Khoury Street
Damascus Street
Saifi Village
Space of debate and policy making
E
Occupy the Egg:
- Ground as a space for TV- shows and interviews
- Cinema: a space of debates and informal courses
- Roof take over
THE RING: FOUAD CHEHAB HIGHWAY
3

CA: Certain spaces in Beirut have maintained social relevance over time despite constant disruptions and transformations. I am speaking particularly of Martyrs Square and its persistent symbolic relevance to locals despite being in a state of *tabula rasa*. In comparison, I would like to highlight a more recently emerged commons, the Port Silos,[9] that acts more as a visual landmark signifying shared city trauma.

How can we distinguish these two spaces of collective value for the city? Can we see both as opportunities rather than dwelling nostalgically on their past or what they represent?

FD: Martyrs' Square and the Silos share a similarity of being paradoxical spaces (Fig. 4). Martyrs' Square has historically served as the focal point of urban agglomeration in Beirut. However, it lost its centrality in the city after the Civil War. During recent protests, it regained this centrality only because of its character as an open field, a terrain vague,[10] and is coincidentally close to the contested Parliament building. So, it is paradoxical that the square, which was historically the center of town, became a node for protests, though no longer holding a central position in shaping Beirut's urban landscape.

The other paradox for the Silos is that, on the one hand, they are a visual mnemonic device reminding us of the destructive explosion, yet on the other, they are too dangerous to preserve but too important to forget (Fig. 5). Preserving them nostalgically as part of an urban park in the name of collective memory would be hazardous due to their compromised condition. So, I find it paradoxical that a building you would want to preserve for its symbolic value is precisely what you should not be preserving for public safety. Both Martyrs' Square and the Silos share this paradoxical connection of occupying opposites. The recognition of this paradox is undeniable.

AHJ: Indeed, I would only add that the fate of the two sites diverges. Martyrs' Square has continuously evolved as a palimpsest, constantly vanishing while new dynamics emerge over time. It has transformed from a populist area to a traffic junction, a site of conflict, a void, and a vibrant space bustling with people. Its metamorphosis remains an ongoing process, showcasing the ever-changing nature of the square (Fig. 6).

For the Silos, they have indeed evolved from being an icon of modern life and infrastructure in Lebanon to a suspended place, both literally and metaphorically. They now represent an undisclosed site of investigation, remaining contested and associated with death. The Silos have shifted from celebrating the modern life of the Republic to representing everything corrupt in our politics and society.

FD: The layers of paradox surrounding the Silos, particularly in the context of the devastating explosion, are evident. The profound criminal negligence that led to this tragedy is truly

Figure 3 Martyrs monument in Martyrs' square with remaining graffiti and artwork done during the Thawra

unfathomable, irrespective of one's political affiliations. It serves as a stark reflection of the deteriorating governance within the republic.

AHJ: I often meet with explosion victims' relatives. To them, the Silos are a monumental tombstone, holding profound significance as the final resting place of over 200 human beings. It goes beyond collective narratives or national debates, becoming almost sacred ground for these individuals.

The site brings to mind the 9/11 ground in New York and its memorial projects. One deeply moving example is the Tribute in Light Installation in commemoration of the 2001 victims.[11] The two beams of light, reminiscent of the Twin Towers, symbolize the lingering sense of phantom pain, even after the physical presence is gone. This could be a relevant reference for the future of the silos' site, opposite to Martyrs Square's transformation, which was banalized by the constant rewriting of its identity.

FD: We must exercise caution, though, and acknowledge that the Silos, as a monumental architectural structure, hold a unique significance compared to other tragic sites in Lebanon. The scale of the silos alone evokes a stronger desire for symbolic representation, which raises questions about why it is perceived as more significant than other sites with higher casualty rates.

The event's magnitude also gives it a significant aura, emphasizing its larger scale. It is important to remember that many other sites of tragedy in Lebanon do not receive the same level of attention.

Sandra Frem: The explosion devastated a vast portion of the city within mere seconds. The power of the Silos lies in the indiscriminate impact of the tragedy, unlike other contested sites of death. It unifies all Beirutis, carrying remnants of salvation by preventing the complete destruction of the entire city. The structure's presence is significant, unlike voids in cases like 9/11. Preserving a physical trace is vital in any memorial or future development, even in a new form. The issue with the silos is that they serve as a constant reminder, contradicting the politicians' reliance on collective forgetting to move past this chapter. This aspect is worth noting as a form of resistance.

AHJ: We recently debated the future of the Port Silos in a civil society meeting with the World Bank; should the site be considered a neutral ground or a memorial site? Two important designations were agreed upon while keeping the idea of a memorial open: it should not be a place for the port's daily business and should be considered a site,

9 The remaining part of the Beirut Port Silos after the 2020 August blast.
10 *Terrain Vague*, a notion described by Ignasi Di Solà Morales, referring to an abandoned urban space in limbo.
11 "*Tribute in Light* (composed of twin beams that reach up to four miles into the sky) is a commemorative public art installation first presented six months after 9/11 and then every year thereafter, from dusk to dawn, on the night of September 11." As viewed on (https://www.911memorial.org/visit/memorial/tribute-light).

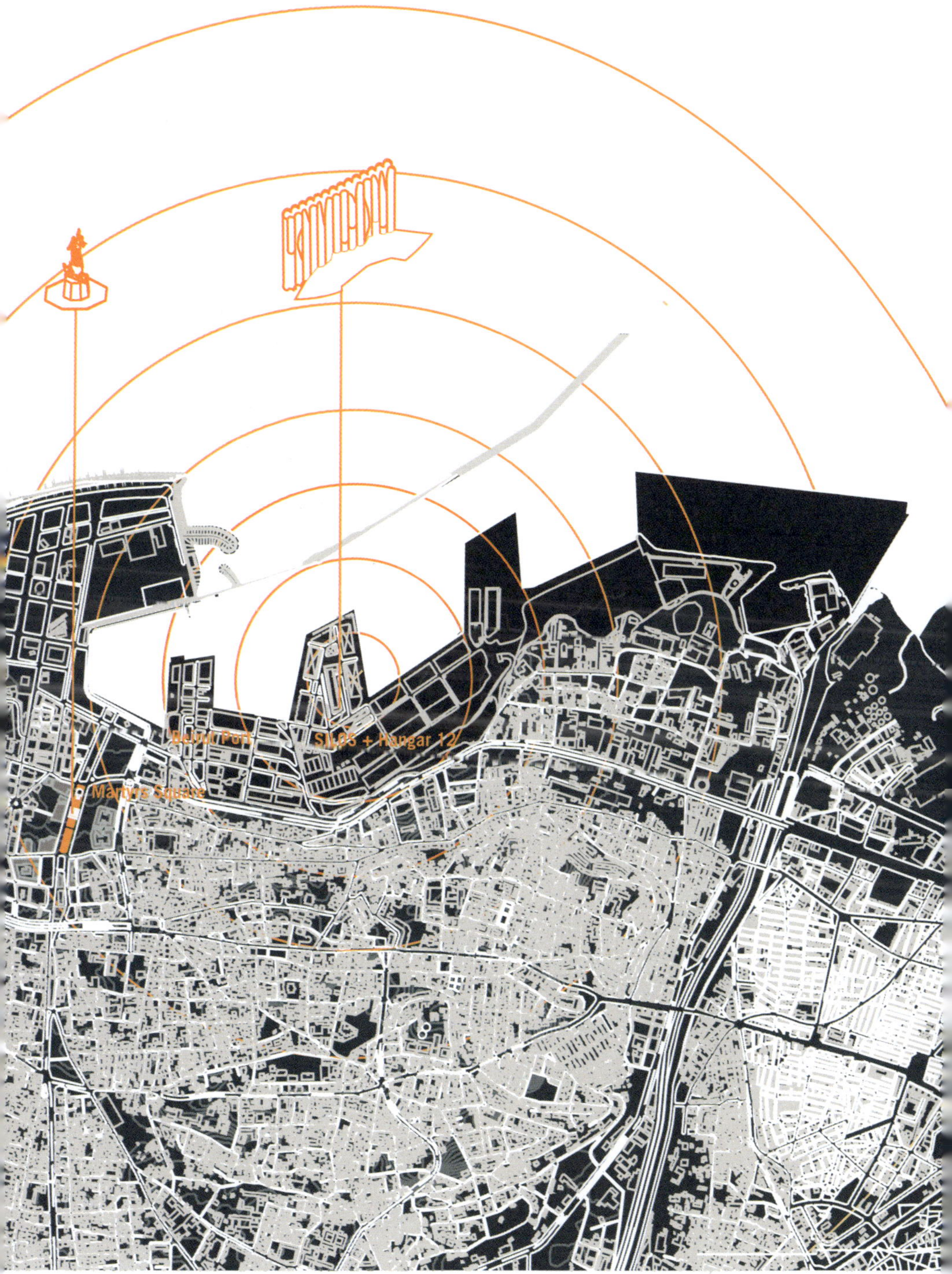

Figure 4 - A map of Beirut showing the proximity of Martyrs' square and the Port Silos

not an object. I even oppose using this site's edges for any function like a cruise terminal and leave this area out of the mundane routine of everyday life. With the support of the World Bank, we have suggested keeping options open until the investigation concludes and people get closure before discussing the site's future.

FD: The blast additionally revealed the proximity of this inaccessible space to the city. Now you realize that it is next to abandoned basins, with the actual harbor being closer to the Eastern edge of the port. This is obviously a space that can serve the city, be it as a public memorial or other, but certainly, a space that can be given back to reconnect the city's urban center to the sea.

CA: When considering the act of preserving memory, we cannot but talk about forms of representation and consider the role drawing can play in capturing the fleeting memory of a place. Can we discuss the important role that visual instruments and archives could play in retaining or even interpreting the city's collective memory? What could be the various modes of these instruments?

FD: Our goal deals with the question of preserving ephemera, even if it ceases to be ephemera when captured in online registries. Events like the Port blast and protests in Martyrs Square warrant capturing their ephemera because of their significance. In other words, we should mine ephemera and create registries to prevent historical amnesia, whether through maps that show change over time, image repositories, or crowd-sourced platforms, to capture the significance of a physical place digitally.

Figure 5 - Port Silos after the explosion in 2022

CA: This also suggests the need to diversify the methods and tools of archiving to broaden our understanding of the city and its collective memory. For example, the memory of Martyrs' Square has historically been shaped by the singularity of its representation, which is prominent in 1970s postcards. Your work with *levantCarta*,[12] in contrast, explores multiple tools and artifacts like maps, aerial photographs, and images to read the city. Can you elaborate more on this diversification of tools in enabling a more comprehensive reading of a place?

FD: The Beirut map we have been working on in *levantCarta*, which has a hint of Orientalism, reflects available information and archival records that are inherently biased. However, it remains agnostic as it focuses solely on longitude and latitude. Where this platform can expand is through a narrative component utilizing these coordinates and dates to tell untold stories. For example, the story of the aftermath of the blast, particularly the heroic efforts of

12 *levantCarta* is a digital archive of Beirut's cartographic history developed by the Spatial Studies Lab at Rice University with support from the New Levant Initiative. The project consists of an online platform that brings together scholarly networks and enables the production of temporally accurate and illustrated maps of Levantine cities over their entire history and across their social, cultural, and religious diversity (https://spatialstudieslab.rice.edu/levantcarta/).

13 Robert Saliba, *Morphological Investigation of Downtown Beirut*, Beirut 1991.

14 Grand Axe vision of Martyrs' Square in Beirut in Solidere's masterplan, connecting the city visually to the sea through its open space.

clinics, hospitals, and medical professionals, should be captured, retold, and remembered.

A cartographic platform to visualize change over time can serve that purpose by incorporating time-based narratives tied to specific locations. It would, therefore, enable us to visualize the large network of mobilized clinics and hospitals and the radius of the wounded that emanated out of Beirut. A digital environment can showcase this information by seamlessly integrating longitude, latitude, and time. Collecting narratives and ephemera thus is crucial for diversifying the archive and enriching the platform.

CA: Abdul-Halim, you mentioned Atallah's drawing of the 'Thawra' as a powerful and iconic representation of that moment. It effectively captured the events and spaces in a simple yet impactful way. Can you elaborate on this example and discuss other similar depictions?

AHJ: Antoine Atallah's drawing is a notable recent example, but I would like to acknowledge an earlier significant example of mental mapping undertaken by the late Robert Saliba and his students from AUB in the early 90s.[13] Saliba's work captured and recorded the spatial memories of different generations in Beirut's downtown after the Civil War. The memories include local favorites like the falafel guy or the best coffee corner and iconic places like Grand Serail, Place de l'Étoile, or Martyrs Square. Ironically, Solidere's initial master plan highlighted superficially these iconic places, as evident in one of their proposed versions of the Grand Axe[14] while still adopting a *tabula rasa* approach.

Thus, it is important to recognize the intricacies and nuances of memory and interpretation in reshaping place. This is very relevant to mental mapping and, evidently, to Atallah's drawing.

CA: Grassroots and local collectives in Beirut, especially after recent socio-political disruptions, have expanded in roles and significance. One can note collectives like Beirut Heritage Initiative (BHI) as playing an essential role in safekeeping the city's heritage while advancing cultural initiatives that build a strong local narrative of history and place.

Can we discuss the importance of creating and expanding such narratives and the role collectives can play in establishing a common imagined understanding of our cultural heritage?

AHJ: As I always say, such initiatives are necessary but not sufficient. I am a strong advocate for regulated bottom-up initiatives. By sheer necessity, this happened organically in the aftermath of the port explosion with initiatives working to bridge the gap between the public sector and the city's needs, like Beirut Heritage Initiative[15] Live Love Beirut, and Offre Joie.[16] Despite their successes in specific areas, limited funding hinders their potential. As soon as the World Bank, the EU, and UNHabitat initiated the 3RF framework[17] it became a classic top-down model loaded with bureaucracy and lucrative overheads.

However, we (BHI) did succeed in producing two significant visual outputs: YouTube lectures and restoration manuals. With the generous support of several colleagues and the Fondation de France, we were able to compile two generations of know-how and expertise into these valuable open-access resources, covering structural, material, architectural, and historical aspects.[18] They demonstrate necessary democratized knowledge, time-honoured skills, and common practice guidelines that can be accessible to all, especially amid the destruction of Beirut's heritage buildings.

This approach bridges the gaping void between people's needs, the city's needs, and the central government's and municipality's limitations and enables contributions from individuals and collectives.

CA: I believe the Beirut Heritage Initiative stands out among post-blast initiatives by emphasizing heritage preservation. Its deliberate selection process and hands-on approach go beyond reconstruction to actively imbue specific parts of the city with cultural significance.

AHJ: Absolutely. From its inception, BHI has taken a deliberate approach to prioritizing 'people within their neighbourhoods in the city'. It aimed to promote an inclusive understanding of heritage beyond grand mansions, to include the city's fabric, streets, cul-de-sacs, and backyards (Fig. 7). Embracing diversity was a key goal, going beyond buildings to encompass a broad range of social and ethnic backgrounds while recognizing the historical significance of certain neighbourhoods like Mar Mikhael, and Karantina. Our goal was to be inclusive and comprehensive within our capacity without competing with humanitarian aid efforts.

CA: Capturing diverse narratives is crucial to building on inclusivity. Collectives, in addition to visual instruments, can thus play a vital role. I would link this to your work, Fares, which aims to be an open-source platform where individuals can contribute data and stories. Do you see this platform also becoming a type of collective?

FD: Definitely. Our ambition is to create a user-friendly cartographic 'Wikipedia', where people can independently reconstruct change over time, without the need for complex software. The goal is to empower others to conduct their

Figure 6 - View of Martyrs Square today with Thawra symbol
Figure 7 - A heritage building in the Mar Mikhael neighborhood in Beirut

15 Beirut Heritage Initiative, an independent collective, founded on August 26, 2020, in the aftermath of the port blast to safeguard and restore Beirut's heritage buildings.
16 Live Love Beirut and Offre Joie, key NGOs, that had substantive roles in post-blast relief and rebuilding efforts.
17 Reform, Recovery and Reconstruction Framework (3RF) is a unique collaborative process that brings together Lebanon's Government, civil society, the private sector and the international community. As viewed on (https://www.lebanon3rf.org/framework)
18 Link to resources (https://beirutheritageinitiative.com/restoration-manual/).

own research and enable research groups to focus onspecific areas while allowing results to be publicly accessible and shareable.

However, I want to return to another point where civil society was able to take over in a place like Lebanon, which was burdened with unprecedented circumstances. All these collectives and NGOs were able to hold things together amidst chaos and competition for resources, serving as the glue that prevented a complete collapse. It is an anarchistic dream; despite challenges, this approach of collective solidarity continues to function, although not perfectly, filling the void left by the failed state. One missing dimension is the lack of coordination in this collective system where the cloud and digital platforms can come in handy because they allow for core decentralized coordination.

SF: Lastly, I would like to underline two emerging points from our conversation: First, preserving shared memories and creating virtual repositories are critical for shaping the future, especially when physical commons and sites of remembrance are erased, neutralized, or restricted. Second, initiatives like the Beirut Heritage Initiative and the *levantCarta* foster alternative collective memories and are open to multiple interpretations, specifically by creating new knowledge and information. I believe the democratization of knowledge can shape a new common for a better future.

CA: With the hope that collective intelligence may prevail in shaping the city's future. Instead of emphasizing differences among people, like sectarian or social disparities, shifting the narrative to highlight our shared cultural values can enable this collective will to operate better. Thank you, Fares, Abdul-Halim, and Sandra, for this engaging discussion.

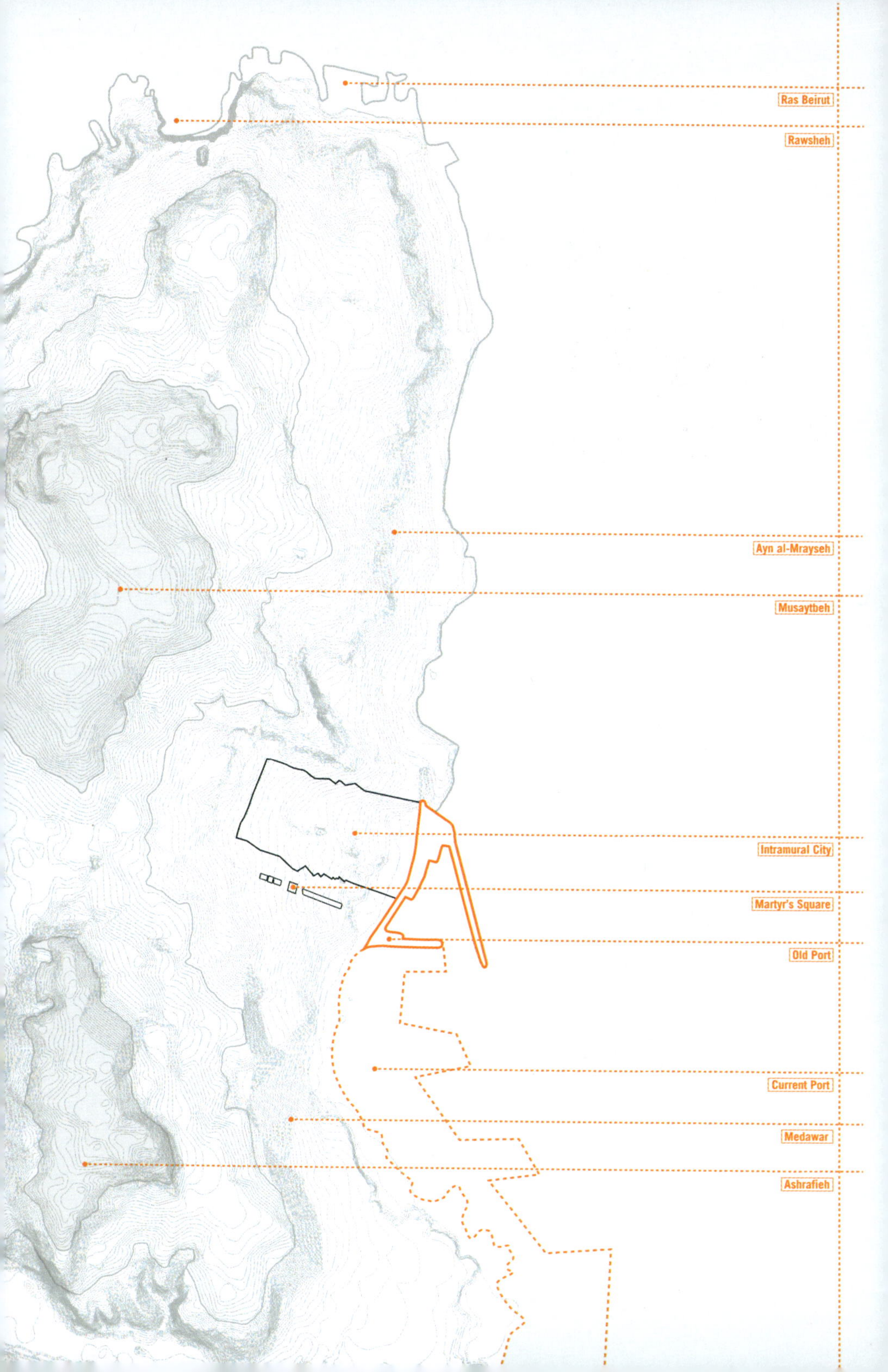
Ras Beirut
Rawsheh
Ayn al-Mrayseh
Musaytbeh
Intramural City
Martyr's Square
Old Port
Current Port
Medawar
Ashrafieh

PORT SILOS AS COMMON GROUND

carla aramouny / stephanie achkar

The port of Beirut is an island—Standing as a logistical agglomeration along the northern coastal edge of the city, this infrastructural mass comprises broad quays, hangars, storage depots, and container yards, forming a boundary between the city and the sea. However, the relationship between the port and the city was not always one of division. Geographically located on the northern side of the peninsula of Beirut, the port historically took advantage of this natural coastal edge that offered protection from southern sea winds and allowed ships to find refuge. Nestled between the hills of Ashrafieh and Musaytbeh, the old intramural city extended down to its port and natural coastline[1], with its eastern wall running parallel to an open plateau, the *'maidan'*, later known as Place des Canons or Martyrs' Square. The natural connection between the port, the city, and the maidan formed a vital artery that linked the sea, the city, and the surrounding region. East of the maidan, the elevated Saifi cliff created a physical barrier with the sea, delineating the port's eventual expansion. This topographical shift and later development of the coastal highway further reinforced isolation and disconnection between the port and its immediate neighborhoods.

1 Samir Kassir, *Beirut*, (University of California Press, 2010), 36.

Figure 1 - Map of Beirut's natural topography and the intramural city limits with its historic port (circa 1840)

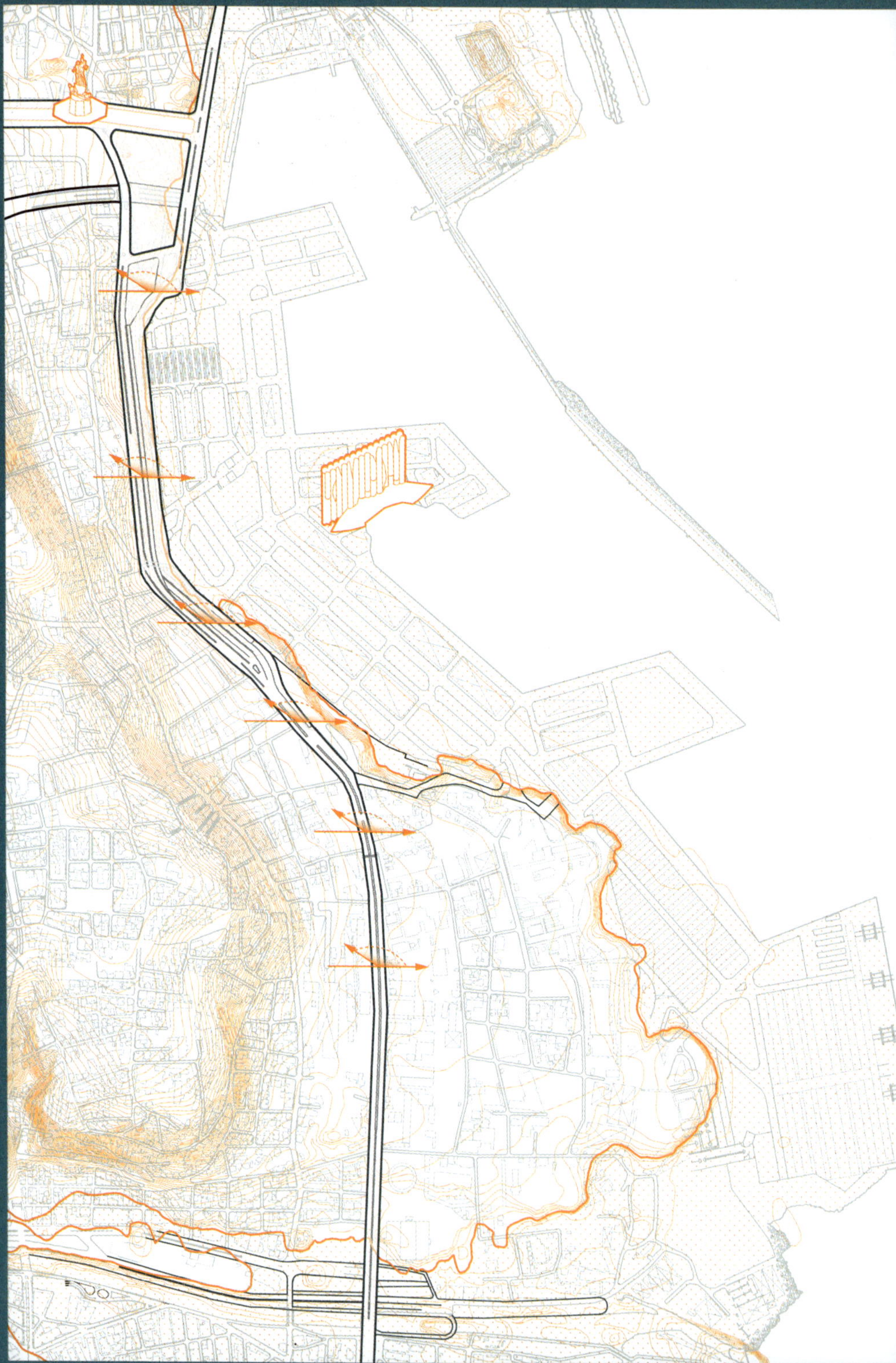

Figure 2 - Current map of Beirut and the immediate vicinity of its port

Figure 3 - Sectional views showing the city/highway/port relationship along the main coastal highway

Historical evidence indicates the presence of a port in Beirut since Greek and Roman times.[2] However, its most significant expansion occurred in the latter half of the nineteenth century, coinciding with a surge in trade. The economic boom in Europe between 1848 and 1873, alongside the opening of the Suez Canal in 1869, shifted global trade dynamics toward the Mediterranean. French and British colonial powers vied for control during this period,[3] which led to the port's expansion under French influence. Parallel developments, such as the establishment of railway infrastructure and the opening of the Damascus Road, which intersects with the maidan, further reinforced the port's regional and national significance.[4]

As the city expanded, eastern neighborhoods like Saifi and Rmeil developed in tandem with the port, facilitating the movement of people, goods, and trade. This growth attracted a diverse population seeking employment in port-related activities and the emerging service sector, leading to the rise of a mercantile community.[5]

During this late Ottoman period, the port was more than just a quay for trade; it aquired a hybrid nature forming a natural extension of the old city and incorporated khans, locandas, a department store, and a bank.[6] While the maidan plateau was separated from direct access to the sea by a cemetery, secondary connections facilitated its growth as a vibrant marketplace and travel hub closely linked to the port. The synergies between the port, the city, and the region persisted throughout the French mandate and into the early years of the Lebanese Republic, continually supported by the urban morphology and geography of the city.

The port's modern expansion and eastward growth benefited from the naturally elevated topography, which helped buffer it from direct urban connections. The Charles Helou highway and bus station, constructed in the early 1970s, further reinforced this separation from the city.[7] The Civil War marked a significant decline in the port's operations and role in the city's economic growth, as infrastructure suffered substantial damage. Trade and shipping were affected, and many businesses relocated away from Beirut. Even after the war ended, it took years for port operations to resume fully. The reconstruction of the downtown area of Beirut shifted the port's main entrance and first quay further east, moving it away from its historical core and disconnecting it from Martyrs' Square.

As a result, the port and city evolved as two distinct entities. While the port remained a part of the city's identity, it became a distant memory of its former prominence. The August 2020 explosion starkly exposed the port's proximity

Figure 4 - Sections along the coastal highway showing the city/highway/port relationship

2 Kassir, *Beirut*, 34-42.
3 Resat Kasaba et. al., "Eastern Mediterranean Port Cities and Their Bourgeoisies: Merchants, Political Projects, and Nation-States". *Review* (Fernand Braudel Center), 10 (1), 121.
4 Fawwaz Traboulsi, *A History of Modern Lebanon*, (Pluto Press, 2007), 54-55.
5 Robert Saliba, *Beirut 1920-1940: Domestic Architecture Between Tradition and Modernity*, (Order of Engineers and Architects, 1998), 7-15.
6 Nadine Hindi, "Urban Forms at Intersection of Imperialism and Colonialism: A Perspective on Beirut", *The 18th International Planning History Society* Conference, (Yokohama: July 2018)
7 Kassir, *Beirut*, 424.

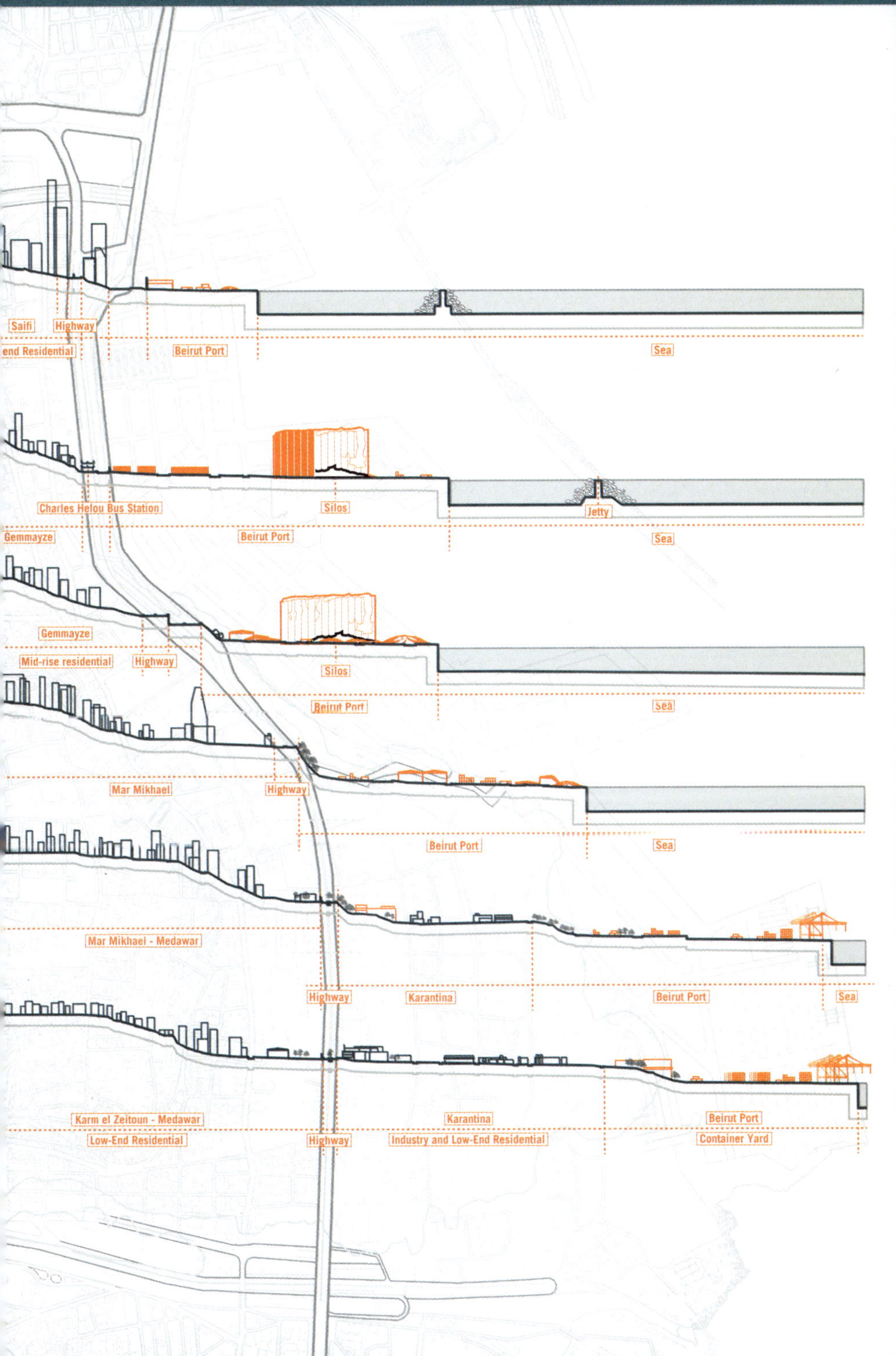
Saifi
Highway
end Residential
Beirut Port
Sea
Charles Helou Bus Station
Silos
Jetty
Gemmayze
Beirut Port
Sea
Gemmayze
Mid-rise residential
Highway
Silos
Beirut Port
Sea
Mar Mikhael
Highway
Beirut Port
Sea
Mar Mikhael - Medawar
Highway
Karantina
Beirut Port
Sea
Karm el Zeitoun - Medawar
Low-End Residential
Highway
Karantina
Industry and Low-End Residential
Beirut Port
Container Yard

to the city. The Port Silos have since emerged as a new 'commons', symbolizing shared trauma and recovery. The blast not only damaged the port and the city but also metaphorically unveiled the once-forgotten relationship between the city and the sea, transforming the logistical port ground into a barren backdrop against the highway. Today, discussions about post-blast reconstruction continue to explore the relationship between the city and its port. Urbanists advocate for an open port policy through a memorial and a reimagined connection to the sea, while politicians and global shipping agglomerates favor maintaining a separation between city life and the port's operations.

In this context, the port holds a paradoxical identity; while it once represented a thriving economic hub for the city, it now symbolizes destruction and the conflict between operational demands and urban needs. The silos, once symbols of abundance and modernity, have become blatant reminders of shared trauma, their presence marked by the crater left by the blast—a physical indent in the ground and a symbolic wound that lingers in the collective memory.

Figure 5 - Collage of the Silos with the backdrop of the city, Martyrs Square, and its martyrs monument

section 3

production

This section scrutinizes spatial production, looking at the ground through the lens of local architecture and construction practices. This practice is particularly important in Beirut, as it has replaced formal planning processes in shaping the built environment and the ground experience over the years. Throughout its recent history, urban development in Beirut was the direct outcome of regulatory frameworks relying on the building code rather than urban master plans, with special decrees allowing exemptions for large-scale market-led projects. In such a condition, construction and real estate became the core of urban transformations of the city, and with this, architecture—in its building culture, regulations, organization, and adopted aesthetics—became the tool at the service of these forces. This is also why Beirut, as a built environment, cannot be understood as a cohesive unit but rather as an assemblage of individual buildings, infrastructures, and urban fragments that form an unplanned whole.

In design and planning disciplines, the spatial production of the urban ground is predominantly discussed as a frame in which activities and socioeconomic relationships develop. It is widely analyzed from regulatory, socioeconomic, and planning lenses[1] that seek to understand processes guiding its formation without necessarily scrutinizing the spatial and architectural typologies that give the ground its form and experience. Seminal works looking at spatial production in Beirut have extensively uncovered the hidden threads linking it with the capitalist and neoliberal political economy that governed the city from the country's Independence in 1943 until today.

The scope of this section is to revert this focus by bringing the architectural connotation of production to the foreground. This is done by conceptualizing architectural typologies and their assessment through qualitative aspects at the ground level; it involves extracting qualities like spatial porosity, plot implantation, definition of street character by buildings, and types of transition between the private and the public. It is also done by scrutinizing mechanisms of architectural production, whether through shifting approaches of building practices and their adopted aesthetics or the evolution of building components and their typical use. The section investigates how such ground practices reflect on (Chapter 1) or transcend (Chapter 2) the dominant building culture, the latter being in constant dialogue with socioeconomic processes, regulatory frameworks, and political agents of space. Finally, this section interprets production as co-production, speculating on formal and organizational characteristics that can transform the ground into an open work, constantly edited and co-edited by its users for a collective role in shaping Beirut.

1 These lenses have been extensively covered in the works of Henri Lefebvre (The Production of Space), David Harvey (Capital, Postmodernism and Neoliberalism), Saskia Sassen (Global City), Richard Sennett (Ethics for the City), Neil Brenner (Planetary Urbanization, Spatial Processes under Capitalism), to name a few.

Figure 1 - Contemporary view of Beirut

architecture as ground shaper

boulos douaihy

This chapter explores a very specific relationship: the role of architecture in creating Beirut's urban ground, explored at the foreground of the massive real estate urbanization (Fig. 1), and its gradual transformation of the city into a concrete jungle.

The chapter sets an initial understanding of how Beirut zoning and planning regulations failed to control the form and space of the ground level, influenced by political and socioeconomic dynamics in different episodes of development: from the strong connectedness of the political and real estate forces that preyed on it to the drastic conflicts Beirut endured and finally, the economic crisis since 2019.

Within the context of the government's weak capacity to set out and enforce urban plans, the argument moves to evaluate how it was in fact architecture that produced Beirut's groundscape through the building code and the single building residential typology.

The chapter examines this relationship through a timeline of building code amendments in Beirut and their impact on the city's urban ground and its evolution, through a detailed catalog of architectural typologies from the early 1930s until 2020. It presents parallels between typologies of the ground and the building code that mutated under constant political and economic pressures, ultimately transforming the ground as a mere base for speculative development.

In the context of the 2019 economic crisis and real estate market crash, the chapter reflects on reevaluating capital and real estate's role in governing the ground's modalities of production, and on halting the destructive development path that disfigured Beirut, proposing to reclaim the ground as an integral part of the city's urban level rather than a threshold for gated communities.

From urban plan to building code

To understand the role of architecture in creating Beirut's ground, it is essential to briefly review the role of political and socioeconomic powers in influencing the modalities of space production in the city and the shift from urban planning to building code as an overarching regulatory framework.

Indeed, Beirut's limited experience with planning has always been ridden with an intrusive encroachment of political powers and economic elites with intersecting interests in real estate development.[1] This "elite cartel" managed to sustain its power structure and reinvent itself—from the "merchant republic" of the 1940s-1970s to the "banking republic" of the 1990s-2020s, feeding on real estate development and speculation as a main source of its economic growth.[2]

This oligarchy's influence hindered several urban plans for Beirut between 1930 and 1954, ultimately approving the city's first plan in 1954, only after it was adjusted to meet their high development ratio requirements.[3] Under this plan, intensive zoning and inadequate urban structures have committed the city to its long-term problems of traffic, extreme density, weakened infrastructure, and haphazard construction.[4] With such foundational weaknesses and and no heritage preservation or open space provisions, the plan was quickly overridden by concrete realities and hindered by the executive weakness of the government.[5]

As formal planning processes proved much slower than the pace of urban development in subsequent decades, the same elites turned to the building code to legislate development increases and private market practices.[6] This is demonstrated by the numerous amendments to the building code (1940, 1954, 1971, 1983, 1992, and 2004) compared to its urban planning laws (1954, 1963).

A building code amendment in 1971 introduced the concept of exemptions for large-scale projects, a modality that later substituted formal urban planning processes. Between 1990 and 2020, this practice became frequent, under which large-scale developments were regulated through exceptional rules and informal decision-making between planning agencies, banks, and developers.[7]

It can be argued that in the absence of effective planning, it was private development and architecture that gave the ground in Beirut its form, guided by an opportunistic building code and amendments that generated discordant relationships for the sake of expanding total built up areas.

1 Assem Salam, "The Role of Government in Shaping the Built Environment" in *Projecting Beirut: episodes in the construction and reconstruction of a modern city*, ed. Peter Rowe and Hashim Sarkis (Prestel, 1998).
2 Bruno Marot, *Developing Post-War Beirut (1990-2016): The political economy of "pegged urbanization,"* Geography (McGill University, 2018).
3 Salam, "The Role of Government in Shaping the Built Environment."
4 Salam, "The Role of Government in Shaping the Built Environment."
5 The duality between Beirut's decision-making (municipal council) and executive power (mohafez), can be one example of why some decisions do not go through into implementation. At the scale of master plans, the authorities in charge of studies and master plans (Directorate General in Urbanism) are different from the authorities in charge of their implementations (Council for Redevelopment and Reconstruction, Ministry of Public Works, etc.).

In a way, the individual building and its architecture, responsible for Beirut's peculiar ground, could be considered a representation of the relationship between the individual and the dysfunctional state and its administration, with all the complexities that this relationship continues to hold today at every turn of the city's evolution.

Figure 2 - Photograph of a street on Sassine, Achrafieh, showing architecture from the five highlighted periods in adjacency to each other.

Architecture of the ground

To understand Beirut's ground evolution under the building code, the transformation of the ground's architecture is traced at the scale of a single building (Fig. 2) and analyzed by cataloging building typologies from 1930 until 2020.

The study emphasizes ground-level taxonomies, scrutinizing their changing relationship with the public realm, such as transition types, edge types, alignments, visual and physical continuity, and level changes.

The study then delves into assessing these changes caused by high-density developments, loss of green areas, land pooling, plot implantation, exemptions, and other factors regulated by building code amendments. To contextualize this evolution, the study simultaneously examines the changing patterns of building regulations that govern the production of space, as well as the political economy associated with it, categorizing them based on their impacts on the ground.

An overview of this evolution and the ground transformations can be categorized into five main periods (Fig. 3):

(1920-1940) Unscripted adaptation—a period where architectural production resulted from a collective building culture that still derived its spatial typologies from earlier vernacular types.

(1940-1970) Hybridization—a period when modernism, capitalism, and informal urbanization shaped the ground divergently under the liberal "laissez-faire" ethos that characterized the first construction boom in Beirut after independence.

(1970-1990) Discordance—a period that witnessed the rise of exception and archaic architectural production during the civil war that translated into ground disjunctions against the backdrop of the ground's sporadic urban growth and military compartmentalization.

(1990-2004) Privatization—a period characterized by a pegged neoliberal economy, in which successive episodes of ground gentrification and post-war reconstruction

6 Abir Saksouk, "Where is Law? Investigations from Beirut," Working paper, American University of Beirut, 2014.
7 Marieke Krijnen and Mona Fawaz, "Exception as the Rule: High-End Developments in Neoliberal Beirut", *Built Environment* Vol. 36 no. 2 (2010).

materialized global capital flows into real estate development and translated into the shift of architectural practices and accommodating regulations.

(2004-2020) High neoliberalism—a period witnessing the rise of exception at the residential tower scale, based on land pooling and built areas increase, ending—or rather halting—with the 2019 financial crisis and market crash.

(1920-1940) Unscripted adaptations

This phase saw the rise of the urban ground and Beirut's expanding urban fabric under a pre-code architecture. Since Beirut did not get a formal building code until the early 1940s, this first growth wave was guided by minimal regulations using legislation dating from 1919 that was adapted from a French document during the Mandate period.[8] Three building practices defined the urban ground in this phase.

The first practice is found in the residential building type, which became instrumental in defining the urban main streets in extramuros neighborhoods like in Gemmayzeh or Msaytbeh, incorporating commercial functions at its ground level and bridging the newly introduced concrete material with traditional construction elements like stone and pitched terracotta roofs. In this typology, architecture incorporated several porous archetypes—stairs, balconies, loggias, porches, and arched passages—that created a dialogue with the urban realm.[9] Semi-open staircases, as stand-alone structures or as part of the building, became ground activators and natural extensions of the ground space (Fig. 4, 5).

The second practice is the use of open space transitions between the inside and outside of private lots. Variations of this typology comprised commercial street fronts as stand-alone structures, with buildings built to the back and articulated around a courtyard, creating two edges with various transitions in between.[10] (Fig. 4)

The third practice is the self-built refugee house. This type is found in refugee neighborhoods with a pre-planned grid, like Bourj Hammoud and Karm El Zeitoun, which were developed for housing Armenian refugees, and where the individual building was conceived as the basis of a linear urban block (Fig. 5). In such a type, land was loaned to the refugees with the responsibility to build their houses.[11] This led to different categories of architectural thresholds that can only emerge from individualized self-build efforts, resulting in an urban morphology adapted to different urban situations and varying topographical conditions.

(1940-1970) Hybridization

Construction in Beirut during the forties was initially guided by its first building law, a 1940 document authorizing the municipality to regulate different aspects of construction, such as building heights, setbacks, materials, implantation in their lots, plots, and areas where construction is banned, etc.[12] Buildings continued using vernacular typologies, presenting similar spatial characteristics in their relationship with the street.[13]

The whole consideration of the ground changed when a code adjustment in 1954 removed the maximum height limit of 26 meters, introducing instead the *gabarit* regulation, which linked the envelope of the building to the proportion of its parcel, with its total height calculated as twice the width of the road (refer to Fig.3). With little specification as to ground implantation, this revision resulted in increased building heights and irregular setbacks to go higher, which undermined ground floor alignments as well as streets' spatial definition[14] (Fig. 6). Starting from this period and under this law, the city's skyline would no longer correlate with its natural topography.

This occurred concurrently with the introduction of reinforced concrete as a novel material, bringing new architectural and structural possibilities. The manifestation of modernism through the *pilotis* in residential architecture became common practice during the fifties and sixties,[15] even though it was not regulated until 1971. Earlier variations of the *pilotis*, still found today in Badaro, managed to nurture generous spatial relationships at the ground level (Fig. 8).

In commercial architecture, modern concepts of spatial continuity were tested in the urban commercial center type. Capturing the flourishing entertainment, economic, and intellectual life of the capital, centers like Gefinor Center, Starco, and many others on Hamra Street, integrated the architectural premise of a porous urban ground with a clear intention to maximize the urban/ commercial realm.[16] The ground was articulated on multiple levels as a visual and spatial hinge between the urban fabric, street level, and upper and/or lower floors (Fig. 7, 9).

Equally, the period between 1958 and 1970—also known as the welfare state or Chehabist period—marked a brief era for the state's commissioning public architecture.[17] Numerous commissions and competitions gave Beirut its modernist landmarks, such as the Ministry of Defense and Électricité du Liban, which were symptomatic of a generous spatial continuum between the public space and the ground levels of such buildings.

In contrast with these ground types, informal architecture shaped the high-density residential quarters in Beirut's southern and eastern suburbs. Built by small-scale builders for migrants and low-income groups, the relationship between public and private ground in such types was reduced to the bare minimum of plot setbacks to accomodate a larger percentage of buildable space (Fig. 8).

(1970-1990) Discordance

In 1971, major amendments to the code introduced rules that largely shaped today's ground.[18] These amendments came both as a response to the greed mobilizing private developers in an unrestricted market, and also to regulate modernist architecture practices that had gained ground, which critically affected their relationship to the ground (Fig. 10).

First, the *gabarit* rule was revised to remove all specifications as to ground implantation, which allowed the removal of

8 Marwan Ghandour, "Building Law: A Critical Reading of the Lebanese Case" in *89th ACSA Annual Meeting Proceedings: Paradoxes of Progress*, 2001.
9 Robert Saliba, *Beirut 1920-1940: Domestic Architecture Between Tradition and Modernity.* (Beirut: Order of Engineers and Architects, 1998).
10 Saliba, *Beirut 1920-1940: Domestic Architecture Between Tradition and Modernity.*
11 Raymond Kévorkian, Lévon Nordiguian, Vahé Tachjian, *Les Arméniens: La quête d'un refuge 1917-1939* (USJ Presse, 2007).
12 Elie El-Achkar, " La Loi de la Construction," in *Réglementation et Formes Urbaines: Le Cas de Beyrouth* (Presses de l'Ifpo 1998), 37-58.
13 Saliba, *Beirut 1920-1940: Domestic Architecture Between Tradition and Modernity.*
14 Elie El-Achkar, *Réglementation et Formes Urbaines : Le cas de Beyrouth.*
15 George Arbid, "Practicing Modernism in Beirut, Architecture in Lebanon 1946-1970" (Doctor of Design Thesis, Harvard University, 2002).
16 Arbid, "Practicing Modernism in Beirut, Architecture in Lebanon 1946-1970."
17 Arbid, "Practicing Modernism in Beirut, Architecture in Lebanon 1946-1970."
18 El-Achkar, *Réglementation et Formes Urbaines : Le cas de Beyrouth.*

BUILDING SECTION

GROUND SECTION

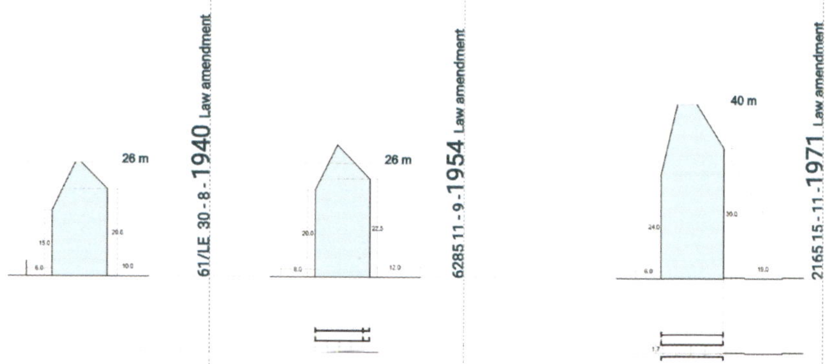

1925 | 1930 | 1935 | 1940 | 1945 | 1950 | 1955 | 1960 | 1965 | 1970

PERIOD	**ADAPTATION**	**HYBRIDIZATION**	
BUILDING CODE AMENDMENT	DECREE 61/LE	LAW 6285/1954	DECREE 2165/1971
OTHER REGULATORY TOOLS		1954 URBAN PLAN DECREE 6285	1964 URBAN PLAN AMENDMENT DECREE 16029-16948/ 1964 MARITIME DOMAIN DECREE 418/1966
AMENDMENTS INTRODUCED	-HEIGHT LIMIT = 26 M -SITE IMPLANTATION -FIXED SETBACKS	-NO HEIGHT LIMIT/ GABARIT -FAR FOLLOWS ZONING -SOME SITE IMPLANTATION -SETBACK= 2 X ROAD WIDTH	-INCREASED FAR (1963 ZONING) -BUILDING ENVELOPE RATIO= 2 -BASEMENT PARKING FOR > 40 M -BUA EXCLUSION FOR PILOTIS & BALCONIES
IMPACT ON GROUND	STREET ALIGNMENT FACADE POROSITY PUBLIC PRIVATE CONTINUITY SKYLINE FOLLOWS TOPOGRAPHY	LOSS OF ALIGNMENT PILOTIS POROSITY SKYLINE/GROUND DISCONNECTION LOSS OF GREEN AREAS	LOSS OF STREET DEFINITION PILOTIS AS PARKING SPACE LOSS OF POROSITY IN UPPER AREAS LOSS OF GREEN AREAS
GROUND PRACTICES	**VERNACULAR INFLUENCE** POROUS ARCHETYPES OPEN SPACE TRANSITIONS SELF BUILT URBAN FRAGMENTS	**MODERN POROSITY** PILOTIS GROUND POROUS TRANSITIONS	**INFORMAL ARCHITECTURE** CONVERTING AGRICULUTRAL GROUND

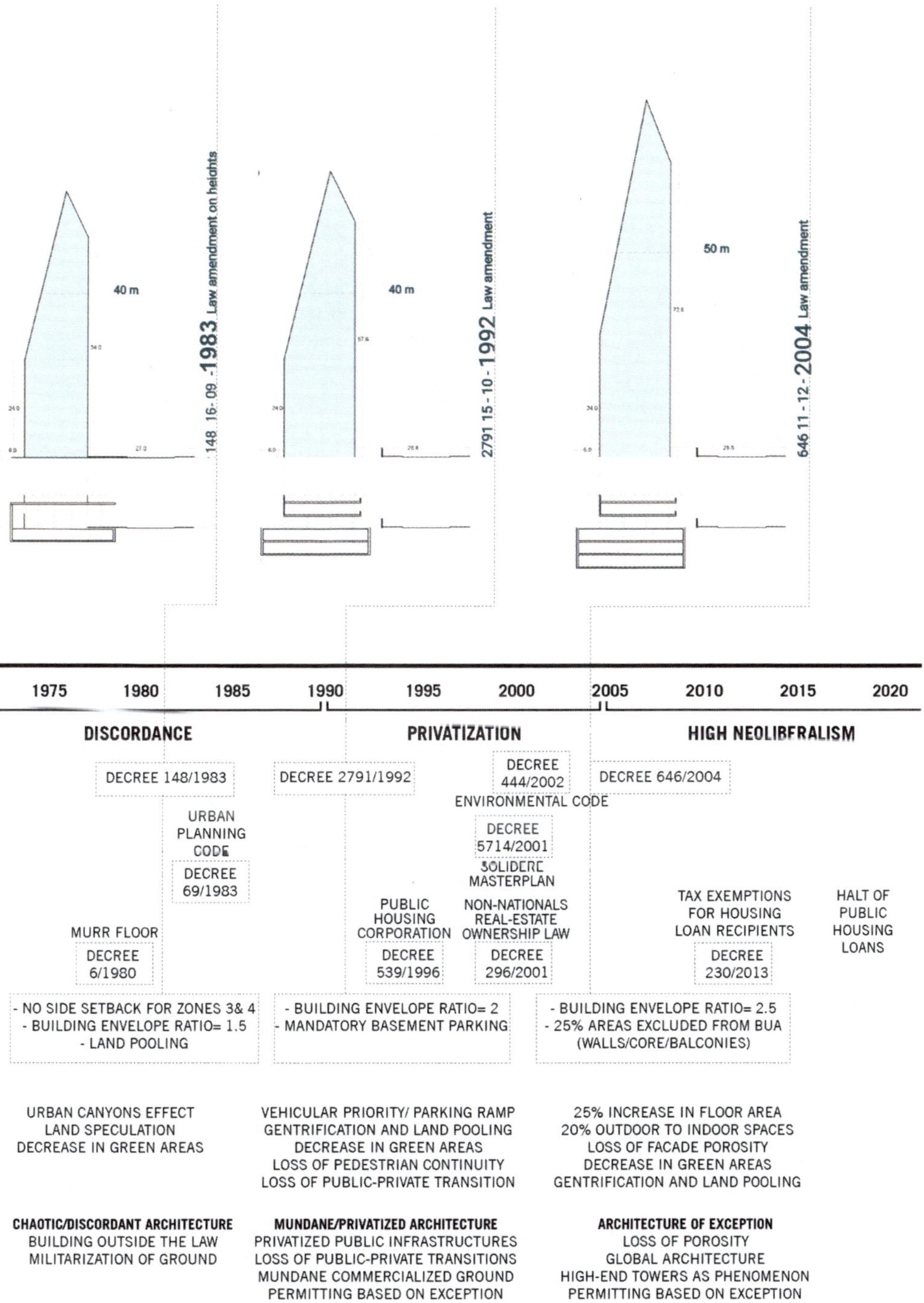

Figure 3 - Timeline of the building code and ground evolution in Beirut

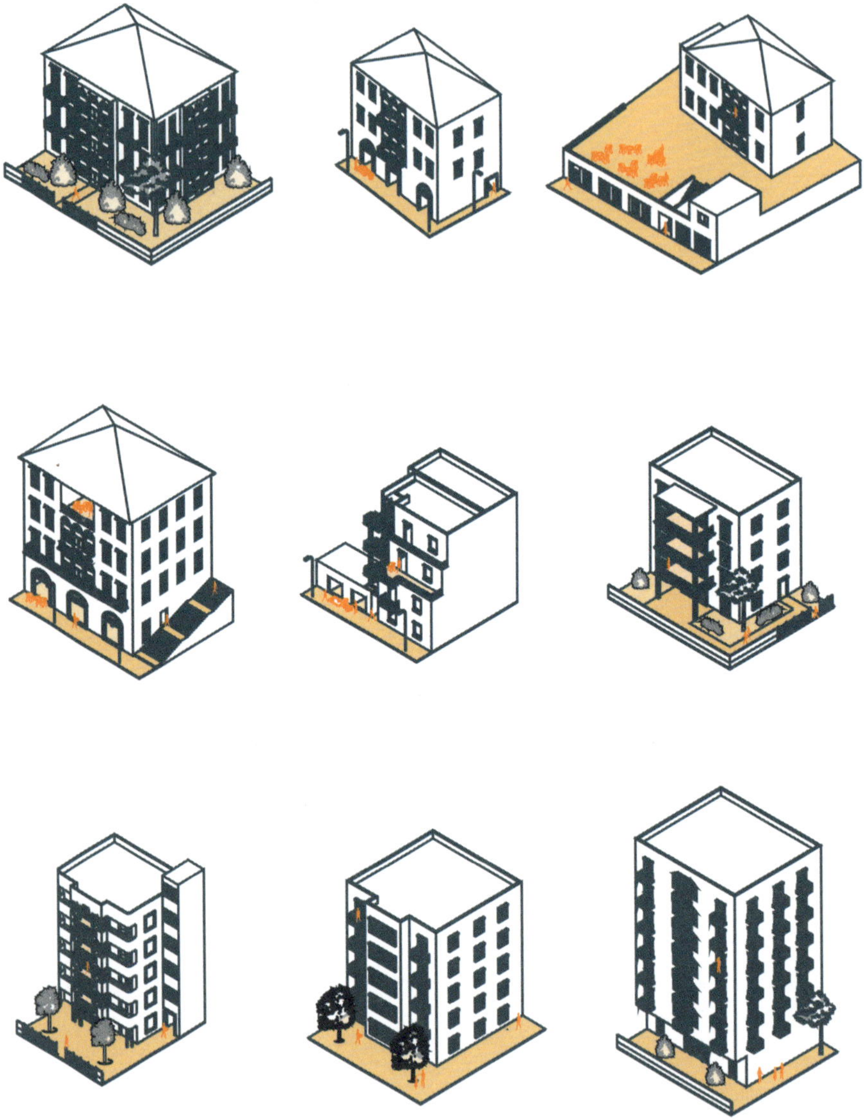

Figure 4 - Diagram showing architectural typologies of the ground from 1920-1940

Figure 5 - 1920-1940 residential urban architecture in Beirut, showing porous archetypes *(top)* and Karm El Zeitoun, a refugee neighborhood from 1930 that developed on the edge of the Achrafieh hill *(bottom)*

Figure 6 - Diagram showing residential architecture during the 1940-1970 period

Figure 7 - Hybridization of the ground during the 1940-1970 between a formal/ modernist architecture (top), and an informal architecture of the periphery (bottom)

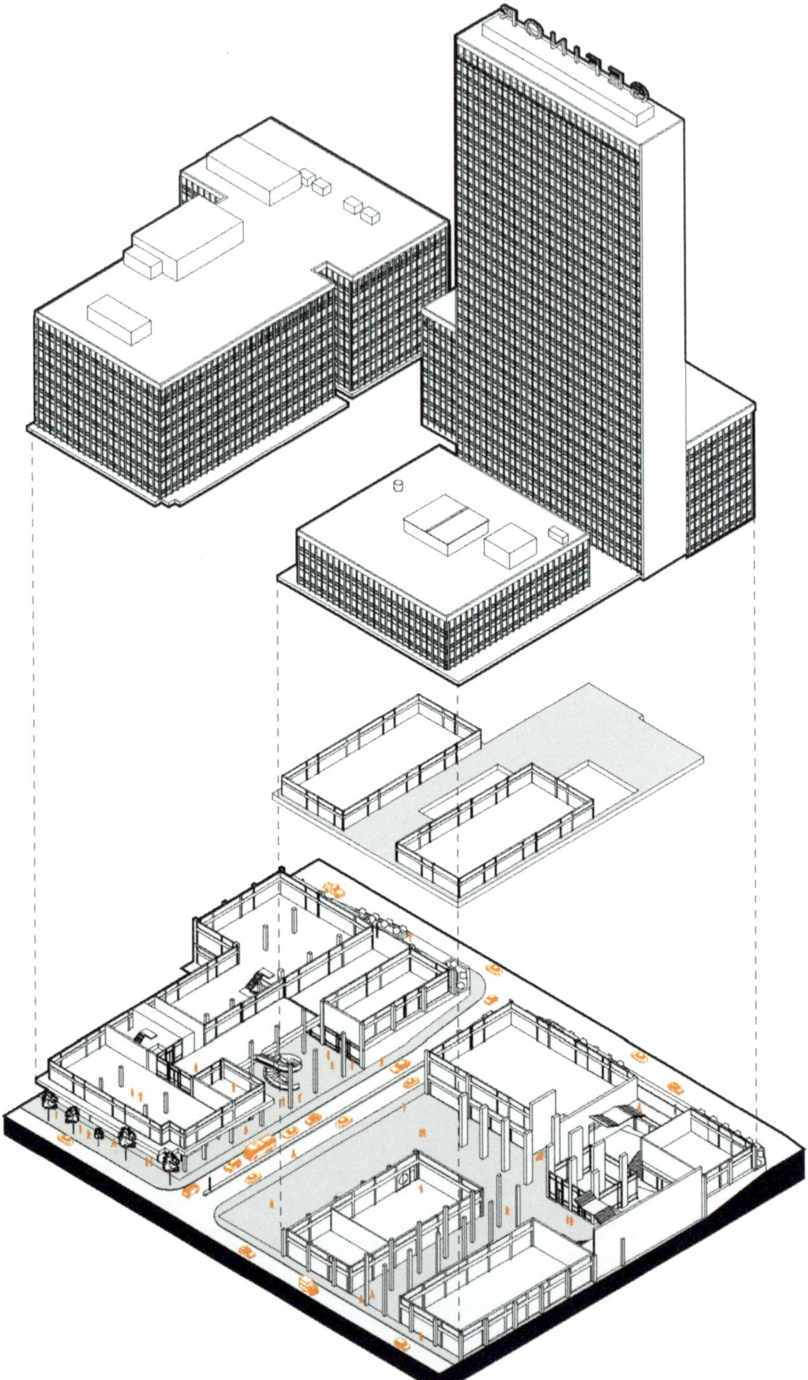

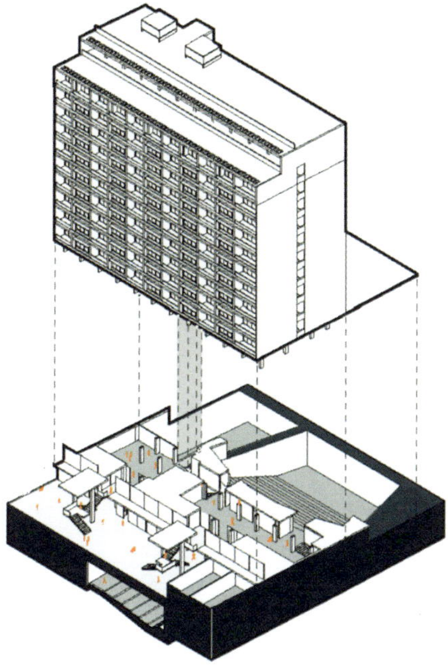

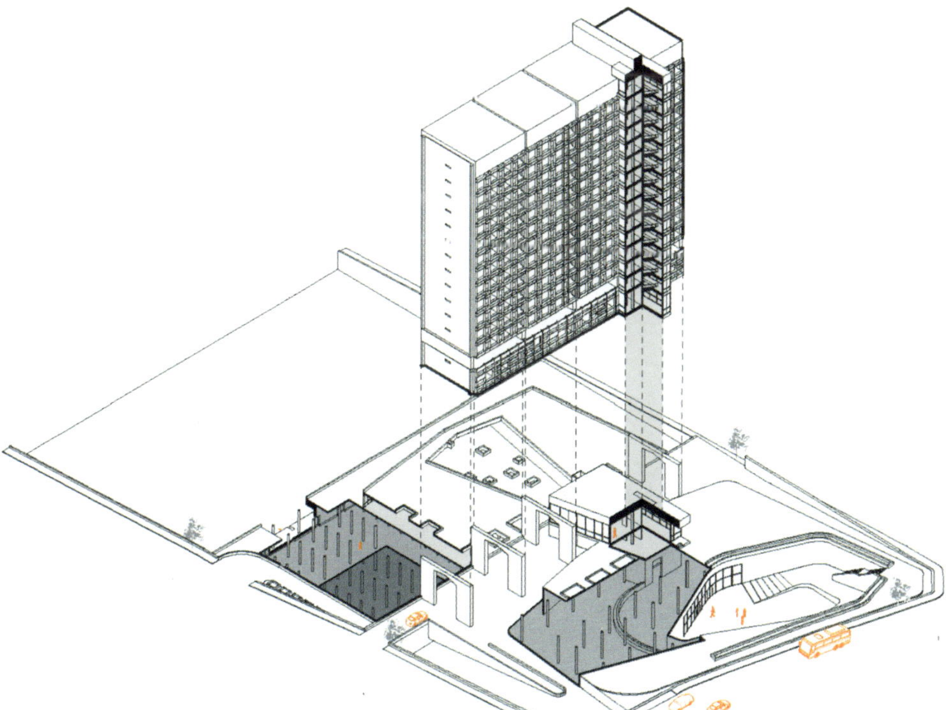

Figure 8 - Diagram showing commercial and public architecture grounds during the 1940-1970 period: Gefinor Center *(left)*, Saroulla Center *(top right)* and Électricité du Liban *(bottom right)*

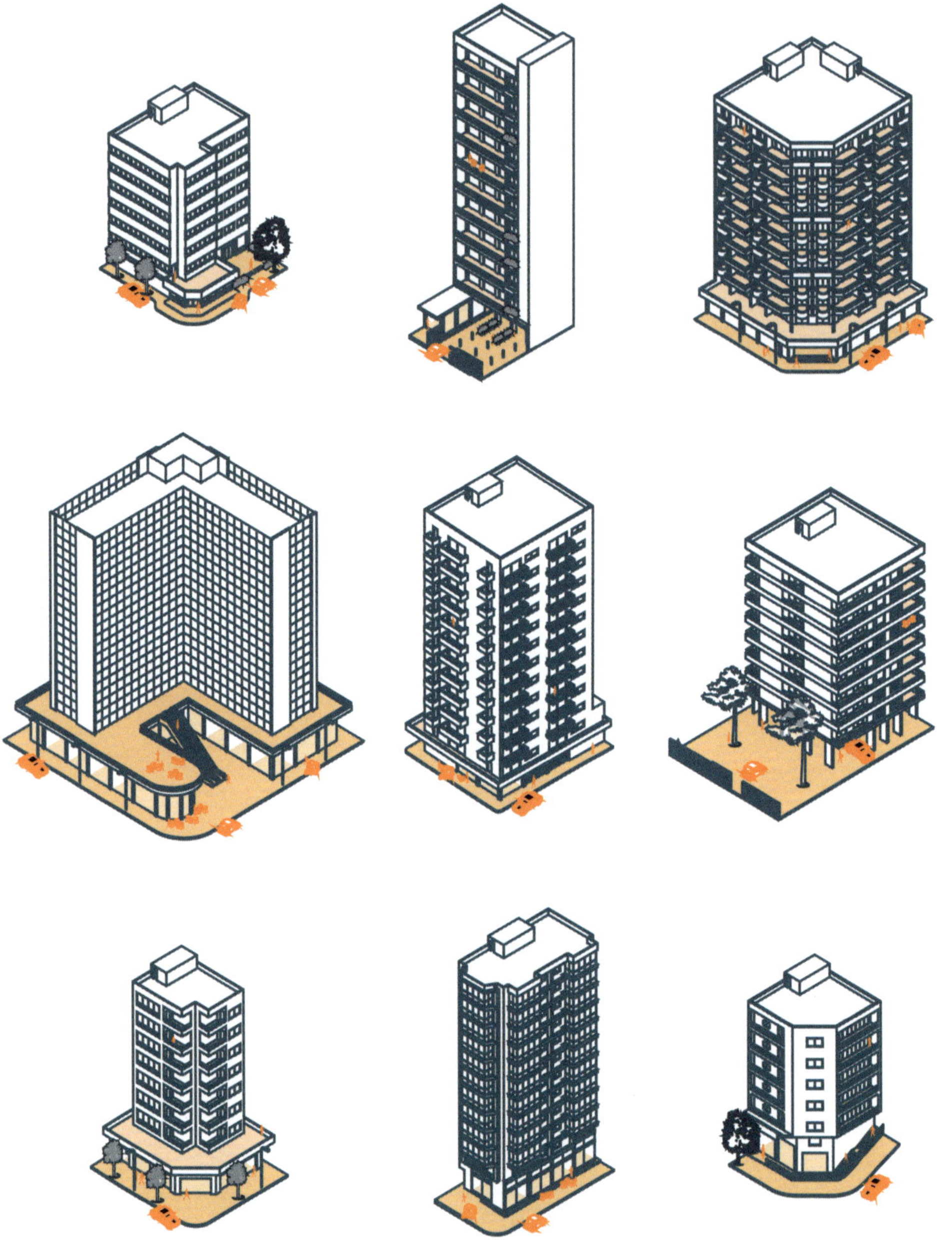

Figure 9 - Diagram showing architectural typologies of the ground from 1970-1990

Figure 10 - Ground conditions emerging during the 1970-1990 period: unresolved adjacencies, redundant pilotis spaces, parking ramps' disconnections of the ground, and inadequate adaptation to topography

YEAR
2000
2001
2002
2003
2004
2005
2006
2007
2008
200
BUILDING PERMITS IN BEIRUT
48
64
88
121
162
170
186
167
231
162

Figure 12 - Photograph showing the Ring—the highway separating Solidere from the rest of Beirut—and, in the background, construction activities in Beirut Central District, a district developed and privatized under Solidere's exceptional jurisdiction. At its bottom, a diagram showing a timeline of permits passed in Beirut between the years 2000 and 2020 is shown.

compulsory fences for setbacks, thereby foregoing street alignments at ground level (Fig. 11)

Second, the *pilotis* areas and balconies were excluded from the net total of built surfaces, allowing additional upper floors on the condition of liberating the ground from any construction and allowing *pilotis* over basements. These amendments harmed these typologies; the *pilotis* became a dead parking space, while the balconies' proportions changed to generic proportions, becoming frequently unused spaces. (Fig. 10)

Third, garage basements became mandatory for buildings over 40 meters in height. In this amendment, which first introduced the basement into residential typologies, the code was written for flat terrains, with simple cut-and-fill sections as the only guidelines for building on a sloping topography. Applied to the hills of Beirut, the implementation came at a terrible cost for the character of the city (Fig. 11). The building ground was calculated from a point that gave developers more floors, resulting in grounds that are sometimes as much as a meter higher or lower than the street, and/or bordered a steep topography with several basement levels visible from afar. Cut and fill leveling resulted in massive retaining walls garnered with small planters to hide their impact on the city's urban landscape.

Finally, large-scale projects, known as "grand ensembles" for plots larger than 10000 m2, were exempted from building law regulations, allowing them to have exceptional building heights and exploitation factors. This regulation became the basis for post-war development under the rule of exception.[19]

The 1983 law amendment canceled side setbacks in zones 3 and 4 in Beirut's zoning plan, creating urban canyon effects on streets and increasing urban density further.[20] The different *gabarit* setbacks and/or infringements to the *pilotis* floor created discontinuous ground alignments with unresolved intersections (refer to Fig. 3). The same amendment introduced regulations of land pooling, allowing the combination of several lots into a larger one; however, this practice did not become common until after the war ended.

During the chaotic and violent years of the civil war, high-volume and uncontrolled construction spread on the outskirts of Beirut while the center was being ravaged by fighting. During this period, informal architecture intensified, and law infringements became routine practices in informal neighborhoods and formal developments. Exacerbated by rampant corruption, these practices impacted the city's

19 Krijnen and Fawaz, "Exception as the Rule: High-End Developments in Neoliberal Beirut."
20 Hiba Mohsen, Rokia Raslan, Ibtihal El-Bastawissi, "The Impact of Changes in Beirut Urban Patterns on the Microclimate: A Review of Urban Policy and Building Regulations," *Architecture and Planning Journal (APJ)*, vol.25 Iss. 1 article 2 (2020).
21 Marot, *Developing Post-War Beirut (1990-2016): The political economy of "pegged urbanization.*
22 Jeremy Arbid, "Higher regulation. Real estate law is complicated, but friendly to developers," *Executive Magazine*, July 16 2014.
23 Saksouk, "Where is Law? Investigations from Beirut."
24 Krijnen and Fawaz, "Exception as the Rule: High-End Developments in Neoliberal Beirut."
25 Saksouk "Where is Law? Investigations from Beirut."
26 Hayat Gebara, N Mona Khechen and Bruno Marot, "Mapping New Constructions in Beirut (2000-2013)" *Jadaliyya*, November 16, 2016. Accessed on March 1, 2014, www.jadaliyya.com/Details/33751/Mapping-New-Constructions-in-Beirut-2000-2013.
27 Lisa Gerbal, Nicolas Hrycaj, Camille Lavoipierre and Marissa Potasiak, *Linking Economic Change With Social Justice In Mar Mikhael, Beirut*, (Gaia Heritage/Sciences Po/Issam Fares Institute for Public Policy and International Affairs, 2016).
28 Beirut Urban Lab, *"Beirut: a city for sale?"* Accessed on March 1, 2024. https://beiruturbanlab.com/en/Details/612/beirut%E2%80%99s-residential-fabric.

ground and, most importantly, increased the people's disregard for the public realm. Unfortunately, this mindset would persist in architectural practices long after the end of the Civil War.

(1990-2004) Privatization

After the end of hostilities in 1990 came a period that was coined the reconstruction era. This was the start of a pegged economic system that would fail 30 years later. This system was based on a neoliberal rentier economy,[21] co-engineered by state actors, the banking sector, and their connections with new real-estate moguls. It introduced new dynamics for spatial production in increasingly deregulated processes, aiming to transform Beirut into a global city for international capital investment. With legal and financial incentives that facilitate the circulation of global capital into high-end real estate,[22] the system had the most severe repercussions on Beirut's urban ground. Treating land and property as a mere financial commodity, it used regulations and legislation to intensify private construction practices to control the city, triggering intense erasure, gentrification, and redevelopment that would continue until 2019.[23]

Initiated under the Hariri mandate (1995-2005), the privatization of public infrastructure and the reconstruction of downtown Beirut under the jurisdiction of Solidere best exemplified the new regime of spatial production (Fig. 12). Paved by the 1971 law amendment, exceptions became the norm[24] in producing a privatized ground: from the abolition of zoning in Solidere to the neo-liberal processes of land pooling and high-rise exemptions in the three decades that followed.

At the scale of the average building, this period started with the 1992 code amendment (refer to Fig. 3) that introduced mandatory parking in all buildings, with the parking ramp as a marking element on the ground floor. The new regulation forfeited corner situations, rhythm, spatial, and pedestrian continuity in favor of optimum column spacing for underground car parking. As a result, the street became congested, putting cars first and prioritizing vehicular access over pedestrian-friendly entrances. Ground floors featured an assemblage of spaces with discordant adjacencies: misaligned party walls, random storefronts, prestigious entrances, illegal additions, and parking ramps, among others.

Most importantly, this amendment marginalized small lots from development as they could not meet parking requirements. It pushed small-lot owners to sell to large-scale development companies and increased land speculation that would change social and spatial dynamics in the different neighborhoods.[25]

This and the 2004 amendment paved the way for real estate companies owned or linked to the same politicians who were ratifying these laws to take over the city's ground and skyline. A construction frenzy and skyrocketing real-estate inflation[26] ensued, fueled by incoming diaspora investments and the banks' high interest rates. This prompted a wave of gentrification in the city that swept through Monot, Gemmayze, Mar Mikhael, Badaro, Ras Beirut, and Hamra (among others), pitting large developments against vulnerable social groups and draining the city from its residents in favor of affluent foreign investors.[27]

Another factor that encouraged gentrification was the "old rent law," which fixed rent fees at a low scale and led to the systematic demolition of old mid-rise buildings in favor of new tall apartment buildings affordable to the upper class and wealthy expatriates. With these sociological changes, gentrification drastically affected the ground, resulting in a high rate of vacancies in the city's building stock.[28]

(2004-2020) High neoliberalism

After Hariri's assassination in 2005, the real estate and construction sectors intensified in a second boom.[29] The practice of exception, first used by Solidere, spread to the rest of the city through land pooling and the construction of residential luxury towers in Beirut.[30]

Significant changes to Lebanese building laws exacerbated the deterioration of the built environment through the 2004 code amendment. First, the building envelope was raised from a ratio of (x 2) to (x 2.5) the width of the road, allowing a 25% increase in development on large plots (refer to Fig. 3).

Exclusions from the total exploitation area were introduced on building elements such as external walls, balconies, and stairs. The rationale behind these revisions was that double walls could function as thermal insulation and that by allowing increased built areas, the housing market would better cater to housing demands. The amendment resulted in a loss of porosity between the building and the street by legalizing the enclosure of balconies with curtain glass. Consequently, the law resulted in an additional 25% increase in floor area due to higher exploitation ratios across all floors, leading to a rise in ground floor density and an increase in building coverage at the expense of green open spaces.

As if all this wasn't enough, the Higher Council for Urban Planning, a public authority controlled by the same "elites", frequently gave exemptions for high rises to surpass their building envelopes or total building allowances.[31] As a result, high-rise towers with impervious boundaries were casually inserted residential neighborhoods, creating islands of large enclosed lots and disrupting the fragile social fabric of these areas.[32]

After the collapse of the pegged economy and real estate bubble in 2019, empty and unfinished projects stood throughout Beirut as the ultimate representation of this failed system that rested too much and for too long on real estate investment as a cornerstone for the economy.

Crisis as possibility

From this typological investigation, it can be argued that the building code and the architectural development of the ground in contemporary Beirut had a reciprocal relationship, albeit to the city's detriment. In this process, code amendments were influenced by the archaic culture that ruled and ruined the city and have, in turn, influenced the architectural exceptions and global development model enacted at the scale of the individual building. This investigation has demonstrated that the manipulations of the building code have systematically disconnected the vertical dimension of development from the horizontal dimension of the ground, encouraging both the amplification of the private production of the city and a transformation of the ground into fractured spatial entities.

As irreversible as it may seem, the financial meltdown brought opportunities. It proved that unbridled development is not the key to a vibrant economy, rather quite the opposite.

The sheer scale of the financial abyss into which the country is currently plunged could be an introspective beginning for reevaluating the role of capital and real estate in deviating development trajectories and moving towards more ethical models of property reuse and ground access that could yield a more equitable Beirut.

Worldwide, neoliberal forces can reshape the private and public interface. When combined with effective governance, building codes can be powerful tools that mitigate such forces by regulating the technical and financial aspects of the construction industry, controlling urban growth, and defining a precise aesthetic of the ground space so it remains livable. Equally, equitable regulations can provide citizens with tools for co-production at the scale of the city, the neighborhood, and the building.[33]

However, such initiatives could only be envisioned locally if the government shifts from promoter to regulator, starting by revising existing laws and the building code to cater to all citizens and reimagine a different relationship between buildings and the city. Through implementation and governance, these initiatives can restore the integrity of the public ground, starting from the scale of the building. Only then would it be possible to envision a reclamation of the ground as an integral part of the city's urban level in its identity, access, and use.

29 This boom occurred under the overlapping impact of the 2004 law amendment, the 2005 withdrawal of the Syrian forces, the hope for a renewed political scene, and finally, the reconstruction following the intense 2006 July war. See Marot, *Developing post-war Beirut (1990-2016): The political economy of "pegged urbanization."*

30 Gebara Hayat, N. Mona Khechen and Bruno Marot. "Mapping New Constructions in Beirut (2000-2013)."

31 To qualify for such exceptional measures, the conditions included a minimum lot size of 4,000 m² and the requirement for demonstrating "special architectural or urban merits", a criterion relying heavily on the personal preferences and interpretations of the High Council members. See Krijnen and Fawaz, "Exception as the Rule: High-End Developments in Neoliberal Beirut."

32 Gerbal, Hrycaj, Lavoipierre and Potasiak, *Linking Economic Change With Social Justice In Mar Mikhael, Beirut.*

33 Many of these regulations and initiatives can be found abundantly in recent scholarship/reports/ publications on co-producing the city, such as Pablo Sendra and Richard Sennett's *Designing Disorder: Experiments and Disruptions in the City* and *Architecture 00's "Compendium for the Civic Economy."*

Figure 1 - Gouraud Street

anatomy of ground sections

nicolas fayad

This chapter examines the spatial intricacies of Beirut's dense groundscape, hypothesizing its constant, iterative, and experimental renewal over time. It is difficult to stumble upon a single ground condition in Beirut that, at one point or another, has not been altered—or originated from a particular social practice—resisting privatization and a typological building code. This chapter singles out four architectural fragments of this ground that offer such conditions, and that became—through form and use—analogous assemblies with transient and sometimes non-tangible urban spaces that unleash new possibilities for Beirut's urban ground. The four fragments are explored through orthographic and three-dimensional ground sections as a systematic reflective tool that can narrate fragments of urban life, in which architecture is inscribed and constantly re-written, addressing the midscale between the morphology of these urban fragments and the intricacies of their small-scale inherent social practices. Through diagrams highlighting continuities between city and urban fragments, the chapter uses visual analysis to argue for better sectional relationships between the vertical/private and horizontal/public datums that are not solely pictorial acts but actively constructed through use and occupation.

Fragments as microcosms of urban life

As a result of unbridled development dictated by real-estate-driven typologies and a sterile building code, today's Beirut can be read as a group of enclaved fragments severed from the falsity of integrated urbanism. As a result, the renewal and adaptation of the city's ground through time reflects a disintegrated perceptual experience rather than a unitary image.

As it is difficult to find a single ground condition in Beirut that has not been altered, it is equally challenging to imagine Beirut's groundscape without capturing its constant, iterative, and experimental renewal over time.

Urban fragments and residual spaces, discreetly extending sidewalks or silently encompassing covered streets (Fig. 1) and concealed patios, have contributed to a unique process of revealing architecture's most essential qualities: reversibility, adaptation, and transformation. Rather than disciplining growth and endowing the city with an orderly construct, new forms of urban life emerged out of building typologies intended to drive modern life's apparatus. Hovering masses, sunken courtyards, and stepped configurations, once built with a didactic purpose, disclose new relationships with the urban ground. Fragments of urban life become analogous assemblies, exploring transient and sometimes non-tangible urban spaces that can unleash new possibilities for Beirut's urban ground.

Therefore, what might it mean—for a given urban typology—to assume and embrace its transformative renewal process? What might it mean to plan for the gradual emergence of urban fragments, the very transference of the urban ideal? More important than the design of cities will be the design of their transience. Would the scalar relationships of those fragments contribute to their vibrancy and the vitality of their existence?

These questions belong to the larger context of the production of site-specific architectural manifestos, not as historical investigations but as critical examinations based on the assumption that site-specific manifestos in general—and the study of urban ground sections in particular—could still constitute significant tools to trace design narratives today. The observation of Beirut's ground becomes a 'rewriting' exercise, simultaneously putting in dialogue the city's massing with the ground and, most importantly, reflecting on the essence of the inherent relationships of such dialogue that delineate an urban scenario for Beirut. Only when closely addressing the complementarity between the urban realm and the architectural scale do typological sections become research tools to better understand the intrinsic qualities of site-specific, historically layered, and formally compelling urban taxonomies.

The anatomy of spatial intricacies found in Beirut's urban fragments thus questions and hypothesizes new design propositions for the urban ground.

Ground sections as method of observation

This typological investigation begins with the assumption that reading urban fragments in a pure orthographic section is an active instrument to change how we look at the urban realm. The section here not only looks at the urban ground as a representation tool segregating form in the autonomous world of architecture but also forces architecture to face reality, testing its potential for the contemporary city and its practices as a way of life, renewal, and transformation.

Ground sections, whether orthographic or three-dimensional, are adopted as reflective or systematic tools to follow or assist predictions. In the wake of constantly evolving tools, ground sections become generators to challenge the morphology of architectural and urban design disciplines, not only mastering the representation of a fragment of urban life but also truly addressing the midscale between the morphology of a given urban fragment and the intricacies of its inherent social practice. Ground sections are not solely pictorial acts but are already and always in active construction. They are the product of multiple generative processes and operative configurations, manifesting figure through matter.

A sectional investigation of Beirut's ground draws insights on the use of participatory observations over time and repeated engagement with the built-up environment.

The section becomes a method rooted in urban form, approaching the city as a 'laboratory' where people, places, and buildings could be studied through observation and interpretation. Following this thinking, the premise of a ground section in Beirut's context becomes an experiment. The superimposition of formal decisions, coincidences, and realities across the twentieth century has given the city its present form. The sectional condition of the current situation becomes a formal interpretation of events in which the traces of history have remained visible. In that sense, the ground section is not a singular unified image but a living collage, a collection of fragments in perpetual construction (Fig. 2).

At the architectural scale, many case studies throughout Beirut exemplify this so-called manifestation of the ground section, not only for its formal qualities or representation of an urban or architectural agenda but also for the recognition of a high degree of human and social agency in certain parts of the city. Rather than represented as islands or closed enclaves, these sectional case studies work as magnets whose basic principle relies on openness, continuity, and cohesion. Most of these case studies rely on clear architectural intentions for the city's future. When designed and constructed, they almost encourage embryonic activities in their respective neighborhoods, intensifying social practices of everyday life within them, proposing an alternative to the existing urban form, and thriving to redefine a new common ground (Fig. 3).

Typological indexing versus iterative transcience

This section looks closer at two fragments built 20 years apart, the residential clusters of Karm El Zeitoun and Horsh Kfoury. The first was built incrementally during the 1930s on the slope of the Achrafieh Hill to house mixed migrants[1]—before passing the 1940 building code,[2] and based on an urban plan that was superimposed over the hilly conditions of the site. The second was built in Badaro between 1940 and 1960 following its commercial boom, based on urban guidelines drafted by Michel Ecochard that integrated the first edition of the building code with the modernist principles of the 'pilotis' on the flat terrain of the pine wood forest in the area.

Looking closer at the cluster in Karm El Zeitoun, one would be faced with an 'autogenetic' architectural process that recognizes the Genius Loci in which it grew over time. The cluster constitutes a specific urban dialectic in conversation with the neighborhood's hilly topographic condition (Fig. 4).

1 During the second half of the 1920s and the early 1930s, different actors (the Nansen office, on behalf of the League of Nations and the French Mandate) came together. They funded the settlements of Armenian Refugees in Karm el Zeitoun. Committees funded land acquisition, road network parceling, and construction materials, whereas the refugees purchased and built the plots and houses.
Raymond Kévorkian, Lévon Nordiguian, Vahé Tachjian, *Les Arméniens: La Quête d'un Refuge 1917-1939* (USJ Presse, 2007).

2 Lebanon's first construction law-number 61- was legislated in 1940, based on a revised version of the French building code that was practised at the time.
Elie El-Achkar, *Réglementation et Formes Urbaines: Le Cas de Beyrouth* (Presses de l'Ifpo, 1998).

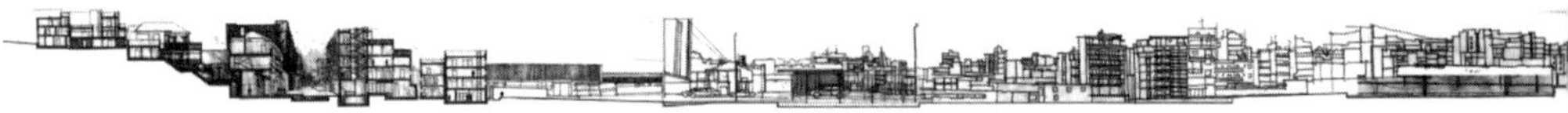

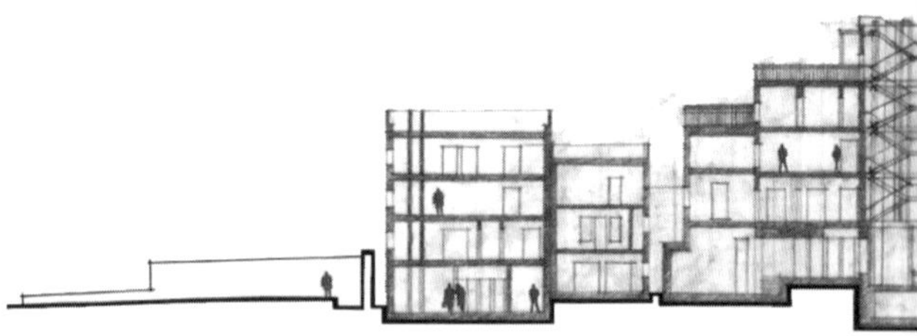

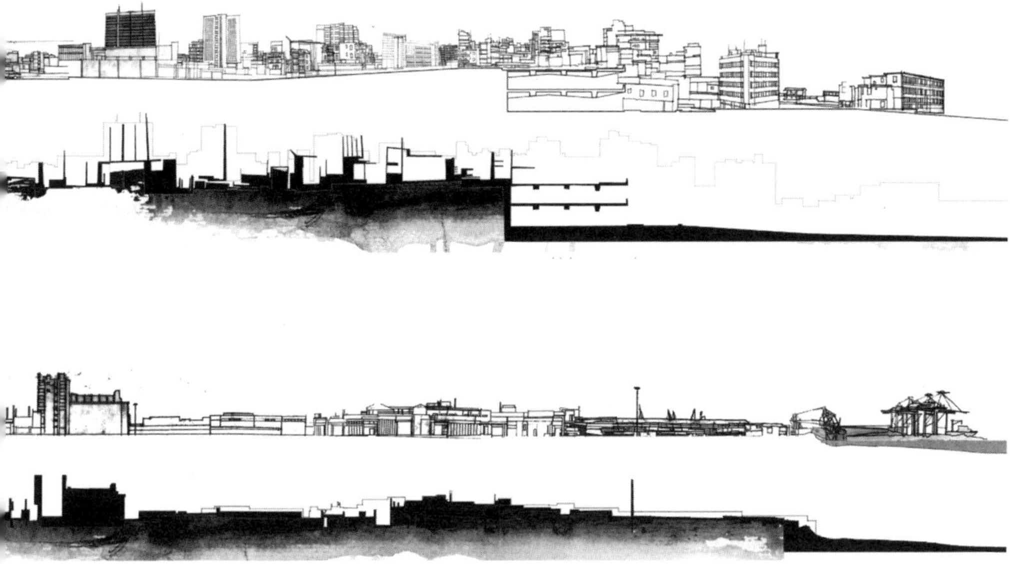

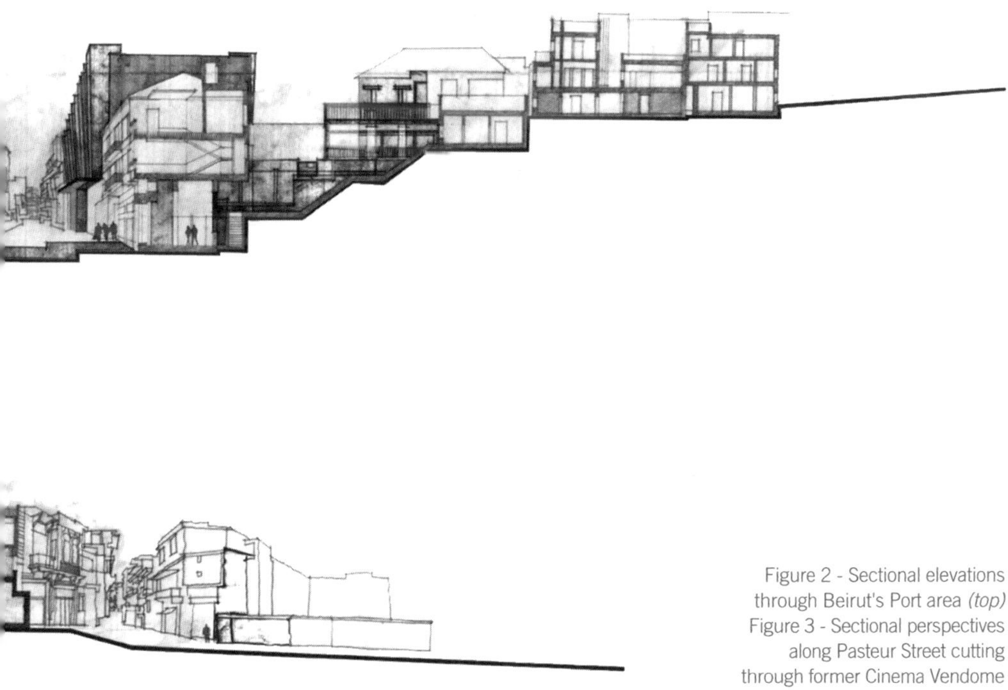

Figure 2 - Sectional elevations through Beirut's Port area *(top)*
Figure 3 - Sectional perspectives along Pasteur Street cutting through former Cinema Vendome *(bottom)*

Figure 4 - Frontal View of Karm El Zeitoun

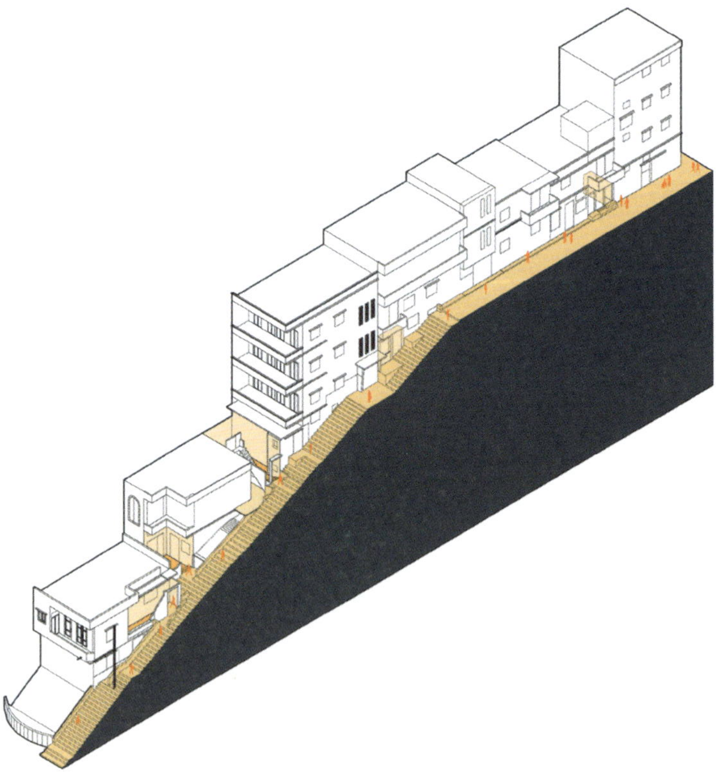

Figure 5 - Sectional axonometric drawing along Karm El Zeitoun

Figure 6 - Street view of Horsh Kfoury

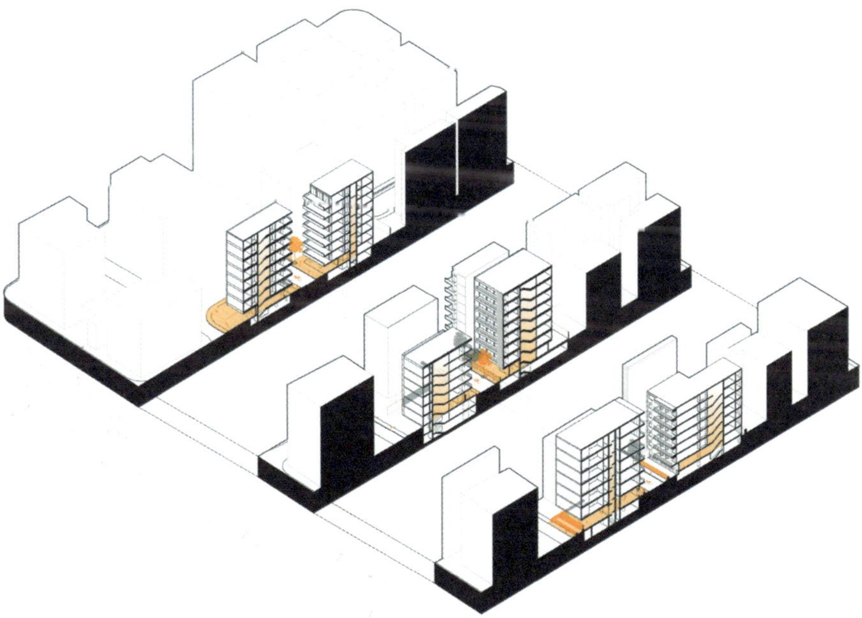

Figure 7 - Sectional axonometric drawing along Horsh Kfoury residential cluster

Figure 9 - Street view of EDL

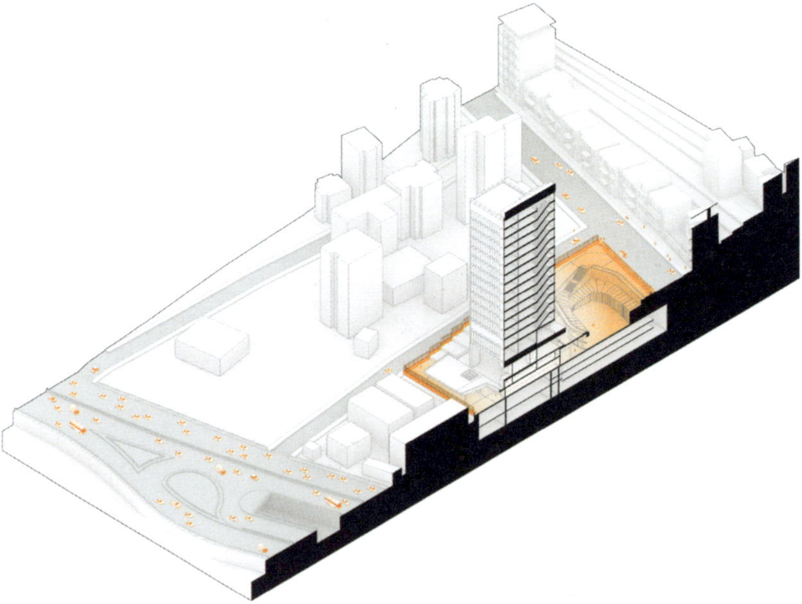

Figure 10 - Sectional axonometric drawing of EDL

Figure 8 – Street view of Gefinor

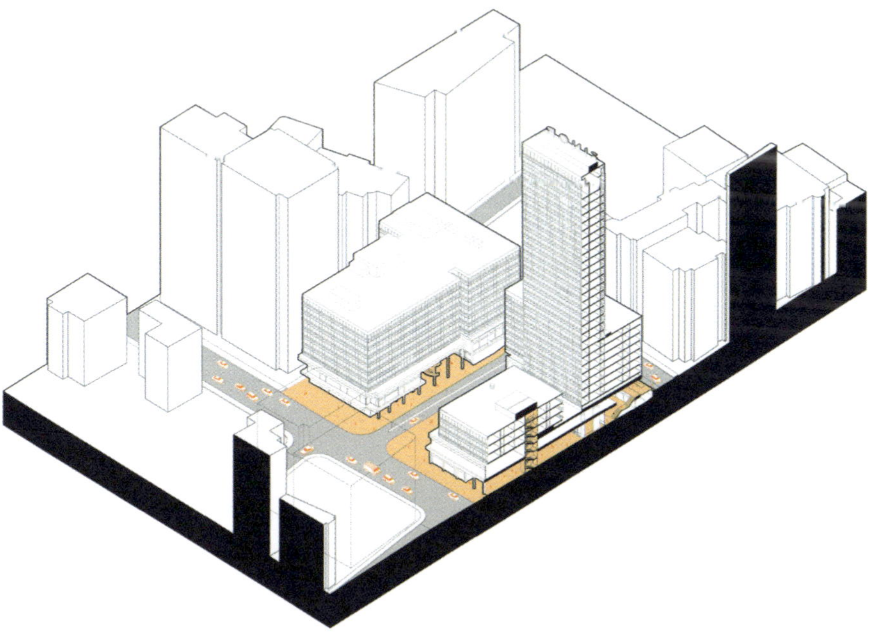

Figure 11 – Sectional axonometric drawing of Gefinor

In this urban condition, expansion is merely an observation of aggregation that incrementally occupies the urban slope with generative housing typologies, organically snapping to one another and simultaneously conversing. The result is an architecture that gradually reclaimed its inherent relationship to the terrain, a stepped configuration in dialogue with the slope. Inevitably, this particular urban section transgresses the urban ground to a new elevated condition—the living roofs of Karm El Zeitoun. Roofs weave the ground with the sky above, denaturalizing urban form and opening up new possibilities and relationships between architecture and urban experience. Over the years, the residents' successful iterations and additions reconfigured the roof's contouring to create several nested spaces, access points to added rooms, and additional units. Tested in a low-income neighborhood in an urban framework implemented before the 1940 code, these urban singularities emancipate urban form from the preconceived parameters of building code and socio-economic pressures, offering an alternative proposition for architecture in direct relationship with an ever-changing ground. In the case of Karm El Zeitoun, the urban ground shifts vertically, cascades, and decomposes, delimiting any act of architecture and stirring away from predetermined order towards entropy (Fig. 5).

In contrast, the Horsh Kfoury residential cluster of Badaro presents a horizontal porosity of the urban ground antithetical to subsequent applications—or deformations—of the 'pilotis' condition in Beirut (Fig. 6).

With its linear series of buildings raised above ground, the fragment optimistically claims a porosity that negotiates the public urban ground with each private residential typology. The simple act of detaching the mass from its horizontal bracing allows the public realm to unfold beyond what was once perceived as private space, inevitably consenting to multiple readings and practices. This suspended urban condition speculates and reveals a singular architectural gesture but, most importantly, it naturally insists on its constant alteration: an occupiable void reveling in a renewed, dense, and struggling urban context, resisting privatization. In fact, Horsh Kfoury is one of the few urban fragments that have riposted their post-modern contemporaries, enacting a visual and intellectual urban integration that fights the unceasing pressures of capitalistic forces (fig. 7). Detachment thus offers an alternative or a less disciplined model for interpreting the city. Surprisingly, it suggests new potentials that confirm the vitality of the urban ground and become a powerful analytical device for discovering architectural essences beyond spatial performance.

Learning from the sectional conditions of Karm El Zeitoun and Horsh Kfoury is key for allowing their architectural particularities to thrive in Beirut's continuously threatened urban realm. These projects embody new urban qualities while introducing an innovative urbanity of different densities. They operate in environments that would otherwise be remote and excluded, giving access to communal spaces, promoting social interaction, and intensifying cultural diversity.

Tran-sectional grounds: 'Gefinor' center versus Électricité du Liban headquarters

Another binomial of buildings, 'Gefinor' Center[3] and Électricité du Liban Headquarters[4] similarly engage with the public realm at ground level and beyond (Fig. 8, 9). Both projects, completed in the early seventies, are pioneering examples of the golden age of modernism in Lebanon celebrating the urban ground. However, their initial gestures yielded paradoxical futures.

Both buildings utilize the street level for public use and adapt to their immediate urban context—a sloping ground by introducing intricate cavities, leveling their respective sites through depression or extrusion. The blatant inventiveness and the innate challenges that emerge from the confluence of the building mass with its urban ground reinterpret the horizontal ground plane and transform it from surface to volume. Where volume is usually understood as solid, in both examples, it often translates into a void, suggesting a spatial and typological transformation of the ground plane, exuding new topographic conditions through an entirely constructed ground, as much carved from the mass of the earth as it is built up from it. When looking closer at both building sections, one is struck by the legibility of the constructed porous ground connecting one part of the city to another, putting architecture into dialogue, negotiation, and ultimately a problematic reconciliation with its surrounding urban fragments, most importantly out of necessity and in order to situate continuities (Fig. 10).

Moving away from the conventions of enclosures, shelter, and singularity, the particularity of those projects lies in the ingenuity of their relationship to the ground. By challenging the generic forces of gravity that pull architecture away from the ground plane, sculpting a new figurative ground mandates a critical approach to weaving a building mass with its natural terrain.

While both projects initially pushed the boundaries of openness and porosity at the ground level, only one of them—'Gefinor' Center—stubbornly endured its inherent fidelity to the public ground (Fig. 11). Through time, the building was saved by its status but also by its morphological and programmatic repertoire. Privately owned, managed, and maintained, it stood the pressures of the constantly shifting urban scape of the area by interestingly stitching many of the building blocks surrounding it. Its matured, porous, and layered ground served as a communal armature, claiming an urban continuity while offering a responsive programmatic solution to the neighborhood. Surrounded by hospitals, clinics, and academic institutions, 'The Gefinor Center became an accessible public nexus, celebrating an intersection and elevating a mixed-use urban ground experience.

Paradoxically, the Électricité du Liban Headquarters building failed to resist the pressures of a declining political environment despite the thriving essence of its original design intent (Fig. 12). A ground condition that was once used and narrated as an extension of the street into an architecture that demanded porosity, now falls in a barricaded, heterotopic, and isolated urban realm. Hampered by the decline of statehood, the building stands in total separation from its peripheral context through the defensive transformation of its ground and street frontage. A victim of its use, where the building itself is (mis) managed by a bankrupt ministry, recounting its continuous failed attempt at lending itself to the city, the periphery of its ground became a seat of repeated manifestations against insolvent governance.

3 Gefinor Center was built in Rue Clemenceau by Australian architect Victor Gruen in the late 1960s. It is a 55,000-square-meter business complex with five blocks of retail and restaurant spaces on the ground floor, which is spanned on two levels due to its sitting on a slope.
George Arbid, "Practicing Modernism in Beirut, Architecture in Lebanon 1946-1970" (PhD diss., Harvard University, 2002).

4 The EDL building was the result of a national competition commissioned by the Lebanese state and won by CETA (J. Aractingi, J. N. Conan, J. Nassar, and P. Neema). It was built between 1964 and 1970 and symbolized the golden era of Lebanon's modernization.
George Arbid and Philipp Oswalt (Ed.), *Designing Modernity: Architecture in the Arab World 1945-1973* (Jovis, 2022).

Ground section as open system

Today's Beirut cannot be rethought as a whole. Public resources are generally too poor to promote significant change. In contrast, private resources push urban development in market-driven directions, coupled with a general political representation crisis, deepening the gap between citizens and politics. A viable strategy on a large scale seems to be promoting a gathering of the city's most creative and active agents into spatially autonomous think tanks or urban magnets. The connection between people and the city, which has been generally blurred or disrupted today, would be given a new impulse as rooted in the compelling ground sections of Karm El Zeitoun and Horsh Kfoury. Since these alternatives could be developed at the core of the urban fabric, their strong contrast would intensify rather than diminish the experience of Beirut. In the same way in which the carcass of a whale is capable of feeding a whole ecosystem of sentient creatures, the city would feed these pulsing urban 'magnets' with open infrastructural layers and sustainable systems, as well as all the other characteristics that would enable these 'magnets' to go beyond their limited autonomy.[5]

These urban concepts that transcend the above-mentioned case studies are pluralistic and almost the antithesis of planning theories, which stem from defining the city as a whole. In the contemporary structure of society, which increasingly incorporates individuals with different demands, desires, and conceptions, unfolding these concepts promotes further individualization of the city. While an autonomous city composed upon a unifying principle provokes a loss of identity and personality, the city dweller in an open system may choose the identity or spatial quality that best corresponds to his or her desires and expectations. Since the actual situation of Beirut's ground is a dynamic process of continuous redefinition, the future task will no longer be protecting and enhancing these phenomena as they are but rather driving them to concentrate into clusters with higher resilience and permanence. This shift in scale would transform the 'magnets' into more extensive laboratories for developing a different urbanity, as a way to develop new proposals for the city's future. As the availability of sustainable and participatory systems is fundamental to these urban 'magnets', more flexibility ought to be strategically realized to support the migration of existing agencies and the hosting of new ones.

5 We expand on such an approach in the following chapter, "The Collective Ground."

Figure 12 - Street view of EDL

Figure 1 - Collective infrastructures of co-production

THE COLLECTIVE GROUND a log of reclamatory actions

sandra frem
(design by boulos douaihy and nicolas fayad)

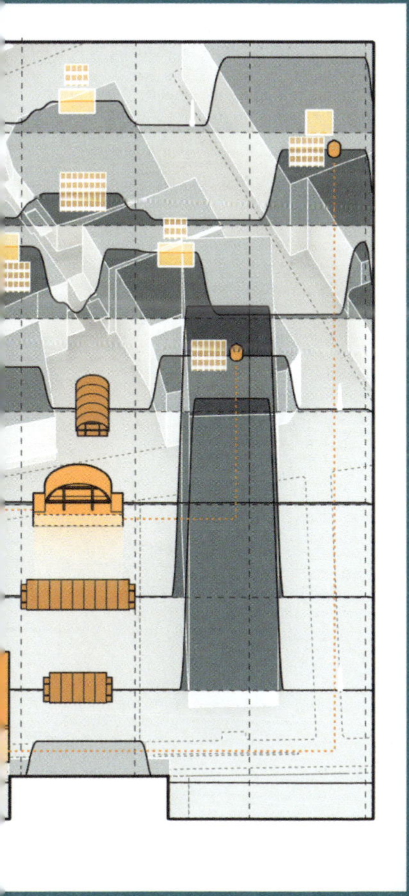

Occurring shortly in the aftermath of the Beirut Port Blast, just as activist groups and NGOs were deployed in the destroyed neighborhoods for humanitarian rescue and reconstruction efforts, a discussion started between the authors around how the ground, in its most vulnerable moments, was also the most collective it has ever been in decades. Inspired from that moment, the discussion moved on to brainstorm design actions that could reinforce Beirut's ground in its mission to support communal uses during times of normalcy but, more importantly, during times of exception.

Indeed, during "normal" times, the ground in Beirut served as a stage for excessive privatization imposed by a globalized real estate industry and neoliberal city governance. This led to a fractured space of chaos and disorder when lots were deemed unworthy of private investment.

While during normal times, the ground was sapped from its collective role in Beirut, it was during periods of exception that its collective dimension resurfaced:

The first significant instance occurred during the October 2019 revolution and the short-lived occupation of Beirut Central District, when people believed it was the tipping point for a radical change and an opportunity to challenge a failed system. This led to the emergence of grassroots leaderless groups through the involvement of first-time activists and regular citizens demanding accountability and seeking alternatives to a corrupt government.

Unsupported by the government in their protests, they had to provide alternative infrastructures for their ground occupation: water, food, data, and shelter, combined with virtual platforms connecting their activities to people outside Beirut and in the diaspora. Their presence on the ground expanded to custodian management and multi-programming of areas under their control: areas of gatherings, waste collection, recycling, programming of rotational activities, food tents, spaces of debate, and collective services such as soup kitchens that were lacking in the public realm for the four past decades under Solidere.[1,2]

The second instance unfolded a couple of months after, following the Port Blast in August 2020, when the ground in the devastated districts was deployed by the civil society NGOs and activist groups, many of which were also present during the previous October. This second experience allowed these groups to advance their organization methods used in the October 2019 protests to achieve a more networked action.[3] Relief activism became an act of contestation and reclamation of the ground, with spaces used for shelter, counseling, soup kitchens, and medical aid units.

However, in both moments, the challenge remained on how to scale up these alternatives from temporary forms of collectivism to citywide initiatives for co-producing the city and how the ground acts as a support infrastructure that encourages public use and, in some cases, occupation. Worldwide, this aim is being repressed by market-influenced planning practices and real estate forces through trends aiming to tame genuine urban life and informality with over-designed and controlled environments.

Hence, the subsequent starting points of our design log were:

How can a support infrastructure be conceived to layer the ground with an open framework that nurtures rather than repress, assembles rather than divides, and remains open to change rather than falls into obsolescence?

How can it be designed while remaining a "low resolution" architecture that orients the collective use of the ground without over-determining it?

What modalities of co-production would underlie such a network, which could become a prototype to be emulated in several host sites in Beirut?

1 Cynthia Bou Aoun. "Reclaiming Public Space and Its Role in Producing the Revolution" Legal Agenda, 2020-01-09. https://english.legal-agenda.com/reclaiming-public-space-and-its-role-in-producing-the-revolution (accessed 10/5/2024).

2 Mariam Hammoud. "Reclaiming Public Space During the Revolution: How We Are Reconnecting With Lebanese Cities" Beirut Today, 20/11/2019. https://beirut-today.com/2019/11/20/reclaiming-public-space-revolution/ (Accessed 10/5/2024).

3 Kareem Chehayeb and Abby Sewell, "Local groups step up to lead Beirut blast response." The New Humanitarian, 10/18/2020. https://www.thenewhumanitarian.org/news-feature/2020/08/18/Lebanon-Beirut-explosion-local-aid-response (accessed 10/5/2024).

4 Pablo Sendra and Richard Sennett. *Designing disorder. Experiments and disruptions in the city*. London and New York, Verso, 2020.

5 The 15-M is an anti-austerity movement in Spain, unfolding in a series of protests, demonstrations, and occupations against austerity policies in Madrid in 2011 and 2012.

6 Barcelona Energia is a municipal company created by an administration born of the 15M revolution, which tackled fuel poverty. Proposing a distributed and collective form of producing energy, the company engages individuals and collectives in energy production, installing panels on top of private or public buildings and selling back to public or private grids as well as combining the possibilities of private or public investment in the infrastructure. In such an example, the municipality assumes the role of redistributing wealth and resources and enlists residents in energy production.

Collective infrastructures of co-production

This design discussion picked up on Richard Sennett and Pablo Sendra's book "Designing Disorder", [4] which looked at how "disorder" could be seeded into cities' urban spaces. This was investigated through design and organization methods in which unplanned collective activities—as part of the collective city-making—could be encouraged at the ground level. As part of this argument, the book documented the 15-M movement in Spain,[5] triggered by activism groups in Madrid against austerity measures, culminating with several activists' wins to the municipal council in the 2015 elections. That electoral win became a departure point for several co-production projects in the city, intersecting community-harnessed resources with municipal-level facilitation, such as Barcelona Energia[6]. According to Sendra, networks and municipalism were two complementary methods to expand the contestation of power to the level of the city.

Picking on parallels between the 15-M movement and the October 2019 experience, we expanded on the idea of a collective infrastructural network that a community-owned trust or company manages, which could allow an exchange of surplus energy (but also could expand to other resources like food, water, or waste) with other collectives (neighborhood groups and collectives on the ground) without necessarily going through the municipal grid. This proposes combining a formal system that ensures equal distribution with other informal systems that allow fluid exchanges for better distribution of resources and circular uses.

To bring such ideas into our design speculation, we borrowed Sendra's notion of "infrastructure as an open system" to think of the ground as a layered infrastructure —physical and social—that keeps an open—yet designed—configuration with elements that support unplanned activities open to additions, modifications, and reconversions.

What ensued is an interpretation of the ground as a base for community-harvested energy points that equip this urban level with data, power, water, and shelter facilities and are open to programming and public use. By embedding collective infrastructures, the ground in Beirut can become an essential enabler of communal life in the city, and by enlisting the community to co-produce services needed for the functioning of infrastructures that are regulated rather than provided by the municipality, new prototypes of co-production could emerge (Fig. 1).

Methodology and criteria

From there, we turned to the neighborhood of Mar Mikhael (Fig. 2), which was severely affected by the Port Blast. There, we defined services like water, power, data, shade, and shelter as networks needed for the ground to empower collective uses.

We contextualized these aspects as potential sponsors for a wide range of community uses that could be facilitated by a collective infrastructural system.

We brainstormed how such a system can be designed —as opposed to remaining accidental without becoming didactic or aesthetic. However, more importantly, we considered how open configurations, socio-spatial contracts, and novel modes of micro-governance could be deployed in complementarity—like in Madrid, where formal/ municipal and informal/ independent types of exchanges can coexist and thrive- to allow for unplanned activities to occur, evolve, and consolidate, the ground's project of collectivity.

Equally influential notions for shaping the formal and organizational features of this network are Sennett's writings on open form[7] and Fumihiko Maki's "Investigations into Collective Form"[8]—among others—in which they acknowledge the need for undrawn backbones and underdetermined forms—that can be collective infrastructures—to organize urban space and new forms of collectives around them.

To materialize such aims, the project became an articulation of two typologies: prototypes—components performing different roles within the larger network, and frameworks—formal organizations defining the correlations between the different components.

Prototypes

Prototypes were developed in three categories (Fig. 3):

Amenity prototypes deployed at ground level, offering amenities to citizens needed for ground use, *powering prototypes* located at intermediate surfaces like roofs, walls, or interior open spaces, supplying the needed resources for the amenities,and *armatures,* connection lines that emphasize the continuity of the collective surface between amenity/ consumption and powering/production/ recycling.

Amenity prototypes are consumption points of the collective infrastructure. They can be potable and non-potable water outlets needed for communal soup kitchens and cleaning after activities; power supply and data points required for developing certain activities and for extended use of the public realm; and shelter and shade structures that include bathrooms and self-use amenities. These points initiate a collective awareness of the shared infrastructure and resources and the negotiation of communal practices to use them.

Powering prototypes are co-production and also recycling points of the collective infrastructure. They can be community-owned solar panels, rainwater tanks, data hotspots connected to an international grid, and waste recycling deposits and units. These points will give rise to the governance committees and community groups to manage and distribute them, allowing the growth of a horizontal hierarchy that can include neighborhood committees and NGOs in the decision-making.

Armatures: In our quest to spatialize these types of communally harnessed infrastructural networks, we needed to differentiate them from municipal infrastructural networks that are usually hidden and concealed. A local precedent to visibility is privately-owned generators and cable television installations whose wirings are visible and take hegemony over the air-scape of neighborhoods through their ad-hoc supply to private residences. The visibility of the proposed networks makes them prone to flexibility, negotiation, and engagement from different stakeholders. Making our proposed elements and connections visible yet non-linear will raise awareness of the production and consumption of collective resources in the public realm.

Frameworks

To materialize the networks organizing the different prototypes, we used three formal criteria for the overarching framework: continuous surface, open/visible/ non-linear networks, and unfinished forms.[9]

Continuous surface (Fig. 2): The idea of a single surface, which is both continuous and porous, can be extended from single buildings to open spaces in which different communities could meet, bringing the notion of ambiguity, which is characteristic of creative disorder. Countering the splintering of open public spaces in Beirut, the single surface can sometimes become vertical, wrapping the public realm in a "carpet" of collectivity.

Open, visible, and non-Linear networks (Fig. 4): The notion of open networks as opposed to closed networks can allow them to evolve and adapt to their communities' unresolved and real-life narratives, which are more often than not non-linear, without falling into the ordered, integrative, and rigid approaches of formal planning.

Unfinished form (Fig. 5): In his writings on the open city, Sennett identifies unfinished form as a characteristic of an open, flexible urban environment, as a form of building that is the antidote to the overdetermined fit-for-purpose city. Using unfinished forms could allow structures to function for simultaneous or rotating activities, break the function-form, and become living, evolving architectures.

The resulting assemblage—collective infrastructural networks, open systems, flexible/multi-use forms, co-design processes, and indeterminate design—can create amenable social and spatial environments that breed the new collective ground in Beirut.

Protocol

To apply this experiment in Mar Mikhael and other sites in Beirut, the process could unfold according to the following protocol:

1. Identify available sites by examining vacant parcels maintained by municipal agencies or private owners and their connections to suitable vacant surfaces on rooftops and inner lots.

2. Once a parcel is identified, issue a "Request for Proposals" (RFP) to the community, particularly local entities active in community organization, to solicit ideas for non-profit community-based amenities that have an infrastructural or civic function and "Request for Interest" (RFI) to identify powering points' suppliers.

3. Based on the RFP, select service needs, which will lead to the selection of relevant prototypes. Depending on the site's size and situation, prototypes will have different combinations of form to provide opportunities for local appropriation.

4. Based on the RFI selected powering points, develop a site-specific armature based on the location of the prototypes and powering points on site to define and organize each location through the provision of circulation and utility access.

5. Establish a collective trust to supervise and manage the infrastructure and propose occasional programs, keeping it predominantly open for collective use.

The municipal role then becomes—like in the Barcelona Energia case—to facilitate the redistribution of resources to the network and the area and to approve the prototypical projects as they become defined in the different locales.

The resulting collective infrastructure provides reliable services and sponsors programmatic innovation on the ground based on the specific needs of the local community. Each site will be recognized as a connected part of the system due to its visible prototypes and armatures but unique due to its locally developed form. This design experiment suggests that such collective infrastructure could be a pathway to promote new forms of co-production and shared experiences; it does this by enabling a distributed network of services provision that acts as both an alibi and sponsor for these collaborative movements.

7 In his book "Building and Dwelling" Richard Sennett, elaborates on the 'Five Open Forms' that should characterize the design of cities based on people's experiences: such forms are synchronous, punctuated, porous, incomplete, and multiple.

8 Maki, Fumihiko, "Investigations in Collective Form" (1964). Books and Monographs. 61.

9 Criteria borrowed from Richard Sennett's essay "The Open City". Richard Sennett, "The Open City", in *The Endless City*, Ricky Burdett and. Deyan Sudjic, eds. London: Phaidon Press, 2007.

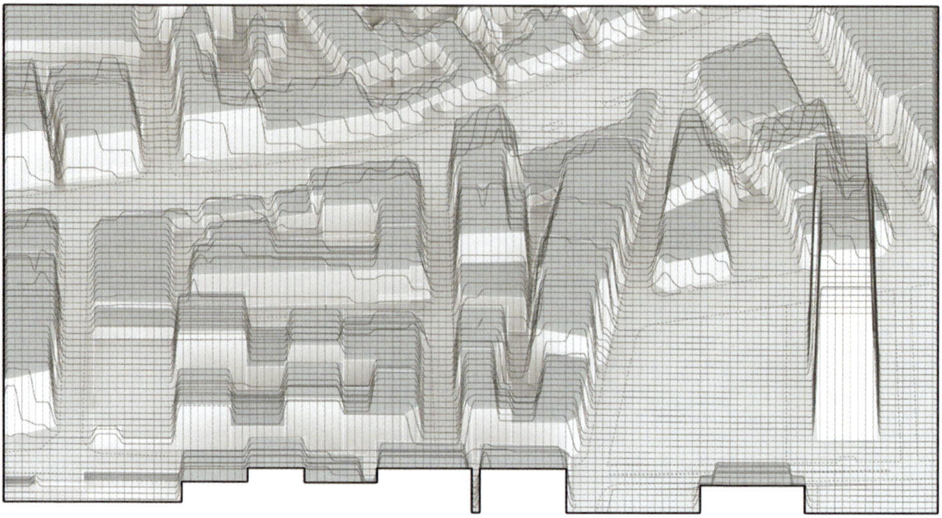

Figure 2 - Site as continuous surface

Figure 3 - Prototypes: amenity points, powering points, and armatures

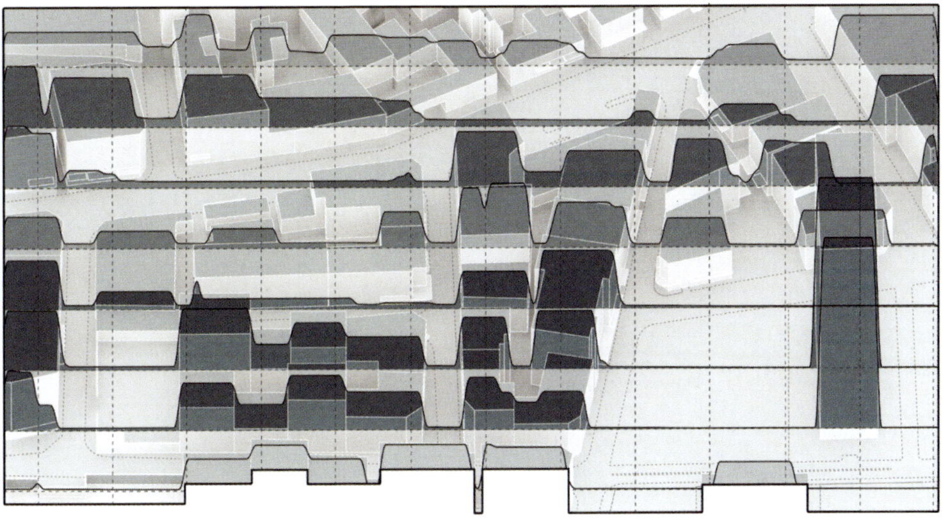

Figure 4 - Open, visible, and non-linear networks

Figure 5 - Unfinished form

section 4

activism

Activism as a ground practice has been particularly transformative for Beirut over the past few years. During periods of public discontent and political stagnation, the ground has served as the common platform from which mobilization efforts arose and as an active space of manifestation and protest. Barricaded, polarized, and neglected spaces became the channels from which citizens and designers alike manifested in and about the city, whether to reclaim their rights for public space or transform street spaces into their collective ground.

Activism in the design discourse has taken multiple shapes and approaches. Generally, it refers to processes that extend the design practice from the sole production of objects or spaces to creating radical change.[1] It can also be articulated as practices that use design to critique or inject change in the city and the built environment at large. Design activism typically revolves around socio-political, cultural, or environmental issues directly impacting the built and natural environments.

A recent publication in Bracket by Mason White and Neeraj Bhatia[2] puts out a call to action, advocating for architecture's spatial agency and accountability toward creating effective change while unpacking various forms of activism in the discipline. Methods like active community engagement, participatory design methods, and design-build projects have long situated the social role of the architect, supported by people like Thomas Fisher[3] and Mass Design group since the early 2000s. A more recent form of activism builds on design methodologies and tools to investigate issues for urban and social justice. Practices like Forensic Architecture or the Beirut-based Public Works utilize tools for 3d simulation, visual analysis, and mapping to reflect and reveal critical spatial problematics.[4]

In an interesting distinction on design activism, Foreign Architects Switzerland[5] distinguishes between strategy-based activism, which involves the engagement of designers in socio-political actions supported by a governing authority, and tactic-based activism, which involves a collective self-organized approach through tactical design interventions to provoke change against the status quo. The latter approach frames the positioning of this book section as it reflects on particular design processes that engage the collective in protest against long-standing issues of the city. Activism is thus explored here through specific recent episodes of bottom-up organization, urban reclamation, and public art installations that have helped transform and mobilize Beirut's ground.

1 Kees Lokman, "Design Activism: Towards Agnostic Pluralism," in *Bracket Takes Action*, ed. Mason White and Neeraj Bhatia (Applied Research and Design Publishers, 2019).

2 Mason White and Neeraj Bhatia (ed.), *Bracket Takes Action* (Applied Research and Design Publishers, 2019).

3 Thomas Fisher, "Public Interest Architecture: A Needed and Inevitable Change" in *Expanding Architecture: Design as Activism*, ed. Bryan Bell and Katie Wakeford (Metropolis books, 2008), 8-13.

4 Carla Aramouny, "Environment, Activism, and Design: Emerging Practices in Lebanon," *World Architecture Magazine*, April issue #358 (Tsinghua University, 2020), 28-33.

5 Two distinctions referencing Michel de Certeau - Foreign Architects Switzerland FAS, "Oh Baby Let's Get Political, A Rant", in *Bracket Takes Action*, ed. Mason White and Neeraj Bhatia (Applied Research and Design Publishers, 2019).

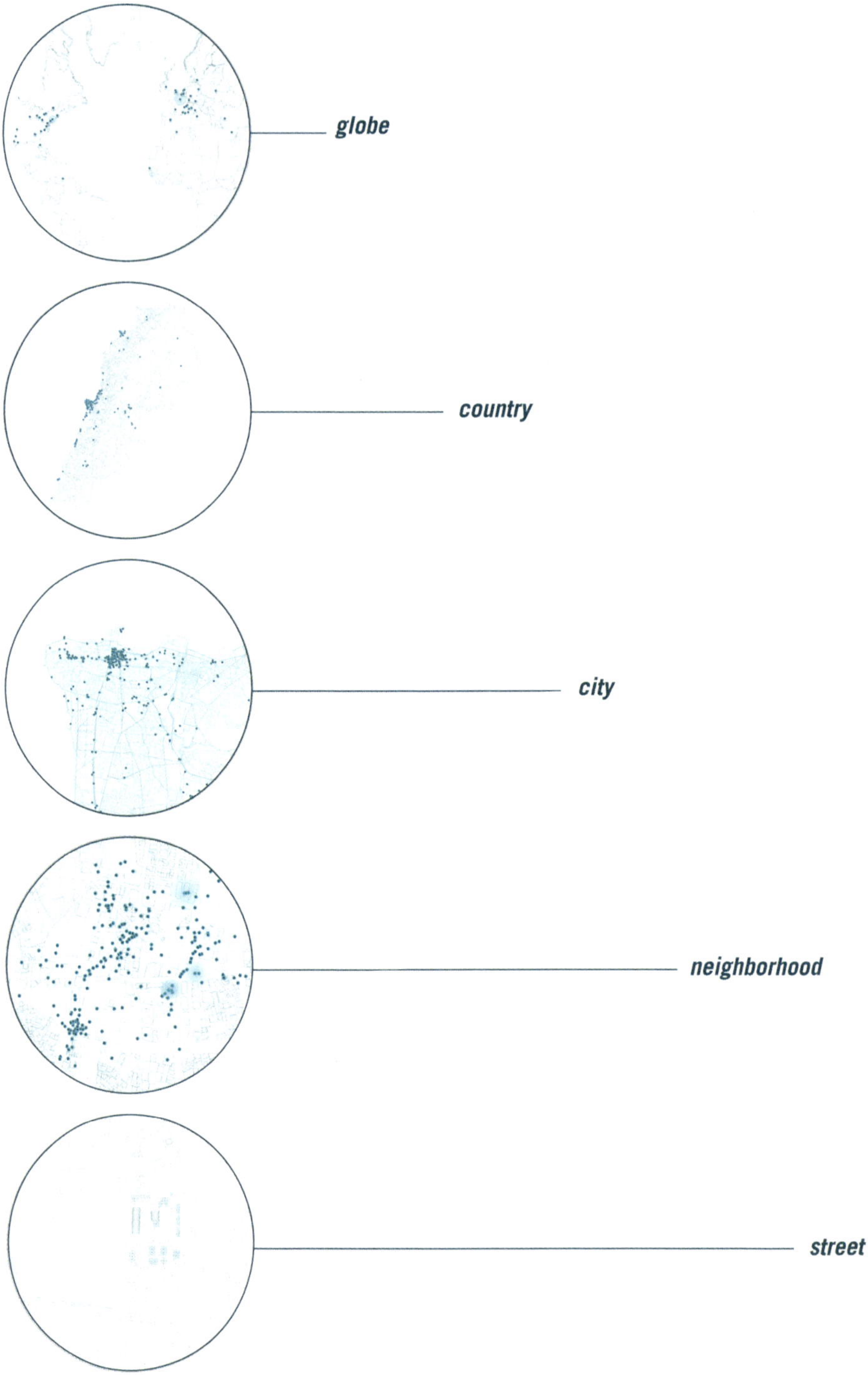

Figure 1

from streets to strategies

beirut's grassroots activism as a case study for participatory planning

joanne hayek

With its multi-layered socio-political history, Beirut has always been an epicentre of change. During the tumultuous events of 2019 and 2020, its urban grounds became dynamic canvases for grassroots activism.

On October 17th, 2019, the Lebanese Revolution, or Thawra,[1] was sparked as a response to proposed taxes, including a tax on WhatsApp calls. This was the tipping point for citizens already burdened by government corruption, economic struggles,[2] and inadequate public services. Lebanese from diverse backgrounds united in non-sectarian protests, demanding transparency and systemic change. The protests, marked by creative expression and community action, centered in Beirut's Martyrs' Square and spread across the country's public grounds, both physically and digitally. This uprising, rooted in previous civic movements and actions, triggered a new era of grassroots activism and hope for political reform.[3]

On August 4th, 2020, Beirut experienced a devastating explosion at its port caused by improperly stored ammonium nitrate, resulting in widespread destruction, loss of life, exacerbating the nation's existing crises.[4] In the aftermath, the Lebanese people united in grief and determination, swiftly mobilized to provide aid and clear rubble and commence the arduous reconstruction process, all while demanding accountability and the comprehensive reforms called for by the Thawra. The post-blast response highlighted once again the urgent need for change and the persistent spirit of grassroots activism in Lebanon.

Through analyzing these two waves of grassroots deployments, this essay endeavors to decode the transformative power of activism, particularly its influence on public grounds and the underlying mechanisms that propel such change. The retrospective mapping of the city's pulse, presented here, reveals a narrative of citizen engagement, self-organization, and bottom-up urban regeneration. While recounting the events that took place during this period, the essay explores the fluidity of urban grounds, emphasizing their evolving roles in societal discourse and their capacity to echo the collective voice of citizens.

Through the lens of Beirut's activism, the analysis uncovers how grassroots movements might inform and rejuvenate urban planning methodologies. It further posits how the dynamism of Beirut's recent experiences could inspire a new form of urban governance that harnesses the collective intelligence of all its actors—citizens, collectives, organizations, and institutions—to co-design the city's future.

Grounds of a revolution

Globally, public space has often been the scene of resistance, especially during times of socio-political upheaval. From the vibrant protests at Cairo's Tahrir Square to the Occupy Wall Street movements at New York's Zuccotti Park, the public ground became emblematic of citizen dissent and aspiration.[5] Beirut, during the Thawra, was no exception.[6] Key areas, such as Martyrs' Square, the Samir Kassir Garden, Downtown Beirut's parking lots, and the Egg, took on new meanings, evolving into dynamic centers of collective action.[7] These sites became focal points for grassroots events tackling various political, cultural, socioeconomic, and ecological concerns (Fig. 2).

The following section attempts to map the processes and acts behind Lebanon's revolution. Through five different scales of mapping—street, neighborhood, city, country, and globe (Fig. 1), the research composes a spatial and temporal narrative that retraces the momentum and hardship of grassroots efforts. The aim is to offer a macro reading of the bottom-up actions to understand the underlying mechanisms and triggers of the pro-activeness and responsiveness of the grassroots efforts and to question their potential to scale, ripple, and mature to long-term systemic change.

A political revolution – manifesting grounds

The Thawra was marked by dynamic political manifestation events, reflecting widespread public discontent. It featured a multitude of protests, strikes, sit-ins, and marches across Lebanon (Fig. 3) as citizens united to voice their frustrations against the existing political system, economic mismanagement, and corruption. The streets of major cities, such as Beirut, Saida, and Tripoli, witnessed large gatherings where people came together, often blocking major roads (Fig. 4) to demand systemic change. These gatherings were characterized by a spirit of solidarity and a demand for accountability and reform. Additionally, the Lebanese diaspora played a key role in organizing support protests in cities worldwide (Fig. 5), bringing international attention to the movement and further amplifying its impact and message.

1 The Lebanese people commonly refer to the October 17th Revolution as the 'Thawra', which translates in English as the 'Revolution'.

2 "Lebanon's October 2019 Protests Were not Just about the 'Whatsapp Tax,'" *Amnesty International*, October 29, 2021, https://www.amnesty.org/en/latest/news/2021/10/lebanons-october-2019-protests-werent-just-about-the-whatsapp-tax/.

3 Dania Koleilat Khatib, "October 17 (2019) Revolution in Lebanon: A Preliminary Analysis," *Perspectives on Development in the Middle East and North Africa (MENA) Region* (2022): 75–93.

4 Lama Fakih and Aya Majzoub, "'They killed us from the inside,'" *Human Rights Watch*, August 3, 2021, https://www.hrw.org/sites/default/files/media_2021/08 lebanon0821_web.pdf.

5 Manuel Castells, *Networks of Outrage and Hope: Social Movements in the Internet Age*, 2nd ed. (Polity Press, 2015).

6 Wael Sinno, "How People Reclaimed Public Spaces in Beirut during the 2019 Lebanese Uprising," *The Journal of Public Space*, no. Vol. 5 n. 1 (January 31, 2020): 193–218.

7 Tarek Fouani, "What Happened to the Public Spaces of the Arab World? From Colonization to Revolution: The Case of Lebanon," *The Journal of Public Space*, no. Vol. 6 n. 1 (April 30, 2021): 203–14

8 Tarek Fouani, "What Happened to the Public Spaces of the Arab World? From Colonisation to Revolution: The Case of Lebanon," *The Journal of Public Space*, no. Vol. 6 n. 1 (April 30, 2021): 203–14.

9 Karim Merhej and Elina Qureshi, "The Lebanese Uprising in the Digital Age" *CyberOrient* 14, no. 2 (January 2020): 85–98.

A cultural revolution – creative grounds

In addition to its political significance, this uprising also represented a collective cultural movement. Diverse cultural events were woven into the fabric of the protests (Fig. 6). Intellectual stimulation flourished through talks, conferences, and discussions, where participants debated solutions and shared ideas, often in impromptu meet-ups or organized forums held in public grounds such as the everyday open daily talks held at the Samir Kassir Garden[8] or the Lazarieh parking lot[9] (Fig. 7 and Fig. 8). Hackathons and brainstorming sessions emerged, harnessing the collective ingenuity of tech-savvy youth to tackle social issues. Open workshops on various themes provided platforms for skill-sharing and learning. The Thawra's vibrant artistic expression[10] transformed the streets into open-air galleries showcasing local talent. Movie screenings and performances offered entertainment and commentary on the unfolding events. Celebrations[11] and games instilled a sense of community and joy amidst the challenging times. At the same time, cultural tours[12] and hikes highlighted Lebanon's rich heritage, connecting participants to their history and landscape, expanding the action to rural areas.[13] These cultural manifestations played a vital role in sustaining the Thawra's momentum, fostering a sense of unity and purpose among the protesters.

A socioeconomic revolution – communal grounds

Beyond its political and cultural dimensions, the Thawra also had a profound socioeconomic and communal impact. Unity events were central, bringing together people from different social, religious, and economic backgrounds, symbolizing the collective aspiration for a better Lebanon.[14] Candlelight vigils and memorials held in honor of the citizens killed during the Thawra created poignant moments of solidarity.[15] Interfaith prayers, collective meditation sessions, and psychological support initiatives offered comfort, reinforcing a sense of communal support and resilience. Numerous donations were collected and distributed to those in need, reflecting the community's generosity. Additionally, establishing free food stations and communal kitchens[16] was a remarkable feature of the Thawra. Erected as temporary structures in the city, these kitchens became hubs of communal bonding, where volunteers cooked and shared meals (Fig. 9), strengthening the sense of unity and support among the protesters. These socioeconomic and communal activities were integral to the Thawra, demonstrating the movement's deep commitment to caring for the well-being of all participants.

10 Rebecca Anne Proctor, "Artists Take a Stand in Lebanon's Peaceful Uprising I Arab News," *Arab News*, November 18, 2019, https://www.arabnews.com/node/1585046/middle-east.

11 Timour Azhari, "Defiant Protesters Hold Rival Parade on Lebanon Independence Day," *Al Jazeera*, November 23, 2019, https://www.aljazeera.com/news/2019/11/23/defiant-protesters-hold-rival-parade-on-lebanon-independence-day.

12 "Tour of Ras Beirut's Ghost and Living Bookshops," Beirut.com, accessed July 25, 2024, https://www.beirut.com/en/directory/tour-of-ras-beiruts-ghost-and-living-bookshops.

13 One particular rural area that witnessed activism was the Bisri Valley through the Save Bisri Campaign.
Roland Nassour, "Environmental Contestation, Planning and Political Change: The Save Bisri Campaign in Lebanon," MUPP Thesis, American University of Beirut, 2020

14 Such as the Human Chain held on the 11th day of the revolution.
Al Jazeera, "Lebanon Protesters Form Nationwide Human Chain," *Al Jazeera*, October 27, 2019, https://www.aljazeera.com/news/2019/10/27/lebanon-protesters-form-human-chain-across-the-country.

15 Such as the candle-lighting events held in memory of Alaa Abou Fakher.
Tamara Kabboul, "A National Mourning across Lebanon for the Revolution Martyr Alaa Abou Fakher," *961*, November 13, 2019, https://www.the961.com/a-national-mourning-across-lebanon-for-the-revolution-martyr-alaa-abou-fakher/.

16 Such as Matbakh el Balad and the Regenerate Lebanon Kitchen.
Rebecca Holland, "Lentil Soup for the Soul: Inside Lebanon's Soup Kitchens," *The National*, December 22, 2019, https://www.thenationalnews.com/lifestyle/food/lentil-soup-for-the-soul-inside lebanon-s-soup-kitchens-1.954968.

Momentum

Pre-planned events

Political
- Protest
- Strike
- Sit-in
- Public Space
- March
- International Support

Cultural
- Conference / Discussion
- Meet Up
- Brainstorming / Workshop / Teaching
- Art Activity / Exhibition
- Movie Screening
- Dance / Performance
- Celebration / Games
- Cultural Tour / Hike

Socio-Economic
- Unity Event
- Candle Lighting
- Memorial
- Prayer
- Collective Meditation
- Free Yoga
- Psychological Support
- Donations / Free
- Free Food / Soup Kitchen

Ecological
- Planting Trees
- Clean-up
- Preservation

Computed based on the Daleel Tharwa calendar and complemented by compiled data from Liveuamap and Emerge Beirut.

Pulse of a Revolution

The first six months of Thawra

Hostility

Instances of violence

Instances of Violence
- ◇ Clashes
- ● Shooting
- ◆ Throwing
- O Arrest
- △ Tear Gas
- ▲ Fire
- ✕ Roadblock

Mentions of Victims
- ■ Killed
- □ Injured

Mentions of Armed Forces
- — Internal Security Forces
- / Police
- I Army

Computed based on crowdsourced data compiled by Liveuamap.com

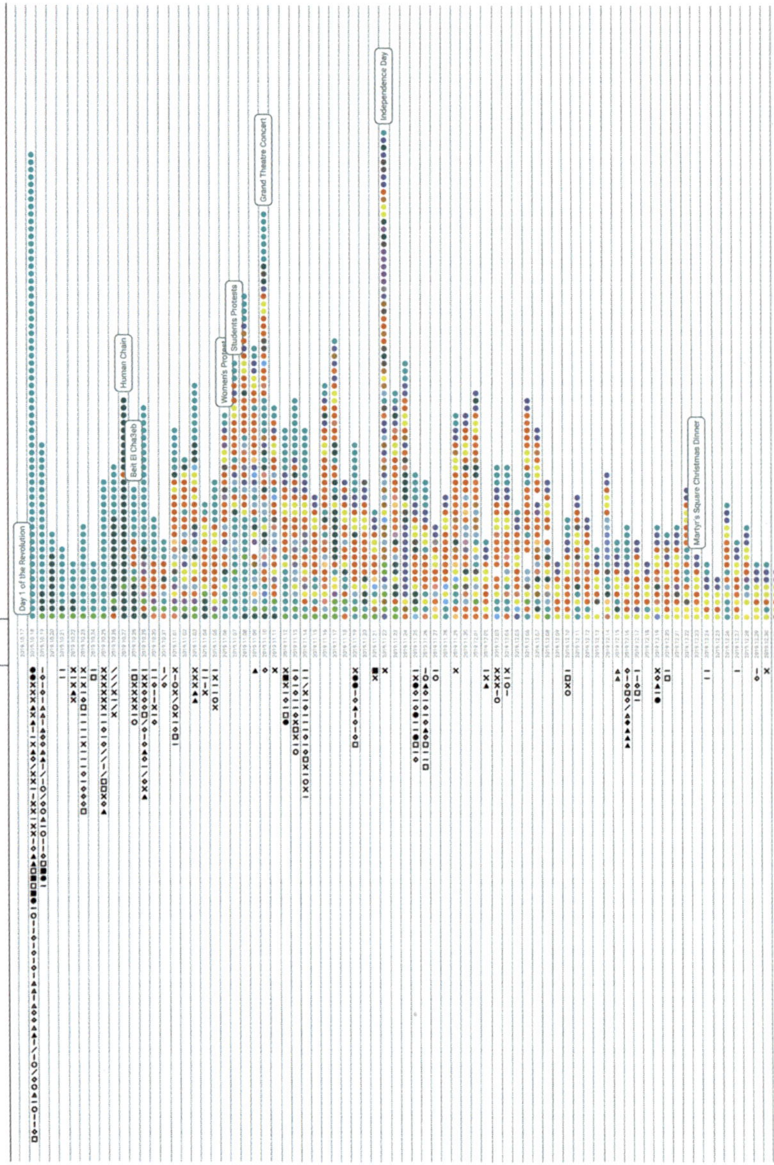

Figure 2

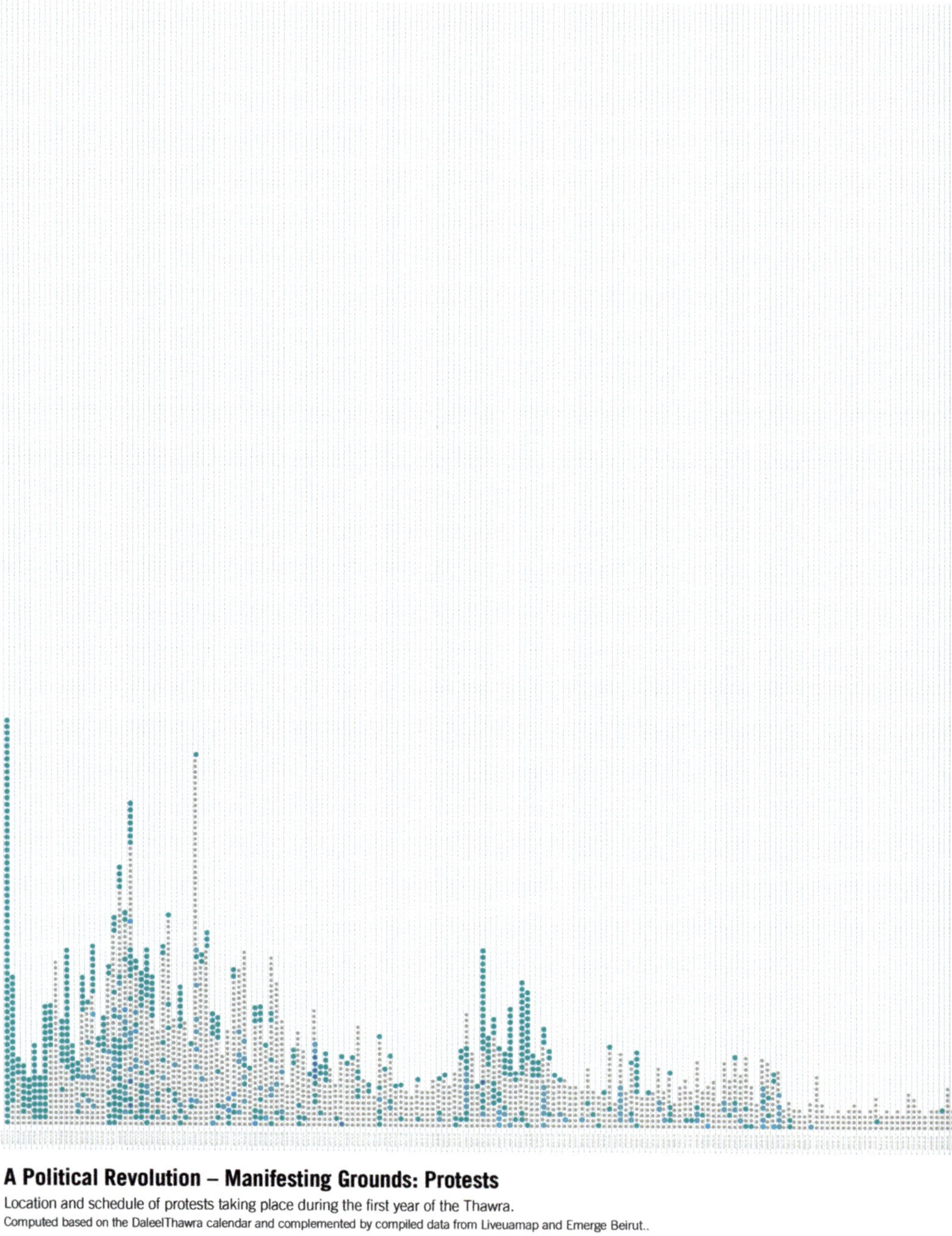

A Political Revolution – Manifesting Grounds: Protests

Location and schedule of protests taking place during the first year of the Thawra.

Computed based on the DaleelThawra calendar and complemented by compiled data from Liveuamap and Emerge Beirut..

● Protest ● Other event

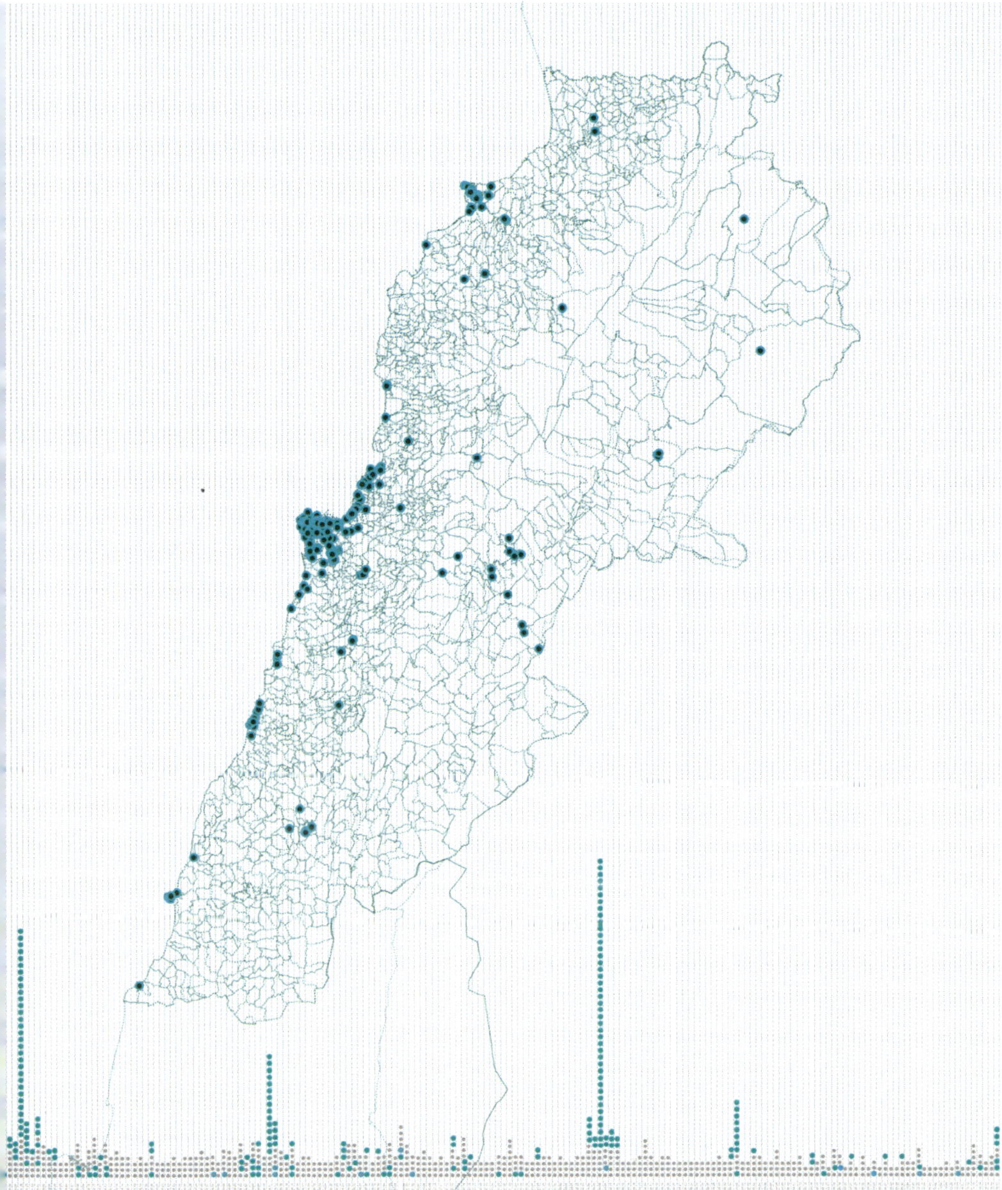

Figure 3

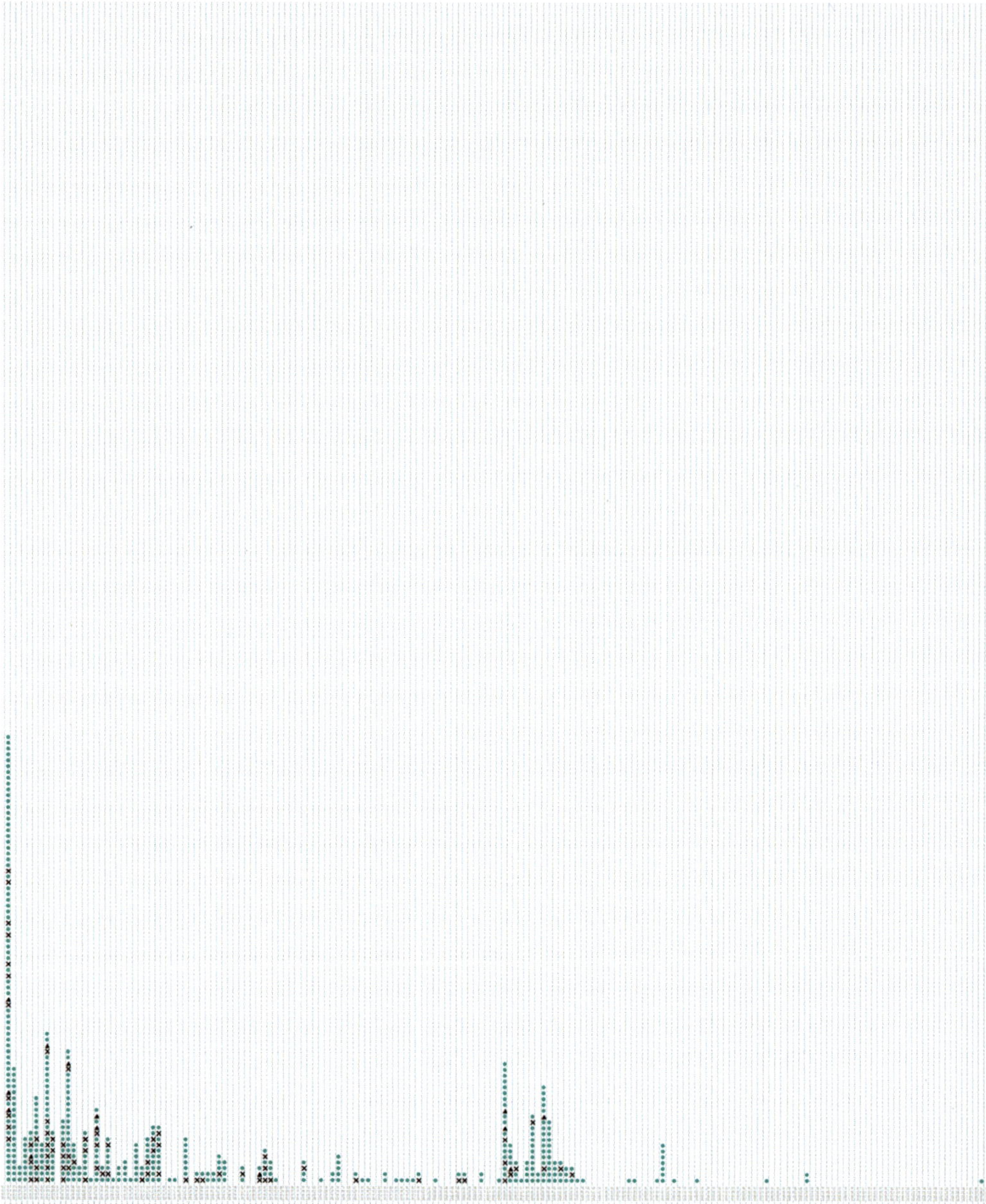

A Political Revolution – Manifesting Grounds: Roadblocks

Spatial and temporal mapping of the roadblocks along the first year of the Thawra

TIMELINE LEGEND

Record of events

- × Roadblocks
- ▲ Burning tires
- ● Protest

MAP LEGEND

Incidence of Roadblocks

- × Roadblocks
- ○ > 20 Roadblocks
- ◯ > 40 Roadblocks

Incidence of Protests

- ● > 20 Protests
- ● > 20 Roadblocks
- ● > 40 Roadblocks

Figure 4

A Political Revolution – Manifesting Grounds: Diaspora Support

Location and schedule of protests taking place during the first year of the Thawra

TIMELINE LEGEND

- Pre-planned International Protest
- Pre-planned Local Event

MAP LEGEND

- International Protest

Figure 5

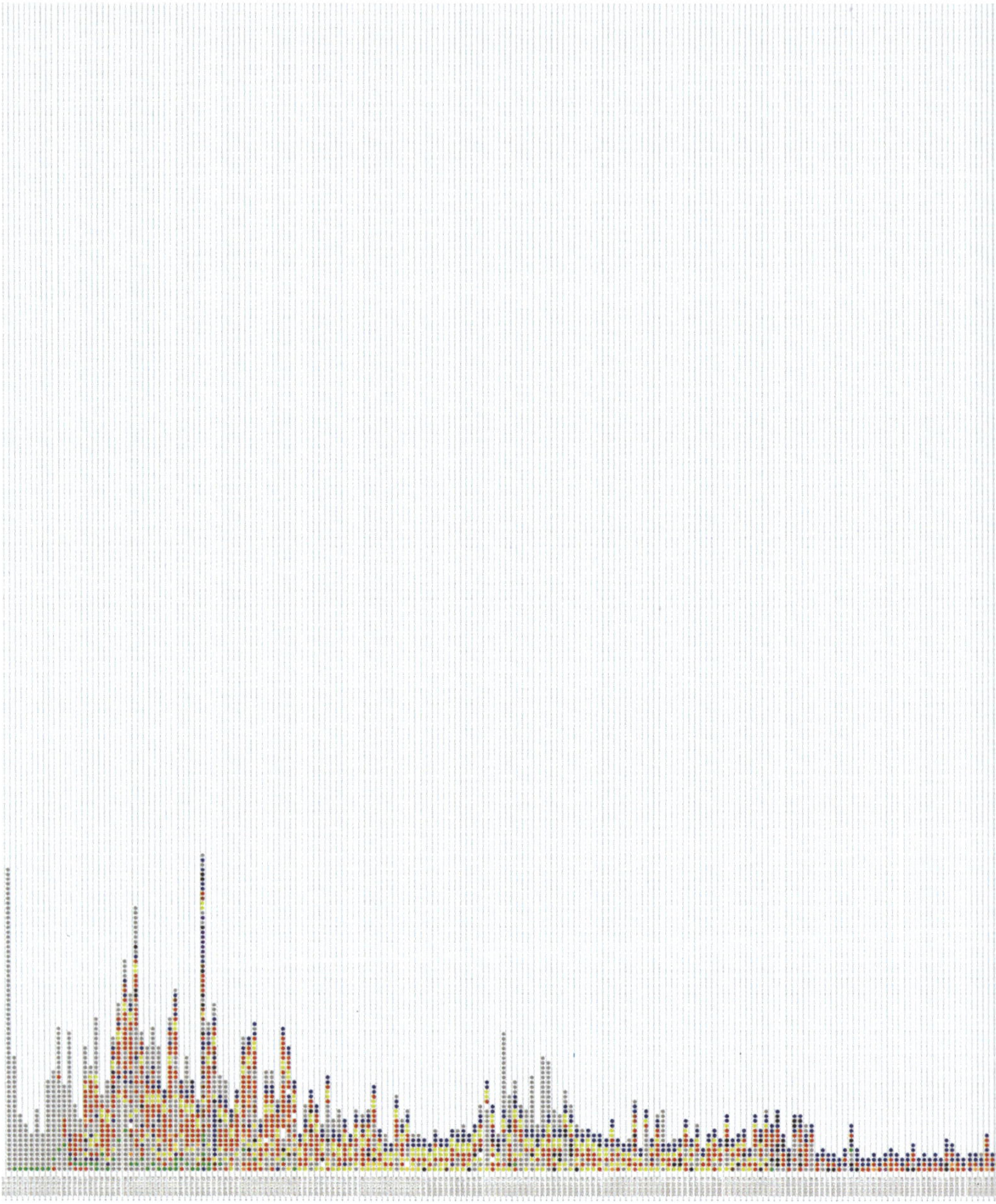

A Cross-sector Revolution – Productive Grounds

Location and schedule of ori-active events taking place during the first year of the Thawra.

Computed based on the DaleelThawra calendar and complemented by compiled data from Liveuamap and Emerge Beirut.

Cultural
- Conference / Discussion
- Meet Up
- Brainstorming / Hackathon
- Workshop / Teaching
- Art Activity / Exhibition
- Movie Screening
- Dance / Performance
- Celebration / Games
- Cultural Tour / Hike

Socio-Economic
- Unity Event
- Candle Lighting
- Memorial
- Prayer
- Collective Meditation
- Free Yoga
- Psychological Support
- Donations / Free Items
- Free Food / Soup Kitchen

Ecological
- Planting Trees
- Clean-up
- Preservation

Political
- Protests

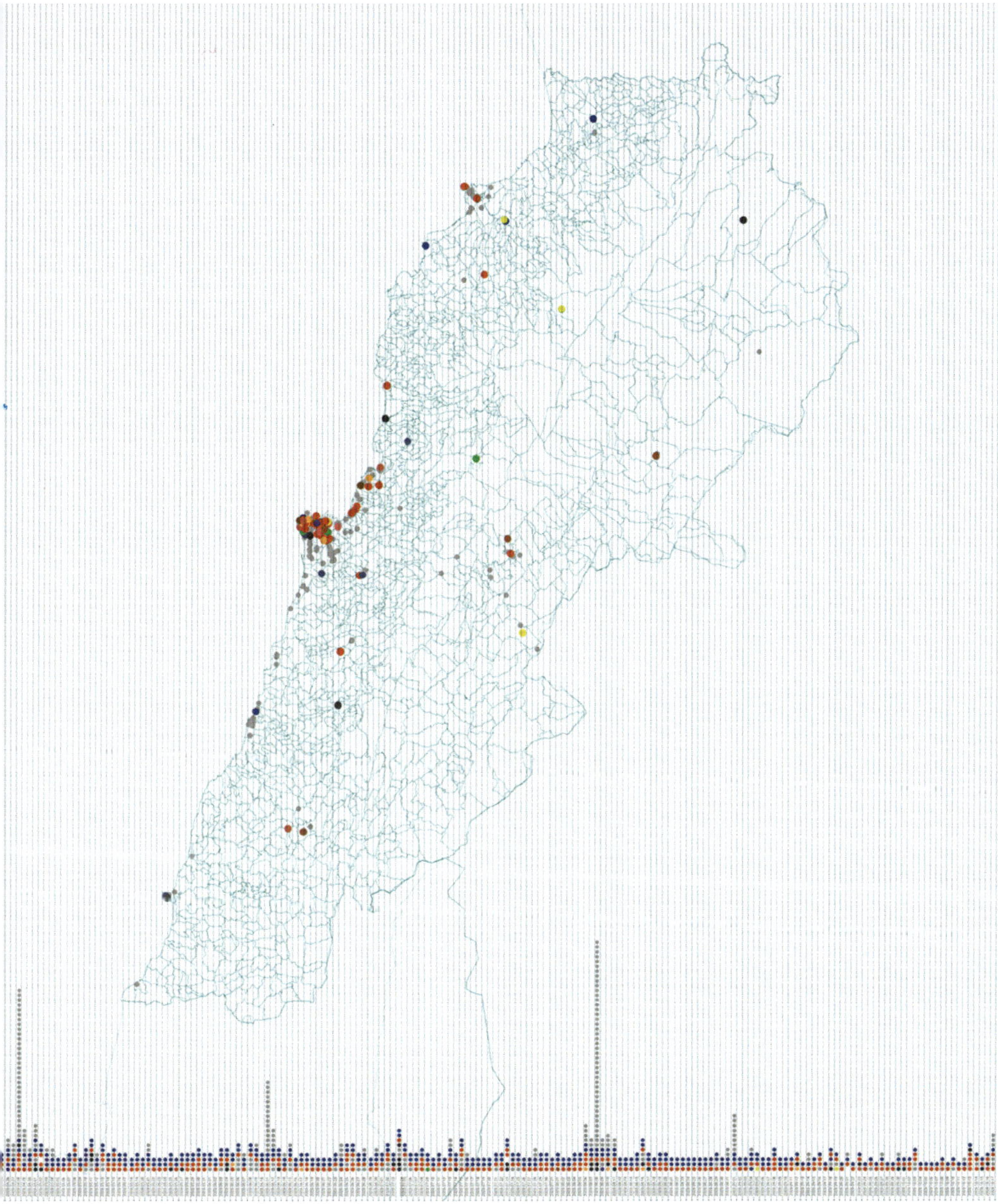

Figure 6

A Cross-sector Revolution – Productive Grounds

Location and type of productive actions taking place during the first year of the Thawra.

Computed based on the DaleelThawra calendar and complemented by compiled data from Liveuamap and Emerge Beirut.

Cultural
- Conference / Discussion
- Meet Up
- Brainstorming / Hackathon
- Workshop / Teaching
- Art Activity / Exhi
- Movie Screening
- Dance / Performa
- Celebration / Gan
- Cultural Tour / Hi

Socio-Economic
- Unity Event
- Candle Lighting
- Memorial
- Prayer
- Collective Medita
- Free Yoga
- Psychological Su
- Donations / Free
- Free Food / Soup

Ecological
- Planting Trees
- Clean-up
- Preservation

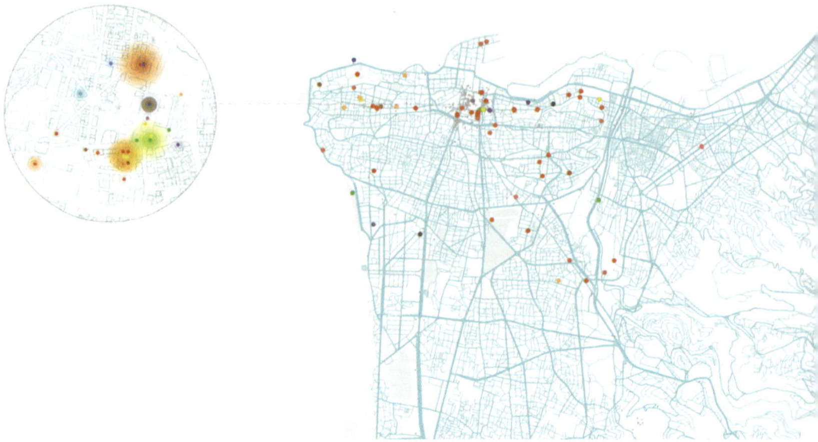

Figure 7

A Cultural Revolution – Creative Grounds

Appropriation of the Lazarieh parking lot by grassroots initiatives, NGOs, and political parties during the first months of the Thawra. The parking and its surrounding abandoned landmarks were transformed into public spaces of debate, policy making, and sharing.

Within the parking
- Political Debates
- Free Kitchen
- Donation Space
- Media Coverage
- Legal Advice
- Military Presence

Around the parking
- Reclamation of 'The Egg'
  Talks, Exhibitions, Conferences
- Reclamation of 'Le Grand Theatre'
  Concert, Sit-In, Art

Drawn approximately based on crowd-shared photographs of the events as well as mapping and research by Antoine Atallah and Dima ElAyash.

Figure 8

A SocioEconomic Revolution – Communal Grounds

Kitchen and Dinner

Free dinner initiative organized in Martyrs' Square on the 23rd of December 2019.

- Dinner Table
- Kitchen
- Dishes Cleaning
- Filtered Water Tanks
- Solar Panels
- Christmas Tree
- Revolution Fist

Drawn approximatively based on crowd-shared photographs of the event.

An Ecological Revolution – Regenerative Grounds

Makeshift waste sorting factory in Downtown Beirut. Day 8 of the clean-up operations led by Muwatin Lebnene - more than 1000 active citizens setting-up and operating a makeshift waste

Tents and zones

- Volunteers Dispatching
- Equipment Supply
- Donation Tents
- Food and Beverage
- Waste Sorting
- Pre-sorted Waste Storage
- Sorted Waste Storage
- Sorted Waste Pick-up Ares
- Logistics and Coordination

Drawn based on drone aerial footage taken on October 27 2019.

A Tactical Revolution – Reclaimed Grounds

Citizen-led transformation of the Independence Street, known as the 'Ring' bridge, into a public space. On October 28th 2019, citizens turned the street into a furnished open living room and free yoga center.

On the street

- Free Yoga Class
- Living Room Furniture

Drawn approximatively based on crowd-shared photographs of the events.

Figures 9, 10, 11 *(from top to bottom)*

An ecological revolution – regenerative grounds

The Thawra also had a significant ecological dimension, highlighting the environmental consciousness of the citizens. Cleanup drives were organized daily,[17] where participants not only cleared the streets of debris from the demonstrations and engaged in waste sorting activities, progressively transforming an open-air parking lot into a makeshift waste management facility (Fig. 10). In addition to collecting and segregating waste, this facility also functioned as a growing deployment center, rallying citizens to clean the streets of Beirut. The initiative, which rippled across the country with similar actions in other cities outside Beirut, such as Jal el Dib and Tripoli, was a testament to the power of collective action, turning an everyday parking space into a hub for environmental activism and community responsibility. It further underscored the idea that in times of crisis, urban spaces could be re-purposed,[18] with citizens taking the lead in driving sustainable change in their city.[19] Moreover, multiple tree-planting campaigns were organized, with citizens converting neglected sidewalks and urban lots into urban oases. These initiatives,[20] which contributed to ecological regeneration, also served as a form of tactical urbanism. Through guerrilla landscaping, these actions constitute an act of placemaking that highlights a core aspect of Beirut's activism: the aim of reclaiming and revitalizing public spaces.[21]

A tactical revolution – reclaimed grounds

The Thawra witnessed this act of reclamation through different forms of collective actions. Activists challenged the privatization of Zaitounay Bay's coastal zone into an upscale development with a public picnic on its piers. Protesters revitalized long-closed landmarks like Beirut's 'Egg' building and The Grand Theater. The 'Egg' was brought back to life[22] with debates, art exhibitions, and film screenings. At the same time, The Grand Theater hosted live concerts, including a cello performance on its sidewalks and a projected opera within its walls.[23] Through bold acts of tactical urbanism, such as hosting a yoga session on a major highway and converting a street into a living room (Fig.11), activists challenged traditional urban space perceptions.[24] Collectively, these interventions reveal a nuanced retake of Beirut's urban grounds; these grounds were not merely reclaimed but also re-envisioned. Each of these actions, rooted in grassroots activism, underscores a re-imagining of Beirut's urban spaces, serving as examples of how citizens can, even amidst adversity, reclaim,

17 Such as Muwatin Lebnene (Lebanese Citizen), a volunteer movement for cleaning and waste sorting in Beirut, which emerged during the Lebanese Thawra and expanded to include a wide range of civic and social activities.
Laura Mackenzie, "Lebanon Protest Cleaning Squads Bring a Lesson in Tidy Logistics," *WIRED Middle East*, October 24, 2019, https://wired.me/science/environment/lebanon-protests-cleaning-recycling/.

18 Carmela Mariano, Ignacio Gràvalos Lacambra, and Patrizia Di Monte, "Open Urban Space Regeneration Strategies Based on Urban Welfare: A Project and Experiment in the San Lorenzo District in Rome, Italy," *Sustainability* 14, no. 24 (December 9, 2022): 16487.

19 John Friedmann, Planning in the Public Domain (Princeton University Press, 1987).

20 Such as Beirut RiverLESS and GROBeirut.
- theOtherDada, "Afforestation," theOtherDada, accessed July 25, 2024, https://theotherdada.com/en/theotherforest/412/beiruts-riverless-forest.
- "Green Sanctuary: Grobeirut Creates Public Garden in the Heart of the City - Beirut Today," *Beirut Today - Independent, community-based news*, October 3, 2022, https://beirut-today.com/2020/12/02/green-sanctuary-grobeirut-creates-public-garden-in-the-heart-of-the-city/.

21 Aseel Naamani and Ruth Simpson, "Public Space as a Venue for Peacebuilding in Lebanon? The Role of Civic Movements in Reclaiming Public Space in Beirut and Tripoli," *The Journal of Public Space*, no. Vol. 6 n. 1 (April 30, 2021): 25–46.

22 Mona Fawaz and Isabela Serhan, "Urban Revolutions: Lebanon's October 2019 Uprising," International Journal of Urban and Regional Research (October 2020).

reshape, and rejuvenate their urban environments. In this sense, the public ground expands beyond its role as a collective platform to become the catalyst for change. These actions demonstrate how tactical urbanism initiatives, driven by community participation, can lead to significant and sustainable urban changes, inspiring long-term transformation in city planning and development.[25]

A connected revolution – resonating grounds

Digital platforms were indispensable in enabling this tactical planning and amplifying the action on the ground. Tools like WhatsApp, Twitter, Instagram, and Facebook became the digital scaffolds of the movement, facilitating swift information dissemination and coordination. WhatsApp groups, for instance, emerged among neighborhood communities or professional clusters, facilitating coordination about planned gatherings or critical alerts. New digital platforms and social media pages were created to act as guides, announcing and covering the daily planned events of the revolution.[26] The digital and physical realms were intertwined,[27] with networks ensuring real-time coordination, information dissemination, and resource allocation. This synchronized the ground's pulse and enabled the scaling and rippling of certain localized actions across cities and countries (Fig. 1 and 5). The confluence of activism and technology in Beirut had profound implications for the city's urban ground. As digital interventions intersected with physical spaces, they created dynamic layers of interaction, transforming how public spaces were experienced, used, and governed. The urban ground, once a static canvas, pulsed with digital imprints, adding depth to the urban narrative and inviting new forms of engagement. This multi-dimensional vision of Beirut was co-created, continually evolving, and resonant with its inhabitants' aspirations.

23 Maghie Ghali, "Abandoned Lebanese Theater resurrected by music with ghostly virtual concert," *Al Arabiya English*, December 2, 2020, https://english.alarabiya.net/features/2020/12/02/Lebanon-crisis-Abandoned-Lebanese-theater-resurrected-by-music.

24 Deen Sharp and May Farhat, "The October 2019 Uprising," Lebanon Unsettled, accessed July 25, 2024, https://lebanonunsettled.org/archive/the-october-2019-uprising.

25 Alessandro Cariello, Rossella Ferorelli, and Francesco Rotondo, "Tactical Urbanism in Italy: From Grassroots to Institutional Tool—Assessing Value of Public Space Experiments," *Sustainability* 13, no. 20 (October 18, 2021): 11482.

26 Such as Daleel Thawra and Akhbar el Saha.
Merhej and Qureshi, "The Lebanese Uprising in the Digital Age," 85-98

27 Resonating with Castells' concept of the Space of Autonomy as a hybrid of internet and urban space.
Castells, *Networks of Outrage and Hope: Social Movements in the Internet Age.*

A polarized revolution – charged grounds

While the urban ground resonated with the cadences of hope and morphed into arenas of democratic expression and collective action, it also witnessed episodes of violence and grief.[28] The positive charge was mirrored by a negative one: a polarization, simultaneous and at times consecutive, through which the urban grounds pulsated (Fig. 2), as a dance between bottom-up and top-down, resilience and repression, hope and despair. As this cyclical pattern of action-reaction unfolded, activism progressed from roadblocks to public space, from vandalism to waste management, from economic precarity to communal circular systems, and from protests to political parties.

What enabled this progression from individual street actions to coordinated cross-sector strategies? How can this inform future urban governance models?

Grounds of a recovery

The grassroots system of cross-sector action of the Thawra planted the seeds for the Post-Blast Recovery action that took form following the August 4 blast in Beirut. The following section investigates the inception, scaling, and replication of these self-organization mechanisms through two scales of actor-relational network mapping: the neighborhood scale, focusing on Mar Mikhael, heavily affected by the blast, and the city scale, offering a macro view of the action and the emergent network of planning actors. Borrowing from natural principles of emergence and group-forming networks theory,[29] the analysis offers insights into potential avenues for smarter and more inclusive urban governance systems. Such systems engage citizens in managing, designing, and planning their future cities by harnessing their collective intelligence.

A bottom-up recovery – self-organized grounds

In the wake of the Beirut blast, the city saw an immediate outpouring of citizen-led support. People spontaneously descended onto the streets, assisting victims, clearing debris, and offering aid (Fig. 12). This organic solidarity quickly gained structure as bases emerged in key areas.[30] At these hubs, volunteers coordinated tasks and established zones for first aid, debris collection, and food distribution. As days passed, these bases transformed from impromptu gathering points into more structured entities. Self-organizational hierarchies began forming

28 "Lebanon: Military Forces Must End Arbitrary Arrests and Torture of Protesters," Amnesty International, November 29, 2019, https://www.amnesty.org/en/latest/press-release/2019/11/lebanon-military-forces-must-end-arbitrary-arrests-and-torture-of-protesters/.

29 Hani Asfour, "Parallel Lines: The Meeting of Aesthetic and Network Theories in Post-Critical Design Practice," Academia.edu, March 7, 2015, https://www.academia.edu/8463735/Parallel_Lines_The_Meeting_of_Aesthetic_and_Network_Theories_in_Post_Critical_Design_Practice?auto=download.

30 Such as Basecamp and Nation Station - Caline Malek, "Lebanon's Basecamp Sets the Pace for Citizens' Initiatives in Fragile States I Arab News," *Arab News*, November 13, 2020, https://www.arabnews.com/node/1762641/middle-east. - Vivian Yee, "Desperate to Leave Beirut, Young Lebanese Are Also the Ones Fixing It," *The New York Times*, August 27, 2020, https://www.nytimes.com/2020/08/27/world/middleeast/beirut-explosion-volunteers.html.

with designated teams, creating ad hoc hierarchies and roles mirrored emergent systems in nature—where simple individual actions combine to form complex adaptive structures "by footprint, not fiat".[31] Similarly to the Thawra, activists appropriated public spaces to erect makeshift structures addressing pressing needs, such as temporary wood workshops in some alleyways of Mar Mikhael for rehabilitating windows and doors. Day by day, the grassroots response became more efficient and sophisticated, demonstrating how decentralized coordination can lead to a powerful collective impact.

A data-driven recovery – sensing grounds

In parallel with grassroots relief efforts, a systematic approach to data collection began, crucial for identifying pressing needs, setting priorities, coordinating volunteer dispatch,[32] and efficiently distributing resources. Digital platforms and tools became invaluable to facilitating crowd-mapping initiatives, enabling the collaborative documentation of the vast amount of information.[33] The rise of a dedicated community of mappers[34] highlighted the transformative power of digital collaboration in urban disaster response and recovery planning. Meanwhile, collaborative mappings[35] also contributed to updating the city's cadastral maps.[36] Specialized groups and collectives of architects and engineers surveyed the city's built fabric, mapping the level of damage to the architectural heritage and assessing the structural integrity of the buildings (Fig. 13, 14, 15). In parallel, the army surveyed the buildings one by one. It kept a record of the progression of the action on its collaborative mapping platform, allowing the relief actors to coordinate through the allocation of zones and ensuring that all areas were properly covered.[37]

A collaborative recovery – group-forming grounds

A detailed look at the Mar Mikhael area during the reconstruction phase highlights the diverse range of relief actors that contributed to the recovery efforts (Fig. 16). While a few of these actors were already involved in such work before the blast,[38] others assumed new roles during this phase to fill in the gaps,[39] and new groups emerged[40] in response to the extensive reconstruction needs following the blast.[41]

These various actors collaborated on the ground (Fig. 17). Buildings and zones were assigned coordinators to guarantee full coverage and avoid redundancy (Fig. 18, 19).

31 Steven Johnson's concept of "by footprint, not fiat" suggests that complex systems and intelligence emerge from the bottom-up interactions of individual elements rather than being directed by a top-down command or control. Steven Johnson, *Emergence: The Connected Lives of Ants, Brains, Cities, and Software* (Touchstone, 2002).

32 The platform The Volunteer Circle played an important role during the post-blast recovery effort through their Crisis Action Section. "The Volunteer Circle," The Volunteer Circle I Knowledge Portal on Volunteerism, accessed July 25, 2024, https://knowledge.unv.org/practices-and-experiences/the-volunteer-circle.

33 Joanne Hayek and Balsam Madi, "Learning from Post-Blast Beirut. Humanitarian Data-Driven Mapping and Co-Planning Efforts. Piloting an Agile Data-Visualization and Co-Planning Tool," *SSRN Electronic Journal* (2022), https://doi.org/10.2139/ssrn.4176603.

34 "Open Map Lebanon," Open Map Lebanon, accessed July 25, 2024, https://openmaplebanon.

35 Beirut Recovery Map - Rice University, accessed July 25, 2024, https://beirutrecovery.org/.

36 Beirut Urban Lab, "Critical Mapping of the Beirut Blast Damage Assessments and Repair Efforts," Beirut Urban Lab, accessed July 25, 2024, http://beiruturbanlab.com/en/Details/782.

37 Beirut Forward Emergency Room, accessed on April 15, 2021, http://www.beirutfer.com/.

38 Such as the March NGO.

39 Such as the NGO Beit el Baraka or groups like Baytna Baytak and Nusaned, which emerged out of the Revolution, adapted their role, and took on reconstruction.

Gioia Sawaya, "Bebeirut Architects Partners with Beb W Shebbek to Rebuild Homes after the Beirut Blast," *designboom*, September 24, 2020, https://www.designboom.com/architecture/bebeirut-architects-beb-w-shebbek-rebuild-homes-beirut-blast-09-24-2020/.

41 More than 77,000 apartments were damaged by the blast. Fakih and Majzoub, "They Killed Us from the Inside."

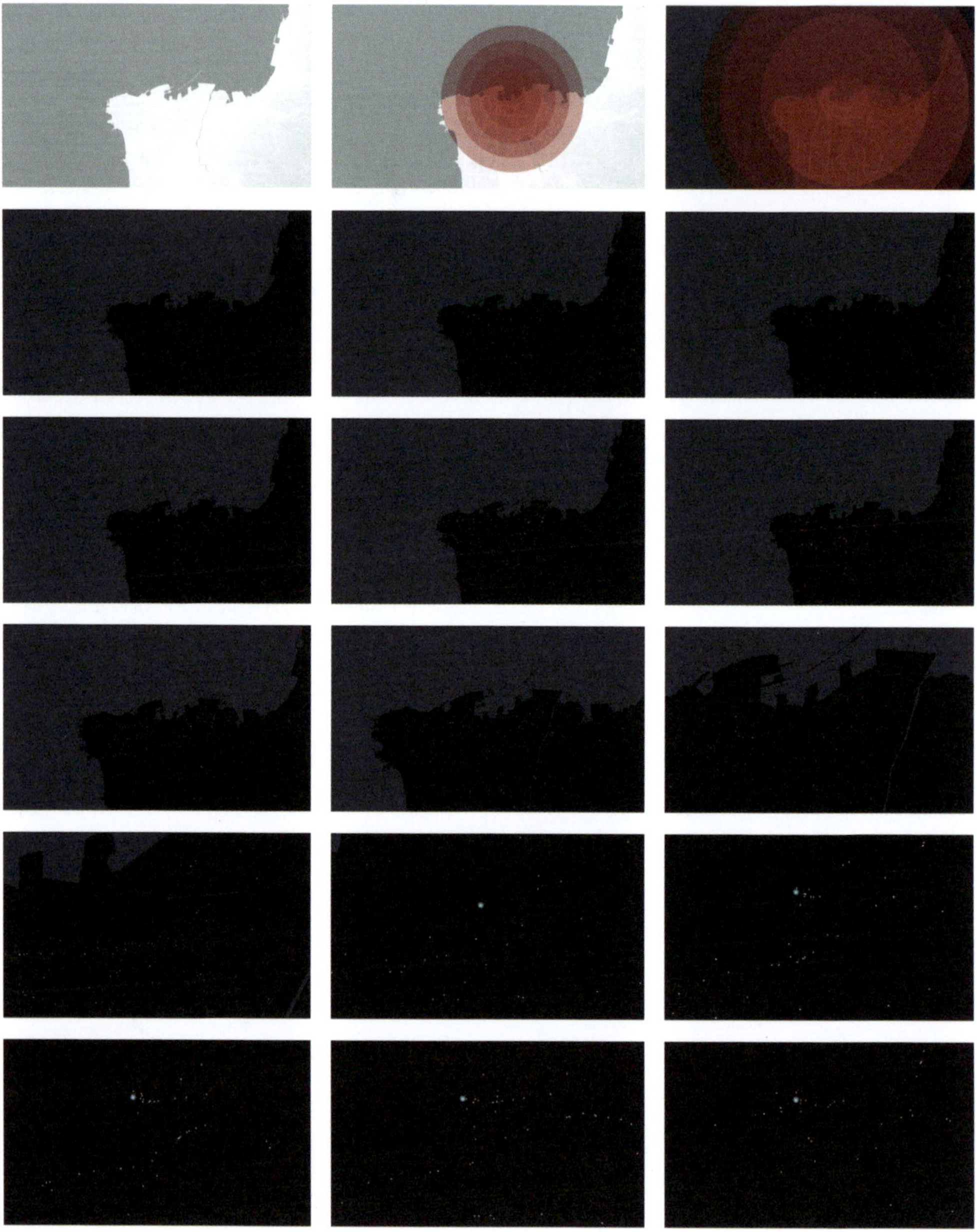

A Bottom-up Recovery – Self-organized Grounds

Retrospective geospatial mapping of citizen deployment at the wake of the blast.

Extracts from animated map of post-blast citizen deployment. Documenting the spontaneous citizen mobilization to help with post-blast ground relief.

Computed based on video footage and interviews with citizens

THE AFTERMATH

Victims' Routes
- Trying to access hospitals
- Fleeing Beirut
- Mobilizing to help

Emergency Units
- Hospitals
- Red Cross

THE DAY AFTER

Progressive Dispatchment
- Rescuing
- Cleaning
- Surveying

Self-organization Structures
- Ground Relief Base
  Basecamp Location #1

Figure 12

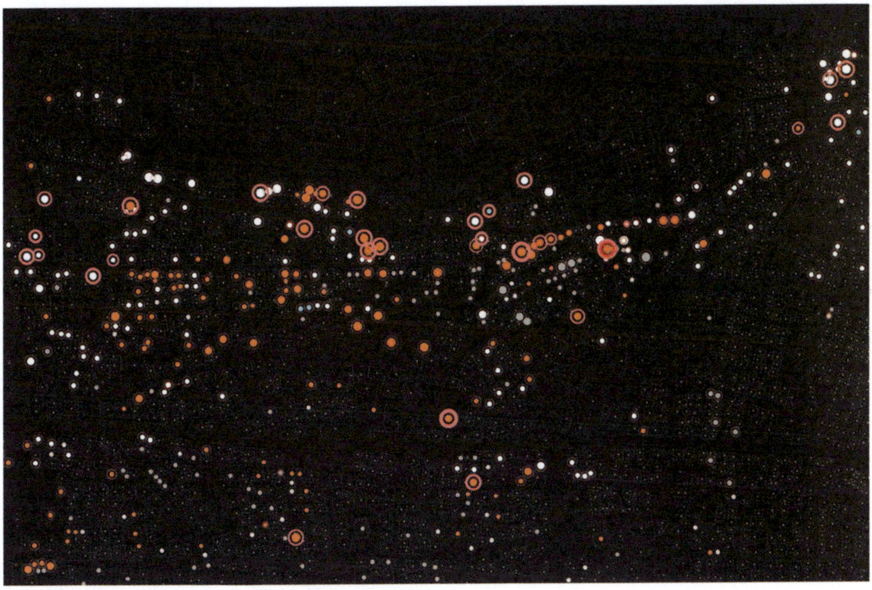

A Data-driven Recovery – Sensing Grounds

Collaborative Surveys of Damage on Architectural Heritage of the City

Computed based on data compiled by the Beirut Heritage Initiative (BHI) in November 2020, based on post-blast surveys of heritage buildings by the Beirut Built Heritage Rescue (BBHR), the Arab Center for Architecture (ACA), and BHI.

Construction Period
1860 - 1920
1920 - 1945
1945 - 1960
Undefined

Roof Status
Roof Collapsed
Partially Collapsed
In Bad Condition
Moderate Damage
In Good Condition

Surveyed Building Status
Building Collapsed
In Very Bad Condition
In Bad Condition
Moderate Damage
In Good Condition

Other Building Reference
Building Instance out of Survey Scope

Figure 13

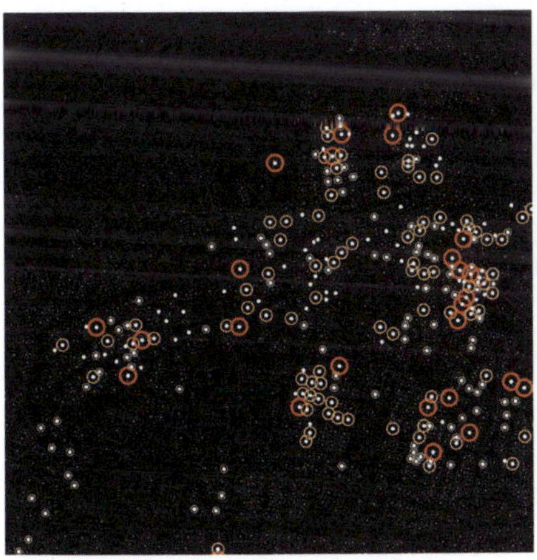

Collaborative Structural Surveys of Buildings

Computed based in surveys conducted by the RELIEF Centre and Catalytic Action as part of the research 'Assessing Vulnerabilities in Post Blast Beirut' funded by the UKRI Global Challenges Research Fund.

Structural Assessment
No longer structurally sound
Partially affected
Not affected

Survey Scope
Surveyed building
Other building reference

Figure 14

Collaborative Surveys of Architectural Heritage

Computed based on data compiled by the Beirut Heritage Initiative (BHI) in November 2020, based on post-blast surveys of heritage buildings by the Beirut Built Heritage Rescue (BBHR), the Arab Center for Architecture (ACA), and BHI.

Building Typologies
Central Hall
Vernacular
Composite
Gallery
Vault
Other/Undefined

Figure 15

A Collaborative Recovery – Group-Forming Grounds: Variety of Reconstruction Partners in each Building

- Each colored dot represents an action from an acting reconstruction partner: an NGO, an INGO, or a Grassroots Initiative. Each color refers to one of these partners.
- Hollow dots refer to buildings with no recorded action at the time of mapping.

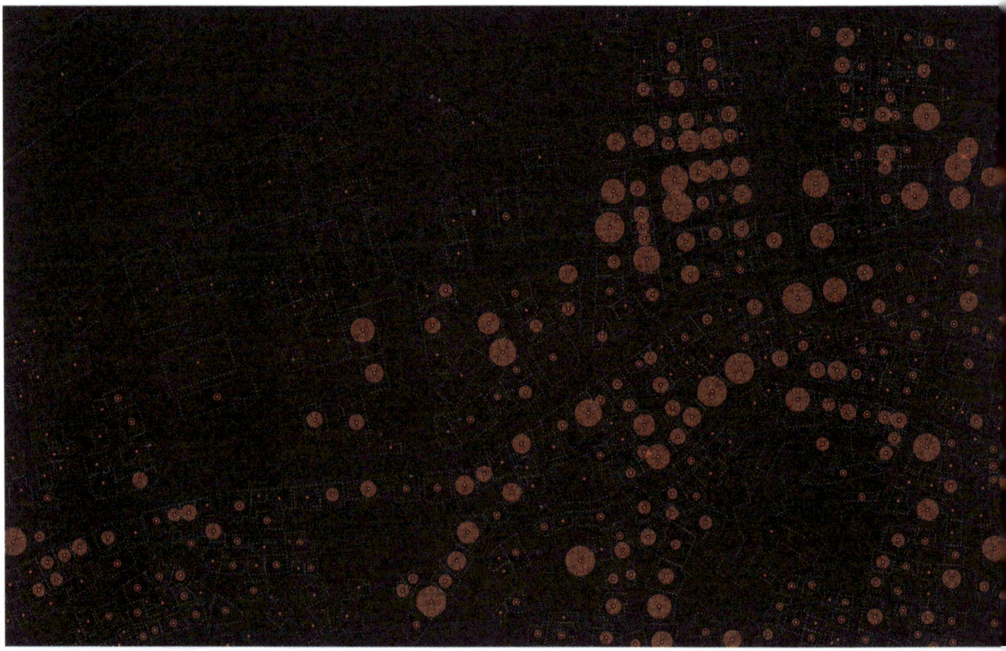

A Collaborative Recovery – Group-Forming Grounds: Multiplicity of Reconstruction Partners per Building

8 partners · 7 partners · 6 partners · 5 partners · 4 partners · 3 partners · 2 partners · 1 partner

Figure 16 *(top)* / Figure 17 *(bottom)*

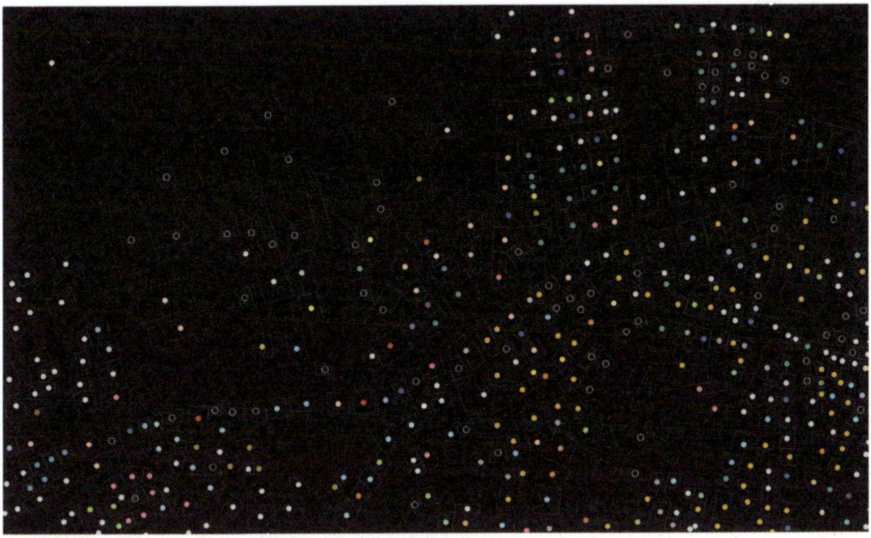

Coordination of Reconstruction in each Building

Computed based on data collected through BeirutFER and Emerge Beirut in April 2021.

- Each colored dot represents the reconstruction partner in charge of coordinating the action on that building
- Hollow dots refer to buildings with no recorded action at the time of mapping.

Figure 18

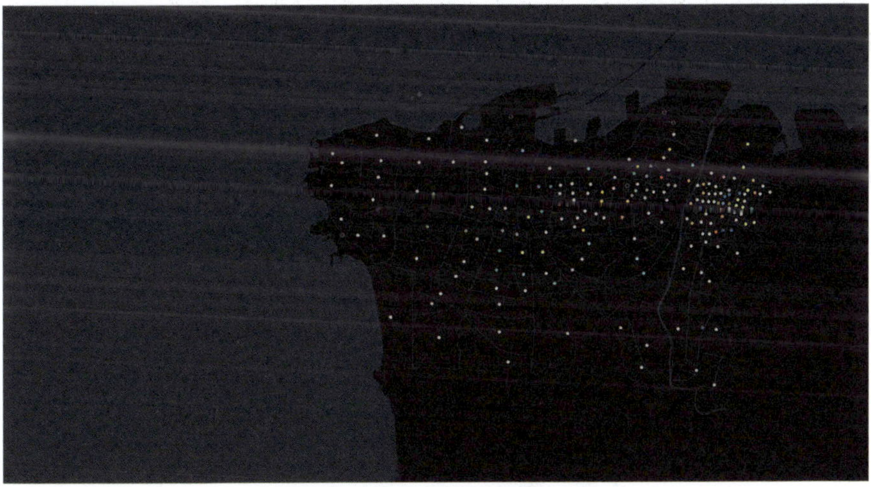

A Collaborative Recovery – Group-Forming Grounds: Coordination through Zones

Computed based on data collected through BeirutFER in March 2021.

- Each colored dot represents the reconstruction partner in charge of coordinating the action on that zone.
- Hollow dots refer to non-residential zones. White dots refer to zones with no specified coordinator.

Figure 19

A Long-term Recovery – Planning Grounds: Constellation of Emerging and Traditional Planning Actors

Headquarters of the institutions, associations and collectives involved in urban planning during post-blast Beirut. Computed based on data compiled by Emerge Beirut.

Traditional
Local Authority · Central Government

Emerging
Collective · Syndicates · Academia · Private Sector · UN Entity · International Entity

Relief Actors
NGO / INGO

Figure 20

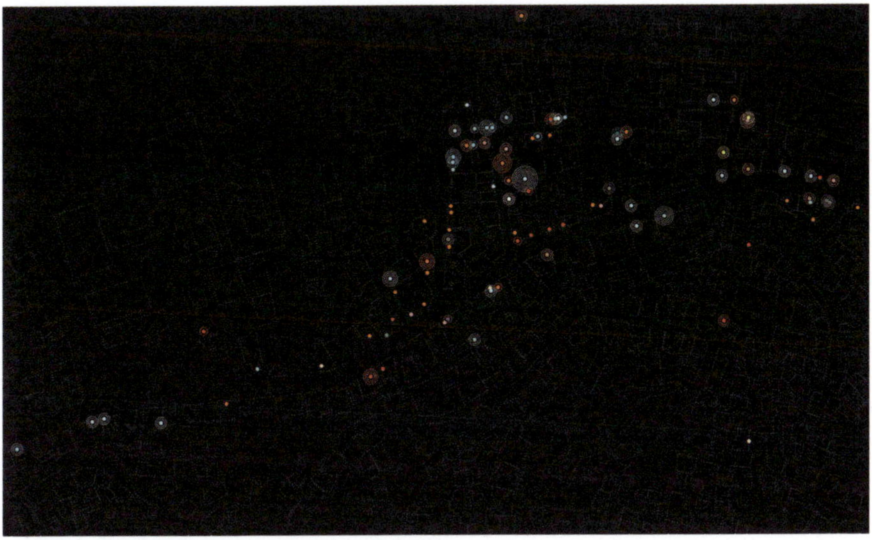

Support of Reconstruction of Commercial Units

Computed based on data collected in April 2021 from Emerge Beirut, AlFanar, Stand for Women, and Together LiBeirut.

Commerce Type

- Bar
- Restaurant
- Coffeeshop
- Butcher
- Bakery
- Market
- Mobility
- Shop
- Bookstore
- Designer Studio
- Gallery
- Flower Shop
- Beauty Care
- Fitness
- Laundry
- Guesthouse
- Administrative
- Pharmacy

Collaborative Support

Number of Partners
Each outer ring refers to one support partner

Figure 21

Focused Rehabilitation

Case Study of a Reconstruction Partners' Scope

Post-blast restauration of doors by Beb W' Shebbek.
Computed based on data shared by Beb W' Shebbek on April 9 2021.

Types of Doors

- Wooden Doors
- Aluminum Doors
- Steel Doors
- Iron Doors

Number of Doors Fixed

- 16 Doors
- 12 Doors
- 8 Doors
- 4 Doors

Figure 22

Progressive Rehabilitation

Case Study of a Reconstruction Partners' Scope

Mapping the progress of one of the actors of the post-blast reconstruction: Bayntna Baytak. Computed based on data shared by Beb W' Shebbek in March 2021.

- House Assessed
- House Measured
- Contract Signed
- Work in Progress
- Installed
- Completed

Figure 23

A Long-term Recovery – Planning Grounds: From Reactive to Proactive Responses

Mapping the collaborative planning process through an attempt to categorize the post-blast urban interventions. Computed based on data collected by Emerge Beirut in March 2021

Type of Response

- Community Center
- Neighborhood Community Project
- Community Kitchen
- Participatory Construction Workshop
- Debris Collection
- Park
- Public Stairs Activation
- Playground
- Farmers Market

Response Category

PROJECTS
Responses that remains at the level of a single reactive intervention (Sfeir, 2014).

PRACTICES
Non-orchestrated reactive responses under the umbrella of a communitarian interest to develop (Farah & Teller, 2012).

LOCAL PRO-ACTIVE SYSTEMIZATION
Responses are categorized sectorally and implemented according to urgency and available resources.

PRO-ACTIVE PLANNING
Responses involve designing a desired future and then inventing ways to create that future state. Not only is the future the preferred state, but the organization can actively control the outcome.

Response Timeframe

- Temporary / Short Term
- Permanent / Long Term

Figure 24

A Long-term Recovery – Planning Grounds: From Reactive to Proactive Responses

Mapping the collaborative planning process through an attempt to categorize the post-blast urban interventions. Computed based on data collected by Emerge Beirut in March 2021

Type of Response **Response Category** **Response Timeframe**

Figure 25

In some cases, such as the rehabilitation of businesses in the Mar Mikhael neighborhood,[42] the effort grouped various types of actors, each bringing a different aspect to the work (Fig. 21). The spread was quite organic, with some actors expanding across different neighborhoods of the city (Figs. 22 and 23). As more volunteer-driven groups formed, the collaborative network of actors became denser and more robust, resulting in a powerful force for urban renewal.[43]

A participatory eecovery – catalytic Grounds

Within the framework of activism and relief efforts, specialized groups have emerged, each honing in on niche areas of urban recovery. Organizations have focused on heritage preservation,[44] while others have been pivotal in coordinating fundraising[45] and relief efforts.[46] These groups have brought expertise, enthusiasm, and a progressive drive for urban change. The interdisciplinary nature of these coalitions has facilitated collaborations that intertwine the expertise of architects, urban planners, artists, environmentalists, and residents, ensuring that city projects are envisioned holistically. Through these collaborative efforts, grassroots initiatives have shifted from being reactive to proactive (Fig. 24 and 25). Immediate emergency responses have evolved into long-term urban visions for neighborhoods,[47] building clusters,[48] playgrounds,[49] and parks,[50] crafted through a bottom-up participatory approach.[51] These co-designed solutions, specifically tailored to address individual neighborhoods' unique challenges, histories, and aspirations, underscore the importance of a resident-centric approach to urban recovery and serve as catalysts for long-term sustainable development.

A long-term recovery – co-planning grounds

In conjunction with these localized efforts, some collectives have assumed the responsibility of assessing needs at the neighborhood scale[52] or at the city's scale,[53] to help strategize the response.[54] The confluence of localized and overarching efforts has given rise to a dynamic network of planning stakeholders (Fig. 20). This network included everyone from individual activists to large organizations, all deeply involved in urban recovery. Their strategic efforts demonstrated the potential for an adaptable, self-directed entity that evolves with the city's needs. This agile network could reshape traditional urban governance models,

42 Such as the initiatives conducted by Alfanar and Together li Beirut.

43 This phenomenon echoed Reed's law, which posits that the value of group-forming networks can scale exponentially with the number of participants.

44 Such as the Beirut Heritage Initiative.
Beirut Heritage Initiative, accessed July 25, 2024, https://beirutheritageinitiative.com/.

45 Such as Impact Lebanon.
Impact Lebanon - a fundraiser to provide disaster relief after the Beirut Port Explosion, accessed July 25, 2024, https://www.impactlebanon.org/fundraisers/1-we-re-raising-7-500-000-to-provide-disaster-relief-after-the-explosion-in-beirut.

46 Such as the Beirut Relief Coalition.
Impact Report - Beirut Relief Initiative https://ungcnlebanon.org/wp-content/uploads/2021/01/Impact-Report-Beirut-Relief-Initiative-1.pdf

47 Such as the Urban Recovery Strategy for Post-Blast Karantina. Beirut Urban Lab, accessed on July 23, 2024, https://beiruturbanlab.com/en/Details/889.

48 Such as the Gholam Heritage Cluster.
American University of Beirut, "Rehabilitation of the Gholam Heritage Cluster - Building 1137," accessed on July 23, 2024, https://www.aub.edu.lb/Neighborhood/Pages/Rehabilitation_Gholam_Heritage_Cluster_lot1137.aspx.

49 Such as the school playgrounds revived by the Let's Play Initiative.
"Let's Play - the Initiative Bringing Beirut's Playgrounds Back to Life," Lebanon Traveler, June 16, 2021, accessed on July 23, 2024, https://www.lebanontraveler.com/en/magazine/lets-play/.

50 Such as the Karantina Public Park.
Catalytic Action, "Karantina Park Rehabilitation," accessed on July 23, 2024, https://catalyticaction.org/karantina-park-rehabitilation/.

51 Howayda Al-Harithy and Batoul Yassine. "The Co-Production of a Shared Community Space in al-Khodor, Karantina, in the Aftermath of the Beirut Port Blast." Land 12, no. 7 (July 12, 2023): 1400, https://doi.org/10.3390/land12071400.

promoting a more inclusive and collaborative approach to planning.[55] Platforms that blend grassroots insights with structured urban planning engage all parties and leverage collective intelligence for holistic city development.[56] Such integration requires adaptive governance that evolves with real-time feedback, emphasizing inclusivity and ensuring every voice is heard in decision-making processes. Recognizing the city as a resilient network allows urban governance to respond swiftly to socio-political, economic, and natural challenges. Beirut's activism emphasizes the need to rethink urban planning, consolidating bottom-up grassroots knowledge with top-down formal governance and envisioning cities not just built but organically molded and nurtured by their people.

Conclusion

These recent activism events in Beirut underscore the impact of the urban ground on social and political dynamics and mark a turning point in urban consciousness. Once perceived as static backdrops, these urban spaces have emerged as dynamic arenas, adaptable and responsive to the needs of their inhabitants, and pivotal to the emergence and mobilization of activists. Though deeply rooted in its unique context, Beirut's journey offers lessons that transcend its borders. It stands as a powerful testament to the transformative potential of grassroots mobilization and the consequential shifts that can occur on public grounds, further augmented by leveraging technology. Moreover, Beirut's experiences emphasize the indispensable role of citizen participation in sculpting and reclaiming urban narratives.[57] As cities around the globe face urban challenges, Beirut serves as a case study highlighting the potential for sustainable, citizen-driven urban regeneration amidst adversity.

52 Elisabetta Pietrostefani, Joana Dabaj, Yara Sleiman, Mayssa Jallad, Sara Maassarani, and Efrosini Charalambous, "Assessing Vulnerabilities for Urban Recovery Solutions in Beirut Post-Explosion: The Case of Mar Mikhael Neighborhood," UCL Institute for Global Prosperity, February 10, 2022, accessed November 1, 2022, https://www.ucl.ac.uk/bartlett/igp/publications/2022/feb/assessing-vulnerabilities-urban-recovery-solutions-beirut-post-explosion.

53 Such as the needs assessment conducted by a team of consultants at Strategy&.
Beirut Explosion Impact Assessment - strategyand.pwc.com, accessed July 25, 2024, https://www.strategyand.pwc.com/m1/en/beirut-explosion/beirut-explosion-impact-assessment.pdf.

54 Such as the working "Beirut Explosion: Drafting a National Social Investment Strategy to Fund a Citizen-Centered Emergency Response."
"ZP: Beirut Explosion - Underfunded Needs Working Paper," ZP I Beirut Explosion - Underfunded needs working paper, accessed July 25, 2024, https://www.zovighianpartnership.com/beirut-explosion/drafting-a-national-social-investment-strategy.

55 Hayek and Madi, "Learning from Post-Blast Beirut."

56 Such as the platform Emerge Beirut, piloted during the post-blast recovery period.
Hayek and Balsam Madi, "Learning from Post-Blast Beirut."

57 'Cities have the capability of providing something for everybody, only because, and only when, they are created by everybody.'
Jane Jacobs, *The Death and Life of Great American Cities* (Vintage Books, 2016), 238.

Figure 1 - 1 Acte / 2 Pièces, Atelier de Recherche at ALBA Installation by Rana Haddad & Pierre Hage Boutros

PUBLIC ART AS ACTIVISM

editors in conversation with rana haddad (BePublic/ 200 Grs)

This conversation with Rana Haddad revolves around public art and the correlation between art activism and the public realm in Beirut. Through reflections on her work and details of public installations and performances that she conducted in the public sphere, we will discuss the mission of public art as an awareness medium that pushes citizens to resituate their eroding relationship to public space in their city. We will further look at its vital role as a provocateur and portrayer of transformative events on the ground, linking to issues of public engagement and dialogue

Carla Aramouny: We will start with the following question: How do you define the role of artwork, particularly public urban installations? Do you see it as an active provocateur?

Rana Haddad: Artwork, especially through public installations, functions on multiple levels. It acts both as an active provocateur and as a public instigator. My work, in particular, is driven by an urgent need emerging from the urban environment—a need for citizens, especially the younger generation, to reconnect with their city. When I returned to Lebanon in 1996 after completing my graduate studies in Architecture at the AA in London, I noticed that university students born in the 1980s had become estranged from Beirut. The aftermath of the Civil War had isolated them from the city, and the process of reconstruction, marked by a *tabula rasa* approach[1], had imposed a forced social amnesia. As a result, we were left without a tangible city center, as though the city had been erased. Consequently, these students felt a stronger affinity for cities like London or Paris, perceiving Beirut as an unappealing and unfamiliar space. This realization motivated me to engage in public installations, collaborating with students to re-engage with the city and address everyday concerns. Current socio-political events or neglected urban spaces often prompt my interventions. The installations at the Barakat Building or the Théâtre de Beyrouth, executed in collaboration with students from ALBA,[2] are prime examples.

Sandra Frem: Can you tell us more about the latter project?

RH: The installation at the Théâtre de Beyrouth was a critical engagement with the theatre's historical significance in Ain el Mraysseh[3]. I sought to use the project to raise awareness about the theatre's role during the Civil War, during which it served as a unique space for public discourse. It was one of the few venues where speakers could openly address socio-political issues in colloquial Arabic, making it a place of remembrance deeply rooted in the lived experiences of ordinary citizens. This partly explains why the government enforced its closure in 2000—an effort to erase its role as a space for debate and war remembrance. To this day, Lebanon's school history textbooks fail to acknowledge the Civil War, with the curriculum ending in 1975. This gap in education leaves us disconnected from our recent history. The theatre symbolized the social and political dynamics of the war era. On the theatre director's invitation, we selected an armchair from the theatre, positioned it prominently in the window, and began a deliberate process of cutting it in half at an excruciatingly slow pace. The installation was a provocative and highly visible artwork designed to engage the public. In conjunction with this, we distributed flyers narrating the theatre's history to passersby (Fig. 1). The installation attracted significant media attention, which helped extend the theatre's operations by 18 months.

SF: It seems you're positioning yourself as an artist engaged in acts of protest rather than reflection.

RH: Absolutely. Protest and activism manifest in various forms, often pushing individuals to confront their history and present,and to take a stance on the past and potential future. By raising awareness and informing the public, you inherently take a stand for them. In that sense, the work is fundamentally public. It is created both for and with the public.

CA: In what way, then, do you distinguish your work specifically from other forms of public installation art?

RH: A crucial element I've recognized in my work is the focus on storytelling. By weaving stories into the artwork,

1 Solidere, a private real-estate company tasked with the reconstruction and management of the Downtown Beirut area since 1994.

2 Academie Libanaise Des Beaux Arts (ALBA). Installation by Rana Haddad and Pierre Hage Boutros was developed under the Ateliers de Recherche with Gregory Buchakajian.

3 Coastal Neighborhoods in Ras Beirut.

4 Corniche Extended - part of Be Public Lab "Public Beirut", 2012 at AUB, with Sandra Richani & Carole Levesque. Students: Jalal Makarem. Farah Harake. Marianne Safi. Mustafa Chehab. Rami Saab (https://ranahaddadworks.com/public-beirut).

5 Radio Silence —part of the Be Public Lab "Silence", 2016 at AUB —with Joanne Hayek and the Sawt w Samt initiative. Students: Betina Abi Habib. Zeina Bekhaazi. Souha Boumatar. Mario El Khouri. Karen Madi (https://ranahaddadworks.com/silence).

6 As conceptualized by Marcel Duchamp.

I aim to make it more accessible to a wider audience and forge a deeper connection with people and their urban environment. The challenge lies in ensuring the work resonates with everyone, regardless of their background. My approach seeks to create a horizontal understanding, avoiding hierarchical interpretations so that the artwork can be grasped and appreciated across different levels of education and social class. It's no coincidence that our projects have found the most success in low-income areas, where people have engaged with and understood the artwork on a more profound level. Examples include the *Corniche extended* project[4] (Fig. 2), *Radio Silence*[5], and Karm el Zeitoun, among others.

SF: It's interesting how your work inherently and explicitly centers on the public. There was a time in Beirut's art scene when much of the artwork seemed to target only a select intellectual circle. However, your work stands in stark contrast to this. It creates a dynamic interaction between the public and art, transforming art from a sterile elitist pursuit into an active ground-level engagement.

RH: Absolutely. Challenging oneself to engage with the public means recognizing that art is not for the artist but for the people. The work must communicate its intended message to the public, both in terms of the narrative it conveys and the artist's position. So, if I take up the challenge of bringing my art to the streets, my primary concern is the public. If I fail to engage them, then I have failed in my role as an artist.

Figure 2 - 'Corniche Extended' installation on Beirut's corniche - part of BePublic Lab Public Beirut, 2012

SF: Are there other methods you use to further define your approach to engaging the city and its people?

RH: My studies abroad gave me the opportunity to reflect and develop an approach that is uniquely contextual to Beirut by seeking out spaces within the city that exist in the 'here and now' while employing the concept of the ready-made as a key tool of expression[6]. The ready-made, with its versatility in interpretation and scale, can be a building, an object, a pavement, etc. It's always something pre-existing that triggers an event, leading to the unfolding of its story. Another vital component of my work is the incorporation of playfulness and lightness, which are essential for fostering dialogue (Fig. 3). This is what differentiates art in public from art for the public. As an architect, I am trained to anticipate the needs of my client, and in my public work, the client is the public on the street. Their experience becomes my responsibility. I believe that incorporating a performative aspect into the work is crucial. As Michel de Certeau[7] suggests, everyday practices in urban spaces often involve creative and tactical engagements with the environment. By leveraging these spontaneous and inventive uses, my work aims to activate the street scene and engage the public in a dynamic dialogue.

CA: How does playfulness impact people's interaction with your installations and their understanding of public space in the city?

RH: Playfulness is integral to altering the conventional approach to urban space. Each installation is developed and implemented within a relatively brief timeframe, encompassing several phases of conceptualization, approval, and execution. Given the complexity and often rigorous nature of these processes, infusing an element of playfulness mitigates the potentially overwhelming aspects of the work. It allows the installation to transcend the mundanity of bureaucratic procedures, yielding a distinct outcome and perspective. This approach facilitates a deeper engagement with the work, allowing audiences to grasp the subtleties of the intended message. The use of the ready-made technique is particularly effective in this regard, as pre-existing objects carry inherent connotations that audiences can readily connect with.

For example, consider the seesaw project "Radio Silence"[8] (Fig. 4). The gate's lock served as a symbolic element representing privatization and segregation in Horsh Beirut[9]. The seesaw, positioned through the lock, directly references play, a concept readily understood by children. Unlike adults, who might be preoccupied with segregation or sectarianism, children engage with the seesaw purely as a plaything. This interaction effectively activated both sides of the divided park. In this manner, children acted as catalysts, indirectly prompting adults to reconsider their perceptions. Although the physical gate remained intact, the installation conceptually undermined its barrier.

Another example is the "Air Rights"[10] project (Fig. 5). We identified an enclosed green plot that was restricted due to its proximity to a local politician's residence. During our investigation into potential interventions, we encountered resistance from private security. who informed us of a 5-meter security buffer zone from the perimeter fence. An electric pole situated just outside this buffer zone presented an ideal location for our installation. The installation featured a chair and a motorized pulley system mounted on the pole, allowing visitors to sit and be elevated to experience the view of the green lot. However, the chair could only rise to the height of the fence when occupied, while it could ascend to the top of the 6-meter pole when unoccupied. This setup was a commentary on the restrictive practices governing public space in Beirut.

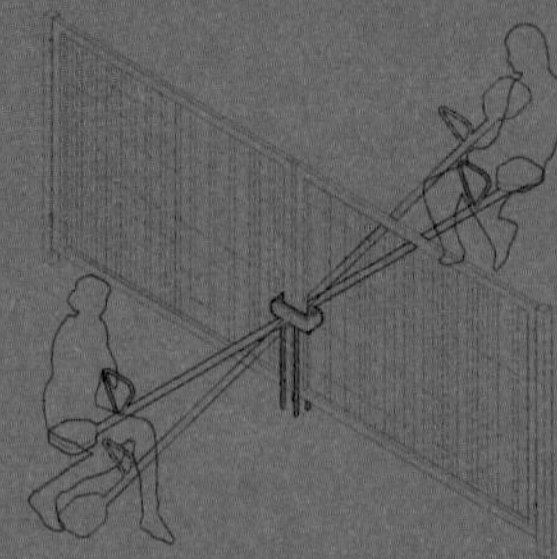

7 De Certeau, Michel, *The Practice of Everyday Life*, (University of California Press, 1984).
8 See the Radio Silence project in the previous note.
9 The Horsh Beirut Park is one of the largest remaining parks in Beirut. However, it remained closed for 25 years after its renovation in 1995. Sections of the park were additionally segregated between neighborhoods of different sectarian affiliations.
10 Air Rights - part of Be Public Lab "Public Beirut", 2012 at AUB with Sandra Richani & Carole Levesque. Students: Youssef Ibrahim. Jana Aridi. Loulwa Achkar.Thea Hallak. Micheline Nahra- https://ranahaddadworks.com/public-beirut

Figure 4 a & b - 'Radio Silence' installation of a seesaw on Horsh Beirut's gate—part of BePublic Lab, "Silence", 2016

Figure 5 a & b - 'Air rights' installation on a vertical electric pole - part of BePublic Lab 'Public Beirut', 2012

Figure 3 - 'In Contemplation' two chairs installation on St. Nicolas Stairs in Gemmayzeh neighborhood—part of AA Visiting School program

CA: Several of your projects were carried out through academic engagement with architecture students. What compelled you to delve into working with students?

RH: As I mentioned earlier, the indifference exhibited by the younger generation after the war, coupled with the over-privatization of the city and loss of public space, sparked my interest in working for the public while involving students in the process. At that time, Beirut had undergone a dramatic transformation, with much of its urban fabric and key landmarks erased, either due to the war's destruction or the post-war reconstruction strategy. The erasure and privatization were, at their core, government-led control mechanisms designed to fragment our diverse community. Public spaces, which could serve as sites for collective gathering and potential uprisings, were deliberately deprioritized in post-war development plans.

This shift solidified my focus on public space, which I later incorporated into academia through several initiatives[11]. The most recent is the teaching lab I established at AUB called BePublic. BePublic centers on the present moment, leveraging academic research and practice to raise awareness through the public sphere among both students and the wider public about the growing issues of over-privatization and the lack of common ground. The initiative also capitalizes on the spatial frameworks of architectural education and its inherent connection to the city and public space.

SF: A key issue you raise is that Beirut's ground evolved from a pre-war, more accessible state to a more privatized and militarized dimension, where capitalism and militarism joined forces to fragment our experience of the ground.

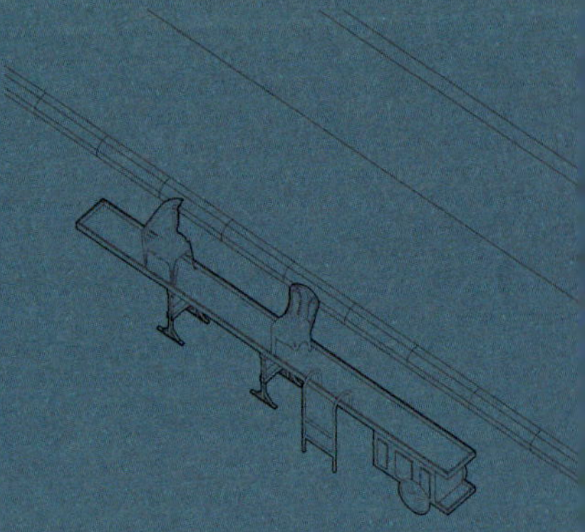

RH: Exactly, and as public spaces in the city became increasingly restricted, our installations adapted by becoming lighter, more transient, and more interactive. Some projects were as simple as sitting on a plastic chair in a parking zone and holding a paid parking ticket to prevent cars or valet parking staff from occupying the space. The lightness of this approach enabled the message to resonate more effectively. This was a particularly impactful installation, the Parking Ticket project[12] (Fig. 6), in which residents of the neighborhood joined in protesting the prioritization of cars over public use and the appropriation of parking spots by valet services. Coincidentally, these valet services often use a white plastic chair to reserve parking spaces, the same type of chair we employed. Through this simple act, we were able to temporarily empower locals to reclaim their space and challenge the disregard and exploitation of their public rights.

Figure 6 - 'Valet Parking' Project, part of come-and-play series as part of BePublic Lab 'Appropriate', 2018
Figure 7 a & b - 'Six Meter Cart' Installation also part of the come-and-play series as part of BePublic Lab 'Appropriate', 2018

CA: So, your work evolved in time, reflecting the city's evolution and its ground, from your early work to recent installations, becoming more interactive with direct provocation for public interaction.

RH: Yes, the evolution of my work has indeed shifted towards greater public interaction. However, this change was also influenced by economic constraints. After 2018, we adopted a lighter and more cost-effective approach due to a lack of funding. As a result, our work became more performative, often involving our bodies as part of the installation, alongside using lighter, simpler tools compared to the heavier structures we previously employed. This shift did not compromise the mission or the standards of our work. Instead, it provided an opportunity to rethink our methods and refine our approach.

We began incorporating locally sourced, re-purposed materials such as ladders, plastic chairs, and carts into our installations. This allowed us to significantly reduce costs while maintaining the work's integrity. Additionally, after each installation was completed, the materials were re-purposed and returned to the local community, further embedding the concept of recycling and giving back. Repurposing and integrating found materials became key elements of the process. Nothing is wasted; everything comes from the public and is returned to the public after the project is finished.

SF: Your work not only engages the public but also often raises political questions, sparking debates about citizens' rights to public space. Can you expand on this aspect of your installations?

RH: The Parking Ticket,[13] for example, not only prompted immediate public engagement because it tapped into a shared frustration, but it also sparked a conversation with the valet parking staff. When the valet attempted to remove us, we explained that we had paid for the parking space and thus had the right to remain there. The situation escalated to the point where he tried to physically remove us from the chairs. This interaction was an intentional aspect of the installation, designed to provoke a playful yet meaningful debate. As I mentioned earlier, lightness and humour are essential in defusing conflict, ensuring that the work doesn't become overly serious or confrontational. Without this element of humour, the installation would lose its impact and simply create tension.

CA: by making it humorous, you were actually compelling the valet to engage rather than resist.

RH: Exactly. Humour forced him to participate in the dialogue and recognize the purpose behind his actions.

11 including L'Atelier de Recherche at Alba, BePublic Lab at AUB.
12 Parking Ticket project part of the *come-and-play* series of interventions done in 2018 as part of the Be Public Lab 'Appropriate' at AUB (https://ranahaddadworks.com/appropriate) with Pascal Hachem. Students: Nicolas Abou Haidar, Soraya Hammoud, Nicol Yamin, Lina Akkaoui, Carl Yammine
13 Refer to the previous note on this project.

Through this exchange, we were able to articulate the citizens' right to public space. It became a form of activism, where the goal was not only to occupy the space but also to assert the legitimacy of that occupation through conversation.

Another example of this type of engagement is the six-meter-long cart installation,[14] which we set up during the same period and on the same street (Fig. 7 a & b). On the cart, we placed a small patch of grass with a disproportionately small parasol, too small to provide actual shade, along with a pool ladder. This absurd combination was meant to capture public attention and highlight the lack of green spaces and the increasing privatization of the coast in the city. We thought it would be amusing to offer people a brief respite from the chaos of the city, allowing them to sit, lie down, or read a book on this mobile patch of grass

Once the public understood the message behind the installation, they were eager to participate. One woman, in particular, stood out. She paid for the parking meter, affixed the ticket to the cart, sat down to read a book for 15 minutes, and even returned later in swimwear to underscore her support for the project. Her enthusiasm and willingness to engage with the installation were remarkable and highlighted the potential for public art to inspire collective action.

CA: So, your work evolved from being interactive to more performative and temporal. Is temporality essential to your work's objective?

RH: Yes, the temporality of our projects is indeed critical. None of our installations are designed to last beyond a month. The concept of disappearance is integral to the work. This ephemerality became even more pronounced in my recent projects, particularly following the compounded crises Beirut has faced since 2019.[15] For instance, my intervention in *It's All in the Streets* for the Venice Biennale project, *Beirut Shifting Grounds,* reflects this approach**?**

The project comprised a series of public installations presented through video, reacting to the ongoing events in Beirut at the time of the 2021 Biennale. Four short films—*Pause, Interruption, Grassroots, and Desintegration*—were accessible via a QR code on each visitor's mobile phone, offering a private, immersive experience of Beirut's street life during the city's crises. These videos served as commentary on three central themes: privatization, revolution, and post-blast grief. They aimed to highlight the significance of human-scale interactions in the urban environment and the potential of public interventions to engage and challenge the populace.

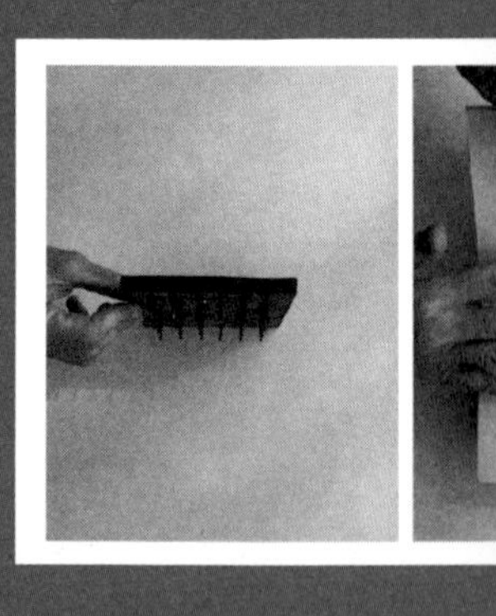

Figure 8a - 'Desintegration' installation on display

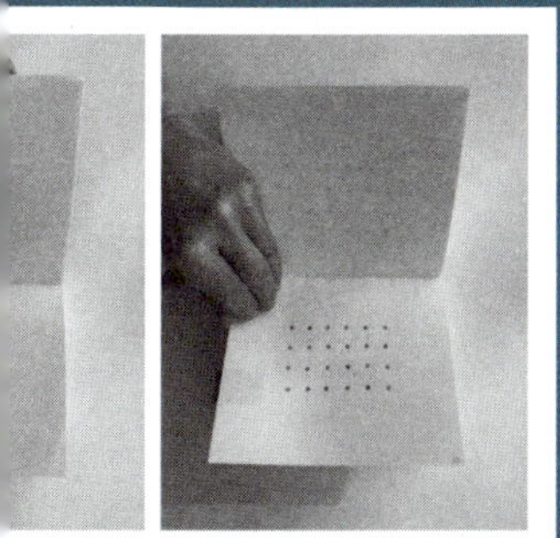

Figure 8b - Still shots showing 'The Making of Desintegration' video

Pause and *Interruption* urged viewers to recognize the extent of privatization in Beirut's public spaces and reclaim their right to the city. *Grassroots* reflected on the informal practices that arose during the Thawra revolution, showcasing the spontaneous actions of people reclaiming the streets. Lastly, *Disintegration* addressed the profound human suffering and loss resulting from the Beirut Port explosion. These digital installations, rooted in street-level experiences, positioned every citizen as author and participant, underscoring the collective nature of the urban experience.

SF: As a follow-up on that transformative period of crises, and beyond the context of the Biennale, how did your art and approach evolve to continue engaging with the public?

RH: During the pandemic, our access to the street and public spaces was severely restricted, making it imperative to transition into the digital realm. Our work is always grounded in the "here and now," so when the pandemic trapped us in lockdown, we had to adapt. It was essential to find a way for our voices to be heard, both in my practice and teaching. I encouraged students to engage the public through online platforms such as Instagram and projects like *Exist, Exit, Act* to tell their stories digitally, reflecting on the crises of the era. Remarkably, two projects from *Exist, Exit, Act* went on to win prestigious awards. For our first online engagement, this recognition was highly rewarding for BePublic and all the students involved. It affirmed the value of the digital approach and the work we put into transitioning public interventions to a virtual format..

Unfortunately, the explosion at the Beirut Port occurred around the same time, erasing vast parts of the city. Intervention on the ground became futile, as the city's people and streets—our usual points of engagement—were devastated. Beirut lost a third of itself in 38 seconds, displacing 3,000 people.

This experience led me to create the project *Desintegration* and *the Making of Desintegration*, for the Biennale[16], and *Debris of Text and Eyeglasses*, initially exhibited in Dresden and later at La Galerie De la Cité Internationale des Arts in Paris. Desintegration (Fig. 9a & b) acknowledged the void and the scar inflicted on Beirut by the blast. It represented the 38 seconds of the explosion, marked through a sketchbook imprinted by 120 nails embedded on a wooden plate. The work evokes the profound sense of loss and absurdity that followed the blast.

I further explored this post-blast trauma with *Debris of Text and Eyeglasses* (Fig. 9), a collaboration with Pascal Hachem.

A version of this work has been acquired by the British Museum. In this project, we exclusively collected abandoned eyeglasses, one of the most fragile yet indispensable everyday objects, which we found scattered throughout the most affected areas. Each pair of eyeglasses carried its own story. We meticulously recorded the location, time, and description of the site, imagining the lives and stories of the potential owners. This collection represents a shattered, everyday practice, embodying the profound impact of the explosion on the city's fabric.

Although it took us time to process these findings, we felt it was necessary to make this work public, despite its difficulty, to ensure that it serves as a lasting reminder of August 4th—a date that must not be forgotten.

CA: It has been an engaging conversation, Rana, to learn more about your work's trajectory and evolution, as well as the nuances with which it addresses the public. It doesn't shy away from being political or dealing with the city's everyday issues. It presents itself actively on the ground through often practical and recognized objects, from the cart to the seesaw, while always being humorous, witty, and intentionally provoking public debate.

14 Cart Installation is also part of the come-and-play series done in 2018 as part of the Be Public studio 'Appropriate' at AUB (https://ranahaddadworks.com/appropriate) with Pascal Hachem. Students: Nicolas Abou Haidar, Soraya Hammoud, Nicol Yamin, Lina Akkaoui, and Carl Yammine.

15 Namely, the 2019 Thawra revolution, the severe economic crash that ensued, the COVID-19 pandemic, and the 2020 August blast. The period's implication on the city, ground, and public life was profound.

16 The Desintegration project was presented at the Galerie de la Cité Internationale des Arts de Paris in 2023, and the Making of Disintegration video was previously presented as part of the Beirut Shifting Grounds project in 2021. https://ranahaddadworks.com/ardesintegration

Figure 9 - 'Debris of Texts and Eyeglasses' installation in collaboration with Pascal Hachem

epilog

the ground as mediator of disruptions and transitions

mona harb

This edited volume shows how Beirut's grounds have been incessantly "shifting" throughout decades of urbanization, modernization, and violent disruptions—brought by wars, crises, and disasters, as well as financialization forces, urban and infrastructural planning, and dysfunctional urban governance. Its co-editors underscore how these shifting grounds also carry what they refer to as "capacities at *transition*" or elements that enable the appropriation and, sometimes, commoning into collective city-making processes.

The ground's dual capacities at disruptions *and* transitions are poignantly revealed as I write this epilog in mid-October 2024, a year into the ongoing genocide in Gaza and the ethnic cleansing of the West Bank, and while Israel is pounding Lebanon's grounds with bunker-buster bombs, killing over 2,000 civilians, injuring over 10,000 and displacing over a million people. As these bombs are breaking open the grounds of Dahiya's neighborhoods, South Lebanon's and Bekaa's towns, swallowing living beings, buildings, and landscapes and exposing the earth's insides, dystopic "shifting grounds" are unfolding before the eyes of the world, threatening of a regional war and foreclosing future collective assembly processes.

However, in Beirut and the other cities and towns of Lebanon that are relatively spared the vicious Israeli war, solidarity and nonprofit initiatives hosting and sheltering the displaced are numerous: a stubborn testimony to the extraordinary "capacities at transition" of Lebanese people who transform dystopic grounds into commoning ones, yet again. Moreover, it is a testimony to how violent disruptions always yield paradoxical outcomes on which people dwell, work, and live; amidst the anguish and aches of rupture and loss, possibilities of being, caring, making, and recovering are collectively crafted.

As this volume argues, Beirut is a city whose grounds have been shifting incessantly throughout its dense urban history, shaping various materialities that may appear stable or permanent. However, because of—or thanks to—the dynamism of these shifts, the volume demonstrates how grounds also transform and enable transitions within stagnant urban lives, practices, and experiences. The Introduction compellingly rewrites the city's urban history through the lens of ground transformations. Readers re-discover how the city's grounds got shaped, un-shaped, and re-shaped through Ottoman reforms, French modernization policies, and Lebanese market-led urban development, up to the civil war's militias' barricades and the post-war's financialized and unequal spatial production, abruptly halted by the 2019 financial collapse. The co-editors focus on the subsequent timeline of interlocking disruptions in/of the city's grounds: the financial collapse combined with nation-wide uprisings, the political-economic crisis, the demographic and societal upheaval, the pandemic, and the Port Blast of August 2020 (Fig. 1). They do so with the scrutinizing eyes of those who have discerned the ambivalence and "duplicity of the ground between the destructive development paths and the bottom-up spatial practices that can hold lessons for inclusive planning and co-production of space" (Introduction).

The book goes on a journey over four sections whereby readers discover, through narratives, timelines, maps, and visuals, how the grounds of Beirut have been appropriated, commoned, produced, and activated, across multiple times, spaces, and scales. They learn that appropriations in Beirut operate through "assemblages" that combine urban, aesthetic, cultural, ecological, pious, and legal artifacts (Frem, Al-Akl, Chaaya). They understand how commoning is a "means to reclaim urban space through collective coming together and shared practices," be it through public spaces, such as Martyrs' Square (Aramouny), data and cultural commons (El-Dahdah and Jabr), or memorialization practices (Aramouny and Achkar). The book also informs on how the ground is shaped by local architecture typologies, building construction laws, and practices (rather than through urban planning), foregrounding how plots, streets, private-public hierarchies, porosities, and aesthetics, are key determinants of urban lives and experiences (Douaihy, Frem), and highlighting the potential of some clusters to become "laboratories for the development of a different urbanity" (Fayad). Additionally, it advocates for design activism that mobilizes and reclaims the ground for social justice, through participatory design methods, design-build projects, and public art (Hayek, Haddad).

I want to add a final note on the book's theorization of the grounds as transformative "conveyors of urban lives," which I find closely relatable to Latour's Actor-Network Theory. ANT conceptualizes socio-spatial realities as assemblages connecting human and non-human actants, and has inspired architecture scholars to recognize the profession's role in amplifying these connections, especially for advancing a radical ecological democratic practice, or what Latour terms a "cosmopolitics".[1] According to this framing, the ground would qualify as a capacious "device" that enables the *mediation* of human and non-human relationships in the processes of production—and rupture—of the built environment. Thus, studying the ground as a potential participant in socio-spatial actions entails discovering its complex life as a mediator of nodes, paths, connections, and networks, with other human and non-human actors. This edited volume effectively illustrates Latour's theoretical approach, as through its use of "shifting grounds" as a lens to understand Beirut, it carefully unpacks the city, capturing and illustrating its multiple, intricate, and changing systems and assemblages, amidst transitions and disruptions.

Figure 1 - Contemporary view of Greater Beirut—a concrete jungle after 8 decades of perpetual development—and in the background, the Port Silos catching fire a couple of months after their explosion.

1 Albena Yaneva, *Latour for Architects* (Routledge, 2022); Brett Mommersteeg, *Variations of a Building* (Springer, 2023); Rania Ghosn and El Hadi Jazairy, *Geostories. Another Architecture for the Environment* (Actar, 2019); Jonathan Metzer, "Cultivating Torment: The Cosmopolitics of More-than-Human Urban Planning," *City*, 20(4), 2016: 581-601.

acknowledgements

This book is a work of reverence for Beirut and the Beirutis, whose practices are its main subject. We want to acknowledge their strength, especially as they were enduring war and hardship at the time of its publication.

This book did not materialize without significant support. First, We would like to express our sincere gratitude to the Graham Foundation for Advanced Studies in the Fine Arts for their generous grant in 2023, which made publishing this book possible. We would also like to thank AUB's School of Architecture and Design for its additional funding support.

The book grew from the "Beirut Shifting Grounds" exhibition presented at the Special Section Co-Habitats of the 17th International Architecture Exhibition—La Biennale di Venezia, curated by Hashim Sarkis. We owe the curator special gratitude for offering the platform and motive to develop the research. The Beirut Shifting Grounds project was co-curated by Sandra Frem and Boulos Douaihy, with Carla Aramouny, Rana Haddad, Nicolas Fayad, and Joanne Hayek, and the collaboration of Nayla Al-Akl and Ahmad Nouraldeen. The installation was supported by the School of Architecture and Design, the Maroun Semaan Faculty of Engineering and Architecture at the American University of Beirut, and the Biennale di Venezia.

We are deeply grateful to the production team who carried out the original material featured in this book: The mapping of the ground samples was realized by Sandra Frem/ platau I platform for architecture and urbanism, with the support of Mariana Boughaba, Annabelle Chebat, Dina Chehab, Gina Ghaoui, Joanna Howayek, Lynne Khater, Nathalie Mounzer, Rayanne Njeim, Yasmine Saad, Clara Saade, Lama Salameh, Hala Stouhi, Maya Ziade. Ahmad Nouraldeen conducted the climatic studies with the support of Lama Barhoumi. Nayla Al-Akl conducted the ecological mappings with the support of Tara Kanj and Thea Maria Maroun. Carla Aramouny developed the 3D visualization of Martyrs' Square with the support of Rabih Arasoghli, Sarah Tannir, Yasmine Atoui, Ismail Hutet, Mia Baraka, Christina Battikha, Ghinwa Azzi, and Michelle Azzi. Boulos Douaihy developed the architectural typologies with the support of Mariana Boughaba, Riad Tabbarah and Lama Semaan. The composite sections were developed by Nicolas Fayad with the help of Alissa Homeidan, based on drawings by Nour Balshi, Mariana Boughaba, and Careen Matta. The collective ground design and visuals were co-developed by Nicolas Fayad and Boulos Douaihy. The visuals in "From Streets to Strategies" were developed by Joanne Hayek with Balsam Madi and Hussein Zaarour.

We are particularly grateful to Wissam Chaaya for contributing his photographs of Beirut. We would like to thank the Arab Image Foundation for the archival photographs in this book. Special thanks to Fadi Ghazzaoui, Antoine Atallah, Michael and May Davie, and Camille Tarazi for their generous support of Martyrs' Square's initial research.

The extended research developed for this book has been additionally supported by a 2022-23 University Research Board (URB) grant at the American University of Beirut under the project title: Shifting Grounds – Beirut Spatial Practices at the Architectural Ground. Research Assistants' support was an essential ingredient in the book's development. We want to express our sincere thanks to Batoul Chahine, Ralph Karam, Alissa Homeidan, Stephanie Achkar, and Dina Arnous for supporting this book's visual production and research.

We are especially thankful to Hashim Sarkis, Nayla Al-Akl, Wissam Chaaya, Boulos Douaihy, Nicolas Fayad, Farès El-Dahdah, Abdul-Halim Jabr, Stephanie Achkar, Joanne Hayek, Rana Haddad, and Mona Harb, for their generous contributions to essays and conversations, and Karim Farah for the book's design.

biographies

Editors biography:

Carla Aramouny
Architect and associate professor at the American University of Beirut, School of Architecture and Design, where she is the founder and director of ArD TechLab. She holds the Associate Dean of Student Affairs position at AUB and has previously served as Architecture Convener. Her work and research reflect on intersections of architecture and the expanded environment, focusing on infrastructure and visualization. She holds an M.Arch from the University of Pennsylvania and a B.Arch from the Lebanese American University.

Sandra Frem
Architect and founding partner at platau I platform for architecture and urbanism. She currently holds the position of assistant professor of practice in Architecture at the American University of Beirut, School of Architecture and Design. Her practice and research probe the intersections between architecture, culture, and the environment. Her work was exhibited internationally, notably at the Seoul Biennale 2019 and the Venice Biennale 2021. She holds a SMArchS in Architecture and Urbanism with distinction from the Massachusetts Institute of Technology and a DES in Architecture from the Lebanese University.

Aramouny & Frem are co-recipients of the Graham Foundation Grant and the ACSA / Buell Prize in Climate, Architecture, and Society in 2023.

Authors / Collaborators biography:

Stephanie Achkar
Architect and researcher. She holds a Bachelor of Architecture with a minor in Urban Studies from the American University of Beirut. Her thesis, which explores architecture's agency in enforcing and disrupting inherent power structures, was awarded the First Prize Areen Award for Excellence in Architecture in 2024. In addition to her studies at AUB, Achkar completed an exchange program at the Architectural Association School in London.

Nayla Al-Akl
Assistant Professor of Landscape Architecture, Dean of Student Affairs at the American University of Beirut (AUB), and co-founder and administrative member of the Lebanese Landscape Association (LELA). She has worked on several landscape architecture, planning, and urban design projects in the Middle East, the US, and China. Her research interests lie in the relationship between humans and their environments and the interface of nature/culture/society. She holds a Bachelor of Architecture from AUB and a Master of Landscape Architecture from Harvard University Graduate School of Design.

Wissam Chaaya
Architect, urban planner and photographer. In parallel to his experience as an architect and collaborator at Hashim Sarkis Studios, Wissam has used photography as a medium to approach architecture and society from a different angle. He has long-term experience in architectural and street photography and has exhibited his work internationally. He holds a DES in Architecture and a Master's in urban planning from the Fine Art Institute at the Lebanese University.

Farès el-Dahdah
Professor of Art History and the Mamdouha El-Sayed Bobst Dean of the Faculty of Arts and Sciences at the American University of Beirut. He received his undergraduate degrees in both fine arts and architecture from the Rhode Island School of Design and his graduate studies in urbanism and architectural theory at Harvard University's Graduate School of Design. El-Dahdah has written extensively on Brazil's modern architecture and has been involved in several collaborative projects with Casa de Lucio Costa and Fundação Oscar Niemeyer foundations, on the boards of which he serves. In recent years, data science, digital art history, and cloud adoption have increasingly become central to his research through the creation of online geospatial platforms, such as levantCarta.

Boulos Douaihy
Architect, geographer, and founding partner at platau I platform for architecture and urbanism. He holds a DES in Architecture from the Lebanese University and a Master in "Environment et Aménagement du Territoire" from Université St Joseph. His work uses architecture as a medium to engage cultural, social and environmental concerns.His work has garnered recognition through numerous awards nominations, the Archmarathon Awards, Arab Architects Awards, and Archdaily Building of the Year, and his research has been exhibited internationally, including at the Venice Architecture Biennale, the Seoul Biennale of Architecture and Urbanism.

Nicolas Fayad
Architect and founding partner of EAST Architecture Studio, and currently holds the position of Assistant Professor of Practice at the American University of Beirut (AUB). He studied architecture at AUB before earning a Masters in Architecture with distinction from the Harvard University Graduate School of Design. He is a recipient of the Aga Khan Award for Architecture, 15th Cycle, for EAST's Renovation of Niemeyer Guest House at the Rachid Karami International Fair in Tripoli, Lebanon, and was recently awarded AUB's Distinguished Alumni Award, honouring his achievements.

Rana Haddad
Architecture Association graduate and a prominent figure in Beirut's cultural and international art scene. Over 23 years, she taught architecture at the American University of Beirut, where she held the position of associate professor and founded the BePublic Lab. She co-founded 200Grs., merging activism and art through performances, interventions, and public installations. Haddad's work has reached global platforms, most recently in the Desert X Alula 2024, among many other venues. Her work has been acquired by the Victoria and Albert Museum in London, including "Debris of Texts and Eyeglasses" and the "Stuck Stick" series.

Joanne Hayek
Architect, designer, and coder with a passion for impact-driven innovation. Her work bridges academic research and entrepreneurship, exploring possibilities across scales—from materials to cities—through collaborative design practices. She is an assistant professor at the Dubai Institute of Design and Innovation (DIDI) and previously a senior lecturer at the American University of Beirut (AUB). Joanne co-founded Vanina, a Beirut-based fashion brand with global reach, and co-created Emerge Beirut, a temporary platform that fostered grassroots digital collaboration. She holds a Bachelor of Architecture from AUB and a Master of Science in Advanced Architectural Design from Columbia University GSAPP.

Mona Harb
Professor of Urban Studies and Politics at the American University of Beirut, where she is also co-founder and research lead at the Beirut Urban Lab. Harb is the author and co-author of over eighty publications investigating disaster governance, nonprofits and urban commoning, urban activists and oppositional politics, refugees as city-makers, municipal governance, as well as political-religious actors and service provision. Harb holds a PhD in Political Science from University Aix-Marseille 3, two MA degrees in Urban Geography (University of Tours) and Urbanism (ALBA), and a Bachelor of Architecture from AUB.

Abdul-Halim Jabr
Architect/urban design consultant and director of the Architecture School at the Académie Libanaise des Beaux-Arts (ALBA). He has previously taught at the Holy Spirit University of Kaslik and the American University of Beirut (AUB). Jabr holds a Bachelor of Architecture from AUB and a Master's in Urban Studies and Housing from the Massachusetts Institute of Technology (MIT). He works actively on urban design and governance issues in Greater Beirut, specifically about the environment, old neighborhoods, and public places. He is a co-founding member of the Beirut Heritage Initiative.

Hashim Sarkis
Lebanese educator, architect, and founding principal of Hashim Sarkis Studios since 1998. Since 2015, Sarkis has been Professor and Dean of the School of Architecture and Planning at the Massachusetts Institute of Technology. Sarkis received his Bachelor of Architecture and Bachelor of Fine Arts from the Rhode Island School of Design (1987), his Master of Architecture with distinction (1989), and his Doctor of Philosophy from the Harvard University Graduate School of Design. In 2020 He was the curator of the 17th Venice Biennale of Architecture "How Will We Live Together?".

credits

Table of Content
Drawing by Boulos Douaihy and Sandra Frem

Prolog
Figure 1 - Drawing by Boulos Douaihy and Sandra Frem

Preface
Drawing by Sandra Frem

Introduction: Shifting Grounds, Carla Aramouny / Sandra Frem
Figure 1, 2, 3 - Drawing by Sandra Frem

Section 1 I Appropriation

Sampling the Ground, Sandra Frem
Figures 2 - Drawing by Batoul Chahine with Sandra Frem.
Figures 4 through 26 - Drawings produced by Sandra Frem with Mariana Boughaba, Annabelle Chebat, Batoul Chahine, Dina Chehab, Gina Ghaoui, Joanna Howayek, Lynne Khater, Nathalie Mounzer, Rayanne Njeim, Yasmine Saad, Clara Saade, Lama Salameh, Hala Stouhi, Maya Ziade, with contribution from Ahmad Nouraldeen and Lama Barhoumi.
Figure 1, 3 - photos by Wissam Chaaya

Sources for figures 4, 12, 14, 16, 18, 20, 22, 24:
Population density is based on an estimate. Units' numbers, sizes, and number of people per household are based on field surveying and questionnaires. Floor Area Ratio (FAR) and Zoning information are based on the Lebanese Building Code.
Average units' price per square meter is based on the Lebanese Examiner, "Real estate group reveals average apartment prices in Beirut". https://lebaneseexaminer.com/2015/07/16/real-estate-group-reveals-average-apartment-prices-in-beirut/ Accessed 20.04.2024

Ecology of the Ground, Nayla Al Akl
Figures 7,9,12 - drawings by Nayla Al Akl with Tara Kanj and Thea Maria Maroun
Figures 1 through 6, 8, 10, 11 - photos by Wissam Chaaya

Appropriation As Aesthetic, Wissam Chaaya
photos by Wissam Chaaya

Section 2 I Commoning

Metamorphosis and Manifestations of the Ground, Carla Aramouny
Figure 1a - Photo 0087ch-al001-003-00012. Place des Canons. 1930. Beirut, Lebanon. Gelatin silver developing-out paper print. 5.0 x 7.8 cm. 0087ch - Simone Chemali Collection. Courtesy of the Arab Image Foundation.
Figure 1 b - Photo 0089la00014. Celebration of the Independence Day at the "Place des Canons" photographed by Issa Albert. 1944. Beirut, Lebanon. Gelatin silver developing-out paper print. 11.6 x 17.6 cm. 0089la - Mansour Lahoud Collection. Courtesy of the Arab Image Foundation.
Figures 2, 4, 8, 9, 15, 16 - drawings by Carla Aramouny
Figures 3, 5, 6, 10-14, 17-19 - drawings by Carla Aramouny, Lea Tabaja, Joseph Chalhoub, Carmen Matta
Figure 7 - Photo 0257se00021. M. Tueni is nominated "officer de la legion d'honneur". Unidentified photographer. 1921.Beirut, Lebanon. Gelatin silver developing-out paper print. 10.3 x 16.8 cm. 0257se - Nayla Bustros Sehnaoui Collection. Courtesy of the Arab Image Foundation.

Cultural Commons and Retaining Collective Memory, Conversation
Conversation transcribed by Batoul Chahine and edited by Carla Aramouny

Figure 1, 3, 6, 7 - Photos by Wissam Chaaya
Figure 2, 4 - Drawings by Carla Aramouny
Figure 5 - Photo by Carla Aramouny

Port Silos as Common Ground, Carla Aramouny / Stephanie Achkar
Figure 1-5 - Drawings by Stephanie Achkar - Photos by Wissam Chaaya

Section 3 I Production

Architecture as Ground Shaper, Boulos Douaihy

Figure 1, 2, 5, 7, 9, 10, 13 - Photos by Wissam Chaaya
Figure 3. Drawing by Boulos Douaihy and Sandra Frem
Figure 4, 6, 9 - Drawings by Boulos Douaihy, Riad Tabbarah and Lama Semaan
Figure 8 - Drawing by Boulos Douaihy, Mariana Boughaba
Figure 12 - Photo by Sandra Frem - Drawing by Boulos Douaihy, based on information retrieved from the Beirut Urban Lab research: Beirut a City for Sale? https://beiruturbanlab.com/en/Details/612/beirut%E2%80%99s-residential-fabric

Anatomy of the Ground, Nicolas Fayad

Figure 1, 8 - Photos by Sandra Frem
Figure 2, 3 - Drawings by Nicolas Fayad
Figure 4, 6, 9, 12 - Photo by Wissam Chaaya
Figure 5 - Drawing by Boulos Douaihy
Figure 7, 10, 11 - Drawings by Alissa Homeidan

The Collective Ground, Sandra Frem (design by Boulos Douaihy and Nicolas Fayad)

Figure 1-5 - Drawings by Boulos Douaihy & Nicolas Fayad

Section 4 I Activism

From Streets to Strategies, Joanne Hayek

Figure 1-25 - Drawings by Joanne Hayek in collaboration with Balsam Madi, with the help of Hussein Zaarour, Stephanie Achkar, Mahmoud Baghdadi, Hisham Ismail, and Hawraa el Husseini.

Figure 1-25 sources: The maps feature data aggregated through the Emerge Beirut platform* and collected from Daleel Thawra, Liveuamap, the961, Megaphone News, Akhbar el Seha, BeirutFER, Beirut Heritage Initiative, Antoine Atallah, UNHabitat, OCHA, The Beirut Urban Lab, Center for Research Computing's Spatial Studies Lab at Rice University, Open Map Lebanon, Together LiBeirut, Stand For Women, The Women Collective, AlFanar, The Relief Center, Catalytic Action, Baytna Baytak, Beb W' Shebbek, OffreJoie and Ardkon.

* Given the extensive scope and complexity of grassroots deployments in Beirut during the periods covered, it was challenging to include all actions and actors comprehensively. We extend our apologies to initiatives and individuals not mentioned in this essay and acknowledge their valuable contributions to the movements and transformations discussed.

Public Art As Activism - Conversation with Rana Haddad

Conversation transcribed by Batoul Chahine and edited by Carla Aramouny and Rana Haddad

Figure 1 - Installation by Rana Haddad & Pierre Hage Boutros - Ateliers de Recherche with Gregory Buchakajian - photo courtesy of Rana Haddad
Figure 2 - BePublic Lab "Public Beirut", 2012, AUB - Led by Rana Haddad, Sandra Richani & Carole Levesque (students: Jalal Makarem. Farah Harake. Marianne Safi. Mustafa Chehab. Rami Saab)- photo courtesy of BePublic Lab.
Figure 3 - AA Visiting School program "Things that are Fascinatingly Boring" - led by Rana Haddad & Pascal Hachem, 2018 - photo courtesy of Rana Haddad
Figure 4 a & b - BePublic Lab, "Silence", 2016, AUB - Led by Rana Haddad & Joanne Hayek (students: Betina Abi Habib. Zeina Bekhaazi. Souha Boumatar. Mario El Khouri. Karen Madi)- photo courtesy of BePublic Lab - diagram by Boulos Douaihy
Figure 5 a & b - BePublic Lab "Public Beirut", 2012, AUB - Led by Rana Haddad, Sandra Richani & Carole Levesque (students: Youssef Ibrahim. Jana Aridi. Loulwa Achkar. Thea Hallak. Micheline Nahra)- photo courtesy of BePublic Lab - diagram by Boulos Douaihy
Figure 6 - BePublic Lab "Appropriate", 2018, AUB - Led by Rana Haddad & Pascal Hachem (students: Nicolas Abou Haidar. Soraya Hammoud. Nicol Yamin. Lina Akkaoui. Carl Yammine)- photo courtesy of BePublic Lab
Figure 7 a & b - BePublic Lab "Appropriate", 2018 at AUB - Led by Rana Haddad & Pascal Hachem (students: Nicolas Abou Haidar. Soraya Hammoud. Nicol Yamin. Lina Akkaoui. Carl Yammine)- photo courtesy of BePublic Lab - diagram by Boulos Douaihy
Figure 8a - "Desintegration" installation - "Quand l'Inconcevable Prend Forme", Galerie de la Cité Internationale des Arts de Paris, France, June-July 2023 - photo courtesy of Rana Haddad
Figure 8b - "The Making of Desintegration" video, Beirut Shifting Grounds project, Venice Biennale in 2021– photo courtesy of Rana Haddad
Figure 9 - "Debris of Texts and Eyeglasses" installation in collaboration with Pascal Hachem - "Northeast Southwest", Robotron - Kantine, Dresden, Germany, September-December 2022 - photo courtesy of Rana Haddad

Epilog

Figure 1 - Photo by Wissam Chaaya

bibliography

Prolog, Hashim Sarkis

Locke, John. "The Project Gutenberg eBook of Second Treatise of Government, by John Locke". Archived from the original on May 30 2024. Retrieved June 3 2024.

Introduction: Shifting Grounds: Transformative Periods and Emergent Spatial Practices Carla Aramouny / Sandra Frem

Davie, May. *The History and Evolution of Public Spaces in Beirut Central District.* Solidere, 1997.

Fawaz, Mona, Mona Harb, and Ahmad Gharbieh. "Living Beirut's Security Zones: An Investigation of the Modalities and Practice of Urban Security." *City & Society* 24, no. 2 (2012): 173-195.

Ghorayeb, Marlene. *Beyrouth sous Mandat Français.* Khartala, 2014.

Kabbani, Oussama. "Public Space as Infrastructure." In *Projecting Beirut*, edited by Hashim Sarkis et al., 132-145. Prestel, 1998.

Khalaf, Samir. "Post-War Barbarism in Lebanon." *Annahar*, February 22, 2019. https://en.annahar.com/article/940004-postwar-barbarism-in-lebanon.

Krijnen, Marieke. *Creative Economy, Social Justice and Urban Strategies.* Beirut: Issam Fares Institute for Public Policy and International Affairs, American University of Beirut, 2016.

Section 1 I Appropriation Introduction on Appropriation

DeLanda, Manuel. Assemblage Theory. Edinburgh University Press, 2016.

Deleuze, Gilles, and Félix Guattari. "A Thousand Plateaus: Capitalism and Schizophrenia." *Journal of Interdisciplinary History*, translated by Brian Massumi, ed. (University of Minnesota Press, 1989).

Lara-Hernandez, J. A., et al. "Temporary Appropriation of Public Space As an Emergence Assemblage for the Future Urban Landscape: The Case of Mexico City." *Future Cities and Environment* 5, no. 1 (2019): 1–22.

Lefebvre, Henri. *The Production of Space.* Blackwell, 1991. Originally published in 1974.

Ripoll, F., and V. Veschambre. "L'appropriation de l'espace comme problématique." *Norois* no. 195 (2005).

Sennett, Richard. *The Uses of Disorder: Personal Identity and City Life.* Yale University Press, 2008.

Sampling the Ground, Sandra Frem

Ahn, Chulmin, Carlo Ignaccolo, and Alicia Salazar-Miranda. "Measuring the City: The Power of Urban Metrics." In *Projections*, edited by C. Ahn, C. Ignaccolo, and A. Salazar-Miranda, 16 (MIT Press, 2022): https://projections.pubpub.org/pub/xusawg1f.

"Apartment Prices in Beirut I Beirut RE." n.d. Beirutre.com. https://www.beirutre.com/real-estate-group-reveals-average-apartment-prices-in-beirut/.

Asmar, Fadi Moussa. *Revitalizing Waterfronts or Urban Fragmentations of the Northern Shoreline of Beirut and the Isolation of Bourj Hammoud's Waterfront.* (MUPP Thesis). Faculty of Engineering and Architecture, Department of Architecture and Design, American University of Beirut, 2008.

Davie, Michel. *Beyrouth 1825-1975, un siècle et demi d'urbanisme.* Beyrouth: Ordre des Ingénieurs et architectes de Beyrouth, 2001.

Fleischmann, Marc, Olivera Romice, and Salvatore Porta. "Measuring Urban Form: Overcoming Terminological Inconsistencies for a Quantitative and Comprehensive Morphologic

Analysis of Cities." *Environment and Planning B: Urban Analytics and City Science* 48, no. 8 (2021): 2133-50.

Gehl, Jan, and Birgitte Svarre. *How to Study Public Life*. Island Press, 2013.

Gehl Institute. "How to Use the Public Life Tools." https://gehlpeople.com/tools/ Accessed July 1, 2024.

Kassir, Samir. *Beirut*. University of California Press, 2003.

Khalaf, Samir. *Heart of Beirut: Reclaiming the Bourj*. Saqi Books, 2006.

Kracauer, Siegfried. *Streets in Berlin and Elsewhere*. Polity Press, 2007.

Lefebvre, Henri. *The Production of Space*. Blackwell, 1991.

Nasution, Ivan. "Urban Appropriation: Creativity in Marginalization." *Procedia - Social and Behavioral Sciences* 184 (May 2015): 4–12. https://doi.org/10.1016/j.sbspro.2015.05.047.

Rowe, Colin, and Hashim Sarkis. *Projecting Beirut*. Prestel, 1997.

Ecology of the Ground, Nayla Al-Akl

Bohn, Katrin, and André Viljoen. "The Edible City: Envisioning the Continuous Productive Urban Landscape (CPUL)." *Field* 4, no. 1 (2011).

Ekkel, E. Dinand, and Sjerp de Vries. "Nearby Green Space and Human Health: Evaluating Accessibility Metrics." *Landscape and urban planning* 157 (2017): 214-20.

Fisher, Brendan, and R. Kerry Turner. "Ecosystem Services: Classification for Valuation." *Biological Conservation* 141, no. 5 (2008): 116-69.

Forman, Richard TT. Land Mosaics: *The Ecology of Landscapes and Regions*. Cambridge University Press, 1995.

Forman, Richard TT. *Urban Ecology: Science of Cities*. Cambridge University Press, 2014.

Francis, R. A., Millington, J. D., Perry, G. L., & Minor, E. S. (Eds.). *The Routledge Handbook of Landscape Ecology*. Routledge, 2022.

Jorgensen, Anna, and Paul H. Gobster. "Shades of Green: Measuring the Ecology of Urban Green Space in the Context of Human Health and Well-Being." *Nature and Culture* 5, no. 3 (2010): 338-63.

Krijnen, Marieke, and Mona Fawaz. "Exception as the Rule: High-end developments in neoliberal Beirut." *Built Environment* 36, no. 2 (2010): 245-59.

Li, Gang, G-X. Sun, Yin Ren, X-S. Luo, and Y-G. Zhu. "Urban Soil and Human Health: A Review." *European Journal of Soil Science* 69, no. 1 (2018): 196-215.

Matsuoka, Rodney H., and Rachel Kaplan. "People Needs In The Urban Landscape: Analysis of Landscape and Urban Planning Contributions." *Landscape and urban planning* 84, no. 1 (2008): 7-19.

Meuser, Helmut. *Contaminated Urban Soils*. Vol. 18. Springer Science & Business Media, 2010.

Norton, Briony A., Karl L. Evans, and Philip H. Warren. "Urban Biodiversity and Landscape Ecology: Patterns, Processes, and Planning." *Current Landscape Ecology Reports* 1 (2016): 178-92.

O'Riordan, Roisin, Jess Davies, Carly Stevens, John N. Quinton, and Christopher Boyko. "The Ecosystem Services of Urban Soils: A Review." *Geoderma* 395 (2021): 115076.

Potschin, Marion, and Roy Haines-Young. "Defining and Measuring Ecosystem Services." In *Routledge Handbook of Ecosystem Services*. Routledge, 2016.

Reyes-Riveros, Rosa, Adison Altamirano, Francisco De La Barrera, Daniel Rozas-Vásquez, Lorena Vieli, and Paula Meli. "Linking Public Urban Green Spaces and Human Well-Being: A Systematic Review." *Urban Forestry & Urban Greening* 61 (2021): 127105.

Stein, Anke, Katharina Gerstner, and Holger Kreft. "Environmental Heterogeneity as a Universal Driver of Species Richness Across Taxa, Biomes, and Spatial Scales." *Ecology Letters* 17, no. 7 (2014): 866-80.

Yan, Yongzhi, Scott Jarvie, Qing Zhang, Shuangshuang Zhang, Peng Han, Qingfu Liu, and Pengtao Liu. "Small Patches Are Hotspots For Biodiversity Conservation In Fragmented Landscapes." *Ecological Indicators* 130 (2021): 108086.

Section 2 I Commoning
Introduction on Commoning

Hardin, Garrett. "The Tragedy of the Commons." *Science* 162, no. 3859 (1968): 1243–48.

Harvey, David. "The Future of the Commons." *Radical History Review*, no. 109 (2011): 101–7.

Ostrom, Elinor. *Governing the Commons: The Evolution of Institutions for Collective Action*. Cambridge University Press, 1990.

Stavrides, Stavros. *Common Space: The City as Commons*. Zed Books, 2016.

Metamorphosis and Manifestations of the Ground as Commons in Martyrs Square, Carla Aramouny

Davie, May. T*he History and Evolution of Public Spaces in Beirut Central District*. Beirut: Solidere publication, 1997.

Hanssen, Jens. "Your Beirut is on my Desk: Ottomanizing Beirut under Sultan Abdülhamid II (1876-1909)", *Projecting Beirut. Episodes in the Construction and Reconstruction of a Modern City, Prestel: Munich, London, New York*, (1998), 41-67.

Hindi, Nadine. "Urban forms at intersection of Imperialism and Colonialism: A Perspective on Beirut", *The 18th International Planning History Society* Conference (July 2018).

Khalaf, Samir. "The Bourj as a Cosmopolitan Public Sphere", in the*Heart of Beirut: Reclaiming the Bourj*. Samir Khalaf. Saqi Books, 2006.

Poujoulat, Baptistin. "La Place du Canon en 1861." In El-Bourj. Place de la Liberté et Porte du Levant, edited by Farès Sassine, Ghassan Tueni. Dar an-Nahar Editions, 2003.

Salam, Assem, "The Role of Government in Shaping the Built Environment", in *Projecting Beirut: Episodes in the Construction and Reconstruction of a Modern City*, ed. Peter Rowe and Hashim Sarkis (Prestel, 1998), 41-67.

Saliba, Robert. *Beirut 1920-1940: Domestic architecture between tradition and modernity (1998)*, Order of Engineers and Architects.

Sarkis, Hashim. "A Vital Void." In Two Squares, edited by Hashim Sarkis. Harvard University Press, 2006.

Sharp, Deen. "Lebanon and the fog of reconstruction", *The Politics of Post-conflict Reconstruction* (September 2018), 44-50.

Volk, Lucia. *Memorials and Martyrs in Modern Lebanon*. Indiana University Press, 2010.

Port Silos as Common Ground, Carla Aramouny / Stephanie Achkar

Hindi, Nadine. "Urban forms at intersection of Imperialism and Colonialism: A Perspective on Beirut", *The 18th International Planning History Society* Conference, (July 2018).

Kasaba, Resat., Keyder, Çaglar, & Tabak, Farouk. "Eastern Mediterranean Port Cities and Their Bourgeoisies: Merchants, Political Projects, and Nation-States". *Review* (Fernand Braudel Center), 10 (1), 121–135.

Kassir, Samir. Beirut, University of California Press, 2010.

Saliba, Robert. *Beirut 1920-1940: Domestic architecture between tradition and modernity*. Order of Engineers and Architects, 1998.
Traboulsi, Fawwaz. *A History of Modern Lebanon*. Pluto Press, (2007), 54-55.

Section 3 I Production Architecture as Ground Shaper, Boulos Douaihy

Arbid, George. "Practicing Modernism in Beirut, Architecture in Lebanon 1946-1970". Doctor of Design Thesis, Harvard University, 2002.

Arbid, Jeremy. "Higher regulation. Real estate law is complicated but friendly to developers." *Executive Magazine*, July 16, 2014. http://www.executivemagazine.com/business-finance/real-estate/higherregulation

Beirut Urban Lab. "*Beirut: a city for sale?*" Accessed March 1, 2024. https://beiruturbanlab.com/en/Details/612/beirut%E2%80%99s-residential-fabric

El-Achkar, Elie. *Réglementation et formes urbaines : Le cas de Beyrouth* (Presses de l'Ifpo, 1998).

Gebara, Hayat, N. Mona Khechen, and Bruno Marot. "Mapping New Constructions in Beirut (2000-2013)" *Jadaliyya*, November 16, 2016. Accessed on Mar 01, 2014. www.jadaliyya.com/Details/33751/Mapping-New-Constructions-in-Beirut-2000-2013

Gerbal, Lisa, Nicolas Hrycaj, Camille Lavoipierre and Marissa Potasiak. *Linking Economic Change With Social Justice In Mar Mikhael, Beirut*, Gaia Heritage/Sciences Po/Issam Fares Institute for Public Policy and International Affairs, 2016.

Ghandour, Marwan. "Building Law: A Critical Reading of the Lebanese Case", 89th ACSA, Annual Meeting Proceedings: Paradoxes of Progress, 2001.

Kévorkian, Raymond, Lévon Nordiguian, and Vahé Tachjian. *Les Arméniens: La quête d'un refuge (1917-1939)*. USJ Presse, 2007.

Krijnen, Marieke and Mona Fawaz, "Exception as the Rule: High-End Developments in Neoliberal Beirut", *Built Environment* Vol. 36 no. 2 (2010).

Marot, Bruno. *Developing Post-War Beirut (1990-2016): The political economy of "pegged urbanization"*. Geography. McGill University, 2018.

Mohsen, Hiba, Rokia Raslan, and Ibtihal El Bastawissi. "The Impact of Changes in Beirut Urban Patterns on the Microclimate: A Review of Urban Policy and Building Regulations." *Architecture and Planning Journal* (APJ): Vol. 25: Iss.1, Article 2. 2020. https://doi.org/10.54729/2789-8547.1001.

Mourad, Ali. "Building Permit: A Critical Review of the Legal Framework in Lebanon," *BAU Journal - Health and Wellbeing*: Vol. 1: Iss.3, Article 8. 2008.

Rowe, Peter, and Hashim Sarkis, ed. *Projecting Beirut: episodes in the construction and reconstruction of a modern city*. Prestel, 1998.

Saksouk, Abir. "Where is Law? Investigations from Beirut." Working paper, American University of Beirut, 2014. Accessed on July 01, 2024. https://www.aub.edu.lb/Neighborhood/Documents/aubAbirNIReport.pdf

Saliba, Robert. *Beirut 1920-1940: Domestic architecture between tradition and modernity*. Order of Engineers and Architects, 1998.

Traboulsi, Fawwaz. *A History of Modern Lebanon*. Pluto Press, 2007.

Anatomy of Ground Sections, Nicolas Fayad

Aramouny, Carla. "Électricité du Liban building." *Brownbook* magazine, Issue 66 - Aramco World, 2017, 62-77.

Arbid, George. *Practicing Modernism in Beirut: Architecture in Lebanon 1946-1970*. Harvard University, 2002.

Arbid, George, and Philipp Oswalt, eds. *Designing Modernity: Architecture in the Arab World 1945-1973*. Jovis, 2022.

Azzali, Simona, Silvia Mazzetto, and Attilio Petruccioli, eds. *Urban Challenges in the Globalizing Middle-East: Social Value of Public Spaces*. Springer, 2022.

El-Achkar, Elie. *Réglementation et Formes Urbaines: Le Cas de Beyrouth*. Presses de l'Ifpo, 1998.

Kassab, Maroun Ghassan. "Beirut Modernism: Theoretical Framework and Case Study." Master's thesis, The University of Sydney, 2014.

Kévorkian, Raymond, Lévon Nordiguian, and Vahé Tachjian. *Les Arméniens: La Quête d'un Refuge 1917-1939*. USJ Presse, 2007.

Kesrouany, Maya. "Review of *City of Beginnings: Poetic Modernism in Beirut* by Robyn Creswell." Comparative Literature Studies 58, no. 2 (2021): e-4-e-8.

Mady, Christine. "The Evolutions, Transformations, and Adaptations in Beirut's Public Spaces." In *Urban Planning*, 1: *Urbanisation, Crisis, and Resilience: The Multiple Dimensions of Urban Transformation in Beirut, Lebanon*, vol. 7, 2022.

The Collective Ground: a Log of Reclamatory Actions - Sandra Frem (design by Boulos Douaihy and Nicolas Fayad)

Bou Aoun, Cynthia. "Reclaiming Public Space and Its Role in Producing the Revolution." *Legal Agenda*, January 9, 2020. https://english.legal-agenda.com/reclaiming-public-space-and-its-role-in-producing-the-revolution (accessed October 5, 2024).

Chehayeb, Kareem, and Abby Sewell. "Local Groups Step Up to Lead Beirut Blast Response." *The New Humanitarian*, October 18, 2020. https://www.thenewhumanitarian.org/news-feature/2020/08/18/Lebanon-Beirut-explosion-local-aid-response (accessed October 5, 2024).

Hammoud, Mariam. "Reclaiming Public Space During the Revolution: How We Are Reconnecting With Lebanese Cities." *Beirut Today*, November 20, 2019. https://beirut-today.com/2019/11/20/reclaiming-public-space-revolution/ (accessed October 5, 2024).

Maki, Fumihiko. *Investigations in Collective Form* (1964). Books and Monographs. 61. Also accessed at: https://openscholarship.wustl.edu/books/61.

Sendra, Pablo, and Richard Sennett. *Designing Disorder: Experiments and Disruptions in the City*. Verso, 2020.

Sennett, Richard. *Building and Dwelling: Ethics for the City*. Farrar, Straus and Giroux, 2018.

Sennett, Richard. "The Open City." In *The Endless City*, edited by Ricky Burdett and Deyan Sudjic, Phaidon Press, 2007.

Section 4 I Activism
Introduction on Activism

Aramouny, Carla. "Environment, Activism, and Design: Emerging Practices in Lebanon." *World Architecture Magazine*, no. 358 (April 2020): 28–33. Tsinghua University.

Fisher, Thomas. "Public Interest Architecture: A Needed and Inevitable Change." In *Expanding Architecture: Design as Activism*, edited by Bryan Bell and Katie Wakeford, 8–13. Metropolis Books, 2008.

Foreign Architects Switzerland (FAS). "Oh Baby, Let's Get Political, A Rant." In *Bracket Takes Action*, edited by Mason White and Neeraj Bhatia. Applied Research and Design Publishers, 2019.

Lokman, Kees. "Design Activism: Towards Agnostic Pluralism." In *Bracket Takes Action*, edited by Mason White and Neeraj Bhatia. San Francisco: Applied Research and Design Publishers, 2019.

White, Mason, and Neeraj Bhatia, eds. *Bracket Takes Action*. Applied Research and Design Publishers, 2019.

From Streets to Strategies, Joanne Hayek

Al Jazeera. "Lebanon Protesters Form Nationwide Human Chain." Al Jazeera, October 27, 2019. https://www.aljazeera.com/news/2019/10/27/lebanon-protesters-form-human-chain-across-the-country.

Al-Harithy, Howayda, and Batoul Yassine. "The Co-Production of a Shared Community Space in al-Khodor, Karantina, in the Aftermath of the Beirut Port Blast." Land 12, no. 7 (July 12, 2023): 1400. https://doi.org/10.3390/land12071400.

American University of Beirut. "Rehabilitation of the Gholam Heritage Cluster - Building 1137," accessed on July 23, 2024. https://www.aub.edu.lb/Neighborhood/Pages/Rehabilitation_Gholam_Heritage_Cluster_lot1137.aspx.

Asfour, Hani. "Parallel Lines: The Meeting of Aesthetic and Network Theories in Post-Critical Design Practice." Academia.edu, March 7, 2015. https://www.academia.edu/8463735/Parallel_Lines_The_Meeting_of_Aesthetic_and_Network_Theories_in_Post_Critical_Design_Practice?auto=download.

Azhari, Timour. "Defiant Protesters Hold Rival Parade on Lebanon Independence Day." Al Jazeera, November 23, 2019. https://www.aljazeera.com/news/2019/11/23/defiant-protesters-hold-rival-parade-on-lebanon-independence-day.

Beirut Explosion Impact Assessment - strategyand.pwc.com. Accessed July 25, 2024. https://www.strategyand.pwc.com/m1/en/beirut-explosion/beirut-explosion-impact-assessment.pdf.

Beirut Forward Emergency Room. Accessed April 15, 2021. https://www.beirutfer.com/.

Beirut Heritage Initiative. Accessed July 25, 2024. https://beirutheritageinitiative.com/.

Beirut Recovery Map - Rice University. Accessed July 25, 2024. https://beirutrecovery.org/.

Beirut Urban Lab. "Beirut Urban Lab - an Urban Recovery Strategy for Post-Blast Karantina." BeirutUrbanLab. 2020. https://beiruturbanlab.com/en/Details/889.

Beirut Urban Lab. "Critical Mapping of the Beirut Blast Damage Assessments and Repair Efforts." BeirutUrbanLab. Accessed July 25, 2024. http://beiruturbanlab.com/en/Details/782.

Cariello, Alessandro, Rossella Fororelli, and Francesco Rotondo. "Tactical Urbanism in Italy: From Grassroots to Institutional Tool—Assessing Value of Public Space Experiments." *Sustainability* 13, no. 20 (October 18, 2021): 11482. https://doi.org/10.3390/su132011482.

Castells, Manuel. *Networks of Outrage and Hope: Social Movements in the Internet Age.* 2nd ed. Polity Press, 2015.

Fakih, Lama, and Aya Majzoub. "'They killed us from the inside.'" Human Rights Watch, August 3, 2021. https://www.hrw.org/sites/default/files/media_2021/08/lebanon0821_web.pdf.

Fawaz, Mona, and Isabela Serhan. "Urban Revolutions: Lebanon's October 2019 Uprising." *International Journal of Urban and Regional Research*, October 2020. https://doi.org/10.56949/2hjd9559.

Fouani, Tarek. "What Happened to the Public Spaces of the Arab World? From Colonisation to Revolution: The Case of Lebanon." *The Journal of Public Space*, no. Vol. 6 n. 1 (April 30, 2021): 203–14. https://doi.org/10.32891/jps.v6i1.1308.

Frangieh, Maria. "Let's Play - the Initiative Bringing Beirut's Playgrounds Back to Life." Lebanon Traveler, June 16, 2021. Accessed on July 23, 2024. https://www.lebanontraveler.com/en/magazine/lets-play/.

Friedmann, John. *Planning in the Public Domain: From Knowledge to Action.* Princeton University Press, 1987. https://doi.org/10.2307/j.ctv10crf8d.

Ghali, Maghie. "Abandoned Lebanese Theater Resurrected by Music with Ghostly Virtual Concert." *Al Arabiya English*, December 2, 2020. https://english.alarabiya.net/features/2020/12/02/Lebanon-crisis-Abandoned-Lebanese-theater-resurrected-by-music.

"Green Sanctuary: Grobeirut Creates Public Garden in the Heart of the City - Beirut Today." Beirut Today - Independent, community-based news, October 3, 2022. https://beirut-today.com/2020/12/02/green-sanctuary-grobeirut-creates-public-garden-in-the-heart-of-the-city/.

Hayek, Joanne, and Balsam Madi. "Learning from Post-Blast Beirut Humanitarian Data-Driven Mapping and Co-Planning Efforts Piloting an Agile Data-Visualization and Co-Planning Tool." *SSRN Electronic Journal*, 2022. https://doi.org/10.2139/ssrn.4176603.

Holland, Rebecca. "Lentil Soup for the Soul: Inside Lebanon's Soup Kitchens." *The National*, December 22, 2019. https://www.thenationalnews.com/lifestyle/food/lentil-soup-for-the-soul-inside-lebanon-s-soup-kitchens-1.954968.

Impact Lebanon - fundraiser to provide disaster relief after the Beirut Port Explosion. Accessed July 25, 2024. https://www.impactlebanon.org/fundraisers/1-we-re-raising-7-500-000-to-provide-disaster-relief-after-the-explosion-in-beirut.

"Impact Report: Beirut Relief Initiative." 2020. https://ungcnlebanon.org/wp-content/uploads/2021/01/Impact-Report-Beirut-Relief-Initiative-1.pdf.

Jacobs, Jane. *The Death and Life of Great American Cities.* Vintage Books, 2016. ISBN: 9780525432852.

Johnson, Steven. *Emergence: The Connected Lives of Ants, Brains, Cities, and Software.* Touchstone, 2002.

Kabboul, Tamara. "A National Mourning across Lebanon for the Revolution Martyr Alaa Abou Fakher." *961*, November 13, 2019. https://www.the961.com/a-national-mourning-across-lebanon-for-the-revolution-martyr-alaa-abou-fakher/.

"Karantina Park Rehabilitation: Beirut, Lebanon 2020 - 2021 - Catalytic Action." Catalytic Action, 2020. Accessed on July 23, 2024. https://catalyticaction.org/karantina-park-rehabitilation/.

Khatib, Dania Koleilat. "17 October (2019) Revolution in Lebanon: A Preliminary Analysis." *Perspectives on Development in the Middle East and North Africa (MENA) Region*, 2022, 75–93. https://doi.org/10.1007/978-3-031-15135-4_4.

"Lebanon: Military Forces Must End Arbitrary Arrests and Torture of Protesters." *Amnesty International*, November 29, 2019. https://www.amnesty.org/en/latest/press-release/2019/11/lebanon-military-forces-must-end-arbitrary-arrests-and-torture-of-protesters/.

"Lebanon's October 2019 Protests Weren't Just about the 'WhatsApp Tax.'" *Amnesty International*, October 29, 2021. https://www.amnesty.org/en/

latest/news/2021/10/lebanons-october-2019-protests-werent-just-about-the-whatsapp-tax/.

Mackenzie, Laura. "Lebanon Protest Cleaning Squads Bring a Lesson in Tidy Logistics." *Wired Middle East*, October 24, 2019. https://wired.me/science/environment/lebanon-protests-cleaning-recycling/.

Malek, Caline. "Lebanon's Basecamp Sets the Pace for Citizens' Initiatives in Fragile States I Arab News." *Arab News*, November 13, 2020. https://www.arabnews.com/node/1762641/middle-east.

Mariano, Carmela, Ignacio Gràvalos Lacambra, and Patrizia Di Monte. "Open Urban Space Regeneration Strategies Based on Urban Welfare: A Project and Experiment in the San Lorenzo District in Rome, Italy." *Sustainability* 14, no. 24 (December 9, 2022): 16487. https://doi.org/10.3390/su142416487.

Merhej, Karim, and Elina Qureshi. "The Lebanese Uprising in the Digital Age." *CyberOrient* 14, no. 2 (January 2020): 85–98. https://doi.org/10.1002/j.1804-3194.2020.tb00004.x.

Naamani, Aseel, and Ruth Simpson. "Public Space as a Venue for Peacebuilding in Lebanon? The Role of Civic Movements in Reclaiming Public Space in Beirut and Tripoli." *The Journal of Public Space*, no. Vol. 6 n. 1 (April 30, 2021): 25–46. https://doi.org/10.32891/jps.v6i1.1324.

Nassour, Roland. "Environmental Contestation, Planning and Political Change: The Save Bisri Campaign in Lebanon." AUB ScholarWorks Home, June 1, 2020. https://scholarworks.aub.edu.lb/handle/10938/21887.

"Open Map Lebanon." Open Map Lebanon. Accessed July 25, 2024. https://openmaplebanon.org/.

Pietrostefani, Elisabetta, Joana Dabaj, Yara Sleiman, Mayssa Jallad, Sara Maassarani, and Efrosini Charalambous. "Assessing Vulnerabilities for Urban Recovery Solutions in Beirut Post-Explosion: The Case of Mar Mikhael Neighborhood." UCL Institute for Global Prosperity, February 10, 2022. Accessed November 1, 2022. https://www.ucl.ac.uk/bartlett/igp/publications/2022/feb/assessing-vulnerabilities-urban-recovery-solutions-beirut-post-explosion.

Proctor, Rebecca Anne. "Artists Take a Stand in Lebanon's Peaceful Uprising." *Arab News*, November 18, 2019. https://www.arabnews.com/node/1585046/middle-east.

Sawaya, Gioia. "Bebeirut Architects Partners with Beb W Shebbek to Rebuild Homes after the Beirut Blast." *designboom*, September 24, 2020. https://www.designboom.com/architecture/bebeirut-architects-beb-w-shebbek-rebuild-homes-beirut-blast-09-24-2020/.

Sharp, Deen, and May Farhat. "The October 2019 Uprising." Lebanon Unsettled. Accessed July 25, 2024. https://lebanonunsettled.org/archive/the-october-2019-uprising.

Sinno, Wael. "How People Reclaimed Public Spaces in Beirut during the 2019 Lebanese Uprising." *The Journal of Public Space*, no. Vol. 5 n. 1 (January 31, 2020): 193–218. https://doi.org/10.32891/jps.v5i1.1258.

TheOtherDada. "Afforestation." TheOtherDada, August 27, 2019. https://theotherdada.com/en/theotherforest/412/beiruts-riverless-forest.

"The Volunteer Circle." The Volunteer Circle I Knowledge Portal on Volunteerism. Accessed July 25, 2024. https://knowledge.unv.org/practices-and-experiences/the-volunteer-circle.

"Tour of Ras Beirut's Ghost and Living Bookshops." Beirut.com. Accessed July 25, 2024. https://www.beirut.com/en/directory/tour-of-ras-beiruts-ghost-and-living-bookshops.

Yee, Vivian. "Desperate to Leave Beirut, Young Lebanese Are Also the Ones Fixing It." *The New York Times*, August 27, 2020. https://www.nytimes.com/2020/08/27/world/middleeast/beirut-explosion-volunteers.html.

"ZP: Beirut Explosion - Underfunded Needs Working Paper." *The Zovighian Partnership.* Accessed July 25, 2024. https://www.zovighianpartnership.com/beirut-explosion/drafting-a-national-social-investment-strategy.

Epilog I Mona Harb

Ghosn, Rania and Jazairy, El Hadi. *Geostories. Another Architecture for the Environment.* Actar, 2018.

Metzer, Jonathan. "Cultivating Torment: The Cosmopolitics of More-than-Human Urban Planning," *City*, 20(4), (2016): 581-601.

Mommersteeg, Brett. *Variations of a Building.* Springer, 2023.

Yaneva, Albena. *Latour for Architects.* Routledge, 2022.

SHIFTING GROUNDS
(the ground between form and practice in Beirut)

Published by
Actar Publishers, New York, Barcelona
www.actar.com

Edited by
Carla Aramouny / Sandra Frem
Graphic Design
Karim Farah
With contributions by
Stephanie Achkar / Nayla Al-Akl / Wissam Chaaya / Farès el-Dahdah / Boulos Douaihy / Nicolas Fayad / Rana Haddad / Joanne Hayek / Mona Harb / Abdul-Halim Jabr / Hashim Sarkis
Copy editing and proofreading
James Dove
Printing and binding
Arlequin SL

Distribution
Actar D, Inc. New York, Barcelona.

New York
440 Park Avenue South, 17th Floor
New York, NY 10016, USA
T +1 2129662207
salesnewyork@actar-d.com

Barcelona
Roca i Batlle 2
08023 Barcelona, Spain
T +34 933 282 183
eurosales@actar-d.com

Indexing
English ISBN: 9781638401247
Library of Congress Control Number: 2023950175

Printed in Spain
Publication date: May 2025
Cover image: Unfinished Ground Form.
© Nicolas Fayad and Boulos Douaihy

Supported by a grant from the **Graham Foundation for Advanced Studies in the Fine Arts**.
Additionally supported by the **School of Architecture and Design** and the **University Research Board (URB)** grant at the American University of Beirut.